ALL YE LANDS

Origins of
World Cultures

Make a joyful noise unto the Lord, all ye lands!
Serve the Lord with gladness!
Come before his presence with singing!
Know ye that the Lord he is God;
It is he that hath made us and not we ourselves;
We are his people, and the sheep of his pasture.
Enter into his gates with thanksgiving,
And into his courts with praise.
Be thankful unto him, and bless his name.
For the Lord is good;
His mercy is everlasting;
And his truth endureth to all generations!
         —Psalm 100

ALL YE LANDS

Origins of
World Cultures

Contributors

Ellen Rossini

Carl Rossini

Rollin Lasseter

Anne Carroll

Christopher Zehnder

Mary O. Daly

General Editor

Rollin A. Lasseter

Produced and developed by:

Catholic Textbook Project

Project Manager: Douglas Alexander
Editing: Bridget Neumayr
Design and Production: Hespenheide Design, Gary Hespenheide, Randy Miyake, Patti Zeman, and the DLF group
Acknowledgments: to all of our spiritual, intellectual, and material benefactors, especially Dr. Dominic Aquila, Mr. and Mrs. William Burleigh, Mark Brumley, Sr. John Dominic Rasmussen, O.P., Fr. Joseph Fessio, S.J., Dan Guernsey, Dr. James Hitchcock, Dr. Ken Kaiser, Helen Lasseter, Ruth Lasseter, Ron Lawson, Carolyn Lemon, Mother Assumpta Long, Luke Macik, Esq., Jan Matulka, Dr. John Nieto, Rose Nieto, Fr. Marvin O'Connell, Dr. Andrew Seeley, Luke Seeley, Mary Ann Shapiro, Mr. and Mrs. Charles Van Hecke, Jessie Van Hecke, and Karen Walker (StudioRaphael). In memoriam, Jacqleen Ferrell and Hal Wales, Esq.

Also, gratitude is due the following organizations for their contributions: Ave Maria University, Dominican Sisters of Nashville, Sisters of Mary Mother of the Church, Sisters of Mary Mother of the Eucharist, Joseph and Laurel Moran, and St. Augustine Academy.

Cover Image: All images supplied by Corbis (clockwise from top) Elio Ciol; Gian Berto Vanni; Araldo de Luca; Eric Curry; The Corcoran Gallery of Art
Photo Credits
(t) top; (tl) top left; (tr) top right; (b) bottom; (bl) bottom left; (br) bottom right; (l) left; (r) right; (c) center
p. 1 © Zeljko Radojko/Shutterstock; **p. 10** (bl) © ribeiroantonio/Shutterstock, (br) © nikolpetr/Shutterstock; (br) © lkunl/Shutterstock, **p. 11** © Chendongshan/Shutterstock; **p. 13** © Dudarev Mikhail/Shutterstock; **p. 22** © sarkao/Shutterstock; **p. 23** © AntoinetteW/Shutterstock; **p. 24** Pichugin Dmitry/Shutterstock; **p. 25** © arka38/Shutterstock; **p. 27** © siloto/Shutterstock; **p. 29** © muratart/Shutterstock; **p. 32** © Kamira/Shutterstock; **p. 33** © Ancient Art & Architecture Collection Ltd / Alamy; **p. 34** © Vladimir Korostyshevskiy/Shutterstock; **p. 35** © Fedor Selivanov/Shutterstock; **p. 37** © apiguide/Shutterstock; **p. 38** © BasPhoto/Shutterstock; **p. 39** © Vladimir Korostyshevskiy/Shutterstock; **p. 40** © Mikhail Zahranichny/Shutterstock; **p. 41** © sculpies/Shutterstock; **p. 42** (t) © seamon53/Shutterstock, (b) © mountainpix/Shutterstock; **p. 43** (bl) © PavleMarjanovic/Shutterstock, (br) © mountainpix/Shutterstock; **p. 44** (bl) Everett Historical/Shutterstock, (c) Jose Ignacio Soto/Shutterstock, (br) Vaju Ariel/Shutterstock; **p. 45** © vagabond54/Shutterstock; **p. 47** © jorisvo/Shutterstock; **p. 49** © jorisvo/Shutterstock; **p. 51** (br) © jorisvo/Shutterstock, (bl) © Anton Kozlovsky/Shutterstock; **p. 52** © Nicku/Shutterstock; **p. 54** (tl) © Asaf Eliason/Shutterstock, (tr) © Asaf Eliason/Shutterstock, (br) © blueeyes/Shutterstock; **p. 55** © ruskpp/Shutterstock; **p. 56** © Nicku/Shutterstock; **p. 59** © Kamira/Shutterstock; **p. 60** © jsp/Shutterstock; **p. 61** (tl) © Nik Wheeler/Corbis, (tr) © Svist625/Fotolia; **p. 62** © Nicku/Shutterstock; **p. 63** (t) © jorisvo/Shutterstock, (b) © mountainpix/Shutterstock; **p. 64** © ruskpp/Shutterstock; **p. 67** © Marzolino/Shutterstock; **p. 72** © rook76/Shutterstock; **p. 73** © Anastasios71/Shutterstock; **p. 75** © Nick Pavlakis/Shutterstock; **p. 77** © JeniFoto/Shutterstock; **p. 81** © iStock.com/ZU_09; **p. 82** © Anastasios71/Shutterstock; **p. 83** © iStock.com/ZU_09; **p. 84** (tl), Vladislav Gurfinkel/Shutterstock, (bl) © barbar34/Shutterstock; **p. 85** row 1 © Philip de Bay/Historical Picture Archive/Corbis, row 2 (l) © Philip de Bay/Corbis, row 2 (r) © Historical Picture Archive/Corbis, row 3 (r) © Bettmann/Corbis, row 3 (l), © Archivo Iconografico, S.A./Corbis; row 4 (l) © Michael Nicholson/Corbis, row 4 (r) © Historical Picture Archive/Corbis;

Credits continue on page 407

Table of Contents

Our Lady of Grace

Preface

Many years ago, when embarking upon a career as an educator, I was confronted with only two options in teaching history: beautifully designed secular texts with a definite anti-Catholic bias, or photocopied versions of old Catholic texts, which were outdated and, in many respects, overly parochial. I realized that Catholic schools were forced by default to use one option or the other. This was not serving our students. I was not satisfied with this limitation, and I found others, teachers and parents, who were not satisfied either. The Church has always been a blend of heaven and earth, the material and the spiritual; and we dreamed of a textbook that combined the beauty of secular texts with the expansive and hopeful vision of history that is truly Catholic.

For more than a decade we have been working to make this dream a reality, to answer the prayers of countless teachers and parents. Now educators and families can have both beautiful illustrations and accurate text that is true to the Catholic vision of history as set forth in the Second Vatican Council's guiding document: *Lumen Gentium*.

The Catholic Textbook Project fills the void in the historical education of youth who know little of the accomplishments and contributions of their parents and grandparents, and even less about the men and women who have given us our civilization, our country and, most importantly, our Catholic Faith. This vacuum of historical knowledge is not our true heritage. Ours is a culture of life and of hope, of faith, vast and deep, and rich achievements for the common good.

The Catholic Textbook Project restores what has been lost in the secular texts and offers beautiful illustrations to accompany the story. We extend to teachers and students the first distinctively Catholic history textbooks since the 1960s.

As a teacher and administrator, I cannot fully express my satisfaction at finally having an option for Catholic schools, an option to educate with the tool of a textbook which is balanced and supportive of our Faith. The Catholic Textbook Project restores what has been forgotten—for the good of the Church, for the good of society and for the good of our children.

—Michael J. Van Hecke, M.Ed.
President
The Catholic Textbook Project

Introduction

Since the Second Vatican Council, Catholics have been aware of the deficiencies in religious education which afflict the Church at all levels, from kindergarten to graduate school, and some efforts have been made to correct these.

But the faith is more than theology. Because the Second Person of the Trinity became man, entered human history, that history must have deep religious significance for believers. The Judaeo-Christian tradition sees historical events as governed by Divine Providence, while at the same time warning believers against thinking that they are able to read the meaning of that Providence.

It is not insignificant that the Gospels were written not as theological treatises but as historical narratives, nor is it coincidental that the most radical attacks on Christianity have been on its historicity.

Just as Catholics have been deprived of much of their authentic theology over the past forty years, so also they have been deprived of their history, a deprivation which has been much less noticed. This has several damaging effects. Catholics now have little sense of their tradition, little understanding of how the faith can and should permeate a culture and serve as a leaven in that culture. They have little sense of what the lived faith was like through the centuries. Indeed they are extraordinarily present-minded, with little understanding of the faith as anything beyond their own immediate communities. They have little sense of the Communion of Saints—that they are intimately linked with all those who have gone before them with the sign of faith. They have little sense that history itself has a religious meaning.

The Catholic Textbook Project is one of the most promising enterprises of the post-conciliar era, with its determination to once more make available to Catholics an understanding of "secular" subjects which helps illumine the richness of the faith.

The curricula of the Catholic schools prior to Vatican II has often been criticized for its alleged parochialism, the assumption that there was such a thing as "Catholic mathematics," for example, or the tendency to look at the past exclusively through apologetic eyes. These mistakes, to the extent that they were real, will not be made by the Catholic Textbook Project. As this volume shows, it will be a series which on the one hand honors the Catholic faith and on the other is not afraid to be honest and comprehensive in its treatment of the past. It is a project which deserves the support of every serious Catholic.

—James Hitchcock
St. Louis University

Chapter 1 Introduction to Geography

God's Creation, God's Gift

When you read a story, do you ever try to imagine yourself at the side of the main character, in the places the story describes? Have you ever, for instance, pictured yourself floating on a raft down the Mississippi with Huckleberry Finn? Hiding with Robin Hood in Sherwood Forest? Climbing the snow-covered Alps with Heidi? Walking the foggy London streets with Sherlock Holmes? A good writer can often make you see these places with your imagination, even though you have never seen them with your eyes. And in seeing these places in your mind, you enjoy the story more.

What about the stories of history? When you listen to the story of the Israelites crossing the Red Sea in their exodus from Egypt, do you wonder how wide this sea was and where they crossed? Do you wonder why the Promised Land was called the "land of milk and honey" in the Bible when it is seems so barren and sandy now? Do you ask where the Rubicon is that Julius Caesar crossed to become ruler of Rome? Do you picture with your mind's eye the battlefield at Gettysburg where Robert E. Lee and the Southern cause went down in defeat?

Sunrise over the earth as seen from space

The physical features of a place (its terrain, landscape, mountains, rivers, seas) often shape how a people lives — such as whether it will be nomadic, wandering from place to place like the Indians of the plains, or whether its people will become merchants, buying and selling on the Mediterranean Sea. And how a people lives shapes history.

So it is that knowing more about the physical places where history was made can deepen your understanding of history. It can also help you enjoy the studying of history more.

All these physical places where history has occurred make up our remarkable planet called Earth, created by God to be our first home on the journey to heaven. The planet Earth is ours to enjoy and share. Its different environments range from the **fertile** farmlands of central Europe to the volcanic islands of Japan, from the ice-covered poles to the hot and humid tropics. It is a gift we are to take care of, enjoy, improve, and pass on to future generations.

fertile: producing crops easily

Earth Writing

The study of Earth — including its land and landforms, rivers and seas, and the people that have carved out homes in its various regions — is called *geography*. This word comes from Greek: *geo* for "Earth," and *graph* for "writing." Geography is thus a "writing about" or description of the Earth. By learning how to read this "earth writing," by learning how to describe the world you live in, you will make better sense of the stories in this book and other books. People and events will fill your imagination. When you read, you will travel; and when you travel, you will read, seeing the past in a landscape that does not change much over time.

Reading Maps

People have always had uses for geography, especially those useful tools of geography called maps. Maps are drawings (usually flat) of the world or certain places on it. In one form or another, maps have existed since the earliest civilizations, for people have always been eager to describe where they are or what belongs to them or to someone else. Travelers, for instance, may want to know how far they have gone on a journey, or where they are in relation to a certain river, mountain, or town. An

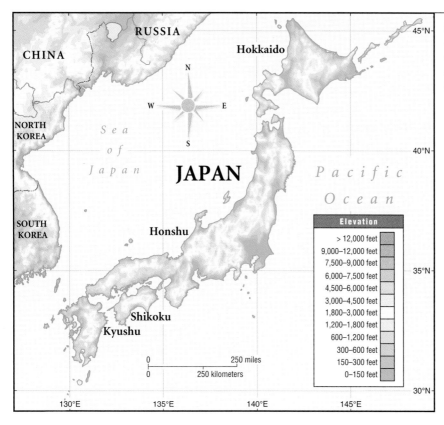

Map of the islands of Japan, showing latitude and longitude lines, and a color-keyed elevation scale

owner of property or the king of a nation may want something to show the boundaries of his property or his kingdom. A student of history will want to know not only *what* happened during a certain time period, but *where* it happened as well. For these, and other purposes, maps are very useful tools.

Depending on what their purpose is, maps show us different things. Some may just indicate the physical characteristics of a place (mountains, valleys, rivers, lakes, etc.) — what we call **physical geography**. Others may show the location of cities, towns, and indicate boundaries between nations and states — that is, they show **political geography**. Most maps show both physical and political geography, for they are very much connected with one another. Nations, for instance, have often used rivers or mountain ranges to mark their political boundaries, and the junctions of rivers have served as the sites for the building of towns and cities.

physical geography: a description of the formations of the Earth (mountains, valleys, rivers, lakes, etc.)

political geography: a description of the boundaries of states and regions, the location of cities and towns, and other aspects of human society that have to do with geography

Maps come in two forms—globes and flat maps. Globes are maps of the entire Earth, showing the continents, islands, oceans, and other features just as they would appear to us if we could see Earth in space. Flat maps show parts of Earth, or the entire earth, but in a way that it does not look like they belong to a sphere.

Flat maps, especially of the entire earth, do not show the various features of Earth as accurately as globes. On a flat map, for instance, Greenland may appear larger than Africa, when it is actually quite smaller. This is a problem with transferring the rounded surface of the globe to a flat surface. To do so, one must make the areas at the top of the map appear larger than they are. Such a flat map is called a *Mercator Projection*, after its inventor, Gerardus Mercator (1589). Today, some maps try to correct this problem by drawing Earth in a rounded shape and depicting the poles as lines, not points. Such a map is called a *Robinson Projection*.

A book of maps is called an *atlas*, a name that comes from ancient Greek mythology, which tells of a giant named Atlas who held up the sky. Early mapmakers liked to draw Atlas underneath a map of the world that he appeared to carry on his shoulders.

You will often hear someone speak of "reading" maps. People speak this way, because maps have their own "language." Maps use symbols that, just like words, convey ideas to those who "read" them. These symbols are the *compass rose*, the *legend* or *key*, *scale*, *direction*, and *latitude* and *longitude lines*. We will now describe each of these symbols in turn.

Mercator Projection—A map showing the meridians parallel to each other and the lines of latitude spaced farther apart as their distance from the Equator increases. This kind of map is especially useful for sea navigation.

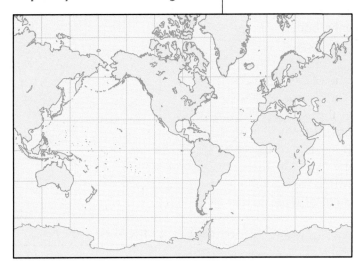

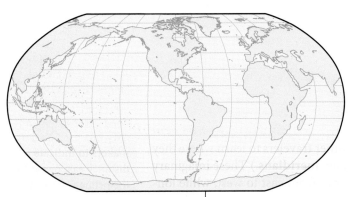

Robinson Projection—A map showing shapes and areas more accurately than other maps. The poles are shown as lines, not points. Lines of latitude are straight, and meridians are curved and get closer as they approach the poles.

The Geographical Directions

Earth is a sphere that spins as it moves around the sun. Of course, that is not what our immediate senses tell us, but what scientists have discovered over the last several centuries. The Greeks, and possibly the Egyptians, knew Earth was a sphere, but they thought it stood still and the heavenly bodies moved around it. They did not think Earth moved around the sun.

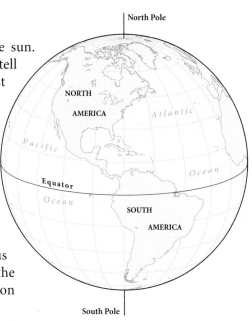

North Pole

NORTH

AMERICA

Atlantic

Pacific

Ocean

Equator

Ocean

SOUTH

AMERICA

South Pole

Globe showing the North and South Poles

The imaginary line that passes through Earth and around which Earth spins is called Earth's **axis**. The ends of the axis are called poles — the North Pole and the South Pole. As Earth spins, the sun's light (day) moves over half the earth. It appears to us that the sun "rises" in the morning and "sets" in the evening. What really happens is that where we are on Earth has moved into the sun's light or out of it as Earth spins.

We give directions based on where the sun rises, where it sets, and on the North and South Poles. The direction where the sun rises is called "east," while the direction where the sun sets is called "west." It has become the custom to draw our maps with the north at the top (the North Pole) and the east on the right.

Latitude and Longitude

Latitude and **longitude** are the imaginary lines used by mapmakers to show places on a map, or by sailors and other travelers to learn where they are on the earth. (Longitude lines are called **meridians**.) These imaginary lines crisscross the globe. Latitude lines run from east to west, while longitude lines run from north to south. The crisscrossing of latitude and longitude lines is the chief way of showing a location on the map.

The latitude line that circles the center of the globe is the **equator.** It runs halfway between the north and south poles. All other latitude lines are parallel to the equator. We number latitude lines in degrees based on how far they are from the equator and how close they are to one of the poles. The equator we say is zero degrees latitude, and the

axis: the line around which a body rotates

latitude: an imaginary line used by mapmakers to indicate a distance north or south of the equator

longitude: an imaginary line used by mapmakers to indicate a distance east or west of the prime meridian

meridian: a longitude line

equator: an imaginary circle equally distant from the two poles, around the middle of the earth

Latitude and longitude lines, as seen on a globe

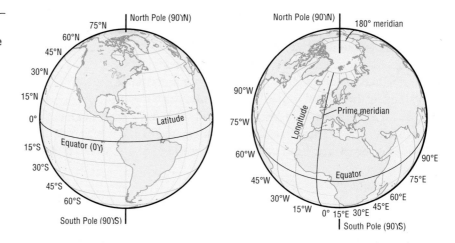

prime meridian: the only great circle of Earth that passes through both poles and the Royal Observatory in Greenwich, England. All other meridians are numbered from this meridian, which is the 0° (degree) meridian.

North Pole, 90 degrees (90°) north latitude. Since the South Pole is the same distance from the equator as the North Pole, but on the opposite side of the earth, it is 90 (90°) degrees south latitude. A latitude line lying between the equator and one of the poles will have a number somewhere between zero and 90 degrees. For instance, the line that runs through Beijing, in China, and Philadelphia, in the United States, is 40° north latitude. The line that runs through Sydney, Australia, is 34° south latitude. If regions have the same latitude, their climates might be the same.

We also measure longitude in degrees; but, instead of the equator, we use a line called the **prime meridian** as our longitude line or meridian of 0°. The prime meridian runs from the North to the South Pole and passes through Greenwich, England. Really, any longitude line could be used as the prime meridian, but in 1884, 25 nations agreed to make the Greenwich meridian the prime meridian. The meridian that runs near Rome, Italy, (east of the prime meridian) is 12° east longitude. The meridian that runs through New York City (west of the prime meridian) is 74° west longitude.

If you started at the prime meridian and traveled westward around the world, you would cross meridians that increase in number. That is, you would go from 0° meridian, through the meridians numbering 10°, 50°, 100°, etc. When you reached 180° meridian (which passes through the Pacific Ocean), you would begin to pass through meridians that decrease in number. That is, you would go from 180° to 150°, 100°, 50°, and 10° meridian. Eventually you would arrive back at the prime meridian.

Map Directions

Most maps are so drawn that north is at the top of the map as you look at it, south at the bottom, west to the left, and east to the right. Some maps, however, may place a different direction than north at the top, so it is important to find on the map what is called the *compass rose*—a small circular symbol that looks like a sun with four long rays shaped like a cross. Each ray will point to a direction, indicated by the letters N (north), S (south), E (east), or W (west). Wherever the N ray points is north for that map.

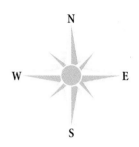

Legend or Key

Because a map is a small picture of a large area, it can include symbols to represent geographical places or features. These symbols will often be found on the map in a small box called a legend or key. A blackened triangle may stand for a mountain and a crooked line for a river or boundary. A dot is usually a city; the larger the dot, the larger the city it represents. A broken line or lines with arrows can show someone's travels or an army's invasion route.

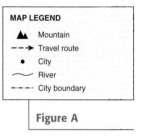

Figure A

Scale

This is a horizontal bar that can be used to show distances on maps. The scale on a map will appear as a straight line, marked by smaller cross lines that indicate various distances. The scale shown in Figure B indicates a distance of 100 miles, along with distances (25, 50, 75 miles) between zero and 100 miles.

A string can be used with the scale to figure out distances between places on a map. If, for instance, you want to discover the distance between San Francisco and Los Angeles, California, you would place one end of the string, say, where San Francisco is on a map and pull out as much string as you need to reach Los Angeles. By measuring the string length with the scale, you will be able to determine the distance between the two cities.

Figure B

tectonics: geological features of Earth's crust
Earth's crust: the solid outer part of the planet

Our Moving Continents

About a hundred years ago, scientists of the earth's history learned something that changed the way everyone thinks about geography. They found that, like puzzle pieces, rock cliffs in South America match and fit cliffs similar to them in Africa. This discovery led scientists to suspect that all the lands of the earth were once one huge landmass above water and that, over millions of years, that landmass broke apart and its different sections drifted away from one another. This theory has thus been called "continental drift." It is also called "plate **tectonics**," because each of the great sections of Earth is called a *plate*. A plate is an enormous, movable piece of **Earth's crust.**

Beneath the oceans are continental plates, which come together to form the surface of the earth. This map shows the boundaries of the plates.

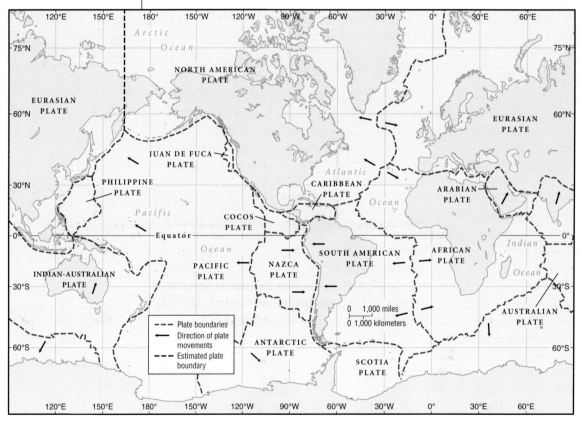

According to scientists, about 120 million years ago, the earth's great landmass began to break up into plates. Some of these plates were already beneath the waters of the oceans; others tipped, throwing up one part of the plate and lowering the other part into the waves. The parts of the plates above the water became continents. A continent is a part of a continental plate that is above water.

Over millions of years, the continental plates have moved apart and been driven against each other. Great mountain ranges rose up when the plates moved against each other; and where they moved apart, ocean waters flowed in to make new bodies of water. In the short history of humankind on Earth, the continents have been just about the same as they are now. They are moving, but so slowly that we cannot detect it. Only measurements at one or two known plate edges give evidence that the theory of continental drift is true.

The Seven Continents and Other Landmasses

The movement of the earth's plates has left three different kinds of landmasses standing above the waters — continents, peninsulas, and islands. The largest of these landmasses are the *continents*, which are seven in number: North America, South America, Asia, Europe, Africa, Australia, and Antarctica.

Of all the continents, Asia and Africa are the largest, while Australia and Antarctica are the smallest. On a map it looks as if Europe and Asia form one continent; but the Ural (YOO-rahl) Mountains, the Caucasus Mountains, the Black Sea and the Caspian Sea separate these two continents. The eastern end of Europe is flat and was once covered with dense forests and wide grasslands. The western end of Asia is also flat, as well as cold or desert-like. These physical boundaries prevented travel and kept the different civilizations that developed on the two continents separate.

The two Americas are connected by the bridge of Central America between the southern boundary of Mexico and the **isthmus** of Panama. Mexico and Central America are parts of North America but are semi-tropical like most of South America.

An *island* is a body of land surrounded on all sides by water. Greenland, the largest island, is a continental island. A continental island is an island separated from a continent by water but connected underwater by one

isthmus: a narrow strip of land, having water on either side, that connects two large bodies of land

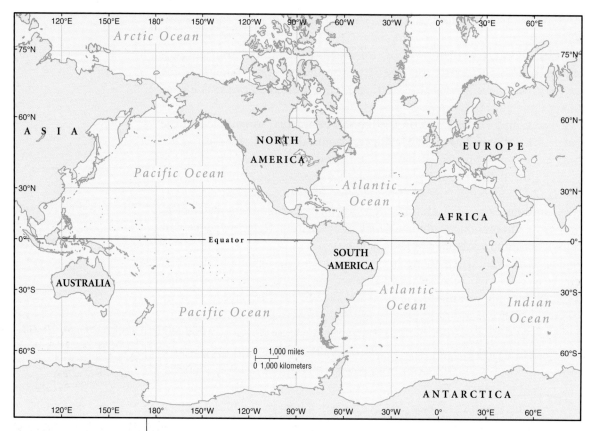

Map of the world showing the continents, the oceans, and the equator

(a) An isthmus; (b) small tropical island; and (c) A peninsula off Croatia's coast

continental plate. Some islands are the top of mountains rising above the waters.

A *peninsula* (from Latin *paene*, meaning "almost," and *insula*, meaning "island" — an "almost island") is a body of land surrounded on three sides by water, but connected to a larger body of land on the fourth side. Greece and Italy are two large peninsulas jutting into the Mediterranean Sea. Spain and Portugal are on the Iberian Peninsula, surrounded by the Atlantic on the west and the Mediterranean on the south and east.

Mountains, Volcanoes, Plains, and Deserts

The landmasses of the earth have various features that give great variety and beauty to our world. We can roughly divide these features into mountains (including volcanoes), plains, and deserts.

Mountains are often made by plates shoving up against each other, cracking, and then reconnecting. The surface of the earth is constantly shifting. Mountain ranges have risen and fallen over the millions of years of Earth's history.

The world's tallest mountain is Asia's Mt. Everest, soaring 29,000 feet high above sea level (that is more than five miles) at the border of Nepal and Tibet (which happens to be the world's largest and highest plateau). Mt. Everest is part of the Himalayas, the world's largest mountain system,

Mount Everest, 29,035 high, located in Nepal is named after an English surveyor Sir George Everest.

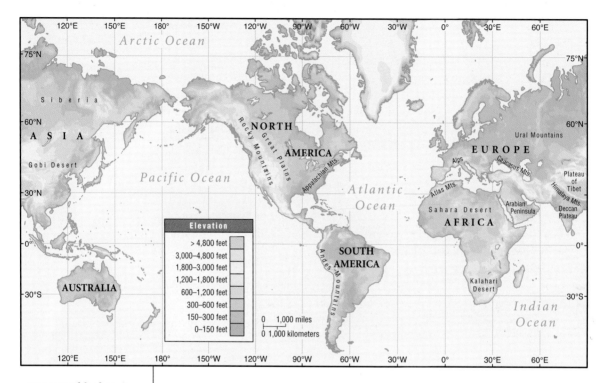

Topographical map showing mountain ranges of the world with color-keyed elevation scale

magma: molten rock material beneath the earth's surface

with eight of the world's ten highest mountains. The higher mountain ranges are the youngest in Earth's history, though still unimaginably old by human history. As a mountain range ages, it is worn down by wind and rain and so becomes smaller.

Some mountains, called *volcanoes*, are formed by molten rock and ash erupting out of the hot **magma** beneath the earth's crust. Breaks in the plates allow the molten rock to pour up to the surface of the earth. Then the molten rock cools and hardens, forming a cone-shaped mountain. Volcanoes surround the Mediterranean Sea and the North Pacific Ocean.

The soil that ash from volcanoes leaves behind is rich and fertile and has produced some of the best farming land in the world. Human beings have chosen to live under volcanoes for the rich farmland. Prehistoric man valued the natural volcanic glass, **obsidian**, since it gave toolmakers the first material for making really sharp knives and cutting tools.

obsidian: dark, natural glass formed by the cooling of molten lava

The most famous volcanoes in history are Mt. Vesuvius in southern Italy and Mt. Aetna on the island of Sicily. In A.D. 79, Vesuvius erupted

Volcanoes in Bromo Tengger Semeru National Park at sunrise, Java, Indonesia

and buried the Roman town of Pompeii in ash, leaving a perfectly preserved ancient town for archaeologists to uncover many centuries later. Mt. Fujiyama, a volcano in Japan, has been revered by the Japanese for its majestic size and beauty. The eruption of Krakatoa in Indonesia during the 1890s sent a cloud into the atmosphere that left ash all over the world.

The large, flat areas of the world are called *plains*. Plains are not truly flat; they have a rolling surface, but no mountain ranges. Plains have been historically the home of **nomadic** peoples, who have no settled homes but follow wandering herds of animals. The plains of eastern Europe and western Asia are huge expanses of thousands of miles of grassland, called **steppes**. The Great Plains of the North American continent were once covered in grasses that grew as tall as a man. Such grasslands are called **prairies**. The plains areas nearer the tropics are too hot to grow tall grasses, but they support **savannahs**, lands with low grasses and stands of scattered trees. **Plateaus** are plains high above sea level; they are usually part of a mountain, where the air is cooler and the winds from the mountains are strong. Central Mexico is a plateau, as are Tibet (north of the Himalayas) and the central portion of India, called the Deccan Plateau.

nomadic: of or belonging to a *nomad*, a member of a people that moves from place to place with no fixed home

steppe: dry, level grasslands with few to no trees

prairie: a large area of flat or rolling land, with no mountains and few trees

savannah: grassland containing scattered trees

plateau: a large area of high land

A *desert* is land with very little or no water. Human life is difficult in deserts, because they are unfriendly to human travel and development. Africa contains the world's largest desert, the Sahara, which stretches the whole width of the continent. The other major deserts that have affected history are the Arabian Desert, in the center of the Arabian Peninsula, and the Gobi Desert, which cuts China off from the West. In North America, the Southwestern Desert may also have affected history by keeping people in the north from invading Mexico and so protecting the development of Mexican and Central American civilization. Between the sea and the Andes Mountains on the west of South America are high, windswept coastal deserts. The civilization of Peru was protected from invasion by the difficulty of crossing those miles of barren waste.

The Waters: Oceans, Seas, Lakes, and Rivers

Most of the earth's surface is actually covered by water. On a map it looks like all the continents are surrounded by one big ocean, which we divide for convenience into four *oceans*: the **Pacific**, the Atlantic, the Indian, and the Arctic. Besides the oceans, the earth has other bodies of water: seas, rivers, and ice.

pacific: calm, peaceful

The largest ocean is the Pacific; it is so large that all the landmasses in the world could fit into it. The Pacific Ocean is more than 64 million square miles, extending from Asia and Australia to North and South America.

The Atlantic Ocean is east of North and South America and west of Africa and Europe.

The Indian Ocean has Africa to the west, Asia to the north, Australia to the east, and Antarctica to the south. The Arab traders sailed across the Indian Ocean to India and Africa and brought their Muslim religion to the islands of Malaysia at the southeastern tip of Asia.

At the top of the world is the Arctic Ocean, encircled by Europe, Asia, and North America. All its waters are frozen much of the year, and a good part of the ocean lies under the northern ice cap all year round.

As you can see by looking at a map, the lands of the continents can enclose parts of oceans. The parts of the oceans enclosed by land are called *seas*. Seas are large bodies of salt water. Some are connected to the larger oceans and are surrounded by land on three sides. Others are really saltwater lakes, such as the Aral and Caspian Seas in Asia, or even large freshwater lakes, such as the Sea of Galilee. Though small compared to the oceans, these seas have nevertheless been important in

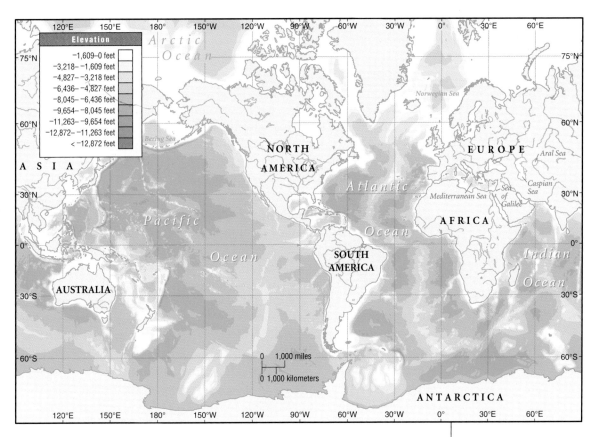

World map showing
seas, oceans, lakes,
and rivers, with an
elevation scale
keyed to the colors
of the map

history. Freshwater bodies of water surrounded by land are called *lakes*. Lakes can be small or as large as some seas — such as the Great Lakes of North America.

A student of history should be able to find the Mediterranean Sea on a map. Our Christian civilization began in the lands about its shores. The Mediterranean (from Latin words meaning "in the middle of land") is surrounded by the three continents of Europe, Asia, and Africa. The ancient peoples of Phoenicia (foh-NEE-shah) and Greece traveled this sea and early on brought Europeans to the north coasts of Africa. The Mediterranean Sea drawn on a map has been said to look like a winged sea horse.

The body of water called a *river* is found on every continent except Antarctica. A river is a large stream that carries fresh water into an ocean, lake, or another river. Rivers are essential to life because their water is

irrigation: the supplying of land with water, especially for growing crops

drinkable and can be used for **irrigation**. It is fresh water, unlike the salt water of oceans.

The world's longest river is the Nile River in Africa; it gave life to the civilization of the ancient Egyptians. The Amazon River in South America is the second longest, although it carries more water than the Nile. At some places, the Amazon is so wide you cannot see across it. The Yangtze River in China is the longest river in Asia; the Mekong of Southeast Asia is the second longest Asian river. The Mississippi River is the longest river in the United States, and combined with the Missouri River that flows into it, is one of the longest rivers in the world. The Danube River and the Rhine River are the longest rivers in Europe; they form the center of much of the continent's history. The great river valleys of the world have been the most hospitable to human life. The first human civilizations began in valleys through which ran rivers with their life-giving waters.

Much of the world's water is frozen. The two poles of the planet are covered with thick layers or caps of *ice*. These ice caps are called the Arctic (North) and the Antarctic (South) ice. The southern continent of Antarctica carries a mile-thick ice cap. The Arctic ice cap is just as thick but smaller in area.

Rivers of ice form in certain high mountain ranges—the Alps, the Himalayas, and the Canadian Rockies—and are almost as huge and thick as the ice caps. The ice rivers are called glaciers. During the long periods of prehistory, called the Ice Ages, the northern ice cap grew or shrank in size, and glaciers descended from it over the continents of Asia, Europe, and North America, pushing animal life into the central parts of the planet.

The Ice Age glaciers carved out clefts and hollows in the land that filled with water and became northern lakes. The glaciers pushed earth and rocks ahead of them, leaving behind glacial hills. Rainfall that might have returned to the oceans was locked up in these glaciers, lowering the level of the oceans so that land bridges could be seen between the continents. They also opened up shorelines that have since returned to the sea.

Climates

The word "climate" refers to all weather conditions, including rainfall and cloud cover, and temperature. Latitudes affect climates because a region farther from the equator is cooler; but other factors also affect climates,

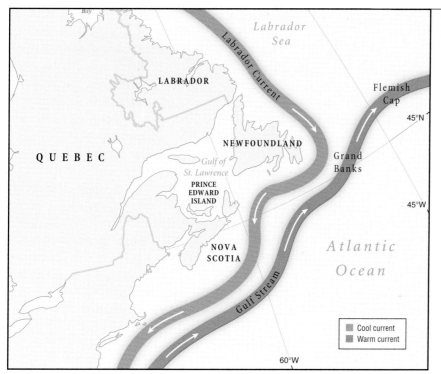

The Gulf Stream and the Labrador Current

such as altitude, the amount of water in an area, and the wind patterns. Water currents can make a difference too. The **Gulf Stream** carries warm water from the Gulf of Mexico to the north, making England's climate moderate. At the same latitude as England is Labrador, a frozen wasteland most of the year because of the icy Labrador Current coming down from the Arctic.

Water is less changeable than air in holding the same temperature. Because they lack water, the world's deserts can undergo extreme temperature changes, even in a single day. This is especially so in central Asia, where temperatures may rise to 130 degrees in the day and then drop to below freezing at night.

The climate regions of the earth are called *zones*, from the Greek word for belt, because they run belt-like around the globe. At the center of the globe are the tropics—the tropic of Cancer (north of the equator) and the tropic of Capricorn (south of the equator). The polar regions are frozen year-round and inhospitable to life. But the **temperate** zones—the

Gulf Stream: a warm-water ocean current that flows in the North Atlantic from the Gulf of Mexico, northward along the coast of the United States, and then to the British Isles

temperate: not too hot, not too cold

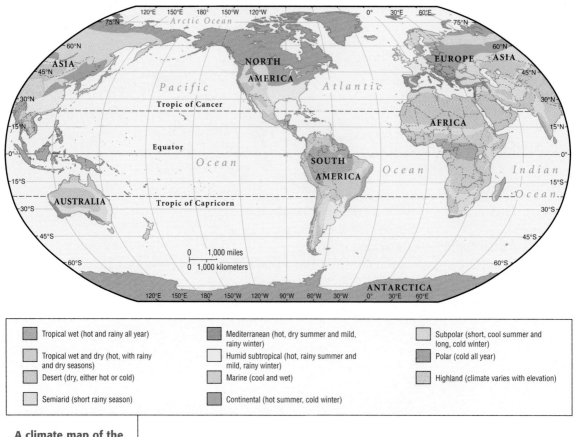

A climate map of the world

tropics: the regions close to the equator

latitudes between the frozen polar zones and the **tropics** — have been where most of human history has occurred.

The regions of the earth have had basically the same climate through all of human history. The cold regions of the polar north and south and of the heights of mountain chains have grown or shortened through the ages, but have basically stayed the same. Europe has enjoyed a temperate and moist climate in recent centuries, as have China and Japan. The Middle East, North Africa, and India have remained warm and semi-tropical. The climate of the Americas has been throughout human history much as it is today.

The chief climate events in human history have been the coming and going of several Ice Ages, when the northern glaciers spread down over parts of Europe, Asia, and North America. No Ice Age has occurred since human beings have been writing and recording their history. Only warming and cooling periods have been noted in recorded history. In the northern half of Africa, the plains of the Sahara were a fertile grassland when the last glaciers withdrew and the world's climate changed. Rainfall shifted away from northern Africa, the rich pastureland dried, and **oases** disappeared. Today, the Sahara is only a dry sand and rock desert.

> **oasis** (*pl.* **oases**): a fertile green area in an arid, or dry, region

Chapter 1 Review

Let's Remember   Please write your answers in complete sentences.
1. What determines the directions east, west, north, and south?
2. Name the seven continents. Which continents touch another continent? Which continents stand alone?
3. What is the difference between an island and a peninsula?
4. How many oceans are there? What are their names?
5. What is the longest river on the earth? What is the second longest? What is the longest river in the U.S.A.?
6. How can scientists tell how old a mountain range is?
7. What is a desert? Where are the largest deserts of the world?
8. Where are the tropics? Where are the temperate zones?

Let's Consider   For silent thinking and a short essay, or for thinking in a group with classroom discussion:
1. Why are deserts very hot in the daytime and very cold at night?
2. Why do you think so many ancient civilizations developed so differently on the one continent of Asia?
3. Why do civilizations begin in major river valleys?

Things to Do

1. Find all the continents on a globe. On a flat surface, make a map of the continents you have seen on the globe. Consider why it is difficult to draw a flat map of a round surface.
2. With your finger, trace the course of the following rivers on a globe or map: the Nile in Africa, the Yangtze in Asia, the Rhine in Europe, the Danube in Europe, and the Mississippi in North America. What

countries do they run through? With a piece of string, measure these rivers on the globe or map as well as you can. Find the legend or key. According to your string measurements, how long is each river?

3. Using your measuring string, find out how far the place where you live is from the equator, and then from the North Pole. Use the legend or key on your map. Consider what other weather-makers (mountains, open plains, winds, seacoast, etc.) make the climate of where you live what it is.

4. Look at a physical map of the world and find the great mountain ranges. Find the Alps in Europe and the Himalayas in Asia, the Rockies in North America and the Andes in South America.

Chapter 2 Prehistory: Beginning Man's Story

The Infancy of Man

The prehistory of our world is a bit like your own childhood. You could not write when you were a baby, nor can you now tell any stories about your infancy. Try as you might, you cannot remember further back than the ages of three or four. Yet, you know that you were once an infant because you see that other people do not come into being at the age of four. They are first formed in the darkness of their mother's womb, emerge at birth, and live as infants, then toddlers. And so, you conclude, the same was true for you.

Yet, though you have no memories of your infancy, you do have your parents' memories. They can tell you stories of what you were like when you were an infant or what you did when you were very young. There are other clues, too, to your earliest years — photographs, baby spoons at the back of the drawer, a baptismal candle, a box of baby toys in the attic, a birth certificate, and medical records.

Like your own life, the life of mankind has periods that we can "remember" and periods that we cannot. The period of the human story that we can remember is the period for which we have written records. But written records of the human story appeared only about 3,500 years before the birth of Christ; and before that, for many, many years, human beings lived, worked, had families, formed communities, and did all that human beings have ever done. The period of human life for which we have written records we call "history." The times before the earliest written records we have is called **prehistory**.

Historians call the time before Christ's coming B.C., or "before Christ." The years after the coming of Christ are called A.D., *Anno Domini*, Latin for "In the Year of the Lord." We live in the 21st century after the coming of Christ. The years before the coming of Christ are counted backwards; the larger the number in B.C., the farther it is from the birth of Christ, as well as from our own time. For instance, 2000 B.C. is older than 200 B.C., while A.D. 200 is older than A.D. 2000.

prehistory: the period of the human past for which we have no written records

Trilobytes

The Prehistory of Mankind

According to scientists, life on our planet is much older than human life. For instance, scientists say the dinosaurs walked the earth for 40 million years—but they disappeared millions of years before the first man and woman were created. Before the dinosaurs, creatures called trilobites lived in the seas for 250 million years, while, even before the trilobytes, there were algae, including creatures called archeons, which still live under unbelievable pressure in the deep places of the earth.

Scientists tell us that creatures that in some ways resembled human beings have existed only for about 1 million years, and they may have been only animals. Our Faith tells us that humankind had two ancestors, a first father and first mother, Adam and Eve. Where those parents lived or when they lived is a mystery. But how our first parents came to be is no mystery. God has told us that he made them, and that—like Adam and Eve—we have his love and special concern. Yet, all of recorded history—that is, the whole life of mankind since anyone was able to write down what was happening—has existed only a little more than six thousand years.

Yet what about all the thousands of years of mankind before there was writing? This time, which we call "prehistory," is not a dark and silent age about which nothing can be known, any more than your life as an infant is dark and unknown. Our earliest ancestors, however, left no written story about themselves and their lives. What they did leave was shards and scraps, skulls, bones, and stone tools.

How do we know our earliest ancestors were human, like us? We know this because they did what humans—not animals—have always done. They left objects that show they were concerned for the soul. They left carefully prepared graves to honor their loved ones who died. They tried to make themselves beautiful with body ornaments. They constructed enormous stone structures all over the world. They made beautiful paintings deep inside caves. They built homes in cliffs and, later, they cultivated the soil and built cities and discovered the arts of writing and music. All these things are the work of thinking creatures—for animals do not paint their surroundings nor carefully bury their dead.

Yet, our earliest ancestors were not innocent or sinless. The evidence shows that they knew how to kill their own kind and went to war with each other. Our Faith explains this tendency to evil as coming from the Fall. That is, revelation tells us that the first parents, Adam and Eve, placed in this beautiful world to guard and improve it, did not know disease or death until they disobeyed the one command of God. When they came to know evil as well as good, they fell from grace and began mankind's sad history of death and disease, domination, conquest, murder, treachery, and deceit.

artifact: an item worked on or made by man
carbon: a substance from which coal, charcoal, and graphite are made. Carbon is found in most animals and plants.

Old and New Stone Age

Scientists who discover and tell the story of prehistoric man are called paleontologists, archaeologists, and anthropologists.

1. **Paleontologists** study the traces left by mankind during those long years before writing. The word paleontologist is from the Greek words *palaea*, meaning the past, and *ontologia*, meaning the study of what is.
2. **Archaeologists** find and dig up the lost cities and campsites of mankind; they study the bones and buildings and rubbish left there for signs of man's life. The word archaeologist comes from the Greek *arche*, beginnings, and *logia*, study.
3. **Anthropologists** study different human cultures and behaviors among ancient peoples. The word comes from the Greek *anthropos*, meaning mankind, and *logia*, study.

These scientists are not actual historians; they do not write history. But by finding human tools and foods, by using the insights of physics to date these findings, and by comparing these findings with the activities of modern people who seem to live like ancient people once did, these scientists can guess a lot about prehistoric mankind.

The paleontologists of the 20th century developed a method to help them learn how old the **artifacts** they discover really are. By learning the age of artifacts, paleontologists can have some idea about how long ago the people who made them lived. This method is called *radiocarbon dating*, because it works by discovering how much **carbon** an artifact contains. All living beings contain carbon, as do things made from living beings, such as wooden posts, weapons, firewood, scraps of food, or bodies

A small, prehistoric stone head from Africa and a scraper made from flint, with a special stone

that were nourished by carbohydrates. Although radiocarbon dating cannot tell us the exact age of something, it can give us a clear idea of the age of things containing carbon that are less than 30,000 years old.

Based on several bits of evidence they have discovered, scientists have concluded that human-like creatures have been on the earth for at least 1 million years. This is not a fact, but a **theory**—an idea we form to explain facts we discover. For instance, a scientist may form an idea to explain some Native American cave paintings. He may decide that the paintings were made for religious rituals—and he may have good reasons to think he is right. Yet, this explanation is just a theory, for later, the same scientist, or another scientist, may find new evidence and so form a different theory—for instance, that the cave paintings were done just for the fun of it. A theory is not the truth but as close to the truth as an interpretation of facts can get. Newer theories replace older theories when more complete facts are discovered.

Scientists call the earliest human-like creatures *homo erectus*, or Upright Man, because their bones show that they walked upright and not on all fours. After Upright Man came another possible ancestor of modern human beings, called *homo sapiens*, or Thinking Man. Modern human beings are called *homo sapiens sapiens,* or Thinking Man, the Wise.

Scientists say Thinking Man was not only our ancient ancestor but the ancestor as well of a line of cousins, called Neanderthal Man (*homo sapiens neanderthalensis*), who no longer walks the earth. Based on the bones of Neanderthals they have found, scientists have described Neanderthal Man as short and stocky, physically strong, with large bones and a thick brow. But he was not an animal, not an ape. In addition to his bones, scientists have found all sorts of remains of the Neanderthal's life, such as body ornaments and distinctive stone tools. Neanderthals adapted to and survived in Arctic-like weather conditions for thousands of years and developed a culture of their own. They made camps and **ritual burial** sites, the traces of which have been found all over Europe and western Asia, as far east as Russia and as far south as Israel and Iran. Neanderthal men and women

theory: an idea used to explain facts we discover or experiences we have had. Theories are not necessarily true.

ritual burial: the burial of the dead done with certain, usually religious, rites

Prehistoric rock paintings from Tassili N'Ajjer in Algeria

lived in family groups, hunted, cooked their food, and honored their dead, just as people have always done. Then, suddenly, in a short period of time, they disappeared from all over the world. What happened to them? Did they die of a sickness that our ancestors survived? Did they intermarry with people of our own kind? Did our own ancestors kill off these distant cousins? Nobody knows.

Old and New Stone Age

Based on the artifacts and tools they have uncovered, the first paleontologists divided the pre-history of man into three ages: the *Stone Age*, the *Bronze Age*, and the *Iron Age*. Though these names are not very exact, they are a useful way to divide pre-history.

Because the tools of earliest human societies were made of stone, the times in which they lived is called the Stone Age. The first metal to be mastered was bronze, and tools and weapons of bronze gave the time in which they were made the name, the Bronze Age. The Iron Age refers to the time when human beings began to make tools out of iron. It has lasted from the time of the ancient Greeks to our own age.

The Stone Age has been divided into two parts: the *Paleolithic* (Old Stone Age) and the *Neolithic* (New Stone Age.) Scientists say that in the Old Stone Age, mankind lived only by hunting, while, in the New Stone Age, farming and city building began to transform human life.

Stone ax head, found in Israel

Life in the Old Stone Age

Scientists tell us that Stone Age men lived in groups with no permanent homes. They were, in other words, nomads, changing their abode in summer and winter, following the herds of animals whose flesh and hides they used for food and clothing.

What else were they like?

Sometimes you see comical pictures of prehistoric "cave men," extremely hairy people, hunched over, holding clubs, and grunting. Such pictures, however, were drawn by those who believed early man was not much different than an ape. But there has never been any evidence that Stone Age people were in any way like this. They were *homo sapiens sapiens,* just like us. They walked upright. They may have had no written language, but we have no reason to think they did not use language at all or that their language had only a few words. Their tools were simple but practical, skillfully crafted, and became more and more refined as the ages passed.

Early people, in fact, used stone well. They used stones to sharpen other stones, and a sharpened stone, tied to a stone-whittled tree branch, became a spear tip. This spear could be used to kill an animal, from which the hunters would get meat for food and, thanks to a stone knife, a hide

Into Distant Lands

The Old Stone Age occurred during the last of Earth's Ice Ages. At the time of their greatest expansion, ice glaciers covered all of northern Europe (including the British Isles, Germany, Poland, and Russia.) They covered North America, as far south as the Missouri and Ohio River valleys, Greenland, and Iceland. The ice heaps had so much water in them that the level of the sea dropped, and land bridges that were once under water appeared between Asia and North America and between Asia and the islands of the East Indies. Using these land bridges, Stone Age people migrated from their original homes into distant lands —for instance, from eastern Asia into North America. When, eventually, the glaciers melted, the seas rose and covered the land bridges, cutting islands off from continents, and North America from Asia. After the end of the Ice Ages, Europe and Asia became lands with valleys and plains teeming with animal life, where nomadic peoples could find good hunting and live well.

This map shows the extent of glaciers covering the Earth about 18,000 years ago.

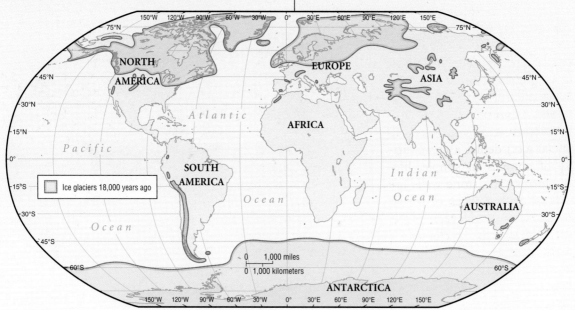

for clothing or for a screen to block the wind or for a roof to stop the rain. Early man used stones to pierce animal bones and so make needles to sew clothing. Tiny stones and bones were made into buttons. Early man's mastery of stone for tools was not only good enough for survival but could produce beautiful works of art as well.

Stone Age man had many talents. He was a craftsman, creating the bow and arrow for better hunting. He was wise about the ways of the animals — a skill he needed to track and hunt them. He was an inventor, making lamps that burned animal fat so he could work at night. And he preserved food by drying or smoking it over fire.

Even though much of what he did was for survival, Stone Age man had a love for beauty and a desire to create beautiful things. For instance, scientists have found a flute made from a bird bone, which, they say, is 30,000 years old. Among other things they have discovered are: an elaborate, 23-ton house, constructed from 400 mammoth bones; 24,000-year old **kilns**, used to fire decorative pottery; and carved ivory jewelry, which scientists say is even older than 24,000 years.

Yet, the most stunning example of early man's artistic nature is a mysterious and lovely treasure, found in the darkness of the earth. Indeed, the oldest paintings in the world are not in museums but on the walls and ceilings of deep caves and rocky gorges in Europe, Africa, Asia, and Australia. These primitive and beautiful cave paintings (dated from 30,000 to 11,000 B.C.) depict a great variety of animals in simple, life-like forms. The stone walls are covered with images of bison, horses, wild cattle, deer, mammoths, wolves, foxes, oxen, owls and the woolly rhinoceros. The

kiln: a furnace or oven for burning, baking, or drying. Kilns have been used for firing or hardening pottery.

A reproduction of a cave painting of a horse at Altamira

ancient artists also made decorations, such as rows of dots or circles, and stencil outlines of their hands.

This remarkable art was first discovered in the mid-1800s in southern France and northern Spain. Two of the largest and best-preserved collections are in Lascaux, France, and Altamira, Spain. Hobbyists and scientists continue to find more cave art. As recently as 1994, the oldest collection of all was discovered in Chauvet, France.

The New Stone Age—Nomads Become Farmers

domesticate: to tame wild animals

After generations of constant wandering, the human family began to settle down. When Stone Age people traveled with the hunt, they gathered and ate the plants they found growing in the wild. Around 9000 B.C., however, people living in the Middle East began cultivating the land to grow these grains themselves. Also around this time, they began to **domesticate** and herd animals, such as sheep and goats, which could supply them with

Map of the Near East; locations of some of the earliest cities

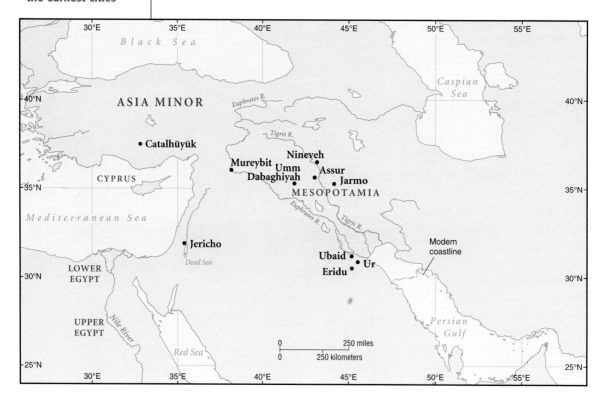

milk, meat, and clothing. Because they could grow food, people could finally grow communities, cities, and civilizations.

An early farming community was not very different from the movable villages of the nomadic hunters. It was a collection of single-family huts clustered near a large, open common area, sometimes with a surrounding wall to keep in animals and keep out intruders. Garden plots and grain fields surrounded the enclosure. Within the common area people milled grain, milked goats, wove baskets, and made pottery. These communities were small and simple, and the people could pick up and move to another area when the farmland was used up.

irrigate: to bring water to land by ditches, canals, or other means; to water

Once people learned how to cultivate and **irrigate** their farms, it became possible to build cities. The oldest known city in the world is Catalhüyük, built in south-central Turkey around 6150 B.C. This unique city looked like a single giant fortress, because the houses were built right up against each other with no streets in between. The citizens entered and left their houses through openings in the ceilings, and to get from place to place they walked across the roofs, using ladders to climb up or down from buildings of different heights. Such a city would have been difficult for an enemy to overcome.

Catalhüyük in Turkey is an ancient city whose residents once worshiped bull-gods and earned a living by trading obsidian blades made from local volcanic rock.

Cities Under the Sand

To look at modern-day Iraq, with its miles of desert sands spreading out to the Persian Gulf, it is hard to imagine that this region was once farmland and the home to the first great civilizations. Iraq, Syria, and Palestine form the area called the Fertile Crescent, a crescent-shaped belt of excellent farmland watered by rivers and the rains from the Mediterranean. Iraq was once called Mesopotamia, which means "middle of the rivers." The land between the historic Tigris and Euphrates rivers, was once rich with farms, bustling with industry, and overlooked by towering temples and huge carved statues.

silt: earth, sand, etc., carried and deposited by moving water

Over time, the courses of the Tigris and Euphrates rivers changed and left behind **silt** that filled part of the Persian Gulf. The coastline then lay further south and the old farmland became dry sand dunes. Though the Old Testament and the historical writings of the Greeks spoke of the ancient Mesopotamian cities of Babylon and Assyria, the sand held a

Map of Mesopotamia showing Sumer and the chief cities

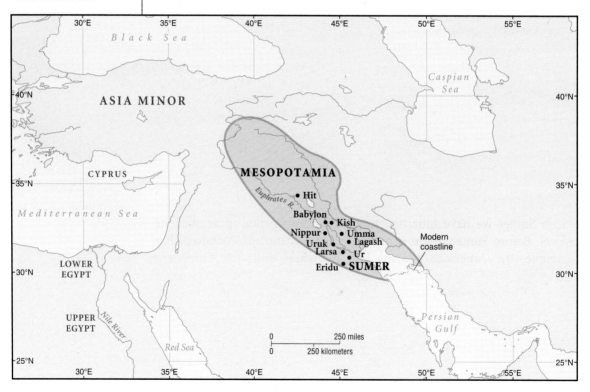

secret that would not be revealed until archaeologists dug it up in the late 1800s. That secret was Sumer (SOO•mer), mankind's first civilization.

A civilization is more than a tribe and greater than a city. The word, civilization, means "the way of life in cities," for a civilization must have cities. But the word means much more. Unlike the simple life of the nomad, a civilization looks beyond day-to-day survival. A civilization looks above, to God, with art and worship. It looks to the future, with education, sciences, and the development of resources (for instance, by farming) to preserve life. Also, a civilization looks back, telling the stories of where it came from. Sumer, which existed from nearly 4000 B.C. until about 2000 B.C., had all the elements that make a civilization.

Sumerian Religion

The True God revealed himself to mankind in the beauty and orderliness of nature. Sadly, fallen human beings did not find God in nature but worshiped the forces of nature as gods. Like all prehistoric peoples, the people of Sumer knew that there were forces greater than themselves. They worshiped these forces in the form of gods of earth and sky.

To be nearer the gods of the sky, Sumerians built the **ziggurats**, solid structures in the shape of layered pyramids, reaching hundreds of feet above ground. There were no interior rooms in the ziggurats, but outside stairways led to the sacred temples located at their peaks. The gods of Sumer were thought to be heavenly landlords for whom human beings were the field hands and slaves. All society was organized to serve and **appease** the angry gods.

ziggurat: a solid, layered stone pyramid structure

appease: to make someone calm and quiet so that he will not grow angry

Sumerian Inventions

From Sumer we have inherited that most fundamental invention, the wheel. Before Sumer, there is no record or evidence of the wheel. For example, the American Indians had no wheel until the Europeans brought it with them in the 15th century A.D. Also, Sumer invented a plow to turn the heavy soil of the Euphrates valley and pontoon boats to sail the rivers.

Sumerians also developed a legal code, a system of formal education for the young, remarkably effective medicine, and buildings made of brick. Probably the most important **legacy** of Sumer was the invention of writing. Called **cuneiform**, meaning "wedge-shaped," this early writing was

legacy: something that has been handed down
cuneiform: wedge-shaped

stylus: a pointed stick used for writing on wax or clay

done by using a sharpened stick called a **stylus** to poke symbols into soft clay tablets that were later baked or dried in the sun.

When archaeologists in the mid-1800s uncovered the great sculptures and temples of Sumer, they discovered many cuneiform tablets. Serious translation efforts moved forward thanks to such intrepid researchers as Henry Rawlinson, an English adventurer, diplomat, scholar, and amateur archaeologist. During a series of dangerous exploits in the 1830s and 1840s, Rawlinson dangled from a mountain precipice to copy inscriptions on the rock face below.

epic: a long poem that tells of heroes and their deeds

In Sumer, the art of writing became very advanced. Writing was used for business but also to maintain temple records, to honor kings, to teach children, and to tell stories. The Sumerian **epic** of Gilgamesh has been found on clay tablets in Ur, and a later version was discovered in Babylon, translated into the Babylonian language.

Life in Sumer

The cities of Sumer were ruled by kings who thought of themselves as gods and who were often buried with riches and even servants. The cities were built within high walls and had at their centers an upraised temple, which the people dedicated to a particular god who watched over them. Like the gods of the later Babylonians, Egyptians, Greeks, and Romans, the gods of Sumer were fickle and powerful—but not too powerful, for they were rather like cartoon superheroes. The religion of the Sumer is filled with deep sadness. The Sumerians believed life is a gift but they thought they had nothing to hope for after they died.

A stone with cuneiform writing and religious images

In spite of the sadness of its religion, Sumer accomplished many great things. The laws drawn up by the Sumerian king, Ur-Nammu, became the basis for the famous law code of Hammurabi, a great king who ruled the Mesopotamian city of Babylon in the 100 years following the death of Ur-Nammu.

Today we can thank the Sumerians for dividing the minute into 60 seconds and the hour into 60 minutes. The Sumerians were the first to divide the circle into 360 degrees.

Gilgamesh

Gilgamesh was the name of a real and very powerful king of Sumer about whom many stories were told. An epic poem telling the story of Gilgamesh, first preserved in 2600 B.C., is full of noble themes of love, friendship, bravery, and the search for the meaning of life. Ultimately, however, it is a tragic tale, for the hero does not find the hope he desperately seeks. Like the broken clay tablets on which Gilgamesh is preserved, this story is somehow incomplete.

As the poem opens, Gilgamesh is the strong and brave king of the city of Uruk, part god and part man; but he is such a bully that the citizens cry out to the gods to put him in his place. The goddess Ishtar hears their cry and creates Enkidu, a man as strong as Gilgamesh but wild and animal-like, with horns on his head. Enkidu lives in the forests outside the city and is a friend to the beasts; but Gilgamesh sends one of Ishtar's priestesses out to the forest to tame Enkidu, and she does so, teaching him to speak and to understand the ways of men.

The priestess also tells Enkidu about Gilgamesh. Eager to challenge the king's power, Enkidu comes to the city of Uruk and steps in Gilgamesh's way as he tries to enter a house to choose a bride. The two giant men begin to wrestle, each one as strong as the other. When the fierce fighting stops, Gilgamesh is the winner; but to the surprise of the townspeople, Gilgamesh

and Enkidu embrace and declare themselves the closest of friends.

The two embark on a series of adventures, including the defeat of a terrifying monster, Humbaba. The heroes engage in a battle with a great bull sent by Ishtar to kill Gilgamesh and destroy Uruk after Gilgamesh refuses to be Ishtar's husband. As punishment for killing the bull, Enkidu is stricken and dies. Anguished at losing his friend and fearing his own death, Gilgamesh sets off in search of eternal life.

He journeys to Utnapishtim, his ancestor, who enjoys immortality on the far side of the Bitter River. But Utnapishtim can offer Gilgamesh no hope. He himself had received eternal life from the gods, but only as a special gift. Utnapishtim however does tell Gilgamesh of a secret plant that can restore youth, but after Gilgamesh pulls the elusive plant from the bottom of the river, a snake steals it from him.

Thus foiled, the great Gilgamesh must suffer death as any common man. The epic ends with the tale of his death.

An ancient seal (2500 B.C.) portraying Gilgamesh with slain lions

Head of an Akkadian ruler, 2300–2000 B.C.

Mesopotamia had no forests, but the Sumerians traded their farm produce and sophisticated crafts with peoples in other lands for wood, from which they made ships on which they sailed on trading expeditions to Africa and India. From the ivory, gold, and precious stones they obtained from these far lands, the Sumerians created magnificent jewelry and handcrafted beautiful instruments, such as lyres and harps.

What Happened to Sumer?

Though we think of Sumer as one, united civilization, it did not have one king or government. Sumer was made up of a number of different cities that had their own kings and so were independent. Constant wars between these kings troubled the Sumerian cities and weakened them. Because Sumer was a rich and fertile land, it became a target for invading tribes from the outlying areas.

So it was that Sargon, one of the first great military leaders in history, conquered Sumer in 2360 B.C. Sargon was a member of the Akkadian tribe that lived in the northern parts of Sumer and learned civilization from the Sumerians. The son of a shepherd, Sargon served in the palace of the kings of Kish, a city in Akkad. He became king himself and commanded a huge army for his time, some 5,000 men. (As far as we know, he was also the first to **draft** young men into his army.)

draft: to select some people for a specific purpose, such as military service; to require them to serve

Sargon devised novel battle plans. Instead of moving in a disorganized crowd, his soldiers fought in formation behind rows of shields, while other warriors in animal-drawn carts attacked the enemy along the sides of the battlefield. With his new methods and conquering spirit, Sargon eventually subdued all of Sumer, then moved back north and west toward the Mediterranean and added Syria to his possessions. He made Akkadian the language of all the Mesopotamian world, replacing the language of Sumer. When he died, he ruled the largest empire of his time. Sargon reigned for 56 years, and his empire lasted through the reigns of his son and grandson.

After the death of Sargon's grandson, the Akkadian Empire broke up. But, because of this empire, the Sumerian way of life, its laws, beliefs, and culture had spread to all of Mesopotamia and to the later empires of Assyria and Babylon.

Ancient Mesopotamian stone carving

Egypt, the First Nation

While Sumer was reaching maturity, another civilization was born 1,000 miles to the west, across the Red Sea in North Africa. This civilization, called Egypt, rose in the fertile valley through which the great Nile River flows. Egypt was perhaps history's first nation state—a unified government for people who speak one language and have a common culture. By 4000 B.C., the Egyptians were one people, speaking a common language, and governed by a single king who ruled over all the Nile Valley.

The Hamitic (hah-MIH-tic) people were the first to settle Egypt in about 6000 B.C. Our name for them comes from the name they gave to Egypt—Khemi. These people farmed along the Nile Valley and in the Delta, the marshy plain where the Nile empties into the Mediterranean Sea. Both the Nile Valley and the Delta were especially good for farming. The land had a warm climate and, more importantly, it was watered and fed by the Nile. Every year, the Nile flooded the nearby fields, and when the waters withdrew, left behind rich silt that renewed the fields' fertility.

Early inventions helped the Hamitic people build their civilization. To irrigate their fields, farmers used a tool called a *shaduf*, which was a long pole balanced over a forked stick, with a water bucket on one end and a **counterweight** on the other. Farmers would dip the bucket into the river, then swing it around to pour the water into a channel, down which the water flowed to irrigate the fields.

counterweight: an equal weight

Map of ancient Egypt showing the Delta, Memphis, Thebes, and the location of the pyramids

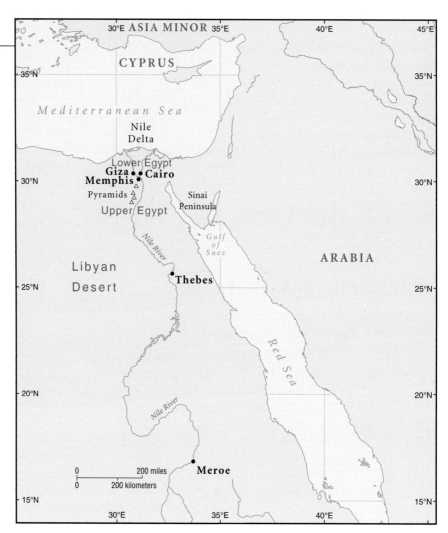

Eventually, two kingdoms developed in Egypt—one in the Nile Delta region (called Lower Egypt, because it was located where the Nile flows into the sea) and the other, upriver and further south, called Upper Egypt. Possibly as early as 3500 B.C., King Menes (MAY-nays) united Lower Egypt and Upper Egypt into one kingdom. This was a great achievement, but not the only achievement of Menes's reign. The king also developed water basins to irrigate the Nile Valley and founded Memphis, a city that later became the capital of Egypt.

Surrounded by a fearsome desert that was hard to cross, Egypt was more protected from constant foreign invasion than Sumer was. The

Egyptian kingdom was so safe and stable that it lasted over 3,000 years under the rule of **dynasties** of pharaohs. The ruler or king of Egypt was called *pharaoh*, a word that meant "the Great House." (The Egyptians called their king "the Great House" much in the same way Americans refer to the United States president as "the White House.") The pharaoh was Egypt's king, but he was thought to be more than a human ruler. Just as the Sumerians did with their kings, the Egyptians revered the pharaohs as gods, and they willingly served them in exchange for their leadership and the magical protection they believed the pharaohs brought them. Ancient Egyptians believed pharaoh called down the gods' favor upon them and brought a heavenly order instead of chaos to the kingdom.

Historians divide Egyptian history into four periods: the Old Kingdom (2670–2198 B.C.), the Middle Kingdom (1938–1759 B.C.), the New Kingdom (1539–1100 B.C.), and the Late Period (1100–332 B.C.) These four periods encompass a total of 30 dynasties.

The World in Pictures

One way we have learned about the culture of ancient Egypt is through the writings of its people that have been preserved to our day. The ancient Egyptians had a very complicated form of writing, which we call hieroglyphics, a Greek word that means "sacred writing." Hieroglyphic writing is made up of several hundred little pictures, each of which could stand for a word or a part of a word. Hieroglyphics also included alphabetic symbols and could be written left to right, right to left, or top to bottom. The Egyptians may have learned the art of writing from Mesopotamia; but since Egyptian hieroglyphic writing is so different from Sumerian cuneiform writing, the Egyptians probably developed writing on their own.

The Egyptians used different writing tools than the Sumerians did. In addition to carving on the walls of tombs and other buildings, the Egyptians invented the first paper, called **papyrus** (pah-PIE-russ). Papyrus came from the papyrus reed that grows in the wetlands of the Nile Delta. Egyptians made their paper by stripping the papyrus reed, pressing and pounding the strips into flat sheets, and hanging the sheets to dry. Using a shredded reed dipped into an ink made from minerals and water, the Egyptians wrote by painting on the sheets of papyrus.

Because hieroglyphic writing was so complex, only 1 percent of the populace of ancient Egypt could read or write. Those who did write,

Papyrus reeds

dynasty: a line of rulers who belong to a single family

papyrus: paper made from pressed and woven reeds

Ancient Egyptian hiero-glyphics carved into stone at the Temple of Luxor in Egypt

the scribes, trained for years to write hieroglyphs and so were greatly honored. In ancient Egyptian society, only the pharaoh received more honor than the scribes.

Life and Death in Egypt

Since Egypt was watered by the Nile and blessed with rich, fertile soil, it is not surprising that most ancient Egyptians were farmers. Yet farming was not their only profession. Ancient Egyptians were also craftsmen, engineers, architects, artists, and laborers of various types. Outside of work, Egyptians honored family life and loved leisure. They drank beer and enjoyed banquets, music, and dancing. They kept their hair short and wore wigs. They dressed themselves in finely woven linen clothes. Both men and women wore makeup.

The ancient Egyptians were great architects and artists. They built enormous public buildings—tombs, great pillared temples to their gods, palaces for their rulers, and great houses for the rich and powerful. They sculpted statues, some very great and massive, others small, delicate, and very beautiful. They made paintings in rich colors, which are quite beautiful though they might look strange to us. And they crafted lovely jewelry

The Rosetta Stone

The hieroglyphs might never have been translated were it not for the Rosetta Stone. This huge basalt slab, recovered on the Nile Delta in 1799, was carved in both Greek and two forms of the Egyptian language, making it a kind of translation dictionary. But even then, it took many years for experts to translate ancient Egyptian inscriptions and documents.

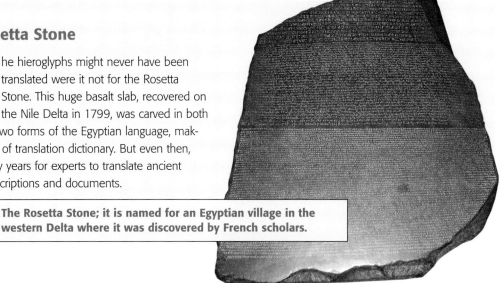

The Rosetta Stone; it is named for an Egyptian village in the western Delta where it was discovered by French scholars.

from gold and precious stones. The Egyptians were ingenious engineers, digging canals to bring water from the Nile to irrigate distant fields, and they were brilliant mathematicians and astronomers. They practiced medicine, as well, and kept time with water clocks and sundials. Indeed, other ancient peoples thought the Egyptians very, very wise.

Like other ancient peoples, the Egyptians believed in many gods. Their supreme god was Ra, the sun god, and they believed that from Ra sprang

The Egyptians told many stories about their gods. One of the more famous ones goes like this.

Geb, god of the earth, and Nut, goddess of the sky, had four children, named Osiris, Set, Isis, and Nephythis. Set was always jealous of his brother Osiris, who ruled Egypt. One day, Set tricked Osiris into lying in a coffin, then nailed it closed and threw the coffin into the river. Isis, who was wife and sister to Osiris, searched for him day and night, distraught and weeping. When she finally found the coffin, Set snatched it from her and chopped Osiris into pieces, scattering the pieces all over Egypt.

Isis wandered over the countryside, gathered the parts of Osiris' body, and put them back together. Osiris and Isis then had a child, Horus, whom Isis raised in secret when Osiris left to become king of the Other World. Horus grew up and conquered his uncle Set and so took his rightful place as king of Egypt.

a whole "family" of gods, some of whom had power over natural elements, such as the sky and the Earth, the Nile and the fertility of the soil. Other gods had power over such things as learning and justice. The Egyptians thought their gods took on animal forms and so often depicted them with animal bodies and human heads, or human bodies with animal heads. But though they appeared as animals, the gods were thought to have human personalities, while the greatest gods were considered to be in no way human or animal. Yet, the Egyptians thought, even the greatest gods, when they appeared, appeared as animals.

The Egyptians believed that death was not the end of human life, but that souls would continue to live after death and could even return to their bodies. This belief led to many unusual practices, such as mummification, a way of preserving dead bodies so that the departed souls could use them again. The word "mummy" comes from an Arab word for wax because the preserved bodies looked wax-like. To mummify dead bodies, the Egyptians soaked them in salts and wrapped them in linen strips. In the later years of the empire, Egyptians mummified animals they believed to be sacred, such as cats, **ibises**, and even crocodiles.

ibis: a wading bird related to the heron

The Mysterious Pyramids

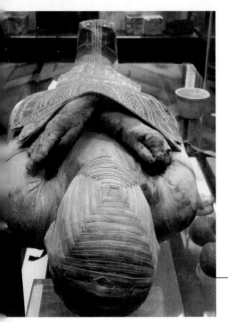

Since they believed in an afterlife, Egyptians developed very elaborate ways to bury their kings and, even, the common people. The earliest Egyptian tomb was a small, rectangular, flat-roofed building made of stone or mud bricks, called a *mastaba*. But in the Third Dynasty of the Old Kingdom, around 2750 B.C., an architect named Imhotep built the first pyramid for Pharaoh Zoser. This 200-foot step pyramid looks like a stack of mastabas, each one of which is smaller than the one below it. The temples built in front of the pyramid had corridors and rooms that held treasures for the pharaoh to enjoy in the afterlife. Pharaohs after Zoser built even more spectacular pyramids, with peaks that pointed towards the gods of the night sky.

The ancient Greek historian, Herodotus, thought the pyramids were built by slave labor, and this belief was held to be true for many centuries. More recent scholars, however, have come to think that farmers and other free workers built the pyramids, both to honor their kings and to have something to do while the flooding of the Nile made working in the fields impossible.

An Egyptian mummy

The most spectacular pyramid, indeed one of the largest buildings in the world, is the Great Pyramid of the pharaoh Khufu, constructed during the Fourth Dynasty, around 2571 B.C. Standing about 348 feet tall, this pyramid was the tallest man-made structure before taller buildings were raised in the 19th century. Each of the pyramid's four sides is 750 feet long, and the area of the whole pyramid covers more than 13 acres — enough to enclose six football fields. The pyramid is constructed of more than 2 million stone blocks, most of them weighing 2½ tons. Although today the sides of the pyramid look rough, at one time it was covered with a smooth layer of brightly polished limestone and capped with marble. Reflecting the light of the bright desert sun, the pyramid could be seen for miles around. What a stunning sight it must have been for the ancient world!

Near the Great Pyramid in Giza (GEE-zah) are two others, also built in the Fourth Dynasty, for Pharaohs Khafre and Menkaure. These smaller pyramids, along with the Great Pyramid, were the last of the most elaborate pyramids to be built. Why did pharaohs stop building

Pyramids of Giza

polytheism: the belief in and worship of many gods
monotheism: the belief in and worship of one god

Ancient portraits of two pharaohs, Akhenaten (top) and Hatshepsut (bottom)

pyramids? We do not know; but perhaps building such enormous structures had become too expensive.

Oddly enough, we have no records to show how pyramids were built. At the time they built the pyramids, the Egyptians had neither pulleys nor wheels. Because of this, some scholars have supposed that workers built ramps of earth around the pyramid so that stones could be dragged to the top over the sloped paths. Without pulleys or wheels, workers must have used rollers, ropes, and human muscle to move the enormous stones.

Giza has another mysterious monument: the Great Sphinx. The giant limestone figure, 240 feet long and 65 feet high, has a lion's body and a man's head. The statue was not called "sphinx" until a long time after it was built, when the Greeks named it after a monster that appeared in their stories. For the Egyptians, the Sphinx represented the sun god, Ra. Its face looks like Pharaoh Khafre's, before whose tomb it appears to stand guard.

The Pharaohs

Only a few of the many pharaohs of Egypt have become well known. One of the famous pharaohs is Akhenaten, who ruled in the New Kingdom from 1353–1335 B.C. He changed his name from Amenhotep IV to Akhenaten to honor Aten, a god of the sun. Abandoning the conquests of foreign peoples, Akhenaten instead tried to change the social and religious life of Egypt. He moved the capital from Thebes, where it had been since the Middle Kingdom, to a grand new city he ordered built. The pharaoah named this after Aten, though today it is known as Tell el-Amarna. Akhenaten then tried to change the **polytheism** (worship of many gods) of his people to a type of **monotheism** (worship of one god), by raising Aten above all other gods and abolishing the temples and worship of all the other gods. When Akhenaten died, however, the nation returned to its traditional polytheistic religion and moved the capital back to Thebes.

Another outstanding pharaoh was Hatshepsut, the mother of Thutmose III, who during the boy's childhood ruled for 15 years of the Eighteenth Dynasty. One of possibly two female pharaohs, she is sometimes depicted in statues as a man, beard and all. Hatshepsut kept a peaceful kingdom and built a number of monuments, including a beautiful temple, Deir-el-Bahri, in western Thebes.

The Nineteenth Dynasty of Egypt began with the reign of Ramses I and his successors, who made Egypt once again a strong military power. Fighting the Hittite people for control of Palestine, Ramses II led an army in the battle of Kadesh, only to be greatly outnumbered by Hittite-led troops from more than twenty Asian peoples. According to a tale recorded on Ramses II's monument, the brave fighting of his army ended the battle in a draw, although history says the Hittites won.

Eventually Ramses II signed a peace treaty with the Hittite king Hattusilis, who later gave one of his daughters to Ramses for his wife. This may be the first peace treaty in the history of the world. The two empires were at peace with each other for more than fifty years, and Ramses II gained a reputation as Egypt's most vigorous builder. In addition to placing his own name and image on the tombs and buildings of former pharaohs, Ramses II left great monuments of his own—including four statues carved from the rock at the Abu Simbel temples.

Ancient Egypt in Our Modern World

Because of its peculiar burial practices, its strange gods, tombs, and statues, ancient Egypt is a mysterious place to us. Egyptian culture was in many ways very different from other ancient cultures. The Egyptians did

Some 1,000 years after construction of the Sphinx, an Egyptian prince, Thutmose IV, was sleeping in its shade after hunting. While he slept, the Sphinx appeared to him in a dream and told him to clear away the sand that nearly buried it, and that if he obeyed he would become king. Thutmose did as he was told, and due to the untimely death of his older brother, he became king during the Eighteenth Dynasty, the first dynasty of the New Kingdom. The story of Thutmose's dream is recorded on a stele, a stone marker placed between the giant lion's paws.

The god Amun gives life (the ankh) to the pharaoh Thutmoses IV

The great Sphinx was once painted in bright colors, while the pyramid of Khufu, shown behind it, was sheathed in polished limestone that gleamed and reflected the sun's rays for many miles around.

The Young King "Tut"

Egyptian pyramids and tombs contained vast storehouses of treasure, which throughout the ages were stolen by clever tomb robbers. Despite the builders' best efforts—installing false doors and passageways going nowhere—the burglars outwitted them. Nearly all the tombs were stripped of their riches, often in the very lifetime of those who buried the kings.

Pharaoh Tutankhamen (TOOT•in•COM•mon) (1333–1323 B.C.) was an exception—his burial chamber was untouched until it was discovered in 1922 by Howard Carter, an English archaeologist. The remains from the tomb included the king's mummy inside three nested coffins, the innermost one of solid gold and the outer two of **gilded** wood.

The pharaoh's **sarcophagus**, bore a beautiful mask of the dead king's head, depicting his face in gold, and around it the symbols of the kingdom, the vulture, and the cobra. The cham-

ber also held jewelry, sacred writings, gilded furniture, clothes, weapons, and other objects.

Though the achievements of this boy king were minor, he became known to all the modern world through the discovery of his tomb. His funeral possessions have traveled around the world, on display in museums.

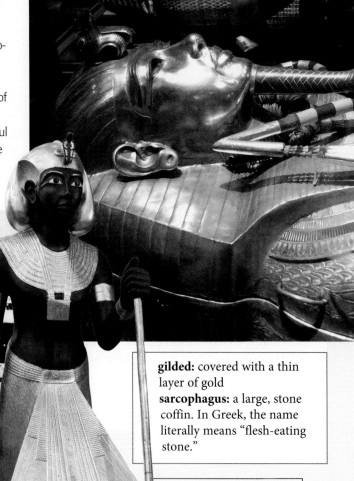

King Tutankhamen's contained artwork and ritual objects for the pharaoh's use in the afterlife.

gilded: covered with a thin layer of gold
sarcophagus: a large, stone coffin. In Greek, the name literally means "flesh-eating stone."

Guardian spirit from Tutankhamun's tomb

not seem to want to extend their culture to other lands nor to allow ideas from other cultures to shape their understanding of the world. In time, Egyptian civilization simply disappeared. Only the great pyramids, tombs, and artwork remained to tell us of its power and mystery.

But this early civilization continues to exist in what it has given to our own civilization. Egyptian papyrus led to the development of our paper, which we manufacture, not from swamp reeds, but wood pulp. The Egyptians divided their year into 12 months and 365 days, as we still do today. They came up with important mathematical formulas. It was the Egyptians, for instance, that taught the world how to find the area of a circle and how to make a true right angle. One Egyptian invention that we have today is the umbrella—though the Egyptians probably used it more to protect themselves from the merciless hot sun of the desert than to shield them from rain.

Today we marvel at Egypt's pyramids, great-pillared monuments, mummified animals, unique art, and sacred writing. Ancient Egyptian culture seems to have nothing in common with the Muslims and Christians who live along the Nile today. Egyptian civilization is unimaginably ancient —so ancient that even the ancient Greeks thought it very, very old. It is perhaps because the civilization of the world's first nation-state is so very old that its majesty and mystery have stirred the imagination of every civilization since.

Ramses II wearing the double crown of Egypt: the tall crown of Lower Egypt inside the short, round crown of Upper Egypt

Chapter 2 Review

Let's Remember   Please write your answers in complete sentences.
1. What are the two divisions of the Stone Age?
2. What was the climate of the world like when the Stone Age took place?
3. How many years did the four periods of Egyptian history cover? How many dynasties were there during those years?
4. What is the Rosetta Stone and why is it important?
5. Who was the pharaoh who tried to change the polytheistic religion of Egypt to monotheism?
6. Who was Tutankhamen?

Let's Consider   For silent thinking and a short essay, or for thinking in a group with classroom discussion:

1. Put the following dates in the order in which they should go, starting from the date farthest away from our time and ending with the one closest to our time: A.D. 35, 1500 B.C., A.D. 1959, A.D. 1200, 30 B.C., 350 B.C., A.D. 1803, 1812 B.C.
2. Three sciences study the past: paleontology, archaeology, and anthropology. How do they differ from the study of history?
3. What sort of people would have made the cave paintings? Why does the fact that they made these painting show they were not just animals?
4. In what ways do you think the invention of the wheel in Sumer made work easier?
5. Do you think Egyptian papyrus paper was a better writing material than wood, stone, or clay? Why or why not?

Things to Do

1. Make a list of the countries and U.S. states that at one time were covered by ice age glaciers.
2. Using the maps in the book as guides, students should draw their own maps of ancient Egypt and Mesopotamia. The map of Mesopotamia should include the following cities: Ur, Babylon, Uruk, and Babylon. It should also indicate where Sumer and Akkad were. The map of Egypt should indicate Upper Egypt and Lower Egypt. Each map should have a compass rose. (Teachers should help the students to discern the geographical directions.)

Let's Eat!

A Stone Age soup could have been made by putting water, meat, and wild onion into a leather container. Stones could then be heated in an open fire and dropped into the leather container to make the water boil.

Chapter 3 The Mission of Israel

God Calls Forth a Nation

All early civilizations grew up in much the same way as Sumer and Egypt did. Groups of families settled in an area to farm. They formed communities, and from these communities, came leaders, who became kings over cities and even nations. Religion was an important part of everyday life; people worshiped many gods—personal, household gods as well as the great gods who were believed to have power over earth, water, and sky. For the people, pagan priests offered sacrifices to appease the unpredictable gods, and the people hoped for good fortune.

The story of the nation of Israel, however, was very different. Israel arose because God wanted to make a special people of his own. God had a plan for Israel and, through Israel, for the world.

God began his nation Israel in a surprising way: by calling an elderly, childless couple, Abram and Sarai. This couple did not remain in their native place, the ancient Sumerian city of Ur. Trusting in the command of God, they moved to a foreign land to make their home among strangers and enemies. They did not reach out to many gods with prayers and sacrifices. Instead, the one, true God of heaven and earth reached out to them.

So begins the story of Israel. Through that nation, all nations would find hope of eternal life through the Son of God, Jesus Christ.

Abraham prepares to sacrifice Isaac, by Andrea Mantegna (1430–1506)

At Haran, a city in Sumer, God broke into human history when he spoke to Abram, saying: "Go forth from the land of your kinsfolk and from your father's house to a land that I will show you. I will make of you a great nation, and I will bless you; I will make your name great, so that you will be a blessing. I will bless those who bless you and curse those who curse you. All the communities of the earth shall find blessing in you" (Genesis 12:1).

Abram obeyed, took his wife Sarai and nephew Lot and all their possessions, and moved into the land of Canaan (KAY•nan), a part of Palestine, west of the Jordan River. When Abram arrived, God made a spectacular promise. Sarai was **barren** and Canaan already belonged to the Canaanite peoples; yet, God told Abram: "To your descendants I will give this land."

barren: not able to have children

God continued to make promises to Abram and tested his faith. Then God made a **covenant** with Abram, an "everlasting pact" to make Abram the father of nations and kings and to make Canaan their permanent home. God asked only that Abram and his people make him their God. God changed Abram's name to Abraham, "Father of Multitudes," and Sarai's name to Sarah, meaning "Princess." In time God proved his word (Genesis 17) to Abraham and Sarah by giving them a son, Isaac. Isaac was the father of Jacob, who received the name, Israel, and became the father of 12 sons. According to the Bible, from these sons came the 12 tribes that made up the chosen people of Israel.

covenant: a solemn agreement between two or more people

The world of Abraham

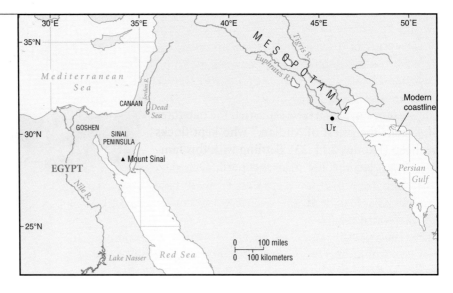

The Exodus

The second book of the Bible, Exodus, tells the story of the next period of Israel's history — the **exodus**, or "going out" from Egypt. The Bible does not tell us when the exodus occurred. It does not name the pharaoh who was ruling Egypt at the time, but simply calls him "Pharaoh." Comparing the biblical story with what we know of Egyptian history, however, it seems that the exodus occurred during the Nineteenth Dynasty, when Ramses II was king over Egypt.

exodus: a large departure or "going out" of people from a place

Ramses II was a great builder, and to carry out his building projects, he needed a large number of workers. Not far from his capital city, called the House of Ramses, was the land of Goshen, a part of the Delta where Abraham's descendants, the Israelites or Hebrews, were then living. Who would be better than these immigrant foreigners to act as laborers to carry out Pharaoh's great building projects? So it was that Pharaoh forced the Hebrews to serve him as slaves.

The Bible tells us that, even though they were treated so badly, the Hebrews grew in numbers. This so worried Pharaoh that he commanded that all Hebrew baby boys had to be killed. One Hebrew mother, however, saved her son by placing him in a basket beside the river. A servant of Pharaoh's daughter found the child and brought him to her mistress, who adopted him and raised him in the palace. Pharaoh's daughter gave the child the name Moses, "because, she said, "I have drawn him out of the water" (Exodus 2:1-10).

When Moses grew to be a man, he killed an Egyptian for striking a Hebrew. Fearing punishment for the killing, Moses escaped to Midian, a land east of Egypt. There he married the daughter of Reuel, "the priest of Midian," who kept flocks of sheep (Exodus 2:11-22). Settling with this family, Moses led the life of a shepherd. One day, while helping with Reuel's flock near "the mountain of God," Mount Horeb, Moses saw an amazing sight. On the mountain above him, a bush was burning but did not disappear into ashes! Moses climbed the mountain, and God spoke to him from the bush. God said to Moses, "Come, I will send you to Pharaoh that

A stained glass window in the cathedral of Brussels depicting Moses and the burning bush

you may bring forth my people, the sons of Israel, out of Egypt" (Exodus 3:10). Moses was to lead the Hebrews from slavery to freedom in the land God had promised to Abraham — Canaan, a "land flowing with milk and honey" (Exodus 3:8).

Though he was a little reluctant, Moses obeyed God and returned to Egypt. But Pharaoh was even more reluctant to follow God's command. He refused to let Israel go, and so, by the hand of Moses, God sent ten plagues upon Egypt. The final plague was the death of all the first-born sons in the land of Egypt (Exodus 7-11). Only the Hebrew children escaped, for God had commanded his people to place the blood of sacrificed lambs on the door posts of their houses. When the "angel of death" saw the blood on the Hebrew's houses, he "passed over" them (Exodus 12:1-32). Ever after, the Israelites have celebrated this event in a feast called the Passover. Each year, the Passover remembrance centers around the Seder (SAY-der), a family prayer ceremony and meal that includes the retelling of the sacred story of Israel's deliverance from slavery in Egypt.

God had said to Moses that he would send plagues on the Egyptians so that they "shall know that I am the Lord" (Exodus 7:5). But God had one more wonder for Pharaoh. After the plague of the firstborn, Pharaoh let Israel leave Egypt. But it was not long before Pharaoh was sorry he had let Israel go. Gathering his army, he pursued the Israelites until they were trapped between the Egyptians and the waters of the Red Sea.

"Lift up your rod," God commanded Moses, "and stretch out your hand over the sea and divide it, that the people of Israel may go on dry ground through the sea." Moses did as God commanded. The waters parted, and Israel passed through the sea. When the Egyptians pursued the Israelites, the waters of the sea washed over and destroyed Pharaoh's army (Exodus 14).

On the far shore of the sea, the Israelites, seeing God's salvation, broke into a song of joy that held a deeper meaning about salvation — not from Pharaoh, but from the power of sin:

"I will sing to the Lord, for he has triumphed gloriously; the horse and rider he has thrown into the sea.

The Lord is my strength and my song, and he has become my salvation;

this is my God, and I will praise him, my father's God, and I will exalt him."

(Exodus 15:1-2)

The Commandments

Moses and the Israelites wandered in the desert for 40 years, a time of testing and trial. Though they had suffered as slaves in Egypt, the Israelites grumbled over their new difficulties on the way to the Promised Land. God, however, provided them with a special bread called manna, and the Israelites journeyed south along the western edge of the Sinai Peninsula, which juts into the Red Sea.

In the southern part of the Sinai Peninsula stands Mt. Horeb or Sinai, where God had appeared to Moses in the burning bush. There God summoned Moses and gave him and his people the Ten Commandments:

1. I am the Lord your God, and you shall not have other gods besides me.
2. You shall not take the name of the Lord your God in vain.
3. Keep holy the Sabbath Day.
4. Honor your father and mother.
5. You shall not kill.
6. You shall not commit adultery.
7. You shall not steal.
8. You shall not bear false witness against your neighbor.
9. You shall not **covet** your neighbor's wife.
10. You shall not covet your neighbor's goods.

covet: to desire that which belongs to another

Stained glass window in the cathedral of Brussels, depicting Moses with the Stone Tablets inscribed with the Ten Commandments

The desert of the Sinai is not like the Sahara. More rocky than sandy, the Sinai desert has hardy trees and enough scrubby plants for sheep and goats to graze on. Today several thousand **Bedouin** (BEH•doo•in) still tend their flocks there.

Bedouin: a nomadic Arab in the deserts of Arabia, Syria, or Northern Africa

Though these commandments were simple, they brought about a tremendous improvement in human civilization. The commandments placed great demands on people in order to lead them to their true purpose in life: the love of God and of one's neighbor for the sake of God. The commandments talk about not just outward action (like stealing) but also the thoughts (like coveting) that lead to these actions. They are meant to set God's people free, not from human slavery, but from the slavery of sin.

The Ten Commandments are based on the knowledge of right and wrong that can be understood just through human reason. Because of this, they do not belong only to the religion of the Hebrews but to all people. Yet God revealed them to his chosen people in a dramatic display of thunder and lightning, and he inscribed them on tablets of stone "with his own finger" (Exodus 31:18).

Joshua commands the sun to stand still.

Israel in the Promised Land

In the book of Numbers, the Bible tells how the Israelites moved from Sinai to the south of Canaan. There the Israelites began to enter Canaan at Kadesh-Barnea, a city ruled by a people called the Amorites. At God's command, Moses sent 12 men, one from each tribe, to scout out the area. They reported that the land had fertile farmlands but was too hard to conquer because of its high-walled cities and the "giant" people who lived in them.

The Israelites were afraid and angry with God. Why had God brought them out of the land of Egypt? The people of Canaan were too strong for them, they cried! The people's lack of faith brought God's punishment on them. He declared that Israel would wander in the desert until every man or woman (except two faithful men, Caleb and Joshua) who had come out of Egypt had died. Not they, but their children, would enter Canaan. When the people heard God's judgment, they changed their minds and decided to invade the Promised Land. Moses warned them not to do this, for God would not be with them; but they would not listen. The invasion was a failure and the Israelites had to complete 40 years of wandering in the desert, outside of the Promised Land (Numbers 14).

After Moses' death in about the year 1200 B.C., the Israelites, led now by Joshua, at last entered Canaan. In the southern part of the land, they conquered the city of Jericho and then turned north to conquer other parts of the land. One by one, the Canaanite cities fell before the victorious Joshua. Joshua then divided up the land between the twelve tribes that made up the people of Israel. The tribes were: Ruben, Simeon, Gad, Judah, Issachar, Zebulon, Dan, Benjamin, Asher, Naphtali, and the two "half tribes," Ephraim and Manassah. The tribe of Levi received no land. Instead, the men of Levi were placed in charge of Israel's tent shrine to God, the Tabernacle, which housed a most sacred object. This was the Ark of the Covenant, a gold-covered chest with two winged figures called cherubim on top. The Ark contained the two stone tablets inscribed with the Ten Commandments, a jar of manna, and the rod of Moses. It was from the Ark that God gave his messages to Israel.

A map showing Phoenicia and the division of ancient Palestine between the twelve tribes of Israel

The Dreaded Philistines

After the conquest of Canaan came the period of the judges, as told in the book of Judges in the Bible, when wise chiefs and military heroes ruled the various tribes of Israel. During this time, the Israelites were not as victorious over their enemies as they had been in the days of Joshua. Instead, God used the peoples around them to test the Israelites' faith. If the Israelites slipped back into idol worship condemned in the First Commandment, God handed them over to their enemies. One such enemy was the Philistines, who dominated Israel for 40 years.

Called the "Sea Peoples" by the Egyptians, the Philistines had moved from the Aegean Sea region around 1200 B.C. and conquered southwest Palestine. The Philistines were known for their skills in metalworking, pottery, and the shipping trade. They were also a mighty military power. They were a formidable foe for the Israelites.

Blood Red Creators of the Alphabet

North of Canaan, stretching along the Mediterranean coast, was the country of a people called the Phoenicians. The name, Phoenician, comes from the Greek word meaning "blood red," referring to the deep purplish dye the Phoenicians made from a shellfish called the murex. But the Phoenicians were not only known for making dye. They were successful seafarers, merchants, and **mercenaries**. The Phoenicians were the inventors of glass and the art of glass blowing.

The Phoenicians formed city-states up and down the coasts of modern-day Syria and Lebanon. These city states were at times independent, but they were usually under the control of other powerful nations, such as the Assyrians or the Babylonians. While under Assyrian rule in the 9th century B.C., the Phoenicians formed colonies in other regions of the Mediterranean world. The greatest Phoenician **colony** was the city of Carthage in northwest Africa, near modern-day Tunis.

As a tool to help them in trading with other lands, the Phoenicians created the first real alphabet. Both Sumerian and Egyptian writing had a large number of symbols; but somewhere between 1500 and

1000 B.C., the Phoenicians simplified Egyptian symbols and came up with a quick method of writing. This method used an alphabet of only 22 letters, instead of hundreds of symbols, such as the Egyptians used. Nearly all the world's languages, except Chinese, Japanese, and other Oriental languages, have come to use alphabets that in one way or another come from the Phoenician alphabet. The Hebrews, too, developed an alphabet for their language from the writing of the Canaanite people they came to live among. Like Phoenician, Hebrew writing is read from right to left, not left to right, as we read our writing.

> **mercenary:** a soldier for hire
> **colony:** a settlement made by a people far from their native country; a territory that is distant from the country that governs it

The Story of Samson

It was during the period of the judges that God raised up one special hero who would weaken Philistine power over the Israelites. This was the hero Samson, whose story is told in the book of Judges, Chapters 13–15.

Manoah of the Israelite tribe of Dan had a wife who could have no children. One day an angel appeared to them and said she and her husband would have a son who would help free their people from the Philistines. The woman was to take no strong drink and to eat no unclean foods, and when the boy was born, he was not to let a razor touch his head, as a sign of his consecration to God.

It came to pass that the woman bore a son and named him Samson. As he grew his mother kept her promise, and Samson's hair grew long. Samson had incredible strength. One day he killed a lion with his bare hands. When he grew up and was married, the Philistines stole his wife and gave her to another man. Samson then caught 300 foxes and, tying torches between the tails of each pair, set fire to all the Philistines' fields and orchards. When the Philistines came after him, Samson took the jawbone of an ass and killed 1,000 of his enemies!

Then Samson fell in love with a Philistine woman named Delilah, to whom her people promised a vast sum of money in exchange for finding out the secret of Samson's great strength. Samson teased her and would not tell her the truth; but when he could take no more of her complaining, he told her that his strength lay in his consecration to God. If a razor touched his head, Samson said, he would be as weak as any other man.

When he fell asleep that night, the treacherous Delilah called for someone to shave off Samson's seven locks of hair. The Philistines then grabbed Samson, blinded his eyes, and threw him into prison.

One night while the Philistines held a huge, riotous party to celebrate Samson's capture, they brought the prisoner to the middle of the temple for their amusement. Samson, whose hair had begun to grow back, prayed to God for one last show of strength. He pushed hard against the two middle columns that supported the temple. In an instant the entire building collapsed, killing everyone, including the hero, Samson.

Samson brings down the temple of their god upon the Philistine leaders for tricking, capturing, and blinding him. Illustration by Gustave Dore.

Israel's First King

In time, the Israelites wanted to unify their nation under a king. "We too must be like other nations, with a king to rule us and to lead us in warfare and fight our battles," they cried (I Samuel 8:20). Israel's last judge, the prophet Samuel, did not approve of this request. Samuel knew the people wanted a king for the wrong reason — not to help them keep the covenant with God, but rather for power and prestige. Finally, at God's command, Samuel gave in to the people's request. Inspired by God, Samuel anointed Saul, the son of Kish, of the tribe of Benjamin, to rule over Israel. And the people of Israel **acclaimed** him their king.

acclaim: to applaud and show approval

Saul had a tragic reign. He disobeyed God several times, which brought upon him the wrath of the prophet Samuel. God at last rejected Saul as king and revealed to Samuel whom he had chosen to succeed him as king. This was a young man named David, the youngest son of Jesse of Bethlehem. David was a shepherd who wrestled wild animals and, later, killed a Philistine giant, Goliath, with only a stone from a slingshot. After he was anointed by Samuel, David served in Saul's army and became the king's best warrior.

Though Samuel had anointed David as king, Saul continued to rule. Saul suffered from an affliction, an evil spirit that caused him to lose consciousness. Only David, playing music, could calm the mad king. Saul suffered many misfortunes and grew jealous of David, who had become a great hero for Israel. In the end, Saul plotted to kill David, forcing him to flee into the wilderness with a band of followers. When the Philistines overcame the Israelites in a battle on Mount Gilboa, Saul, filled with despair, killed himself by falling on his sword.

David slays Goliath. Illustration by Gustave Dore.

Upon learning of Saul's death, the men of Judah — the Israelites who lived in the southern part of the kingdom

—declared David their king, while the rest of Israel chose Saul's son, Ishbaal, to rule over them. Seven years later, after Ishbaal's death, David was anointed king of all Israel. He was 30 years old when he began his reign, and he reigned for 40 years. David was Israel's greatest king.

David, Hero-King of a Golden Age

Scripture calls David a "man after God's own heart," for, unlike Saul, David did all he could to please God. David was also a military master. He defeated the many peoples in and surrounding Palestine — Philistines, Moabites, Arameans, Ammonites, Amalekites, and Edomites. Ultimately, he extended his empire from the Sinai peninsula to the Euphrates River, thus beginning the golden age of Israel. David pushed the Jebusites out of Jerusalem and made it Israel's capital city, called the City of David.

It was to this city that David, by God's command, brought the Ark of the Covenant and danced before it with a heart full of joy and love for God (2 Samuel 6:14). Scripture tells us that David was a poet and musician, and tradition says he composed most of the psalms found in the Old Testament. Because of David's faithfulness, God made a covenant with him — to establish his throne forever This covenant was fulfilled in Jesus of Nazareth, who was born to the House of David.

During these years of peace and prosperity, David was favored by God and admired by his people. His battle against Goliath tells of the ultimate victory of right over wrong, no matter the odds. But a second famous story about David teaches another truth: that pride goes before a fall.

Because David was a man of power, he came to think that he could have whatever he wanted. So, when he saw a woman named Bathsheba, and liked her, he took her for his wife, though she was already married to one of David's soldiers, Uriah (you-RYE-ah), a Hittite by birth. To cover up his sin of adultery, David added another sin: he ordered Uriah moved to the front lines in a battle, where he was killed.

God was angry with David for these sins and sent the prophet Nathan to him. Nathan told David a **parable** about a poor man who had one little lamb that was taken by a rich man, even though the rich man had many lambs of his own. Stung to anger by this act of injustice, David cried out against the rich man: "The man who has done this deserves to die!" Nathan replied, "You are the man!" David now understood his sin — by taking Uriah's wife, he had done a far worse deed than the rich man in the parable. Moved to sorrow for his sins, David repented, but

parable: a moral lesson told through a story

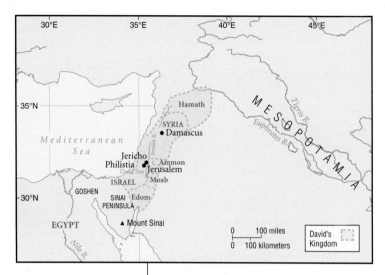

Map showing the full extent of David's kingdom from Egypt to the Euphrates

he still had to face God's punishment—the death of a baby son Bathsheba had borne for him. (2 Samuel 11-12)

But this was not the end of God's punishment for David's sin. By Nathan, God had told David that "the sword shall never depart from your house because you have despised me," and this was fulfilled when David's son, Absalom, rebelled against him. Yet, David's repentance was sincere and God had mercy on him. In the end, he overcame his enemies, and died peacefully at a ripe old age. He was succeeded as king by Solomon, the second son he had with Bathsheba.

The Reign of Wise King Solomon

In his younger days, Solomon, like his father David, loved God and pleased him. God was especially pleased when Solomon asked him, not for riches or a long life or for victory over his enemies, but for wisdom and understanding. God granted Solomon his request, and the king was ever after known for his great wisdom (1 Kings 3:3-15). God also gave Solomon great riches, with which the king built Jerusalem from a little frontier castle into a great city with fine buildings and palaces. But Solomon's greatest contribution was the building of the magnificent Temple for the worship of God. When the priests brought the Ark of the Covenant into the Temple, Scripture says a cloud, which was the glory of the Lord, "filled the house of the Lord" (1 Kings 8:10-11).

Scripture tells how Solomon married many wives, including foreign women who worshiped foreign gods. In spite of his wisdom, Solomon, as he grew old, also began worshiping these gods. Nearly 1,000 years after Abraham was called by God to worship him alone, his people were still being pulled back into the worship of idols. For this sin, God punished Solomon by destroying the glory of his kingdom. After Solomon's death, the ten northern tribes of Israel refused to accept his son, Rehoboam, as king, and, instead, chose a king of their own — Jeroboam, the son of Nebat. It was this Jeroboam who led the northern kingdom, called Israel, into the worship of idols.

Thus only the tribes of Judah and Benjamin remained faithful to the House of David. Like the kings of the northern kingdom, many of the kings of Judah worshiped idols and led their people into sin. Yet, unlike the northern kingdom, Judah had some kings who pleased God, just as David their forefather had done. The two Israelite kingdoms struggled with each other for many years, until a great empire conquered the northern kingdom and led its people into captivity, far from their land. That empire was Assyria.

Assyria, the Cruel

Assyria was a major civilization in Mesopotamia that in about 1350 B.C. grew out of the city of Ashur on the Tigris River, north of Babylon. The Assyrian civilization lasted until 650 B.C. During its last years, the Assyrians had control over an enormous region, having conquered eastern Egypt, and all of Mesopotamia and Syria. Assyria fought hard and developed into a ruthless warrior state.

Every Assyrian man was trained to use weapons and had to fight if summoned. To lay siege to and invade walled cities, the Assyrians used battering rams, scaling ladders, horse-drawn chariots, cavalry, bows, spears, and even giant slings. Assyrian art works mostly picture war, killing, and battles. This is especially true of the stone-cut **bas-reliefs** on the palace walls of Ashur and Ninevah, the greatest Assyrian cities.

Ancient relief of Assyrian warriors fighting with bows, arrows, and spears

The Assyrians were very bloodthirsty and even boasted of it. They did not just kill their enemies, but sometimes beheaded, impaled, burned, or even skinned them. The greatest (and cruelest) Assyrian conqueror was Ashurnasirpal. He was succeeded by Tiglath-pileser, whose forces swarmed into the northern kingdom of Israel in the 8th century B.C. The Assyrians conquered the cities of Israel but stopped at Jerusalem, the capital of Judah. Instead of conquering Jerusalem, Tiglath-pileser demanded a

bas-relief: a fairly flat sculpture in which the design is raised slightly from the background

huge sum of money, which King Ahaz of Jerusalem ended up taking from the Temple (2 Kings 16:8).

Tiglath-pileser died in 727 B.C. and was succeeded by Shalmanaser V, who in 721 B.C. captured Samaria, the capital of the northern kingdom of Israel. The conquest of Israel was finished by Sargon II, who forced the Israelites of the ten northern tribes to go into captivity far from their homeland (2 Kings 17:6). Only the kingdom of Judah remained in Palestine, but it was forced to pay **tribute** to the Assyrian king. Assyria remained the master of Mesopotamia, Syria, and Palestine until it, too, was conquered by another Mesopotamian empire—the empire of Babylon.

tribute: money paid by one nation to another in return for peace or protection

Babylon, Successor to Sumer

The city of Babylon on the Euphrates River in Mesopotamia had been the center of a rich civilization for hundreds of years before the Assyrians came to power. The people of Babylonia—the lands surrounding Babylon—had adopted much of Sumerian culture. Like the Sumerians, the Babylonians wrote on clay tablets and even had their own version of the Sumerian epic, *Gilgamesh*. They worshiped many gods and built ziggurats to reach them. It is likely that the Tower of Babel named in the book of Genesis refers to a ziggurat in the city of Babylon, the highest ever built.

Hammurabi was a great king of Babylon who lived about 1800 B.C. His most significant contribution to history was a list of 282 laws that all people of his kingdom had to obey.

Hammurabi's laws had two good effects. They prevented the strong and rich Babylonians, and officials, from being unjust to the common man, and they discouraged crime by letting everyone know what the laws forbade and what the punishments were. Some of the 282 laws are quite a bit harsher than our laws today. For instance, if a Babylonian hurt another person's eye or tooth, he would have his own eye or tooth put out. Also, the death penalty was the punishment for many crimes, from murder, accidental killing, and kidnapping, to breaking into a house or bearing false witness in court.

Hammurabi receiving the law from Shamash, the sun god; a detail from a basalt stele that records the Code of Hammurabi, (c. 1790 B.C.)

The Babylonians were perhaps the first to try to read the future to discover the gods' will. The pictures formed by the constellations became linked with fortune-telling using horoscopes. The Babylonians were so anxious to know the future that they even tried to read the livers of dead animals to discover it.

It was King Nebuchadnezzar II who made Babylon the center of a great empire. Nebuchadnezzar destroyed the power of Assyria. He conquered all the lands from Elam to Egypt, including Syria and Palestine. The kingdom of Judah was forced to pay tribute to Nebuchadnezzar; but, later, in 586 B.C., when the king of Judah attempted to revolt against Babylon, Nebuchadnezzar stormed Jerusalem and utterly destroyed it (2 Kings 24-25). His army burned the king's palace, all the houses, and even the great Temple built by Solomon. Nebuchadnezzar forced the inhabitants of Jerusalem to leave their land and go into exile in Mesopotamia. Thus

Above: How the Hanging Gardens of Babylon may have looked. Below: The Ishtar Gate, a main entrance in the walls of ancient Babylon, recently rebuilt.

Shadrach, Meshach, and Abednego in the fiery furnace to which Nebuchadnezzar had condemned them. Illustration by Gustave Dore.

began the period of Jewish history, known as the Babylonian Captivity.

Nebuchadnezzar not only conquered foreign lands but restored the ancient city of Babylon. An 11-mile wall with a road on top encircled the city. Nebuchadnezzar built the 30-foot Ishtar gate with its bright blue, glazed brick decorations. Above this gate, the king constructed the magnificent "Hanging Gardens," which the Greeks called one of the Seven Wonders of the World. Archaeologists have discovered some remains of the gardens, which, it appears, were built on a giant step pyramid.

The Prophets

Through all the years of Israel's history, God spoke to his people to give them courage, hope, and direction, as well as to warn them to abandon their sinful ways. God sent his messages to Israel through holy men, the prophets, some of whom served as direct advisers to the king. Among the prophets were Isaiah, Jeremiah, Ezekiel, and Daniel, who are called the "major prophets." Their books of prophecies are the longest prophetic books in the Old Testament. We speak also of the twelve "minor prophets," who wrote the shorter books of prophecy found in the Old Testament. Some prophets do not have books in the Bible; one of these is Nathan, another is Elijah, one of the most famous prophets in Israel's history.

The prophets' message to Israel can be summed up in the two great commandments: love God, love your neighbor. When the Israelites turned to pagan worship, the prophets called them back to their covenant with the one, true God of Abraham and Moses (Jeremiah 10:1-16). When the Israelites broke the commandments of God and ignored the laws of Moses, the prophets urged them to turn from sin. At times the prophets described Israel as an unfaithful spouse and God as a patient, forgiving husband (Hosea 1-4; Ezekiel 16). The prophets called on Israel to care for the poor, especially widows and orphans, to show justice to workers, and to free the oppressed (Isaiah 10:1-4; Isaiah 58).

Yet, along with their woes and warnings, the prophets spoke to Israel of God's love and his power as the Lord of history. God, said the prophets, will not utterly abandon his children, no matter how disobedient they are, but will send a "**Messiah**" (an "anointed one") to save them. Especially in Isaiah's prophecy of God's suffering servant and the glorious city of Zion (Isaiah 7-12, 52-53), we see a foretelling of Jesus Christ and his reign over all of humanity.

Stained glass window in the cathedral of Dinant, Belgium depicting the Prophet Isaiah

Jeremiah, the Suffering Prophet

After the conquest of Israel by Assyria in 721 B.C., the small kingdom of Judah found itself surrounded by powerful enemies — Assyria, Egypt, and the growing might of Babylon. Under King Josiah of the House of David, the people of Judah returned to the worship of God alone; but when that king died and his son took the throne, the people again took to idol worship. God, however, did not abandon his people but sent them a prophet to call them back — the prophet Jeremiah.

Jeremiah was born into a priestly family about the year 600 B.C. in a small village near Jerusalem. In the 13th year of the reign of Josiah, God called Jeremiah, who was then only 22, to be his prophet. Jeremiah's prophecies to Judah were filled with severe warnings. For these prophecies, the powerful of the land rewarded Jeremiah with scourging and imprisonment.

Messiah: a form of a Hebrew word that means the "Anointed One." In Greek, it is *Christos*, from which we get Christ.

Yet, despite these sufferings, Jeremiah continued to prophesy — even foretelling the capture of Jerusalem by the Babylonians. When he prophesied doom at the Temple, priests and false prophets seized him, calling for his death. He was spared and lived to see the fall of Jerusalem in 586 B.C. During the period of Judah's exile to Babylon, Jeremiah foretold that God

The Prophet Jeremiah holding one of his scrolls, from the Basilica of St. Vitalis in Ravenna, Italy

The Handwriting on the Wall

Daniel, a Hebrew prince, served in the royal court of King Nebuchadnezzar and was renowned for his goodness and his accurate interpretation of dreams.

One night during the reign of a later king of Babylon, named Belshazzar, a mysterious thing happened. The king was in the midst of a great banquet with laughter, music, and wine, when suddenly he saw a human hand appear in midair. The hand began writing unknown words on the palace wall—*Mene, Tekel, Peres.*

The frightened king searched for a magician or astrologer to interpret the words, but none could. Then the queen suddenly remembered Daniel, and the king summoned the Hebrew prince to the palace. Daniel told him the meaning of the words: "*Mene* means God has ended your kingdom, *Tekel* means you have been measured and found wanting, and *Peres* means your kingdom will be divided between the Medes and Persians." Daniel's interpretation came true. King Belshazzar was slain that very night, and, the next morning, Babylon fell to the Persians.

covenant: a solemn agreement

would form a new **covenant** with Israel. This was a prophecy of Christ's coming.

At last, some of his countrymen forced Jeremiah to flee with them to Egypt. In that land of exile he died, according to legend, at the hands of a fellow Israelite.

The Book of Daniel in the Bible tells of three Jewish youths with the melodious names of Shadrach, Meschach, and Abednego who refused to bow down before a golden statue made by King Nebuchadnezzar. The king flew into a rage and had his soldiers tie up the three youths and throw them into a white-hot furnace. Miraculously, the three did not die nor were they even harmed by the flames. Instead they walked around singing praises to God. Nebuchadnezzar called them out of the furnace, and seeing that their clothes were not even singed, gave honor to God and made Shadrach, Meschach, and Abednego leaders in his kingdom.

Exile and Return

The sorrow of the Judahite (or Jewish) exile in Babylon is expressed most beautifully in the Book of the Lamentations of Jeremiah:

"Is it nothing to you, all you who pass by?
    Look and see
if there is any sorrow like my sorrow
    which was brought upon me,
which the Lord inflicted
    on the day of his fierce anger."

(Lamentations 1:12)

The books of Baruch, Ezekiel, and Isaiah, on the other hand, speak not so much of sorrow but of the hope for a new day:

"It shall come to pass in the latter days
    that the mountain of the house of the Lord
shall be established as the highest of the mountains,
    and shall be raised above the hills;
and all nations shall flow to it. . . ."

(Isaiah. 2:2-3)

The exile in Babylon was very sorrowful, yet it proved to be good for the Jewish people. It brought them to repentance, devotion, and a zeal to preserve their faith in God. Two stories from the book of Daniel — the stories of the fiery furnace and the writing on the wall — show this deepening faith and foretell the end of the exile.

Persia, a Burst of Power

The Jewish exile did come to an end, and in less than 50 years after the fall of Jerusalem. In 539 B.C., Babylon was conquered by the Persians, a sudden superpower that rolled across the whole civilized world west of China. By 400 B.C. Persia ruled the largest empire the world had known. Persia's conquests stretched from southeastern Europe, across all of Mesopotamia and Egypt, and as far into Asia as the Indus River in Pakistan.

Where did the Persians come from, and why did they become powerful so quickly?

The tiny Persian state of Anshan in Elam (part of modern-day Iran) was home to Cyrus II. This gifted general conquered the Medes, the people that had taken over Assyria for good in 609 B.C. With the former Assyrian

Empire under his belt, Cyrus moved west toward Europe. He funded his army by conquering the wealthy King Croesus of Lydia, and then returned to Mesopotamia, where he took Babylon in a surprise attack. The Persians, though militarily strong like the Assyrians had been, were not as cruel. They allowed the conquered nations to keep their cultures and religions. This was a blessing for the Jews and others.

Persian religion itself took one of three forms. The common people worshiped many gods. The magi, the name of a tribe that produced priests and astrologers, revered angelic beings and spirits. The royal court and the nobility followed Zoroastrianism, a religion that started with a prophet named Zoroaster in the 6th or 7th centuries B.C. Zoroaster had taught that there are two gods, a good god and an evil god. These gods, said Zoroaster, are always at war with one another.

Map of the Persian Empire showing its extent and its major cities

The Persians' cultural achievements included a system of roads linking all parts of the empire, a canal connecting the Red Sea and the Nile, and the construction of a grand capital city, called Persepolis by the Greeks.

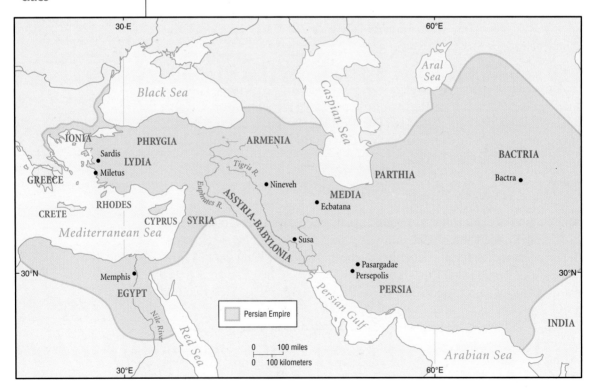

Only carved staircases and a few of the original 100 columns remain from this grand city, which was either accidentally or intentionally burned when it was taken by Alexander the Great of Macedon in 331 B.C.

Under Persian rule, the Jews were able to return home. In 515 B.C., they rebuilt the Temple, which became the center of worship for Jews over all the world. But, having kept the faith through the exile, the Jews had found that they could worship God even without the Temple. They met in their own local gathering places on the Sabbath to read the books of the Law and the prophets, to pray and study. The site for their local gatherings is called a synagogue, from the Greek word meaning, "gathering place."

The Jews held fast to their faith as Persia fell to Greece and Greece gave way to Rome. Jews moved all over the Mediterranean world and took their faith with them. From this faith would come the Christian Church. It can be said that no other ancient nation has had such an impact on the world as Israel, which for 2,000 years upheld the worship of one God in a polytheistic world.

An old illustration of a synagogue in Jerusalem

Chapter 3 Review

Let's Remember Please write your answers in complete sentences.

1. What were the new names given to Abram and Sarai?
2. In the reign of what pharaoh did the Exodus probably take place?
3. What were the Ten Commandments that Moses gave to the Israelites? Please list them.
4. The land of Palestine was divided up among how many Israelite tribes? Please name them.
5. What does the name "Phoenician" mean in Greek? Why did Greece give the Phoenicians this name?
6. What do we call the exile of the Jews after the fall of Jerusalem in 586 B.C.?
7. Who are the major prophets? Who are the minor prophets?

Let's Consider For silent thinking and a short essay, or for thinking in a group with classroom discussion:

1. The summary of the Law of Moses is contained in the commandments to love God and to love your neighbor. Consider how different this is from the hundreds of rules that existed elsewhere, for instance the 282 laws of the Code of Hammurabi.
2. Consider the courage of the Jews who kept their faith alive as they studied and prayed in their local cities during the Babylonian captivity. Why do you think keeping the Jewish religion required great courage in the ancient world?
3. Why do you think monotheism (the worship of one God) is a more hopeful religion than polytheism (the worship of many gods)?

Things to Do

1. The teachers should help students to make maps showing the path of the Exodus from Egypt, through the Sinai Peninsula, and into Palestine. The map should indicate the Red Sea, Mt. Sinai, the Dead Sea, and the Jordan River. Be sure to include a compass rose and a legend.
2. The teachers should help students make maps showing the lands the Assyrian and Babylonian empires covered. The map should include the cities of Nineveh, Babylon, and Jerusalem. Be sure to include a compass rose and a legend.

Let's Eat!

The Jewish Passover meal is a ritual observed in Jewish families to this day. The meal replays the Exodus of the Jewish people from Egypt and consists of a roasted lamb and unleavened bread, bitter herbs and wine. It was this Passover meal that Jesus ate with his disciples and that became known to Christians as the Last Supper, when Jesus instituted the Blessed Sacrament of the Eucharist.

Chapter 4 The Marvelous Greeks

Introduction

The land of the Greeks lies on a peninsula that reaches out into the Mediterranean Sea east of Italy. Long before the time of Christ, a remarkable nation arose in this beautiful land of jagged mountains and crystal harbors. Ancient Greece was the home of adventurous warriors and traders, of **philosophers** who defined excellence and virtue, of poets who gave us stories of duty and love, of architects and sculptors who created works of timeless beauty. These Greeks called

philosopher: lover of wisdom

Map of ancient Greece

themselves Hellenes and their land Hellas. Our name for them and their land comes from the Romans, who referred to Hellas as Graecia.

We call ancient Greece the "Cradle of Western Civilization," which means that these Hellenes were the first people to ask such important questions as, "how do we know truth? How do we know what is just or what is right or wrong? What is the best way to govern society? How do we create beauty and order?" Such questions have always been very important to Christian Civilization.

The Geography of Greece

Greece is the southern part of the Balkan Peninsula, the farthest east of the three peninsulas of southern Europe (the Balkan, Italian, and Iberian peninsulas.) Greece juts out into the Mediterranean Sea. To the west, between Greece and Italy, lies the Ionian Sea, and to the east, between Greece and Asia Minor, sits the Aegean Sea. A long arm of the Ionian Sea, called the Gulf of Corinth, almost divides northern Greece from what is called the Peloponnesus or Morea. The Peloponnesus would be an island, except for the fact that it is connected to the rest of Greece by a narrow neck of land, called the Isthmus of Corinth.

Greek colonization

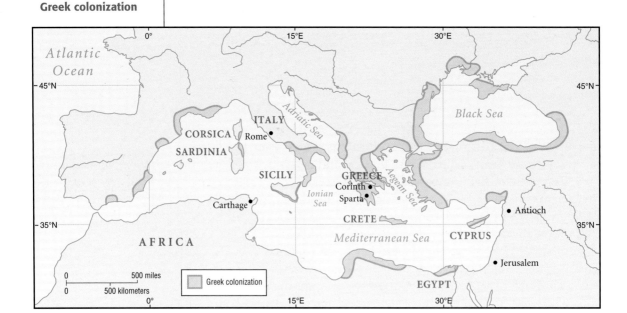

The land of Greece is very mountainous, which makes it difficult to farm there. Partly because of this, the Greeks from the earliest times have tried to make their living from the sea. They have been fishermen, merchants, and pirates.

Ancient Greece, however, did not include just Balkan lands. Greek peoples settled the many islands of the Aegean Sea, as well as those in the Ionian Sea. The Greeks founded colonies along the coasts of the Black Sea as well as the western coast of Asia Minor. The Mediterranean island of Crete formed a part of ancient Greece, and Greek cities rose in Italy and the island of Sicily. In time, Greeks founded cities and colonies on the islands of Corsica and Sardinia, along the coast of what is now southern France, as well as the eastern coast of modern Spain, and on the shores of North Africa.

The Homeric Myths

The Greeks treasured their historic myths. These stories were sung and later written down by Greek poets to explain where their culture came from and to give examples of how to live. The greatest of these poems are the *Iliad* and the *Odyssey* by the poet Homer. They tell stories from the Trojan War, a war that we know now only from these stories. Later Greeks believed that the events in the stories actually took place and wanted to imitate the struggle for excellence, the noble characters, and devotion to family and city that Homer described.

The story of the Trojan War begins with a beautiful woman and a goddess.

Aphrodite, the goddess of love, had caused Paris (son of the Trojan king) to fall in love with Helen. Though married to a Spartan king, Helen eloped with Paris to Troy. In response to this grave insult, the Greeks gathered a large army, sailed across the sea, and **lay siege to** the city of Troy. Ten years of fighting passed, but the Greeks could not take Troy. Great heroes died on both sides — including the Trojan prince Hektor, slain by the Greek hero, Achilles. Only the oaths of the Greek princes and their sense of honor kept them fighting on the windswept plains of Troy.

Ultimately, trickery succeeded where brute strength did not. The wily Greek warrior, Odysseus, thought of a plan to get into the city. The Greeks withdrew from Troy, leaving a large wooden horse for the Trojans to find. The horse, however, held several Greek warriors inside its hollow

lay siege to: to surround and try to capture; *besiege*

A Legendary Writer of Fables

Many different stories have been told about Aesop. One account says he was a slave who lived in the 6th century B.C. Another says he was the advisor to Croesus, the fabulously rich king of Lydia in Asia Minor. Modern scholars doubt that Aesop ever even existed. But whether he existed or not, Aesop has gone down in legend as the writer of fables whose main characters are for the most part beasts.

Fables are stories. Aesop's fables are short stories that generally give a moral lesson. The following Aesop fable shows the danger of spending time with bad companions. It is called "The Farmer and the Stork."

A farmer placed nets on his newly-sown plowlands and caught a number of cranes, which came to pick up his seed. With them he trapped a stork that had fractured his leg in the net and was earnestly beseeching the farmer to spare his life. "Pray save me, Master," he said, "and let me go free this once. My broken limb should excite your pity. Besides, I am no crane, I am a stork, a bird of excellent character; and see how I love and slave for my father and mother. Look too, at my feathers—they are not the least like those of a crane." The farmer laughed aloud and said, "It may be all as you say, I only know this: I have taken you with these robbers, the cranes, and you must die in their company."

—Translation by George Fyler Townsend

An ancient Greek depiction of the Trojan horse

belly. Sinon, a Greek spy, pretended that he had escaped just before his fellow Greeks could sacrifice him to the gods. He told the Trojans that the key to victory was to possess the large wooden statue of the horse.

When the horse was brought into Troy, the hidden Greeks emerged from it by night. They let waiting Greek soldiers into the city, and Troy was destroyed.

Homer's *Iliad* tells only a part of this story—of the anger of the great Greek warrior, Achilles, against the Greek high king, Agamemnon, and of his refusal to fight for the king. Without Achilles—and with the gods against them—the Greeks began to lose to the Trojans. It is only when his friend, Patroklos, dies that Achilles returns to battle, drives the enemy back toward Troy, and kills the

Trojans' greatest warrior, Hektor. Achilles takes revenge on Hektor's dead body. He refuses to allow it to be buried until Hektor's father, Priam, the king of Troy, humbles himself to ask his son's murderer for his son's body. Moved to pity, Achilles grants Priam's request.

The *Odyssey* tells of how the Greek hero, Odysseus, struggles to return home from the war at Troy. Opposed by the sea god Poseidon, Odysseus wanders for ten years, until, aided by the goddess Athene, he returns to his home island of Ithaka. There he fights to rescue his wife and son from treacherous men who want to possess his property and household.

Many years after they were written, the *Iliad* and the *Odyssey* became schoolbooks for Greek boys and the respected literature of older men. Homer's poems formed the ideas of generations of Greeks about how men ought to live and behave. They have since become one of the foundations of European literature — the literature of our Christian civilization.

The Greek City-State

For many centuries, Greece did not have one, united government but was divided into city-states. A **city-state** is a city that, with its surrounding territory, is an independent country. Though all Greeks thought of themselves as Hellenes, they gave their loyalty as citizens only to the city-state in which they lived.

The two primary city-states of Greece were Athens, in the north, and Sparta, on the Peloponnesus. Athens and Sparta had very different, even opposing, ways of living out the Greek way of life.

city-state: a city, along with its surrounding territory, that is an independent country

Sparta—A Military Oligarchy

Sparta was known over all the world, then and now, as a land of military sacrifice and discipline. All of life in Sparta was directed to making strong warriors. Its citizens were soldiers, first and foremost, and its armies were the best trained in Greece.

Spartan warrior

Yet, Sparta was not always so warlike; it was once a land of poets and artists. That all changed around 800 B.C. when Sparta's king, Lycurgus, forced strict new laws on his people. These laws turned Sparta from a festive city into an armed camp.

Childhood was short for both the girls and boys of Sparta. At the age of seven they left their homes and lived in a military barracks where they were trained in physical fitness, discipline, and the ways of war. Boys hunted to supply part of their daily food and endured hardships to strengthen their mind and body. Spartan men were expected to serve the city as warriors until they were 50 years old. At the age of 30, they were allowed to marry and start a household. Women, however, were married much younger, approximately at about age 14.

The Spartans were forced to be constantly on guard because they made slaves of the people they conquered in war. The slaves, called helots (meaning "the captured" in Greek), had a miserable life and so always wanted to revolt. A secret police killed any helots thought to be too independent or troublesome. When the secret police failed to control the helots, the Spartans used the army.

The Spartans used their army not just to control the helots but to carry on wars of conquest in Greece. The Spartans had two goals in waging war: to supply food and other necessary goods for their growing population and to force other city-states to give in to Spartan demands.

oligarchy: political rule by a small group

The form of government Sparta had is called an **oligarchy** (the rule by a few of the citizens). Judges, two generals, and a small council of elders made the decisions for all the people of Sparta. Sparta had originally been formed from two cities, each with its own king. United Sparta kept both kings who, later, became the generals of the city's army. Because it con-

A Laconic Answer

The ancient Spartans of Greece lived in a valley called Laconia. Because they valued feats of arms more than fine speeches, Spartans were taught to use as few words as possible at all times. It is for this reason that using the fewest words possible is called **"laconic** speech."

An example of laconic speech was the Spartan reply to King Phillip of Macedon, who sent the Spartans this message: "If I come down to your country, I will level your great city to the ground." A few days later, the king received a letter from the Spartans. When Phillip opened the letter, he found only one word —"If."

laconic: using very few words

Visible from far out to sea, the ancient temples of the Acropolis still rise over the city of Athens; once a fortified mountain, the Acropolis, or "high town," has always stood at the heart of the city.

tinued to be ruled by kings, Sparta thought of itself, not as an oligarchy, but as a **monarchy**.

monarchy: government by a king, queen, emperor, etc.

Athens—a Direct Democracy

The foremost city of Greece was Athens. Though, like other Greek city states, Athens was originally ruled by a king and then became an oligarchy, it eventually developed into a **democracy**.

Athens was a direct democracy—that is, a government where every **citizen** has the right to vote for or against laws. In countries that are not direct democracies, like the United States or Canada, the citizens elect representatives, who meet in an assembly called a congress or parliament and vote for or against laws on behalf of the citizens. In Athens, citizens themselves met in the assembly, where each one represented himself and his family. Athenian citizens were male adults who usually owned property.

democracy: political rule by all of the people governed
citizen: one who belongs to a state and who has the rights, privileges, and duties of a freeman

In Athens, ordinary citizens not only sat in the assembly but served in the government as judges or **magistrates**. The highest magistrates were the first archon, who oversaw the life of the city; the "king-archon," a kind of religious leader; and the polemarch, the head military general. When a citizen was not taking care of his own business, he was busy looking after the affairs of the city. Every citizen, too, was required to serve in the army in time of war. Athens did have slaves to perform the most distasteful tasks, such as mining, but it had far fewer slaves than Sparta did. Unlike the Spartans, freeborn Athenians farmed their own lands and worked at manual labor and crafts. And while Athens was willing to go to war to

magistrate: an officer of the government who has the power to enforce laws

protect itself, it had no permanent army. The Athenians were interested in leading their neighbors, not enslaving them.

So that they would become good citizens, Athenian boys were taught to read and write, do mathematics, and to speak persuasively. They learned also the history of Greece, including its military history, so that they all could serve as army officers in time of war. Although their military training was not as strict as that of the Spartans, the Athenians had a tremendous love for their democracy and fought very hard to defend their city and its families.

Draco and Solon

Athens's journey to democracy was long and difficult. For a long time, the rich landowners of Athens, the aristocracy, had been struggling with the common farmers and workers, called the *demos* (tribesmen). The struggle between rich and poor in Athens grew so great in the early part of the sixth century B.C. that the city almost plunged into civil war.

It was an Athenian leader named Draco who settled the quarrel by composing the first written laws for Athens. These laws had such severe punishments that we now call harsh laws **draconian**, after Draco. This written law, though harsh, was an important step in protecting the rights of the ordinary citizen. Over time, however, ordinary farmers began losing their land to rich moneylenders, and some people even had to sell themselves into slavery to pay off their debts. As a result, law and order broke down, and it looked as if civil war would break out in Athens.

draconian: cruel or harsh

In 543 B.C., a soldier named Peisistratus with a powerful private army of bodyguards made himself ruler of Athens. The Greek word for a ruler who sets himself up by force and not by the people's choice is *tyrannos*, a "tyrant." Though tyrants in other city-states could be unjust and cruel, Peisistratus was a **benevolent** tyrant. He saved the poor farmers from losing their farms and encouraged the wealthy to invest their fortunes in trade and expansion of the city. He gave money for public works and especially encouraged artists to come to Athens. Peisistratus paid to have the works of Homer written down for the first time in a standard text.

benevolent: kindly

It was an Athenian noble remembered as "Solon the Lawgiver" who found a way to bring peace between the rich and the poor in Athens. To stop the civil war that was brewing in Athens, Solon returned all lands that had been lost on account of debts back to their original owners. He freed from slavery everyone who was paying off debt, and forbade people to sell themselves into slavery because they were in debt. Solon opened part of the government to all citizens but kept the highest positions for the wealthiest citizens. He did not take lands away from the rich and give them to the poor but maintained the traditional social order of Athens.

While Solon's reform of the laws prevented civil war, the weakened nobles and strengthened workers continued to clash with one another. In time, three factions emerged: the Plain (representing the nobility who resisted Solon's reforms), the Coast (mostly businessmen and farmers who supported Solon's laws), and the Hill (farm workers and shepherds who did not think Solon went far enough).

The porch of the Caryatids overlooking Athens

Cleisthenes and the Council of 500

It was the statesman Cleisthenes who, around 500 years before the birth of Christ, finished the job of forming Athens' democracy. The first written laws of Athens were Draco's harsh precepts. Then Solon modified those laws. Now Cleisthenes made another major change, one that would last for many years. He composed a new constitution for Athens.

Although Cleisthenes made many changes to Athens' laws, two changes were the most important. The first change was to abolish the political power of the four old tribes of Athens by replacing them with ten new artificial tribes, called *demes*. The *demes* were not related to the old families and did not have wealth or social status. In this way, Cleisthenes was able to include in the government many citizens who were previously "outsiders" because they were not from the old tribes.

Aristides the Just

In the turbulent times of the war against Persia, Athens had a military and political leader, named Aristides, whom his fellow citizens called "the Just." Aristides was one of the ten generals in the famous battle of Marathon.

After being exiled because of political disagreements with powerful rivals, Aristides was recalled to Athens to help defeat the Persians' second invasion. Aristides was also trusted to determine the amount owed to Athens by each of its allies to defend Greece against Persia.

A story is told that when the Athenians were taking a vote on whether to send him into exile, Aristides came on a poor peasant trying to write something on a ballot. Aristides asked if he could help. The man did not recognize him and asked how to spell "Aristides." "Why do you want to vote for Aristides' exile?" the statesman asked. The poor man replied, "Because he is always being called 'the Just.'" Aristides then wrote his own name on the poor man's ballot.

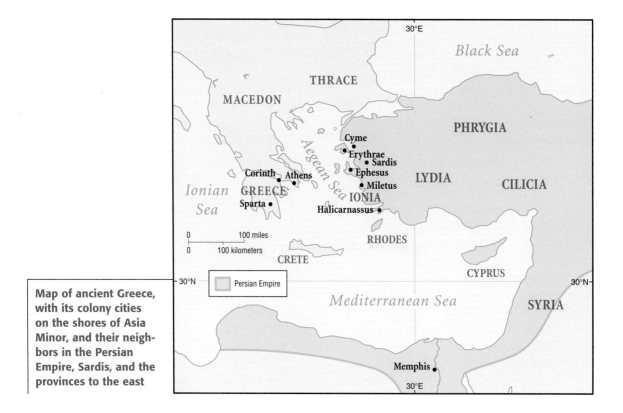

Map of ancient Greece, with its colony cities on the shores of Asia Minor, and their neighbors in the Persian Empire, Sardis, and the provinces to the east

Cleisthenes' second major change in the law was to establish the "Council of 500," which shared power with the assembly. Each new tribe provided 50 representatives to the council, and the council proposed laws to the assembly and enacted the laws that were passed by the assembly. The council also appointed ten generals, one from each tribe. The assembly was still made up of all citizens.

The changes Cleisthenes made in Athens' government weakened the power of the nobles. The changes also made the government more stable and stopped one faction or person from taking control of the government. Perhaps, most importantly, Cleisthenes' constitution made many more people (though not everyone in Athens) a citizen. In other words, not only the rich and powerful but those who belonged to the poorer classes now had a say in how the government was run and what laws were made. Both rich and poor, too, had duties to perform towards the city-state — for this was part of being a citizen, too.

For instance, every citizen in Athens had to bear arms in defense of the city. All those who could afford the heavy and expensive armor of a Greek soldier, a **hoplite**, had to purchase it and learn to fight in formation with the men of their division of the city. Those who were very wealthy had to supply a warhorse and fight from horseback in the city cavalry. The poorer citizens had to learn to use less expensive arms, such as bows and slings. They could form support battalions for the heavy armored troops or serve in the city's navy as rowers on the warships.

hoplite: a heavily armed infantry soldier in ancient Greece

From the days of ancient Athens to our own, citizenship has remained a high ideal of government. A citizen is not just the subject of a king — he is certainly not a slave! A citizen is a free man who receives benefits from the human society in which he lives but, more importantly, gives back to society by fulfilling certain duties, such as paying taxes, voting, serving in government, or, at times, defending his homeland. Citizenship brings many benefits, but it comes with responsibility to the common good of all.

War with Persia

Living along the coasts of the sea, the Greeks early on became a seafaring people. Their journeys to trade with lands and peoples across the Mediterranean led them, in time, to establish settlements along the coasts of Asia Minor, the Black Sea, and as far away as North Africa, southern

Italy, Sicily, and what is today southern France and eastern Spain. These settlements developed into Greek city states that, even though they were independent, they kept close ties with the cities of Greece that had founded them.

Across the Adriatic Sea, along the western coast of Asia Minor, Greeks had early on established settlements that in time became independent city states. This region was known as Ionia because it was settled by Greeks who, like the Athenians, spoke the Ionian **dialect** of the Greek language. (Other Greeks, such as the Spartans, were called Dorians because of the dialect they spoke.) The Greek city states of Ionia grew rich, founding colonies along the Black Sea and the western Mediterranean. But, in the middle of the 6th century B.C. (from about 560–545 B.C.), the Ionian city states were conquered by Croesus, the king of Lydia. When Cyrus of Persia conquered Lydia, Ionia passed under the power of the Persian Empire.

dialect: a form of speaking a particular language that belongs to a certain group or class of people

The Persian Empire was the greatest power of the time. By 500 B.C., the Persian king governed lands stretching from India to Asia Minor, and from the mountains of Armenia to Egypt. He was the master of millions of people and was fabulously wealthy. Yet, despite the Persian king's power and wealth, the Ionians revolted against him in about 500 B.C. With the help of Athens, the Ionians burned the Persian-controlled city of Sardis to the ground. After burning Sardis, the Athenians returned home, and the Persian king Darius reconquered all the Ionian cities.

Darius, however, was outraged at the Athenians for the help they had given the Ionians. Vowing revenge, he sent a **flotilla** of ships, carrying Persian soldiers, to Athens. He was determined to conquer Athens and bring it under his power. Matters looked very dark indeed for the Athenians.

flotilla: a fleet of small ships

The Battle of Marathon

The Athenians were left to face the Persian fleet and army without the help of Sparta or any other Greek city-state, except the small city of Plataea. The small Greek army was badly outnumbered when the Persians landed near Athens, on a plain called Marathon.

As the two sides prepared for battle, the Athenian general, Miltiades, put most of his army on the flanks (or ends) of his battle line and then attacked the Persians at a dead run. Protected from Persian arrows by their metal armor, the Greeks beat back the Persians in sharp hand-to-hand fighting.

At last, the Greeks encircled the Persians and crushed their line. Many of the fleeing Persians were killed after they fled into nearby swamps.

Following their victory at Marathon, the Athenian army returned to Athens as quickly as possible to protect the city from the Persian fleet and army. They arrived in time to defend the city, and the Persians gave up the attempt to conquer Athens and returned home.

Thermopylae and the Brave 300

News of the defeat of his army at Marathon enraged King Darius, and he began organizing another invasion of Greece—this time, a massive one that, he thought, could not fail. Darius, however, died before the invasion began, and it fell to his son, King Xerxes (ZERK-sees), to lead it. When Xerxes had organized the force, he led it to the Hellespont, a narrow sea passage between Asia Minor and Greece. Making a **pontoon bridge** to cross the **strait**, the enormous Persian army moved into Greece. Xerxes was certain the Greeks would surrender to his army—but what was his surprise when the Greeks took up arms to resist the invasion!

Led by their king, Leonidas, a force of 300 Spartans along with allies from the city of Thebes, were determined to stop

The Battle of Thermopylae

pontoon bridge: a temporary bridge built on low, flat-bottomed boats called *pontoons*
strait: a narrow channel of water that connects two larger bodies of water

Pheidippides's Marathon Run

Following the Persian defeat at Marathon, the Athenian army feared that before they could return to Athens, their countrymen would surrender the city to the Persians. Thus, according to legend, the Athenian commanders sent a runner, named Pheidippides, to the city to announce the victory. Pheidippides had already run the 140 miles to Sparta and back, to seek the city's help against the Persian invaders—a feat he accomplished in two days. He had returned to Athens just before the battle with the disappointing news that the Spartans would give the city no aid.

In his run from Marathon to Athens—a distance of 26 miles—Pheidippides was bringing much better news. Running into the city, he brought the joyful message—"Rejoice, we win!" But no sooner had the words passed his lips, than Pheidippides fell dead. He had given his last strength, sacrificing himself for the people and the soil of Athens.

Detail of the Leonidas monument at Thermopylae

the Persian invasion. Leonidas took up a position at Thermopylae, a narrow mountain pass through which the Persians had to pass if they were to invade Attica (as the lands surrounding Athens are called) and the other Greek lands of the south. The pass was so small that the Spartans could use their skill at hand-to-hand fighting to beat back the vastly larger Persian force. When told that the arrows shot by the Persian archers would be so numerous that they would blot out the sun as they flew through the air, the Spartans gave the courageous reply: "That's good, we'll get to fight in the shade."

With his small force, Leonidas was able to keep the Persians from entering the pass. At last, however, a Greek told the Persian commander of a hunter's path by which the Persian army could march around Thermopylae and attack the Spartans from behind. Learning that the Persians were advancing along this path, Leonidas did not retreat but chose to defend the pass to the last with only the 300 men of his royal guard. The rest, he sent away so they could fight another day.

The Persians attacked the Spartans with all their might; the brave 300, however, would not surrender but fought with their swords in a desperate hand-to-hand combat. Two days later, Leonidas and the Spartans were all slain. But the fight at Thermopylae was not a failure, for not only had the Spartans slain thousands of Persians, but they had held the Persians back two extra days—enough time to allow the Greek cities to organize their army against the invaders. Years later, the grateful people of Greece built a monument at Thermopylae to Leonidas and his brave 300, and on the monument were written these words:

> Go tell the Spartans, passerby,
> That here, obedient to their word, we lie.

Victory over the Persians

Following the battle at Thermopylae, the Persians marched against Athens, to destroy it. Learning that the Persians were moving against their city, Athenian men, women, and children fled to the Peloponnesus or across the straits, to the island of Salamis. When Xerxes and his army arrived at Athens, they took the city, pillaged, and burned it.

Xerxes had at last punished Athens for helping the Ionian city states rebel against his father. He was now determined to punish Sparta as well. The great Persian fleet now prepared for an invasion of the Peloponnesus — but first it had to destroy the Greek fleet, anchored in the narrow strait between the island of Salamis and the mainland of Attica. Led by the Athenian leader, Themistocles, the Greek fleet attacked the Persians. Because the Greek ships were smaller and so were easier to maneuver, they had an advantage over the Persians. The Greek ships rammed the Persians ships, which the Greeks boarded, attacking the Persians in fierce hand-to-hand encounters. By the end of the battle, the Greeks had won a great victory over the Persians.

It was Themistocles who was responsible for the great sea victory. It had been he who had persuaded the Athenians to build a large fleet of ships. It was he who chose Salamis as the place for the battle and had kept the Greek allies together so that they could fight as a group against the Persians. Finally, it had been Themistocles who had directed the Greek forces to victory in the narrow waters off Salamis island.

The Golden Age of Greece

After the defeat of the mighty Persian fleet at Salamis, Athens and its allies formed a league to protect each other from the Persians. The league was called the Delian League because

An Oracle at Delphi Speaks — "Wooden Walls Will Save the City"

After the battle of Thermopylae, the Greeks consulted the **oracle** at Delphi to find the best way to defend Athens against the Persians. (They believed that the priests at Delphi spoke for the gods.) The oracle said, "Wooden walls will save the city."

Themistocles, the Athenian leader, understood the oracle's puzzling message to mean that Athens should abandon their city and meet the Persians on water, defended by "the wooden walls" of Athens' ships. Following the oracle's advice, Themistocles trusted the defense of the city to the navy. This resulted in the great victory over the Persians in the Battle of Salamis.

> **oracle:** a priest or some other person through whom the gods were thought to send a message; also, the message sent by a god

In the sea battle off the island of Salamis in 480 B.C., the warships of Greece, led by the Athenian navy, gained a complete victory over the Persian fleet.

Stone bust of Pericles, the young politician who led Athens when it first flourished as an empire after the defeat of the Persians. Created about 500 B.C.

the allies kept their treasury on Delos, an island they thought was sacred to the god Apollo. For several years, the Delian League defended Greece from the power of the Persians.

Athens was the most powerful member of the Delian League, and in time it used its power to force the other league members to pay tribute to it. The Athenians also took control of the league's treasury, removing it from Delos to Athens because, the Athenians said, Delos was no longer safe. So it was that the Delian League went from being a group of allies to become an Athenian empire. The Athenians made it harder to become a citizen of Athens, which meant fewer Greeks could benefit from belonging to the empire, even if they came to live in Athens. Only those whose parents were both Athenians could become Athenian citizens.

During this time, Athens made its government more democratic than it had been before. The assembly of the people became the chief lawmaking body in Athens and chose the ten generals who ruled the city. The generals chose one of themselves to be the chief political leader. In 461 B.C., the generals appointed a man named Pericles to be the chief political leader. For the next 33 years, Pericles was the most powerful man in Athens.

Many great and beautiful public buildings were built under Pericles' direction. The greatest of these was a temple built to the goddess Athena Parthenos (Athena "the Maiden") and called the Parthenon. Built on the Acropolis, a high hill of stone overlooking the city, the Parthenon has been called the most beautiful structure ever built. The Acropolis held several other temples, which could be seen for miles out at sea, as well as enormous statues.

So many great works of art were made in the years Pericles directed the life of Athens that this period has been called Athens' Golden Age. Some of these works were beautiful statues that were so real to life that they captured the personality and human spirit of the people they represented. The greatest Greek sculptor was Phidias, who was in charge of building the Parthenon. It was Phidias who sculpted the statue of Athena inside the Parthenon and who made an even

The Parthenon, the principal temple on the Acropolis of Athens, built between 447 and 438 B.C. Originally a giant statue of Athena Parthenos, or the Virgin Athena, stood within.

greater statue of Zeus at Olympia, where the Greeks held their Olympic games. So enormous was Phidias's Zeus that it has been called one of the Seven Wonders of the Ancient World.

The Seven Wonders of the Ancient World (clockwise from top): the Temple of Artemis at Ephesus, the Hanging Gardens of Babylon, the Lighthouse of Alexandria, the Pyramids of Egypt, the Mausoleum of Halicarnassus, the Colossus at Rhodes, and the Zeus at Olympia.

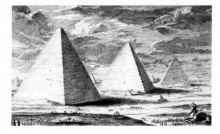

The Greek Styles

When you look at classical Greek buildings, you will notice three different styles of **architecture**: the *Dorian*, *Ionian*, and *Corinthian* styles. You can tell each style by the stone caps or "capitals" on the columns that hold up the roofs of the buildings. The "Dorian" style has a simple, **fluted** column, with a simple, round capital. The Ionian style has capitals carved like scrolls, while the Corinthian style has more ornate capitals, carved in the shape of flower petals.

> **architecture:** the art of building or designing buildings (houses, churches, public buildings, etc.)
> **fluted:** having long, parallel grooves

Some of the world's greatest works of stage drama were written during Greece's Golden Age. Aristophanes of Athens wrote comic plays that made fun of many aspects of Greek life, from war to politics. The Athenian playwrights Aeschylus, Sophocles, and Euripides wrote **tragedy**—a dramatic art form that describes the downfall of the great and good, usually on account of some small fault in their character. Greek tragedy tried to find meaning in human suffering, exploring the beauty in life even when death and pain occur.

> **tragedy:** a serious play or story having an unhappy ending; ancient Greek tragedy tells about something sad happening to a great and good person because of some small fault he has or mistake he has made

The Peloponnesian War

But even while Athens was enjoying its Golden Age, trouble was brewing. Sparta had not joined the Delian League and was alarmed over Athens' growing power. So, when Athens clashed with city states in the Peloponnesus, Sparta came to their aid. Wanting to rule all of Greece, Pericles and Athens did not avoid war with Sparta. Instead, by war, they hoped to destroy the power of Sparta, Athens' chief rival in Greece. The story of this war has been passed down to us in the work of a great historian, Thucydides (ca. 460–ca. 404 B.C.)

Thus Pericles led Athens into a ruinous war with the cities of the Peloponnesus, led by Sparta. Sparta invaded the north and laid waste to the farm country around Athens. Even worse, a plague broke out in overcrowded Athens. A great part of the population died, including Pericles himself, whom the plague struck down in the second year of the war. The war, however, continued another eight years until the two rivals, Athens and Sparta, made a truce with each other in 421 B.C.

Alcibiades and the Defeat of Athens

Peace between Athens and Sparta did not last long. Under the leadership of the general Alcibiades, Athens again tried to break Sparta's power. Athens' invasion of the Peloponnesus, however, failed in August 418 B.C. when the Spartans defeated the Athenian army at the battle of Mantinea.

The defeat at Mantinea, however, did not discourage Alcibiades. Instead, he suggested that Athens fight a war with the Greek city of Syracuse on the island of Sicily. Once Syracuse was defeated, he said, the Athenians could conquer the North African city of Carthage and then return to Greece with added strength and wealth to take care of Sparta once and for all. The Athenians eagerly approved Alcibiades' plan.

Alcibiades was one of the three generals commanding the fleet sent against Syracuse. But, while he was at sea, Alcibiades' enemies in Athens accused him of **sacrilegious** acts and sent a message ordering him to return to Athens to face trial. Refusing the summons, Alcibiades instead fled to Sparta, where he encouraged the Spartans to send a fleet against the Athenians at Syracuse. And so it happened that the Athenians met disaster in Syracuse. Caught in the city's harbor, they were defeated by the Spartan fleet. **Famine** and disease further weakened the Athenians. Finally, in 413 B.C., forces of the Spartans and the men of Syracuse attacked and slaughtered the Athenian troops.

sacrilegious: referring to a thing or person who causes *sacrilege*, an act insulting to what is dedicated to God

famine: a lack of food, a time of starving

Left: A shield-wall of Greek hoplites (heavily armed soldiers) faces an attack of enemy chariots—a tribute to the gods carved in 525 B.C. on a wall of the Siphnian Treasury in Delphi.

Right: A vase depicting Greek hoplites

The Retreat of the Ten Thousand

After the end of the Peloponnesian War, many young Athenian men felt betrayed and angry at the defeat of their city. One such young soldier was Xenophon (ZEH-neh-fon), who answered a letter from an older friend to come to Asia Minor and join him in a Greek regiment. The 10,000 Greek soldiers, most of them young and inex- perienced, were going to help a Persian prince named Cyrus to take the Persian throne from his brother.

Xenophon, the valiant Athenian general

When Cyrus was slain in battle, the Greeks found themselves alone and in the heart of a hostile continent. They tried to make an agreement with Tissaphernes, the victorious Persian general. Tissaphernes called the Greek officers to a meeting under a flag of truce and than treacherously slew them all. The young Greek soldiers were terrified.

It was at this point that Xenophon said to himself: "Who is left to do this? Who other than I? Am I not an Athenian, used to taking responsibility for the city when I vote? I am old enough to take command of myself, I am old enough to take command of others." He summoned the assembly and explained that the only hope lay in their weapons and strong right arms. He himself, he said, was willing to follow another leader, if anyone would come forward, or to lead if necessary. The Greek soldiers acclaimed Xenophon their leader and began at once to make preparations for their retreat.

After burning their baggage, the Greeks, led by Xenophon, set out at night, crossed a broad river, and ran into the first attack of the enemy. Xenophon tried to repel the attack; the Persians cut them off from the coast of the Mediterranean. They were forced north. Soon the winter weather brought snow and ice. Buffeted by storms, drenched and blinded by snow, the Greeks strug- gled on through snow six feet deep. The able-bodied car- ried many sick and wounded. The column kept formation as well as it could, while the enemy harried it from the rear. At the last pass out of the mountains, the Greeks found their way blocked by wild mountain tribesmen. With the resolve that was now their habit, the strongest of the column ran at the wild men and drove them off. The column finally came to the edge of the mountains and saw far below them, shining in the distance, the blue water of the sea.

The men cried with pleasure, "The sea! The sea!" They ran and stumbled down the slope toward the plain below. Then with a sudden impulse they stopped and set themselves to gather stones. Where they had first gazed upon the sea, they raised a monument. The rem- nant of the 10,000 had forced their way to safety.

A count showed that about 6,000 of the original 10,000 had made it. In true Greek fashion, the healthy and sound sent the wounded home first and themselves awaited ships the wounded would send back to them. Relief arrived soon, and the survivors went home. Their fame spread throughout Greece and their glorious march became an inspiring legend to be celebrated ever after.

Athens lost most of its fighting force at Syracuse. In the years following the disaster there, Athens enjoyed some victories over the Spartans; but constant raids by Sparta on land and sea exhausted Athens until, at last, it was forced to surrender. In 404 B.C., Athens agreed to pull down the walls protecting the city and join the Spartan alliance. The Athenian empire was ended — a result that must have seemed only a little better than death to that proud people.

Socrates, Plato, and Aristotle

Socrates was a Greek philosopher (or "lover of wisdom," in the Greek language) who lived through the Peloponnesian War and the defeat of Athens. He believed that the purpose of men's lives is to understand what is right and good, and then to do it. This, he said, was virtue.

The House of Socrates

One summer Socrates, the philosopher, built himself a house. His neighbors were surprised by the size of the house; it was by far the smallest in the neighborhood.

"Why have you built such a tiny box for a house," they said, "when you are one of the most famous men in all of Greece?"

"I have little reason," replied Socrates, "but small as it is, I will be happy if I can fill this house with true friends."

Socrates, the Athenian philosopher, intently awaiting a student's reply. An ancient Roman bust

The Death of Socrates, by Jacques Louis David (1787)

Plato points up to the heavens while Aristotle gestures downward to this world, in a detail from *The School of Athens* by Raphael.

dialogue: a conversation
apology: a formal defense

Socrates' method of teaching and the depth of his questions were unique. He would not teach by speaking what he knew, but rather "pulled the truth" from his students by patient questioning. He searched to know the truth about the basic questions of human life—how one should live and what his responsibilities were. Perhaps his questions made some in Athens uncomfortable. At any rate, in the defeated city his enemies found others who would go along with their attacks on the old man. Falsely charged with corrupting youth, Socrates was condemned to death in public trial. Refusing exile, he obeyed the court and drank the poison hemlock it had commanded him to drink.

Socrates' death did not stop his influence, however. His student, Plato, wrote many books about Socrates' conversations, or **dialogues**, with his students. In Plato's account of Socrates' trial, *The **Apology** of Socrates*, the old man tells his judges that he would rather die than stop asking questions and calling men to virtue; for, said Socrates, "the unexamined life is not worth living."

The *Republic*, another work by Plato, asks the questions: "What is justice?" and "How should men live together in society?" Plato says that all men live as if chained in a cave; they are able to see only shadows thrown on the cave's walls and think that the shadows are the real things. The man who wants the truth must free himself from those chains and climb out of the cave into the sunlight and look directly on the Truth. Such men will understand justice and live as men are supposed to live. The *Republic* is still read by people today who want to understand what is true and good.

Another great philosopher who studied with Plato and followed the tradition of Socrates was Aristotle. Aristotle believed that we learn the truth about the world by observing it and making logical conclusions from what we see. In this he is the father of modern science. He also taught that God is "the unmoved mover"; that is, God is the first power in the universe, for there is no power above God.

Aristotle composed lectures on logic, science, theology, ethics, and politics. Until modern times, his works were accepted as the final authority on many questions. Even in the modern world, all philosophy must grapple with the questions and answers developed by Aristotle in Greece many centuries ago.

Hippocrates, the Father of Medicine

The first great medical doctor in history whom we can name lived through the period of the Peloponnesian War. He was Hippocrates, from the Greek island of Cos. Hippocrates' family for many generations had practiced medicine and was believed to be descended from Asclepius, the god of healing. It is Hippocrates himself, however, who has been called the "Father of Medicine," for he is the first who removed **superstitious** ideas from the study of the human body.

Hippocrates thought the human body was part of nature and so could be understood by the human mind. Though he knew little about the structure of the human body, he had some correct ideas about what the heart and brain do. Hippocrates discovered that each part of the body has a special function or task it performs, and that to cure sickness a physician has to discover which part of the body is not working properly. He found, as well, that by listening to the beating of the heart or the pumping of the lungs, a physician could discover what disease a person had. He studied how herbs and exercise bring about health in the body.

Hippocrates founded a guild of physicians whose members had to swear an oath to heal, do no harm with their art, poison no one, reveal patients' secrets to no one, and perform no abortions. Until the end of the 20th century, all new physicians took the "Hippocratic Oath."

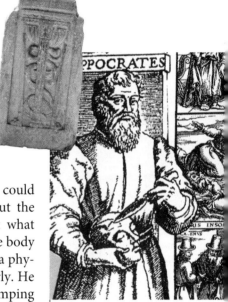

Above left: An ancient relief of the caduceus, a symbol of professional medical doctors —a staff entwined with two snakes. It was carried by ambassadors and heralds as a sign that they were not to be harmed.

Below: Hippocrates, the father of medicine

Alexander the Great (356–323 B.C.)

The long Peloponnesian War had so weakened the Greek city states that, only about 40 years after the surrender of Athens, they all were conquered by Philip, the king of Macedon, a country just north of Greece. The

Alexander the Great at the decisive battle of Issus, a plain in southern Turkey, as shown in an ancient Roman mosaic created in the 1st century A.D.

Macedonians shared in Greek culture, though they were not as civilized as the Greeks living in the city states to the south. Yet, Philip thought of himself as a Greek, and as king he hoped to unite all Greeks in a war to overthrow Persia so that it would never again be a threat to the freedom of Greece.

But Philip was assassinated before he could carry out his plans. His son, Alexander, was only 20 years old in 336, when he became king, but he set out to fulfill his father's dream. What followed was an amazing series of military victories. Over the next 13 years, Alexander overthrew the Persian Empire and conquered Egypt, Mesopotamia, and parts of India. In Egypt, he established a great new city, which was to become a center of learning and culture for centuries to come. This city he named Alexandria, after himself.

Alexander died young, in 323 B.C., and, after his death, his great empire was divided up into smaller realms. Yet the deeds of Alexander "the Great" were greatly important; for the lands he conquered became "hellenized" — that is, they took on Greek (or Hellenic) culture. From Egypt to India, and along the Mediterranean coastline, people began speaking Greek and took on Greek dress and Greek habits. Because of Alexander's conquests, Greek culture spread from Greece to much of the known world of that time.

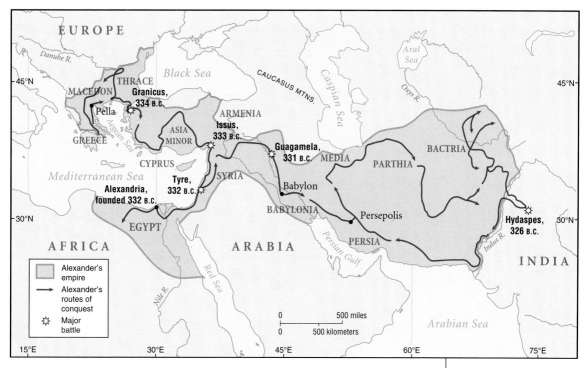

Map showing the marches of Alexander's army and the extent of the Greek Empire he created

The Greek Legacy

Just as furniture fills a house, the thoughts of the Greeks furnish the mind of the modern world. Arts like logic and disciplines such as philosophy come from the Greeks. So do democratic government and many of our ideas of justice. Modern science received its method from Greek philosophers and their discoveries. Our mathematics has benefited from such great Greek mathematicians as Euclid (who wrote the *Elements of Geometry*) and the astronomer Ptolemy. The beauty and proportion of Greek art, sculpture, and architecture have inspired and influenced artists from ancient days down to our own time. Greek tragedy reveals the worth and beauty of human life amidst suffering and pain.

In short, the Greeks left us an incredibly rich deposit of culture. Alexander spread the Greek legacy across the lands from Egypt to India. As we shall see, another conquering people, the Romans, would spread this legacy even farther. Before the Roman advance was halted, it would bring Greek civilization to the peoples surrounding the Mediterranean Sea, modern day Europe, and the island of Britain.

Chapter 4 Review

Let's Remember   Please write your answers in complete sentences.
1. What are the two great epics written by the Greek poet Homer?
2. What is a city-state? What were the two main city-states of Greece?
3. Why was the Battle of Marathon important?
4. What were the two sides that fought each other in the Peloponnesian War?
5. Name the Seven Wonders of the World.
6. Who were the three most famous Greek philosophers?
7. What was the name of Philip of Macedon's son who spread Greek culture from Egypt to India?

Let's Consider   For silent thinking and a short essay, or for thinking in a group with classroom discussion:
1. Why is Greece, and not Sumer or Egypt or Israel, called the Cradle of Western Civilization?
2. Think of all the writing, arts, and drama that flourished in the Golden Age of Athens. Why do you think Athens produced so much great art?
3. Why do you think the Hippocratic Oath, which insisted that doctors had, above all else, to practice healing, is so important?

Things to Do

1. On a blank outline map of Greece, locate the following places: the Peloponnesus, Attica, the Aegean and Ionian Seas, the Isthmus of Corinth, the Gulf of Corinth, Athens, and Sparta.
2. On a blank outline map of Greece, locate Thermopylae, Marathon, Plataea, and Salamis.

Let's Eat!

Since ancient days, the Greeks and all peoples of the Mediterranean have enjoyed a simple combination of flat fried bread wrapped around grilled or roasted meat. They may have added cucumbers, which were available to them. Today, we can enjoy this ancient food as a gyros sandwich or a stuffed pita. It is usually eaten with tomatoes, onions, and a cucumber sauce.

Chapter 5 Eternal Rome

The great city of Rome had very humble beginnings. About 700 B.C., Rome was only a small group of families living in huts on a hilltop near a river in central Italy. In their Latin language, the people called their village *Roma*, the river *Tiberis* or Tiber, and themselves, *Romani* or Romans. By 100 B.C., the descendants of these Romans had raised a great city on the site of the original village, and from this city they had gone forth to conquer the entire Mediterranean world. For centuries, the Roman conquest united the Mediterranean world under one language, one set of laws, one system of roads, and one ruler.

An ancient Roman coin showing the image of the Emperor Hadrian

Geography of Italy

Rome is located in Italy, a European peninsula extending into the Mediterranean Sea. On a map, Italy looks like a large boot that is about to kick a triangular football. The "football" is the island of Sicily. The northern boundary of Italy is the huge mountain range called the Alps, which cuts the peninsula off from northern winds and snows, leaving it a warm and sheltered land, sunny and mild—ideal for living. A chain of mountains, called the Apennines, runs through the center of Italy. The Apennines contain several extinct volcanoes and one active volcano, Mt. Vesuvius. This volcanic mountain range extends into Sicily, where another volcano, Mt. Etna, is also active.

Map of Italy, showing mountains, rivers, and some important cities

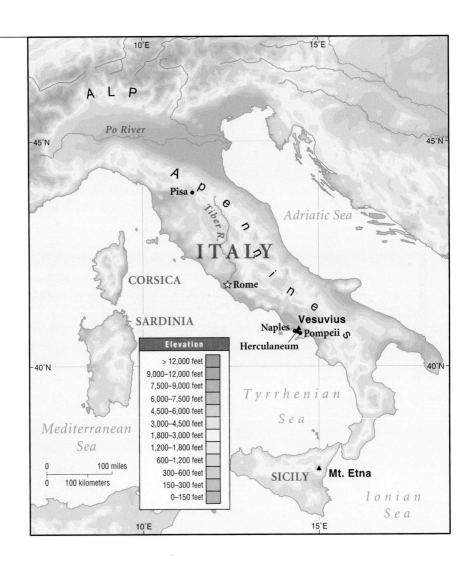

On the eastern side of the Italian peninsula is the Adriatic Sea, and on the western side is the Mediterranean itself. These two warm seas keep the temperatures of Italy temperate. Northern Italy has a wide and fertile valley watered by the Po River, which flows eastward into the Adriatic Sea.

Italy's two coasts are quite different from each other. The eastern coast is abrupt and rocky; but, where it is flat, it is swampy. The western coast is broad and, in ancient times, it had the best farmland. Both coasts are watered by small rivers that rise in the Apennine Mountains. Among the rivers flowing westward from the Apennines is the Tiber, on whose banks Rome was built.

Legendary Beginnings

In the stories they told about themselves, the Romans claimed that their ancestors escaped from the burning city of Troy following its conquest by the Greeks. The Roman poet Publius Vergilius Maro, who lived many centuries later in the times of Caesar Augustus, made this story famous in his epic poem, the *Aeneid*.

Vergilius (or Virgil, as we remember him) modeled his poem on the *Iliad* and *Odyssey* of Homer. The *Aeneid* tells of a Trojan prince, Aeneas, who escapes from the burning city of Troy with a band of followers and sails off to find a safe homeland for the last survivors of Troy.

After many adventures and false starts, Aeneas and his Trojans arrive at the city of Carthage and are taken in and given shelter by the widowed queen, Dido. Aeneas and Dido fall in love and plan to join their peoples into one people; but the gods tell Aeneas that he must sail on to Italy to find the land that is destined to be his. Crushed because Aeneas is leaving her, Dido curses him and his descendants before taking her own life. Virgil presents this curse as the root of the future wars between Rome and Carthage.

From Carthage, Aeneas sails to Italy, to the mouth of the Tiber River. There, Latinus, the king of Latium, welcomes the fugitives. But a war breaks out between the Trojans and the Latins. Only after the intervention of the gods does Aeneas make peace and, as prophesied, unite his Trojans and the Latin people into one.

Other legends tell of the founding of Rome itself. The Roman historian, Titus Livius, or Livy (59 B.C.–A.D. 17), tells how Rhea Silvia, the daughter of the Latin king of Alba Longa, gave birth to twin sons, Romulus and Remus. To protect her infant sons from enemies, Rhea Silvia placed them in a basket and set them adrift on the Tiber River.

An ancient statue showing Rome's founders, Romulus and Remus, being suckled by a she-wolf

When at last they drifted to the bank, they were found in the woods where the future Rome would be. In the forest, the boys were suckled by a she-wolf and guarded by a woodpecker.

In time, the boys grew to manhood and returned to Alba Longa to avenge their mother. Later they set off with a band of young friends to find a new home. Returning to the place on the Tiber where their basket had come to shore, the brothers founded a village; but, when building a wall around the village, Romulus killed Remus over a petty quarrel. Romulus' friends named the village after him, calling it Rome.

According to the legend, Romulus gave Rome its first government and became the city's first king. From the original families, he chose elders ("senators" — from the Latin word, *senex*, meaning "old man") to be his advisors. These senators formed a council called the Senate, which became a permanent part of the government of Rome. Later, the people of Rome spoke of their government as *Senatus Populusque Romanus* — "The Senate and People of Rome." The Romans placed initials for the Latin name, SPQR, on their banners and **insignia**.

insignia: the marks of authority, such as medals, badges, and crowns

Horatius at the Bridge

The Tiber River as it flows through Rome today

The Etruscans, a neighboring people, had been carrying on a war against Rome. When an Etruscan force was about to cross the bridge across the Tiber and enter the city, Horatius, a young and strong soldier of Rome, told his fellows to chop down the supports to the bridge quickly, while he and two companions held off the advancing enemy. The skill, strength, and courage of the three Roman soldiers kept the Etruscans from crossing the bridge. Finally, the Romans who were destroying the bridge shouted that they were almost finished and that the three brave defenders should return to the Roman side. At this Horatius dismissed his friends and carried on the battle alone, fighting furiously until the bridge collapsed behind him. He then plunged into the Tiber's waters.

Rome was safe, but all who watched from the Roman side were sure Horatius, with his heavy armor, would perish in the swirling waters. Even the Etruscans watched with expectation — would the brave Roman survive or would he be drowned in the mighty river? A huge cheer for Horatius went up from both sides as he came to the surface, and with almost superhuman effort, swam to the Roman bank to be pulled to shore by his friends.

The Sixteen Days of Cincinnatus

Cincinnatus had been a wealthy general of Rome. But bad fortune had reduced his wealth, and he had to turn to tending his farm in the hills outside Rome to make a living. In those days there was honor in working one's own farm.

While Cincinnatus worked his own fields, the army of Rome was trapped and defeated by northern tribes. No one was left to defend Rome from the enemy but boys, old men, and the few guards of the city. In desperation the leaders of the city sent a delegation to Cincinnatus, and they found him at his plow. After they explained the emergency at hand, Cincinnatus came to the city to meet with the leaders of Rome. They explained that they would make him absolute ruler of Rome so that he could deal with the terrible threat.

It took 16 days for Cincinnatus to organize his small troop of men and defeat the enemy. Given the threat involved, it was an amazing feat of leadership. But what came next revealed the great character of Cincinnatus. After he told the city leaders that he had defeated the enemy, he laid down his spear and shield, and simply returned to his plow.

Many over the centuries have admired Cincinnatus for his citizenship, with no ambition for honor, glory, or riches. The officers of the American Revolution formed a club called the Society of Cincinnatus in his honor, and the city of Cincinnati, Ohio, was named for him.

The members of the original families of Rome became known as the **patricians** — a name that comes from the Latin word *pater*, meaning "father." Fathers played a very important role in Roman culture. Under the ancient Roman system, the father of a family had absolute power over the members of his family, which included slaves and even his adult sons. The father literally had the power of life and death over everyone in his household. In practice, however, the father's power over his family was influenced by his advisors, which included older adult relatives.

patrician: a person of noble birth, an aristocrat

The Founding of the Roman Republic

For many years after 753 B.C., when Rome was founded, kings ruled over the land with the help of land-owning farmers, who also served, when needed, as foot soldiers for the king. The last king, Tarquinius, was cruel and immoral. His crimes at last became so great that, in 509 B.C., the patrician families, led by Lucius Junius Brutus, drove him out of Rome.

Brutus and the patricians did not replace Tarquinius with another king; instead, they formed a **republic** — a government controlled by its citizens. Every year, the Senate, made up of the leaders of the patrician families,

republic: a government controlled by its citizens

A True Story of the Geese that Kept Guard Over Rome

Rome was under siege. An army of tall, fierce, golden-haired warriors from the tribes of Gaul (now France) had swept down upon the city and defeated Rome's soldiers. The barbarians were beating on the gates of the city. Fierce battles were fought in the streets of the city itself as the tired Roman soldiers retreated with their families to the fortress on top of the Capitol Hill. The Gauls were not only strong, they were fearless and fought with a kind of madness that terrified the Romans. At last the Romans were safe in their fortress, for who could think of climbing the steep rock and the high walls on its top? But when the men and women looked down from those high walls at the burning homes they had left behind, they saw that the Gauls kept up their assaults. They had settled down to a siege of the Capitol.

Weeks went by, and the Romans could not break out or the Gauls break in. But the Romans inside grew very hungry. Many times they looked at the sacred geese of the Temple of Juno and thought that it might not be so great a crime to eat these fat, gray birds. But to kill them would be a sacrilege.

One night, a brave young Roman named Manlius was supposed to be on watch, but he fell asleep near the Temple of Juno. A strange sound came through his troubled dreams and woke him up suddenly. He sprang to his feet and grabbed his spear. He recognized the sound at once. It was the hissing of the sacred geese. What had upset the birds?

Manlius ran to look inside the temple compound and he came face to face with a Gaul. The leader of the Gauls had led his men up the rock and to the walls where they joined the temple. Manlius saw that the first man already had his hands on the parapet to haul himself over. Manlius struck at those hands and hurled the man back down the hill. Louder and louder the geese clamored. The other Romans woke from sleep to see what it could be. They found Manlius defending the walls alone. With shouts and spears they rushed to his rescue and in a few minutes all the Romans were awake. The Gauls were beaten back and scrambled down the rock the way they had climbed up.

A bronze goose in the Capitoline Museums in Rome, from the imperial period

elected two rulers or "consuls," who would direct the affairs of the city. It may seem that the consuls had great power, but there were checks placed on it. For one thing, no action could be taken unless both consuls agreed to it. The fact, too, that the consuls could hold office only for one year, greatly limited their power. Ex-consuls could become members of the Senate, from which they could use their experience to guide the consuls who were in power.

A republic is a government that is supposed to look out for the good of all citizens. Since, however, the early Roman republic was controlled by the patricians, the government did little to protect the common people, called the **plebeians** — the members of families who came to Rome later than the patricians. The plebeians did not have enough land to make a living on. To survive they had to take on many debts, and to pay off these debts, they had to become servants of wealthy patricians. In time, the plebeians refused to put up with this ill treatment. They left Rome and said they would not return to work or serve in the army unless the patricians agreed to listen to their complaints.

The rulers of Rome did listen to the plebeians' complaints and appointed a new magistrate, called a tribune, who would represent the plebeians in government. A tribune could represent a plebeian in court and had the power to stop government actions (to veto laws) that they thought were harmful to the plebeians. In this way, the Republic of Rome was able to satisfy the political desires of both patricians and the common laborers.

plebeian: a commoner
commerce: trade or buying and selling of goods between different places

A Roman standard with the initials "SPQR"— *Senatus Populusque Romanus*

Rome Extends Its Empire

The Punic Wars

In time Rome became more and more powerful; eventually it made itself the ruler of Italy. Rome, too, began building ships and took to trading with other peoples around the Mediterranean Sea. Rome's growing **commerce** made it the enemy of the other great power on the Mediterranean — the city of Carthage, located on the northern coast of Africa. The Romans called the people of Carthage *Punici* (Phoenicians), because the city had originally been founded as a Phoenician colony.

decisive: settling something beyond any doubt or question; a decisive battle is a battle in which one side clearly wins.

The rivalry between Rome and Carthage flamed into war in 264 B.C. because each power wanted complete control of the island of Sicily. The war—called the First Punic War—lasted for more than 20 years, and because of it several major cities on Sicily were totally destroyed, causing untold misery to the Sicilians. Rome too suffered enormous losses—about 100,000 soldiers and 500 ships. Eventually, though, Rome defeated Carthage (in 241 B.C.) in a **decisive** sea battle off the western coast of Sicily. Rome forced Carthage then to leave Sicily, return all captured Roman soldiers, and pay a large sum of money to Rome over ten years' time. Unlike the various peoples of Italy over which Rome ruled, the people of Sicily were not made citizens of Rome. Instead, Rome made Sicily a province and ruled it like a foreign territory.

But Carthage was a strong and proud city that did not easily accept defeat. It soon regained its strength and sent armies under Hannibal, the son of Carthage's ruler, Hamilcar, to conquer southern Spain. Hannibal however was not happy just with conquering parts of Spain. He was determined to take revenge on the Romans and crush their power. He would do so by leading his army from Spain, north across Gaul (modern-day France), and into Italy from the north over the daunting peaks of the Alps.

A painting of Hannibal on an elephant with his army on the wall of the Palazzo dei Conservatori, Capitoline Museum, Rome

So began what came to be known as the Second Punic War. Hannibal's march was a tremendous task. He picked up allies in Gaul and crossed the Alps with thousands of men, mules, and elephants — an amazing achievement. He was also successful in defeating the Romans in several battles fought in Italy.

But though they were defeated time and again by Hannibal, the Romans would not make peace with him. Roman generals made sure they fought no direct battles with him so that their armies would not be destroyed; and so for 16 years, Hannibal was forced to fight in Italy until he and his armies were exhausted. Rome ended Hannibal's war in Italy by sending a fleet and army to attack Carthage itself. Forced to return to Africa to defend his native city, Hannibal was defeated by the Romans at the battle of Zama in 202 B.C.

The end of the Second Punic War allowed Rome to continue expanding its empire. In northern Italy, Gaul, and Spain, Rome waged war against Gallic tribes and expanded the size of its western provinces. In the east, in Greece and Macedonia, Rome made many allies and allowed local peoples to rule themselves as long as they did not rebel against Roman

The Oath of Regulus

The stories nations tell about themselves can give us an idea of their highest ideals. Such a story is an ancient Roman legend about the Roman general, Marcus Atilius Regulus. After he had been captured in battle during the First Punic War, Regulus was told by Carthage's leaders that they would let him return to Rome with an offer of peace—but only if he would give his word as a Roman that he would return to Carthage if Rome rejected peace. Regulus gave his word and was allowed to return to Rome.

But when Regulus reached Rome, he refused to enter the city. "No longer am I a citizen or a senator of this great city," he said. "I will neither enter her walls nor take my seat in her Senate." When some senators came out to him to ask his advice whether Rome should make peace with Carthage, Regulus stoutly answered, no. Nor would he accept a **ransom**, so he would not have to return to Carthage. "It is to no purpose to ransom those who have surrendered while they still hold their weapons," he said. "Let them be left to perish. Let war with Carthage go on until Carthage be conquered."

Neither his wife nor his children could convince Regulus not to return to Carthage. The Senate said it would send someone else in his place, but Regulus refused to break his oath. He returned to Carthage, where he died in prison. "I am spent with battle and near death," said Regulus, "and what will the peoples think of Rome if her generals will not keep their oaths?"

> **ransom:** a price to be paid before a captive is set free

domination: control or rule of another

domination. When anyone did, Roman armies arrived to show what would happen to any nation that dared to resist Roman power.

The Second Punic War was not the last struggle between Rome and Carthage. The final war between these powers (called the Third Punic War) ended in 146 B.C. when Rome leveled Carthage to the ground and sowed salt in its fields so that no crops would ever grow in them again. From that time on, Rome was the only great power in the Mediterranean world.

From Village to Empire

It took 500 years for Rome to grow from a village on the Tiber River to become the supreme power of the Mediterranean world. During that period of time, Rome and its people underwent many changes. The city of Rome went from being a small village of huts to become a great city. The Roman army and navy grew in numbers and skill. Rome's merchant ships brought great wealth to the Roman people.

Such changes may seem good, but other changes were not at all good. Rome's new power and wealth changed its army. At first, the Roman army was made up of Roman citizens, many of them farmers who took up arms because they loved Rome and wanted to make her safe, powerful, and glorious. In later Rome, however, men who were not Roman citizens filled the army. Such men served for 25 years and then were given citizenship, some money, and a farm. Non-citizen soldiers tended, however, to be more loyal to their generals, who provided for them, than to Rome and its people.

When Romans began conquering lands outside of Italy, they forced many people who opposed them into slavery. Men, women, and children were forced to work the large farms owned by the patricians. Roman citizen farmers could not compete with these large farms and so were forced to sell their small farms and move to Rome. In Rome, these once independent farmers relied on the government for food, which was handed out daily. In this way, Rome's empire destroyed the small citizen farmers who had made Rome great in the first place.

The Roman government not only provided food to the common citizens, but free entertainment as well. Such entertainment was called the "Games," which were held in a large stadium called the *Circus* (a Latin word meaning "circular") because it contained a racecourse for horse and chariot races. Besides such races, the Games featured athletic con-

ΜΑΡΓΑΡΕΙΤΗC   ΕΛΛΗΝΙΚΟC

An ancient mosaic depicting gladiators

tests, men fighting animals to the death, and battles between gladiators. Gladiators were mostly slaves who were forced to fight and kill each other for the amusement of the Romans. A gladiator could in time earn his freedom, but he was more likely to end his life of brutal slavery by an early death.

Rome's power and wealth changed the patricians as well. Many of these once patriotic men who served as senators and generals became selfish and greedy. As senators they became more concerned with their own success than what benefited all Romans. So it was that Romans came to lose the virtues of courage, loyalty, and self-control — the virtues that had made Rome great.

The Rise of the Caesars

The Start of the Civil Wars

As the patricians became wealthier and the plebeians poorer, friendship between the classes broke down. When the Roman armies were made up of citizen farmers, the plebeians could force wealthy citizens to give in to their demands. But when the army filled with non-citizens and slaves produced the food for the city, the patricians thought they no longer needed to pay attention to the plebeians. For their part, the plebeians did not give in easily to patrician control, and conflicts broke out between the two classes.

In time, Roman generals with private armies took advantage of these conflicts. Some generals took sides with the plebeians while others joined the patricians. For 100 years, civil war shook Rome. Laws were ignored and trampled on, while powerful men seized control of the government, condemned their rivals as traitors, taking their families' money, and giving their offices to friends. The Senate was too weak to control this turmoil. Rome needed a strongman who could stop the civil war and bring peace. Rome eventually found that strongman. His name was Julius Caesar.

Julius Caesar

In the struggles between the rich and the poor in Rome, some patricians took the side of the plebeians instead of their own class. One such patrician was the senator, Gaius Julius Caesar. Caesar won the affection of Rome's poor by paying for elaborate spectacles for them in the Circus.

In time Caesar became important in Roman politics and was elected a consul. At his own request, the Senate then made Caesar the governor of a Roman province in Gaul. Commanding the Roman armies in the province, Caesar went on to conquer all of Gaul for Rome and even made a raid into Britain. These victories made Caesar very popular with the Roman people.

Patricians in the Senate, however, did not love Caesar. Among his opponents was the senator, Cicero, who was not only a politician but a philosopher who had brought Greek ideas to Rome. Cicero was a master of the Latin language (his philosophical works are read with respect even today) and a powerful speaker. He was a dangerous opponent whom Caesar could not lightly ignore.

Gaius was Julius Caesar's given name, and Julius was his family name. Caesar was the name of his branch of the Julian family. He was called Julius Caesar to honor both families.

Crossing the Rubicon

The term "crossing the Rubicon" means to take an irreversible step. This term came into our language when Julius Caesar and his army crossed the small Rubicon River, the official border of Italy, on their way to Rome.

Roman law and tradition strictly held that no governor of a province could enter Italy with his army. When he crossed the Rubicon, Caesar was defying the Senate and plunging Rome into a bloody civil war.

Ancient Roman bridge over the Rubicon, at Rimini in Italy

Yet, Caesar was not a man to be frightened by a bunch of old senators, including the eloquent Cicero. Knowing it was determined to destroy him, Caesar disobeyed the Senate and led his army south across the Rubicon River, the border of Roman Italy, and marched against Rome. For the next four years, Caesar waged war with his enemies until, at last, he defeated them. In 46 B.C., he was made **dictator** — the sole ruler of Rome — for ten years. As dictator, Caesar reduced the amount of money the poor had to pay in debt, gave lands in the provinces to many poor and former soldiers, and gave Roman citizenship to more people, including those whom Rome had conquered in Gaul. Caesar also doubled the pay of Roman soldiers.

dictator: a person who rules absolutely with no checks on his power

In spite of the good things Rome received from Caesar's strong leadership, the patricians feared Caesar. He ignored the Senate. He was taking on too many honors and, like the kings of the East, was allowing himself to be treated like a god. This was too much for the patricians. Several senators plotted together, and, on March 15 (the **Ides** of March), 44 B.C., they attacked Caesar with their daggers. Among those who assaulted Caesar was his old friend, Marcus Junius Brutus, a descendant of the Brutus who

Ides: the middle day of the month in the Roman calendar

Our word emperor comes from the Latin word, *imperator*—the title Augustus Caesar took as commander-in-chief of Rome's armies. After Augustus, all rulers of Rome took his family name, Caesar, as their title and mark of authority. From Caesar come the titles of European monarchs, *Czar* or *Tsar* in Russia, and *Kaiser* in Germany.

had driven out Rome's last king. Recognizing Brutus as one of his assassins, Caesar said sorrowfully, *Et tu, Brute?*—"Even you, Brutus?" Then Caesar died.

Pax Romana: The Roman Peace

After the murder of Julius Caesar, his nephew and adopted son, Octavius (later called Augustus), took control of Rome and its empire, calling himself its *imperator* (supreme general) or emperor. Although he held on to enormous power, Augustus shared the rule of the vast empire with the Senate. This pleased the patricians, who helped Augustus rule the vast Roman holdings.

The Roman Empire during this period included all the lands around the Mediterranean Sea and stretched from the Atlantic Ocean to the shores of the Black Sea. The Roman Empire brought law and order to these lands, as well as paved roads, orderly commerce, good food, hot baths, sanitation, and Roman citizenship. Most of all, the empire brought peace to the Mediterranean world—the *Pax Romana* or "Roman Peace."

The Romans were wise rulers, for they were able to keep the people they conquered fairly happy by granting them many rights. Some of the conquered peoples were able to have their own local governments under Roman rule. Local men of wealth or talent could reach high positions in the Roman world. Many men from the provinces became senators and even consuls. This achievement is perhaps the greatest feat of government the world has ever known.

The Slaves of Rome

The Roman Empire, however, was not a land of freedom for large numbers of people, for it was built on slavery. Slaves worked in the fields, producing food for the empire. They labored in the mines. They built

Caesar Augustus

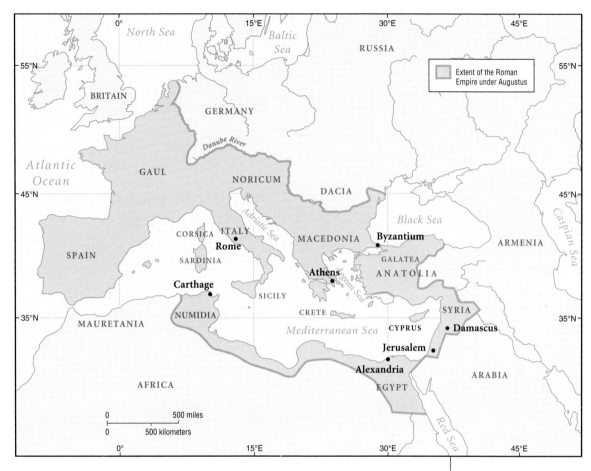

Map of the Roman Empire at the time of Caesar Augustus

roads. The state itself owned slaves for building public works. Everyday housework as well as the task of educating children belonged to slaves. Slaves even managed businesses.

It has been said that one-third of all those who lived in Rome were slaves. They were mostly captured enemies and the sons and daughters of slaves. Although slaves could not win their freedom, masters could free their own slaves. Upon their death, many slave owners **manumitted** their slaves as a reward to them for good service, making them "freedmen." Freedmen had a lower place than Roman citizens in Roman society but a higher place than slaves. Some freedmen who were

manumit: to free another from slavery (noun, *manumission*) well educated and skilled in government, business, or the arts became wealthy and influential.

The Growth and Decline of the Roman Empire

After Augustus' death in A.D. 14, the Roman Empire fell under the rule of his adopted son, Tiberius. Tiberius was not as great a ruler as Augustus, but he was not a bad ruler, either. This was not true of all his successors. After Tiberius' death in A.D. 37, Caligula, a madman, became emperor. Caligula was followed by Claudius, under whose reign Rome conquered Britain. Claudius, however, was followed by Nero, a man who murdered

Rome and the Jews

In the years following the death of Nero, first the Roman general, Flavius Vespasian, and then his son, Titus, ably ruled the empire. It was Vespasian and Titus who had to deal with a great rebellion—a revolt of the Jews in Judea. The Romans subdued this revolt, known as the First Jewish War, only after a three-year siege of Jerusalem. The siege ended with the destruction of Jerusalem and its temple in A.D. 71. The Arch of Titus that greets visitors to the now-ruined forum in Rome shows scenes of that siege and the Roman triumph.

The First Jewish War was not the last time the Jews revolted against Roman rule. In the year 130, Emperor Hadrian ordered the rebuilding of Jerusalem—but not as a Jewish but a Hellenized city, called Aelia Capitolina. Hadrian even had a temple dedicated to Jupiter built on the ruins of the Jewish temple.

Furious at this desecration of the sacred city, in 132 the Jews, led by one Simeon Bar Kokhba, rose in another revolt against the Romans. Under Bar

Kokhba, the Jews defeated a Roman legion and even retook Jerusalem. Yet, once again, the power of Rome proved too great for the Jews. By 135, the Romans had crushed the revolt The emperor ordered mass executions that brought the population of Jerusalem down to that of a small town. Jews who had not been killed in the war were exiled, and Jerusalem was repopulated, but not with Jews. Instead, Gentile legionary veterans came to live there. Indeed, Hadrian forbade Jews even to enter their sacred city.

The destruction of Jerusalem in the year 71 and the defeat of the Jewish revolts caused more and more Jews to leave Israel for other lands and cities in the empire. In their new homes, the Jewish people formed communities centered on their synagogues, where they met to sing praises to God and to read from their sacred books. In this way, the Jews were able to preserve their identity as a unique people—an identity they have kept through all the centuries, even to our own day.

his own mother, was said to have started a great fire in Rome, and was the first emperor to persecute the Christian Church. Nero was so cruel a ruler that a civil war drove him from Rome. He died by committing suicide in A.D. 68.

Nero was the last emperor to belong to the Julian family—the family of Julius Caesar and Augustus. The emperors who followed Nero were mostly strong and able rulers. They included the "Good Emperors"—Nerva, Trajan, Hadrian, Antoninus Pius, and Marcus Aurelius. It was under these emperors that the Roman Empire reached its greatest strength and glory.

When the last of the Good Emperors, Marcus Aurelius, died in 180, the empire began its long, slow decline. There were different reasons why the empire began to grow weaker and weaker. One reason was the constant wars the empire had to fight against German tribes, who were attacking along the empire's borders in the north. Another enemy the empire faced was the Persian Empire in the east.

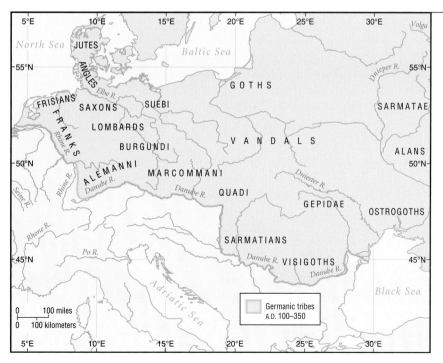

Map showing the locations of the many Germanic tribes in Europe between A.D. 100 and 350

Another thing that weakened the empire was the wars waged by some Roman generals against other Roman generals for the control of the empire. From 218–268 (only 50 years) the empire had 50 different emperors, all of them generals. These struggles for the throne brought **chaos** and disorder to the empire.

chaos: very great confusion or disorder

By the year 290, it was clear that the empire had grown too large to be ruled by one man. In that year, a Roman general named Diocletian became emperor. He changed the government of the empire in the hope that he could save the empire. Diocletian kept the empire going longer than it might have if he had not made his changes, but he could not stop the empire from growing ever weaker. The Romans and Italian citizens no longer wanted to spend their lives protecting the enormous empire, and so the government was forced fill its army with non-Italians and even Germans. To keep some German tribes from invading the empire, the empire had to hire other German tribes for protection. And if the government did not pay all the money agreed on, these German tribes would go from being friends to becoming enemies of Rome. In the late 300s and into the 400s, the empire had to fight off invasions from Germans, Huns, and Persians. After 476, the empire in the west (including Italy and Rome) had entirely ceased to exist.

But perhaps the chief reason for the decline of the Roman Empire was that Roman citizens had lost the courage and self-control that they once had had. The need to pay for the large armies to protect the empire meant common people had to pay very high taxes, which made many of them poor. So many people had been forced to move to the cities, where they spent their lives being fed and entertained by the government. The wealthy lived lives of selfish pleasure. The Roman Senate was filled with men who no longer had the courage or wisdom to make the hard decisions they needed to make to save the empire. The Romans had gone soft and so were unable to stand up against their strong, brave, and warlike enemies.

The Legacy of Rome

Human civilization has received many benefits from ancient Rome. One of the chief benefits is that it was through Rome that Greek civilization has come to us. The Romans learned Greek philosophy, drama, art, architecture, and science; they copied it and imitated it and so preserved it for future generations. Perhaps, without the Romans, Greek culture would have died just as Sumerian and ancient Egyptian culture did. Instead, the culture of Greece continues to live on in our own Western and Christian civilization.

Rome, too, had its own legacy from which the world has benefited. Ancient Roman courage, self-control, and love of country have inspired people throughout history. The Roman belief that governments should follow law and not the desires of kings and dictators has been a very influential ideal. The Romans thought that all citizens, from the highest to the lowest, were supposed to obey the law. Roman law courts tried to apply the law justly for everyone, rich and poor, the powerful and those without power. Such ideals continue to be important for us, who live in the 21st century.

Roman law and government have given an example to all the peoples of the earth of how states can be ruled justly. They have ever been an example of how citizens should live, by doing their duty for the good of all.

Chapter 5 Review

Let's Remember   Please write your answers in complete sentences.
1. What does SPQR mean?
2. What two rival cities fought each other in the Punic Wars?
3. Who was Hannibal?
4. Who were the opponents in the Roman civil wars?
5. Why did the Roman senators want to kill Julius Caesar?
6. What was the *Pax Romana*?
7. Who was Diocletian? What did he do?

Let's Consider   For silent thinking and a short essay, or for thinking in a group with classroom discussion:
1. How much did the Roman Empire, and Western civilization afterwards, owe to the Greeks?
2. How did the government of Rome ensure the good of all citizens?
3. How did the lives of Roman patricians or plebeians differ?
4. What virtues made Rome great?
5. Why did Rome decline as a great power?

Things to Do

1. Using the map of Italy on page 86, with a measuring string and the scale, measure the length of Italy from the Alps to Rome. Next, measure the distance from Rome to Naples. How far is it by sea from Naples to Sicily?
2. With a string, and using the map on page 96, measure the Roman Empire at its greatest length and width. Do the same with the map of Alexander's empire on page 83. Which empire seems to cover more land?

Let's Eat!

The Romans put a sauce called *liquamen* on almost everything they ate, much as we put ketchup or soy sauce on our food today. *Liquamen* is a very salty, fishy-tasting sauce, similar to anchovy paste, and can be found in supermarkets. Try this authentic Roman side-dish for dinner: Put 1 large package of frozen green beans in water; add 1 tablespoon anchovy paste, 2 tablespoons olive oil, 1 tablespoon coriander seeds, 1 teaspoon cumin, 1 small leek, chopped. Boil together and serve.

Chapter 6 The Christian Church: A Gift from God

The Hinge of History: The Life of Christ

"In the sixth month, the angel Gabriel was sent from God to a town of Galilee called Nazareth, to a virgin betrothed to a man named Joseph, of the house of David, and the virgin's name was Mary." (Luke 1:26-27) So begins the most awe-inspiring story in all of human history—the story of the **Incarnation**, when God became man in the person of Jesus Christ. So great was the Incarnation that it can be called the "hinge of history"; for, like a hinge on a door, the Incarnation is the event on which all history turns. God becoming man opened up all of human life to promises and possibilities never before imagined.

So important has the Incarnation been to history that we tell time by it. For centuries we have labeled all the years before the birth of Christ as B.C. ("Before Christ); the years after Jesus' birth are called A.D. (*Anno Domini*, Latin for "in the year of the Lord). This way of telling time witnesses to the important fact that the coming of Jesus into the world is the most important event in human history.

> **Incarnation:** the uniting of devine and human natures in Jesus Christ

A Byzantine Greek icon of the birth of Christ

The World at the Incarnation

Jesus was born over 2,000 years ago in Bethlehem, the hometown of King David, in the land of

Palestine at the time of Christ

Judea. Judea was then a very small place in a much larger, Roman world; it was the homeland of the Jewish people, the descendants of the ancient Israelites. Judea was located in the region the Greeks and Romans called Palestine. Since the Jews had returned from captivity in Babylon, they had been ruled by foreign powers — the Persians, the Greek empire of Alexander the Great, and the Greek kingdoms of Egypt and Syria. For about 80 years, the Jews again had an independent kingdom under the Maccabees (whose story the Bible tells in the books of I and II Maccabees); but in 63 B.C., Jerusalem and Judea came under the rule of the Romans.

In 47 B.C., the Roman general Pompey appointed a young Jewish man named Herod as governor of Galilee — a region just north of Judea. Within ten years, the Romans made Herod king of Galilee, Judea, and of regions on the other side of the Jordan River.

Though he followed the Jewish religion, Herod spread pagan Greek culture in Palestine. This angered many Jews, because they thought Greek culture was opposed to their own culture and religion. Herod built Greek-style theaters, stadiums, and the Roman city of Caesarea on the coast of Judea. At the same time, he took the small temple the Jews had built in Jerusalem after their return from Babylon and turned it into a gloriously beautiful building.

Yet, we remember Herod more for his great cruelty than for building projects. As king of Judea, he murdered three of his sons, two of his wives, and various political enemies. His most famous act of cruelty is told in the Gospel of Matthew — the massacre of the innocent male children of Bethlehem.

Under this bloody ruler, five main factions of Jews quarreled with one another. One faction, the *Herodians*, supported the Roman government for the comfort and peace they thought it brought to Palestine. The *Zealots*, on the other hand, wanted to drive the Romans from Palestine and restore an independent Jewish state. The *Sadducees* were the religious authorities — the party of the priests and the Sandhedrin, which was the supreme court of justice for the Jews. The *Pharisees* saw themselves as defenders of the Law of Moses; they were religious teachers who insisted that every Jew keep the Law of Moses most strictly. Like the Pharisees, the *Essenes* were also devoted to the Law, but they lived a quiet life of prayer and study.

There were also the common people, faithful Jews awaiting the Messiah — the promised leader who would deliver Israel from its enemies.

A Buried History

The Essenes disappeared many centuries ago, but they gave the world a great gift that was not discovered until our own time. In the year 1947, a shepherd boy in the Qumran region near the Dead Sea accidentally discovered hundreds of ancient Essene scrolls. These scrolls, which had been tucked into clay jars and buried in caves around A.D. 70, contain parts of nearly every book of the Old Testament. Bible and historical scholars have been very interested in these scrolls because they shed light on the lives of the Qumran Essenes who kept and hid the writings. The scrolls also have given us information about the ideas of the Jews who lived during the time of Christ. More importantly, the copies of the Hebrew Scriptures found at Qumran are very much like the same Scriptures found in the Bible as we have it today. Some people have claimed that the books of the Bible have changed greatly over the centuries. The Qumran scrolls have shown that this claim is not true.

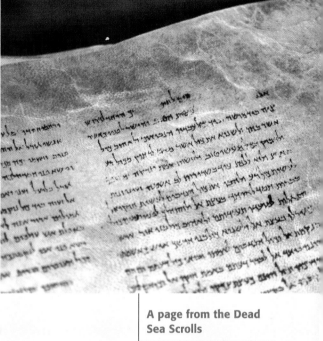

A page from the Dead Sea Scrolls

Among these common people were Mary, the mother of Jesus, and his foster father, Joseph, a carpenter. Few people would have thought that so important a person as Jesus would come from the humble Jewish poor. The Romans would never have thought that anyone from the tiny Jewish nation would do anything very important. Though the life of Jesus is very important to us, it meant little or nothing to the Roman world—which is why very little was written about Jesus by outsiders.

What we know about Jesus' earthly life comes almost only from four books—the Gospels of Matthew, Mark, Luke, and John. The Gospels were written by Jesus' friends, his **disciples**, or those who later knew his disciples. The Evangelists, or Gospel writers, were: *Matthew*, a tax collector and one of Jesus' disciples; *Mark*, an early convert and companion of the apostles Peter and Paul; *Luke*, a **Gentile** Greek, physician, and companion of Paul; and *John*, an apostle.

disciple: a follower or student of another

Gentile: a person who is not Jewish

The Life of Jesus

According to the evangelist Matthew, only a band of shepherds were present at the birth of the most important person of history — Jesus, the **Christ**. Later, some magi or "wise men" came "from the East," to honor the king whose coming was made known to them by a special bright star. King Herod learned of the birth of this baby king from the magi. Fearing that Jesus would take his kingdom, Herod was determined to destroy him and ordered the murder of all of Bethlehem's male children, two years old and younger. Warned in a dream of Herod's murderous plan, Joseph fled with his family to Egypt. After Herod's death, Joseph, Mary and Jesus returned to Palestine and settled in Nazareth, in Galilee.

Christ: a form of the Greek word for the Hebrew word, *Messiah*, meaning "anointed one"

The Gospels say very little about the first 30 years of Jesus' life, and so it has been called his "hidden life." The Gospel writers again take up the story with Jesus' cousin, John, called "the Baptist" — telling of his preaching in the desert, dressed in rough clothes and living off wild food. Like an Old Testament prophet, John told people to repent of their sins, baptized them, and announced that the Messiah would soon come. Jesus' hidden life came to end when he came to John, asking for baptism — not because he needed to repent of any sins, but, as Jesus said, "to fulfill all righteousness." When John baptized Jesus in the Jordan River, the voice of God the Father declared Jesus to be his beloved Son. Those witnessing the baptism thought the voice was a clap of thunder.

The baptism of Christ, from an ancient baptistry ceiling in Ravenna, Italy

After his baptism, Jesus went into the desert, where, for forty days, he faced and overcame the devil in a trial of temptations. When Jesus left the desert, he called 12 men (most of them uneducated fishermen) to be his disciples. He began to journey throughout the region, preaching to the people about the Kingdom of God. This kingdom, he said, was a spiritual rather than a political kingdom. It took a while for the people to understand this message; even Jesus' disciples did not fully understand what he was saying.

It was Simon, the leader of the twelve disciples, who was the first to call Jesus, not just the Messiah, but the Son of God. "Who do you

The Last Supper, the First Eucharist

One of Jesus' last important acts was to celebrate the Passover with his apostles. This was not an ordinary Passover meal, however, but the first Eucharist. At this meal, Jesus made his disciples his priests. They were to wash others' feet as he washed theirs (John 13:1–17), and to break bread and offer the cup of wine in his name. But the bread and the cup they were to offer were not ordinary food and drink, but Jesus' body and blood that would to be offered in every Mass until the end of time (Matt. 26:26–28).

say that I am?" Jesus asked his disciples. Simon answered, "You are the Christ, the Son of the living God." Because of his faith, Jesus called Simon *Petros* or Peter — "rock." Simon Peter was to be the rock upon which Jesus would build his Church (Matt. 16:18). Jesus gave Peter the "keys of the kingdom of heaven — meaning that Peter would serve Jesus as the leader of his Church, with the power to forgive sins and to rule the Church in Jesus' name. (Matt. 16:19).

Jesus worked many miracles. His first miracle was at a wedding, where, at his mother's request, he made the bride and groom happy by quietly seeing to it that there was enough wine for the celebration. From that time on, he worked many wonders: healing lepers and other sick people, expelling demons, restoring eyesight and hearing, calming a storm at sea, walking on water, multiplying food for the crowds, and raising people from the dead. Jesus spoke to his countrymen in simple stories, called parables, using examples from everyday life to explain deeper truths. Jesus attracted many disciples, but many rejected him as well, especially when he told them that if they wanted to live forever, they would have to eat his body and drink his blood (John 6:25–66).

Jesus especially offended many of the Jewish leaders because they thought he was disobeying the Law of Moses when, on the Sabbath day of rest, he healed people and allowed his disciples to pluck ears of grain because they were hungry. Jesus, however, told these leaders that it is always right to do good on the Sabbath. Jesus called the Pharisees **hypocrites**, because, he said, they demanded others to do things they would not do themselves. The Pharisees especially grew angry when Jesus called himself God (John 10:30, 13:14). In their pride and unbelief, they accused Jesus of **blasphemy** and plotted to arrest him.

Jesus' three years of preaching, teaching, and healing the sick and troubled came to an end when one of his disciples, Judas Iscariot, betrayed him to the Jewish leaders. After being tried by both the Sanhedrin and the Roman governor of Judea, Pontius Pilate, Jesus was condemned to death, whipped, beaten, and mocked. Finally he was nailed to a cross and died between two criminals. It seemed like Jesus' short life of 33 years had come to a tragic end.

But, his death was not the end of Jesus. On the third day after his death, he rose from the tomb and, for the next forty days, appeared to his disciples at various times and places in his glorious, resurrected body. At last, telling his disciples he would send them the Holy Spirit to give them the power to spread the good news of salvation to all the world, Jesus ascended bodily into heaven.

hypocrite: a person who pretends to be virtuous but who is not

blasphemy: the act of insulting God or claiming to have the powers or characteristics of God

The crucifixion of Christ, with the Virgin Mary and St. John. An 11th century Greek mosaic

The Church—A Perpetual Gift

While on earth, Jesus said he would establish a church (Matt. 16:18), but when did this church, the Catholic Church, actually begin? Was it when Jesus was born? When he called his disciples? Or when he declared that Peter was the rock? The event sometimes called the birthday of the Church actually occurred after Jesus' resurrection, on the Jewish feast of Pentecost (Greek for "50th"), celebrated 50 days after Passover.

On the Pentecost following Jesus' ascension into heaven, while Jews from around the world gathered in Jerusalem, the apostles and Jesus' mother and close relatives were gathered in a house in the city for prayer. While they prayed, suddenly the room was filled with the sound of a great wind, and "tongues as of fire" appeared over the heads of everyone gathered there. Filled with the power of the Holy Spirit, the disciples went out to the crowds and spoke about Jesus and the meaning of his life, death, and resurrection. Miraculously, the people in their own various languages could understand what the disciples were saying to them (Acts 2:1-41).

The first Christians were eager and bold. Jesus' 12 followers were no longer just his disciples, but the **apostles** he wanted them to be—messengers of the Kingdom of God to all the earth. Even Peter hardly seemed to be the same man who had fearfully denied Jesus three times (Matthew 26: 69–75; Mark 14:66–72; Luke 22:54–62; John 18:15–18, 25–27). The young Church attracted more and more followers, and the apostles, under Peter's leadership, appointed men called deacons to care for the everyday needs of the new **converts**. The Christians lived a common life, like a family. They attended the "breaking of bread" on Sundays and listened to the teaching of the apostles. They shared property and daily meals; and just as in a family, the stronger members cared for their weaker brothers and sisters.

Yet, just like Jesus, the growing Church had enemies. The Jewish authorities feared the new religion. They imprisoned the apostles, Peter, James, and John, and condemned the young deacon, Stephen, to be

apostle: the name given to Jesus' 12 disciples after Pentecost; from a Greek word meaning *messenger*

convert: to change or turn from one belief or religion to another (noun form, *conversion*)

The First Sermon

"Then Peter stood up with the Eleven, raised his voice, and proclaimed to them…'You who are Israelites, hear these words. Jesus the Nazarene was a man commended to you by God with mighty deeds, wonders, and signs, which God worked through him in your midst, as you yourselves know. This man, delivered up by the set plan and foreknowledge of God, you killed, using lawless men to crucify him. But God raised him up, releasing him from the throes of death, because it was impossible for him to be held by it…. Therefore let the whole house of Israel know for certain that God has made him both Lord and Messiah, this Jesus whom you crucified….' Now when they heard this, they were cut to the heart, and they asked Peter and the other apostles, 'What are we to do, my brothers?' Peter said to them, 'Repent and be baptized, every one of you, in the name of Jesus Christ for the forgiveness of your sins; and you will receive the gift of the Holy Spirit. For the promise is made to you and to your children and to all those far off, whomever the Lord our God will call.' He testified with many other arguments, and was exhorting them, 'Save yourselves from this corrupt generation.' Those who accepted his message were baptized, and about three thousand persons were added that day" (Acts 2:14, 22–24, 36–41).

The martyrdom of St. Stephen, from the Church of St. Stephen in Vienna, Austria

martyr: a person who chooses to die rather than deny his faith
sect: a group of people sharing the same beliefs

stoned to death. Stephen accepted death rather than deny his faith, and so became the Church's first **martyr** or "witness" for Christ. Like Stephen, others would suffer for the Faith, but this did not weaken the Church. Instead, it brought it new strength.

Why did the witness of the martyrs strengthen the Church? There are two reasons. First, because the courage of the martyrs helped stir up faith in the hearts of unbelievers, and many joined the Church. Secondly, many Christians left Jerusalem because of the persecutions, and these preached the Gospel in the distant regions to which they fled. In this way, the Church spread from Judea, into Samaria, and then into the lands of the Gentiles and all the Mediterranean world. As a later Christian writer named Tertullian said, "the blood of the martyrs is the seed of the Church."

No one reached more of the world of his time with the story of Christ than a man who once himself had persecuted Christians. This man, named Saul, had been a Pharisee and one of Church's greatest enemies; but, after a miraculous conversion, he went from being Saul, the persecutor, to Paul, the Apostle. It was St. Paul, more than anyone else, who opened up the Christian Faith to Gentiles as well as Jews. At first, it seemed the Church would be just another Jewish **sect** or group, but by Paul's preaching and writing, it truly became a religion for the entire world.

The Growth of the Church

Driven from Jerusalem by persecution, some believers in Christ found their way to Antioch, a large and important city in Syria. It was in Antioch that Jewish believers began preaching the Gospel to Gentiles and where, for the first time, believers were called "Christians." Antioch soon became the second largest Christian center after Jerusalem. It was from Antioch that Paul began the first of his many missionary journeys, spreading the Gospel in Asia Minor and Greece and going even to Hispania (modern Spain and Portugal) in the far west.

The task of spreading the Gospel was helped by the network of roads the Romans had built across the empire. Over the paved Roman roads, missionaries could travel safely and rather easily. Greek philosophy also helped the missionaries, for it opened up minds to the spread of new ideas, such as the Gospel. The fact that two languages, Latin and Greek, were spoken all over the empire made it easier for the missionaries to communicate with people wherever they were.

Poor people and slaves were the first to embrace the Christian Faith. These people were not satisfied with the worship of the Roman emperor or the pagan gods. The story of Jesus brought them a hope they had never known before. They learned that God loved them as much as he loved the rich and powerful—that he sent his Son to die even for them. In God's sight, and in the Church, it did not matter whether someone was a Jew or a Gentile, a slave or a freeman, rich or poor, for all were brothers and sisters in Christ Jesus. These teachings gave the poor a religion to live for, and to die for.

The Twelve Apostles themselves did not stay in Jerusalem but became missionaries both within and outside the Roman Empire. Tradition says Peter traveled to Rome, John to Ephesus, James to Hispania (before returning again to Jerusalem), Bartholomew

A mosaic portrait of Saint Peter, in the Byzantine basilica of Saint Vitalis, Ravenna, Italy

The Bones of St. Peter

The high altar in St. Peter's Basilica in Rome is erected over the tomb of the Prince of Apostles, St. Peter, the first pope. It is certain that Peter lived in Rome, and history and tradition both say that he died there around A.D. 67.

Peter was buried in the pagan cemetery on the slope of Vatican hill. Probably in the 200s, the remains of Peter along with those of St. Paul were placed in another tomb to protect them during a persecution when Christian burial-places were **desecrated**. Later, St. Peter's bones were returned to their original burial site, over which, in the 4th century, Emperor Constantine built the first church of St. Peter. The basilica that stands there today was built in the 15th and 16th centuries.

Although it was believed for centuries that the altar in Constantine's church was built over St. Peter's tomb, there was no archaeological evidence to prove it. Then, the 1940s, Pope Pius XII allowed archaeologists to excavate under the main altar of St. Peter's Basilica. There, surrounded by Christian graves and inscriptions asking for St. Peter's prayers, they discovered a burial niche built by Pope Anicetus (A.D. 155–166) for St. Peter's remains, and in this niche, they found the bones of an elderly, powerfully built man. By radiocarbon dating they found these bones dated back to the first century, when St. Peter lived. In 1968, Pope Paul VI declared the bones to be the bones of St. Peter.

desecrate: to treat irreverently; to treat a sacred thing with insult

Circumcision, Baptism, and the New Covenant

Since the earliest Christians were mostly Jews, it was not clear to them at first how much of the old Jewish rituals they should follow. For instance, what about circumcision, the sign of God's covenant with Israel? Did boy babies have to be **circumcised**, as the Law of Moses demanded? Did Gentiles who wanted to become Christian first have to be circumcised? With so many Gentiles converting to the Faith, these questions threatened to divide the new Church.

It was St. Peter who finally decided the question. Speaking with the guidance of the Holy Spirit, Peter said that Gentile converts did not need to be circumcised; they only had to repent, be baptized, and live in Christ. For the Church, baptism rather than circumcision thus became the new sign of the covenant between God and man and the way a person entered the People of God. The baptism of both adults and children came to take the place of the Jewish rite of circumcision for baby boys.

> to **circumcise:** to cut off a male's foreskin; in Judaism, the act represents the entrance of a boy into Israel

to India and Armenia, Simon and Jude to Persia, Thomas to India, Andrew to Scythia and Epirus, Matthew to Ethiopia or Persia, and Philip to Phrygia. The New Testament tells only of the death of the apostle James (Acts 2:12), who was beheaded by King Herod Agrippa I in Judea in A.D. 44. It is believed, however, that all the apostles were martyred except for John, who died in old age after an exile on the island of Patmos. On Patmos, John received the vision that became the Book of Revelation or Apocalypse in the Bible.

Wherever Christian Churches were established, men called bishops were appointed to govern them. In Greek, a bishop is called an *episkopos*, a word that means "overseer" or "shepherd." Bishops appointed *presbyters* to help them govern the Christian people and to administer the sacraments. In time, presbyters also were called priests.

At first, the Christian Faith spread mainly by preaching and the witness of miracles worked by the apostles and others. In time, Christian teachers and philosophers such as St. Irenaeus of Lyons, Tertullian of Carthage, and Origen of Alexandria composed thoughtful written works about Christian belief and philosophy. Such works appealed to the educated people of the empire and brought more of the learned and powerful into the Church. Yet it was not mostly the intellectual arguments that won people over. Converts were attracted by the joy of the Christians, their courage, and the way they cared for widows, orphans, prisoners, and one another in close-knit communities. According to Tertullian, the pagans used to say of the Christians, "see how they love one another!"

So powerful was the witness of Christian love that, by the 3rd century, the Christian Church had spread throughout the whole Mediterranean region, from Spain to Palestine, and from Gaul to Egypt. Missionaries also had traveled outside the empire into Persia (modern-day Iran), Mesopotamia, and the country of Armenia. It was Armenia that, in the year 301, became the first Christian kingdom in history.

The Christian Scriptures

When the first Christians gathered to read the Scriptures, they did not have the complete Bible that we have today. They did not read the Gospels or the epistles of St. Paul, St. Peter, or St. John, but the books of the Old Testament. Over 200 years before the birth of Christ, the Old Testament had been translated into Greek. It was this Greek version, called the Septuagint, which it seems the early Christians mostly used.

The *Didache*

The oldest Christian writing outside of the New Testament is a work called the *Didache of the Twelve Apostles*. In Greek, *Didache* means "teaching." Written about A.D. 60 by an unknown author in Syria, the *Didache* speaks of **liturgy**, prayer, the Sunday obligation, community rules, and moral teachings. The *Didache* even has the Church's first condemnation of abortion. The *Didache* was an important work in the early Church, but the complete manuscript was lost for 800 years. A monk in a monastery in Constantinople found an 11th-century copy of the manuscript in the 1800s.

> **liturgy:** the prayers and actions organized for public worship; the Mass is a liturgy

A windowpane from Saint Denis church in Paris, showing Jesus surrounded by symbols of the four evangelists: Matthew (angel), Mark (lion), Luke (winged ox), John (eagle)

canon: standard; the list of books the Church recognizes as truly inspired

The word "canon" comes from the Greek word meaning "standard" or "measure." When used to refer to the books of the New or Old Testament, it means the books that tradition and the teaching authority of the Church have said are divinely inspired and sure guides to salvation history. The Bible as we know it was fully formed by 397.

What we call the New Testament came to be bit by bit during the first 70 years of the Church's existence. The first book of the New Testament to be written was probably Paul's first letter to the Church in Thessalonica, in about A.D. 52. As for the Gospels, the most ancient tradition says that Matthew's was the first to be written, but most scholars today think Mark was the first to write his Gospel, about the year A.D. 60. John's Gospel was the last to be composed, in about A.D. 96.

Though the entire New Testament had been written by the year 100, not everyone in the Church agreed about which books were inspired by God. Different churches had different lists or **canons** of books they thought were inspired. Everyone agreed that certain books, such as the four Gospels, were inspired, but they differed about such books as the Apocalypse of St. John and the epistle of St. Jude. Some Christians thought books that most of us have not even heard of (such as the *Shepherd of Hermas* and the *First Epistle of Clement*) were inspired.

It was St. Athanasius, the archbishop of Alexandria in Egypt, who in 367 offered the canon of 27 books we accept today as the New Testament. This canon was approved by the Catholic Church at a bishops' council held in Rome in 382 and at another held at Carthage in 397. These councils also approved the Old Testament canon and so gave to Catholics the Bible that we use today.

Christians Under Siege

You may have heard the period of the early Church called the "Age of the Martyrs." You may have heard stories of the early martyrs—those brave Christians who chose torture and death rather than deny Christ and offer sacrifices to the Roman gods. Such stories may make anyone think that the Roman Empire did not allow much freedom of religion—that one had to follow the Roman religion or face the consequences.

Such a view of the Roman Empire is wrong. The emperors allowed the practice of many religions besides the traditional Roman religion. It is true that Rome commanded people throughout the empire to offer sacrifices to the emperor and the Roman gods, but this would not have bothered anyone besides the Jews and Christians. Since they worshiped many gods already, pagans were not bothered by adding a few more gods to their worship. The Jews refused to offer pagan sacrifices, but Rome made an exception for them because they had an ancient religion and were following the "ways of their fathers."

Why, then, did the Roman Empire persecute the Christians? For one thing, Christians were not Jews and so their refusal to worship the gods and the emperor broke the laws of the empire and made it seem that they were not faithful to their rulers. The fact that Christians gathered before dawn on Sunday made them suspicious to the Romans, for the government forbade people to meet at night for fear they were hatching political plots. Many Christians, too, would not fight in wars, and they settled their disagreements through their own bishops rather than Roman courts. The Romans misunderstood even the Mass or Eucharist. Because the Christians were said to eat the Body and Blood of their god, their pagan neighbors thought they were immoral, or even cannibals!

So it was that the Church was declared illegal in the empire, and Christians at various times and places were arrested and sometimes killed. Christians were not always persecuted, but persecutions broke out against them in various times and places, until 249, when a persecution across the entire empire began. It must be remembered, too, that though we call this time period the Age of Martyrs, Christians have suffered for Christ throughout the entire history of the Church. In fact, more Christians were martyred in the 20th century than in any previous century.

Early Christian fresco in the Catacomb of the Via Latina, Rome

The First Persecutions

The Acts of the Apostles in the Bible tells us of the very first persecutions against Christians. As we have already seen, the Sanhedrin in Jerusalem persecuted the Church in that city. The Sanhedrin even sent Saul as far as the Syrian city of Damascus to arrest the Christians living there. The stories of Paul's missionary journeys, also found in the Acts, tell of persecutions he suffered at the hands both of Jews and Gentiles alike.

The first persecution by a Roman emperor came in A.D. 64. A great fire had severely damaged Rome, and the emperor Nero blamed the Christians for the destruction. They were an easy **scapegoat,** because many people thought Christians were "haters of humanity" for refusing to sacrifice to the gods. Large numbers of Christians suffered terribly in Nero's persecution. Some were covered with pitch and used as torches to light up Nero's gardens at night. Others were crucified and even skinned alive. Sts. Peter and Paul were among the martyrs who died by Nero's command. Paul, being a Roman citizen, was protected from dying a very cruel death and so was beheaded. Peter, who was not a citizen, was sentenced to crucifixion. Before being nailed to the cross, Peter asked to be crucified upside down. He was not, he said, worthy to suffer in the same way as his Lord.

In the years following Nero's death in A.D. 68, persecutions against Christians broke out in different parts of the empire. These persecutions were not frequent, but they could be very bloody. Christians were blamed for any natural disasters that occurred, as though the gods were angry because the Christians did not sacrifice to them. Many Christians died in the Roman Games. Audiences gathered in the Colosseum to watch as Christians and other "criminals" were attacked and devoured by hungry beasts. Those who survived the lions' jaws were killed by the swords of their guards.

scapegoat: a person or thing who takes the blame for a bad act done by another

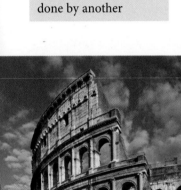

The Colosseum, built in Rome between A.D. 72 and 82, just after the destruction of the Temple of the Lord in Jerusalem. Some of the building stone probably came from the destroyed Temple.

The Great Persecutions

The persecutions against Christians went from being local to becoming empire-wide when Decius became emperor in 249. Emperor Decius wanted to strengthen Rome and his own power, and he thought one way to do this was to force everyone to return to the old Roman religion and make sacrifices to the gods and to him. Every person who offered sacri-

Perpetua's "Day of Victory"

One of the earliest writings by a Christian woman is the prison diary of a 22-year-old noblewoman, Vibia Perpetua. In the year 203 Perpetua and some Christian companions were arrested in Carthage for refusing to offer pagan sacrifices. The darkness and heat of the prison and the cruelty of the soldiers frightened Perpetua, and she also worried about her infant son. "Such cares I suffered for many days," she wrote, "and I obtained that the child should abide with me in prison; and straightway I became well and was lightened of my labor and care for the child; and suddenly the prison was made a palace for me, so that I would sooner be there than anywhere else."

Perpetua's father begged, cursed, and even tore hair from his beard to get his daughter to give up her resolution not to deny Christ. He tried to frighten her with warnings that her baby would die if she died. Yet Perpetua's faith remained strong. She wrote: "'Father,' said I, 'Do you see this vessel lying, a pitcher or whatsoever it may be?' And he said, 'I see it.' And I said to him, 'Can it be called by any other name than that which it is?' And he answered, 'No.' 'So can I call myself nothing other than that which I am, a Christian?'"

Finally Perpetua and her companions received their sentence—to be thrown to wild animals in a public spectacle. A fellow Christian wrote, "Now dawned the day of their victory, and they went forth from the prison into the amphitheater as it were into heaven, cheerful and bright of countenance; if they trembled at all, it was for joy, not for fear." One of Perpetua's companions was her slave, Felicity, who had just given birth to a child. First whipped, then mauled by a wild cow, Perpetua and Felicity shared the kiss of peace with their friends before dying by the sword.

fice was to be given a *libellus* or official letter to prove that he had done so. If someone did not have a *libellus*, he would be executed. Because they refused to offer pagan sacrifices, some bishops, presbyters, and lay Christians suffered death. Some went into hiding, while others did not sacrifice but paid friendly officials to give them a *libellus* saying they had. Some Christians simply gave in to the government and offered the sacrifices.

Decius' persecution ended in 261, and for about 40 years afterwards, the emperors did not persecute Christians. But, beginning in 303, Galerius, an assistant emperor (called a *caesar*) convinced Emperor Diocletian to start a new persecution of the Christians. Issuing edict after edict against the Christians, Diocletian ordered Christian churches to be destroyed and copies of the Scriptures to be burnt. In 304, the emperor ordered Christians throughout the empire to sacrifice or die. Though, once again, some Christians sacrificed to the gods, others bravely refused and so were cruelly tortured and put to death. Whole Christian communities were destroyed.

Yet this, the greatest of Roman persecutions, could not destroy the Church. In 305 Diocletian resigned as emperor, and the caesars in the western half of the empire, Constantius Chlorus and Maxentius, stopped the persecution there. At last, in 311 the dying Galerius proclaimed that Christians in the eastern half of the empire would be allowed to meet and worship in peace. So ended the last Roman persecution of the Church. The Christian Faith was legal throughout empire for the first time in 250 years.

heresy: a teaching that denies a truth of the Faith
orthodoxy: the right or true teaching of the Faith

Heresies of the Early Church

During the persecutions of the first three centuries, Christians enjoyed long periods of peace. During such times they had to work out disagreements they had about the beliefs and practices of their religion. Some Jewish Christians said all Christians had to observe certain Jewish rituals. Gentile converts brought with them ideas from the pagan religions that either agreed with the Faith or had to be rejected. Philosophical debates among the Greeks raised questions that the early Church had to address.

For example, the Gnostics (Gnostic comes from a Greek word, meaning "knowledge") thought the material world, including the human body, was bad. When certain Gnostics came into the Church, they rejected the authority of the apostles and claimed to have "secret teachings" from Jesus that proved that Jesus was divine and not really a man at all. On the other hand, others said Jesus was just a human being whom God had used to work wonders. Because the Church condemned such false beliefs, they are called **heresy**. Heresy is teaching that denies a truth of the Faith. The term **orthodoxy** refers to the right or true teaching of the Faith as handed down by the apostles.

Today it is hard to imagine a time when everyone in the Church did not believe that Jesus is true God and true man or that God is a Trinity—three Divine Persons in one God. Yet these and other questions were discussed

Mosaic of a beardless Christ enthroned between angels. From San Vitale church in Rome, built about A.D. 400.

and fought over in the early Church. The mysteries of the Faith are impossible for man to understand fully. Heresies came about when men attempted to explain Christ and the Trinity in simpler ways. Showing where these simple explanations were wrong and teaching the true Faith to the people was the work of the bishops, under the leadership of the bishop of Rome, the successor to St. Peter — the pope.

Heresies caused some groups to break away from the Church, but in some ways they helped the Church, too. In arguing against the heretics, the Church was able to deepen her understanding of the apostles' teaching.

Does Heresy Matter?

Is heresy a small matter? Is arguing about it a waste of time? The answer is no, because heresy attacks Church teaching, and Church teaching is about our salvation. The early Church understood this and so, even when they were being persecuted, orthodox Christians fought against heresy.

A fresco of the Holy Trinity and the coronation of Mary

Heresies strike at the very root of the Gospel. For instance, if Jesus is not fully human, he could not have died for our sins. If he is not truly God, then the sacraments are powerless; yet, the sacraments are the way we come to the Truth and the Life in Christ. If only those who have a secret knowledge could be saved, as the Gnostics said, then the Church is not for all people but only a special few. Finally, ideas matter because they determine how we live and what we do. This is why the Church was and always has been so concerned with correct doctrine.

An Emperor Converts: The Church Under Constantine

After three centuries of so much difficulty and torment for the Church, a most surprising thing happened. By the end of the 4th century, the most hated religion in the Roman Empire became the official religion of the Roman Empire. The man responsible for this great change was Constantine the Great, who reigned as emperor from 306 until his death in 337. Constantine was not the emperor who made the Christian Faith the state religion, but he did more than anyone to prepare the way for this to happen.

Constantine was born about the year 280 to a Christian mother, St. Helena, and Constantius Chlorus, a caesar in the empire. When he himself became caesar in his father's place in 306, Constantine knew he faced enemies who wanted to destroy him. One of these was Maxentius, who made himself the ruler of Italy. Seeing Maxentius wanted to take control of the entire western empire, Constantine marched against him and defeated him in battle in 312. It is said Constantine won this battle after

The Cross That Won the West

Constantine, the Roman ruler of Britain and Gaul (France), took arms against Maxentius, who occupied the capital city of Rome. Marching with his soldiers toward the city, Constantine suddenly saw a vision. In front of the afternoon sun a kind of cross appeared, bright with light, with the words, "By this sign, conquer." Immediately Constantine had his soldiers decorate their shields with the symbol he had seen—the *Chi-Rho*, a cross made from the letters of the name "Christ" in Greek. (See picture.) Following this vision, Constantine and his men faced down Maxentius' army at the Milvian Bridge that spanned the Tiber River. As the enemy soldiers retreated, the bridge broke, causing Maxentius and his men to fall into the river and drown. In this way Constantine won Italy.

Above: A colossal head of Emperor Constantine, created during the years of his reign

Right: An antique tapestry depicting the battle of Constantine against Maxentius

receiving a vision of a Christian sign, the *Chi-Rho* (the first two letters in Christ in Greek), which he ordered his men to place on their shields. From that time on, Constantine is thought to have been a Christian, although he was not baptized until the end of his life.

In 313, Constantine met with Licinius, the emperor of the East, in Milan, a city in northern Italy. Together they signed the Edict of Milan, which granted full religious freedom to Christians and returned their property to them. Over the next 25 years, life for Christians in the empire continued to improve. Churches that had been damaged were restored, and grand new churches were built with public money.

Under Constantine, the Christian faith now began to influence the empire in a way it had never done before. For instance, coins bearing

Map of Constantine's empire—showing the provinces and the two capitals, Rome and Constantinople

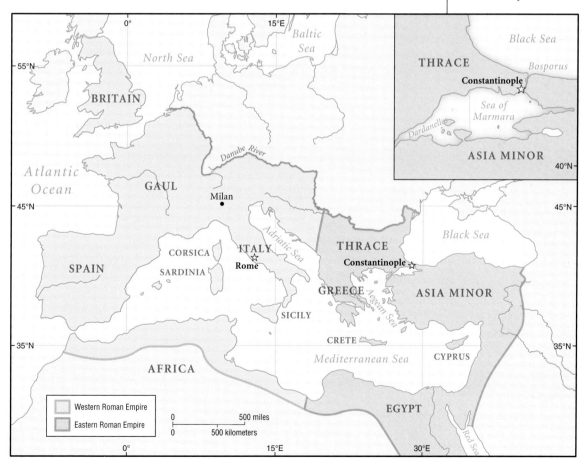

pagan symbols now included Christian symbols as well. Civil laws began to reflect Christian morality and practice. Sunday became an official day of rest. Masters could no longer kill their slaves, nor could they break up slave families. Sins against marriage, such as adultery, were punished more severely. Priests and bishops were excused from service in the military.

When he became the sole ruler of the empire in 324, Constantine's great desire was to unite the empire under his authority. As emperor, he began to see himself as the head of the Church, as well, and he wanted to unite the Church just as he had united the empire.

Uniting the Church, however, was more difficult than Constantine may have thought it would be. Christians were no longer being persecuted, but they were divided among themselves. One question that divided Christians was what to do with those believers who had denied their faith and sacrificed to idols. Should they be forgiven and readmitted to the Church or should they be kept out of the Church forever? The disagreement led to a **schism**, or splitting off from the Church, of a strict group in North Africa called the Donatists. The Donatists thought the Church would be weakened if unfaithful Christians and, especially, unfaithful bishops and priests, were allowed again into the Church. The rest of the Church decided that those who had denied Christ in the persecutions could be forgiven after a period of penance.

schism: a division or split

A worse split in the Church, however, came about when a deacon of Alexandria in Egypt named Arius began teaching that God the Father "created" the Son and that the Son is not fully God. The Church was soon divided between the Arians (those who followed Arius) and the orthodox believers, who said the Son was God, equal to the Father. Across the empire, Christians argued and even fought each other violently over Arianism. To stop the riots and help the desperate bishops, Constantine assembled the first ecumenical council, or worldwide meeting of bishops, in Church history. It met in the city of Nicaea in the year 325 to decide what the true teaching of the Church was. Is the Son true God, or is he less than the Father?

theologian: someone who studies theology – the science that teaches us about God

With the help of the great Alexandrian **theologian**, St. Athanasius, the Council of Nicaea condemned Arianism and declared that the Son of God is true God, equal to the Father. It expressed this teaching in a creed, or statement of belief. This creed eventually became the Nicene Creed we recite today at Mass on Sunday.

But though the Arian heresy had failed to win over the Council of Nicaea, it did not immediately go away. Because several emperors after Constantine supported the heresy, it even looked as if Arianism would eventually take over the entire Church. But, in the end, the truth about Christ won out over the error of Arius, thanks to the work of the bishops gathered at the Council of Nicaea and other Christian writers who, like St. Athanasius, bravely defended the Faith.

The Church Conquers the Empire

Like Diocletian had done, Constantine decided to place the capital of the empire in the eastern

A view of Constantinople (across the bay) and the Bosporus beyond

part of the empire. But, unlike Diocletian, who had made Nicomedia in Asia Minor his capital, Constantine did not choose an already existing city but decided to build a city of his own. So, in 327 Constantine chose the site of the ancient town of Byzantium and there founded his new capital, which he named *Nova Roma* (New Rome). It was later called Constantinople (the city of Constantine).

The location of the city was very important. Constantine built it at the place where Europe and Asia are separated only by a narrow strait, called the Bosporus. All ships sailing from the Aegean Sea into the Black Sea, and from the Black Sea into the Aegean, had to pass through the Bosporus. Many roads both from Europe and Asia met at New Rome, as well. Among the many buildings raised by Constantine was the **cathedral** of Hagia Sophia (Hagia Sophia means Holy Wisdom, in Greek). The building of this cathedral was another sign that Constantine favored the Christian religion.

As we have said, Constantine did not make the Christian Faith the official religion of the Roman Empire but continued to give all religions the same freedom he had given to the Church. This changed in 380, when the Christian emperor Theodosius decreed that the Christian Faith would **thenceforth** be the only official and recognized religion of the empire. Ten years later, he ordered all pagan temples to be closed.

In the days of Constantine and Theodosius, many more people converted to the Christian Faith than during the time of the persecutions. Not everyone, however, during the times of the Christian emperors converted for the best reasons. Under Constantine, being a Christian became a most helpful

cathedral: the chief church of a diocese; the bishop's church. A church is called a cathedral when it contains the *cathedra* — the bishop's chair or throne.

thenceforth: an adverb meaning, "from that time on"

way to a successful and comfortable life in the empire. Under Theodosius, it became necessary to be a Christian if one wanted to get ahead in the world. So it was that, under these emperors, many people perhaps became Christians, not because of a strong faith, but for unworthy reasons.

Fathers and Doctors

While the Roman Empire was becoming Christian, the Church was guided by some the greatest minds in her history. The Church has called these men both "fathers" and "doctors." They are "fathers" because, by studying the Scriptures, they gave us the ideas we use today to understand our Faith. They were the fathers of Christian teaching. They are doctors, too — but not because they took care of sick people. The Latin word, *doctor*, means "teacher"; thus, the men about whom we are speaking were doctors because they were some of the greatest teachers about the Faith that the Church has ever known.

Latin was the major language in the western part of the empire while, in the eastern part, it was Greek. It is for this reason that we speak about "western" or "Latin" fathers and "eastern" or "Greek" fathers (or Latin doctors and Greek doctors.) The Greek fathers were very important, because it was they who, by arguing against the Arians, made what the Church teaches about the Trinity clearer. They also helped us to understand better what it means to say that Jesus Christ is true God and true man. The Latin doctors taught about the Trinity and the Incarnation, but they are better known for helping us to understand such teachings as Original Sin, what baptism does for us, and the need for God's grace in salvation.

Both the Latin and Greek fathers made Church teaching what it is today. They were of immense importance in helping us to understand what God revealed to us in Scripture and the tradition of the Church.

The Greek Fathers

As we have already said, Arianism did not go away immediately after the Council of Nicaea condemned it. Not long after the council, Emperor Constantine himself decided that he did not want to be too hard on the Arians. He had forced Arius to go into **exile** following the council; but, six years after the council ended, the emperor allowed Arius to return to his

exile: banishment; being forced to live away from one's home

home city of Alexandria and even ordered the archbishop of that city to accept Arius as an orthodox believer. The archbishop, however, refused, and for his bravery, Constantine exiled him to the city of Trier in Gaul — a long, long way from Alexandria.

The archbishop who refused to obey Constantine was none other than the great St. Athanasius, who had played such an important part at the Council of Nicaea. This was not to be last time Athanasius was to suffer for the Faith he had so stoutly defended. After Constantine's death, his son, Emperor Constantine II, allowed Athanasius to return to Alexandria. After Constantine II's death, however, a council of eastern bishops who favored Arianism declared that Athanasius was no longer archbishop of Alexandria, and he fled from Egypt and took refuge in Rome, where he received the pope's friendship. Later, in 346, another emperor, Constantius, allowed Athanasius to return to Alexandria. Athanasius was forced to leave Alexandria four more times before his death in 373. He did not, however, die a martyr, but peacefully in his bed, surrounded by his faithful **clergy**.

St. Athanasius of Alexandria was one great Greek father and doctor of the Church, but there were others. These include St. Basil, the bishop of Caesarea in Cappadocia; St. Basil's best friend, St. Gregory Nazianzus, archbishop of Constantinople; and St. Basil's brother, St. Gregory of Nyssa. These men are called the "Three Cappadocians" because they came from a region called Cappadocia in Asia Minor. All three were great defenders of the doctrine of the Trinity against the Arians. The greatest of the three was Basil. Among his many works, Basil wrote a book on the Holy Spirit, showing from Scripture and Church tradition that the Holy Spirit is God, equal to the Father and the Son. In 381, two years after Basil's death, the Council of Constantinople added a section to the Nicene Creed about the Holy Spirit, saying that he is worshiped with the Father and the Son.

Basil was not only a great theologian but an able bishop as well. As bishop he not only cared for the spiritual needs of his flock but did all he could to help the poor. He is famous as well for having written a rule for monks.

Even before the reign of Emperor Constantine I, Christian men and women had been going out into the wilderness and the desert, living lives of penance alone in order to become more like Christ. Some of these

clergy: persons who are official ministers in the Church — deacons, priests, and bishops

A statue of St. Athanasius, Lichfield cathedral, England

hermit: one who goes apart from society and lives alone for religious reasons

monk: one who lives a life of prayer, poverty, and contemplation in a religious community

hermits formed communities that became known as monasteries, where they worked and prayed together. To become closer to God, these ancient **monks** and hermits fasted from food, went without sleep, lived like the very poor, and spent many hours in prayer and reading Scripture. St. Basil wrote two sets of instructions or "rules" for monasteries, and these rules are used in monasteries of Eastern Catholic and Orthodox monasteries even in our time.

Latin Fathers

The life of a monk or hermit attracted Christians not only in the Greek East but in the Latin West as well. One Latin Christian who wanted to live as a monk was Eusebius Hieronymus, who was born in 331 in Dalmatia — on the other side of the Adriatic Sea from Italy. We generally remember Hieronymus by the name, St. Jerome.

The "Vision of St. Jerome" by Jan Janssens

In school, Jerome had been taught to read the works of the great pagan Latin authors, such as Virgil, Horace, and Cicero. He dearly loved the works of these men, especially Cicero, whom all Romans admired for his beautiful writing style. Even after he had become a hermit, Jerome enjoyed reading Cicero — in fact, he enjoyed Cicero so much that he found it hard to read parts of Scripture because he did not like how they were written.

Once, when Jerome had become very sick, he had a vision in which he was standing before the judgment seat of heaven. Asked who he was, Jerome answered, "I am a Christian." The voice that spoke to him answered, "You lie. You belong to Cicero, not Christ!" Asking God to have mercy on him, Jerome abandoned the Roman writers and took up the study of Scripture with great fervor. He even learned Hebrew in order to understand the Old Testament in its original language.

St. Jerome wrote many works, but his greatest service to the Church and our civilization was a work that Pope St. Damasus asked him to complete in 382 — a new translation of the entire Bible from Greek and Hebrew into Latin. Twenty years later, with the help of St. Paula and St. Eustochium (a Roman mother and daughter), Jerome had translated the entire Bible into Latin. Because it was translated into the common or

vulgar language of the western Roman Empire, Jeromes' translation is known as the *Vulgate*. The Vulgate was the Bible used by the Latin Catholic Churches for more than a thousand years.

St. Jerome was a very important Latin Church father and doctor; but, even greater than Jerome was a man who spent many years living a life of sin outside the Church. This man, whom we remember as St. Augustine of Hippo, was born in 354 in Tagaste, a small city in Latin-speaking North Africa. The son of a pagan father and a Christian mother, Augustine as a young man rejected the Christian Faith. This gave his mother, St. Monica, much sorrow, and she spent many years praying that her son would return to the Faith she taught him as a child.

First in the town of Madaura and then in the great North African city of Carthage, Augustine studied the Roman classics and became a master of **rhetoric** — the art of public speaking and writing. Though living an immoral life with a woman who was not his wife, Augustine began hungering for truth. In his search for truth, he began following the Manichees, a religious group that believed in two equal gods, one good and the other evil. The Manichees taught that the human body and material things are evil. Only spiritual things are good.

For nine years, Augustine followed the Manichees — until he moved to Milan, a city in northern Italy. There, he heard the preaching of another great Church father, St. Ambrose, the archbishop of Milan. It was Ambrose who convinced Augustine that the Manichees' teachings were false and that only Christian teaching is true. Because of Ambrose, Augustine wanted to become a Christian.

Augustine wanted very much to be baptized into the Church, but he could not give up his life of sin. He wanted to follow Christ, but he felt he could not. One day, while praying and weeping in a garden, he heard a child's voice say, "Take and read." Augustine opened a book of St. Paul's epistles, and his eyes fell on these words: "put on the Lord Jesus Christ, and make no provision for the desires of the flesh." These words gave Augustine the strength he needed to give himself entirely to Christ.

St. Augustine was baptized in 387, and, soon after, with a little company of friends and relatives, began a type of simple community life of prayer and contemplation. He returned to North Africa and moved to a seaport town called Hippo, hoping to live the life of a monk there. But in 391, at a Mass in the cathedral, he was surrounded by the congregation and brought to the bishop to be ordained a priest. In 395, he was made bishop of Hippo.

vulgar: common, popular

rhetoric: the art of speaking in public

St. Augustine, 354–430

We remember Augustine especially for the works he wrote against a British monk named Pelagius, who said people are born good and can be good without the help of God's grace. Against this teaching, Augustine showed that Scripture teaches that all men are born with Original Sin and need to be cleansed by baptism. Only by God's gift of grace, said Augustine, can anyone become truly holy. By ourselves, we cannot please God. It is for these teachings that St. Augustine is remembered in the Church as the "Doctor of Grace." One of his greatest works is the *City of God*, in which he showed that God's city, the Church, will in the end triumph over the "City of Man." The City of Man is the world of sin.

St. Augustine wrote an astounding number of works, including more than 100 books, 200 letters, and 500 sermons. St. Augustine was the most important doctor in the Latin Church for over 800 years. Even today, the Church greatly honors the works and ideas of this great man.

Beyond The Roman Empire

St. Augustine wrote the *City of God* because of a great disaster in the Roman Empire. In the year 410, a German tribe called the Visigoths attacked the city of Rome and plundered it. This was the first time in many centuries that an enemy army had entered Rome. Pagan Romans said the disaster happened because the empire had abandoned the old gods and become Christian. Augustine began writing the *City of God* to defend the Christian Faith against such pagan attacks.

The Visigoths were not the last barbarian tribe to invade the empire. Twenty years after the Visigoths plundered Rome, another German tribe, the Vandals, invaded North Africa from Spain. St. Augustine died while the Vandals lay siege to his city, Hippo. Hippo fell, and the Vandals then went on to conquer all of North Africa. In 455, the Vandals crossed over into Italy and plundered Rome. The Vandals were very cruel, but more frightening even than they were the Huns, who invaded both the western and eastern Roman Empire from Asia, destroying everything in their path. Other barbarian tribes took advantage of Rome's weakness to invade and conquer different parts of the empire.

In the late 400s, the Roman emperor was very weak indeed. When the Huns appeared before Rome in 452, it was not the emperor who saved the city, but Pope Leo I. He convinced the Huns' leader, Attila, not to enter the city but to receive a payment of gold instead. In 455, Pope Leo could not keep the Vandals from invading Rome, but at least he convinced them not to murder its citizens.

In Italy and the western Roman Empire, the Church was replacing the emperor as the protector of civilization. So, it was not a great shock to anyone when, in 476, the German general Odoacer simply removed the last western Roman emperor from power and made himself king of Italy. The last emperor was just a boy who had been made emperor by his father, a Roman general. The boy emperor was powerless but, at least, he had an interesting name — Romulus Augustus, the name of both Rome's founder and its first emperor.

This map shows the main barbarian invasions that harassed the Roman Empire, and their routes and dates.

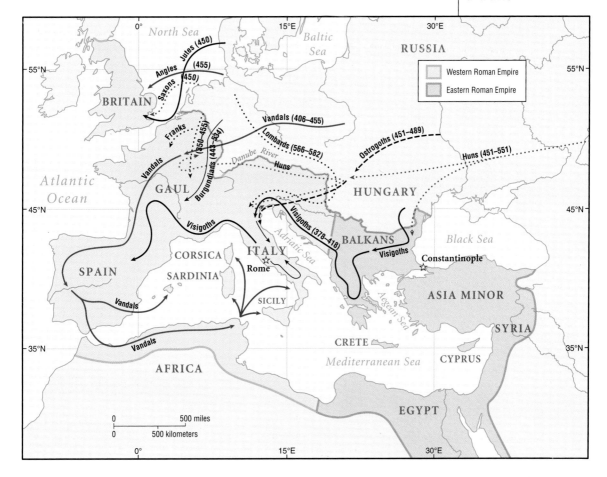

Into the Wider World

The fall of the western Roman Empire left the lands of western Europe in the hands of many German kings. Some of these kings and the tribes they led were pagan, others were Arian Christians. To the civilized Romans who lived in Italy, Gaul, Spain, Britain, and North Africa, the Germans were nothing but barbarians — uncivilized people with very bad manners. With barbarians as their rulers, it looked to the Romans as if civilization had come to an end and the end of the world was near.

The world, of course, did not end, nor did civilization. Though there was no longer any emperor in the West, the Church remained, guided by the pope. The Church saw that the barbarian conquests, though bad, offered a great opportunity — the opportunity of spreading the Gospel. In the centuries following 476, bishops and popes joined with monks in spreading the message of Christ among the German nations. It was not long before missionaries were spreading the Gospel all over western Europe and new Churches, with cathedrals, parishes, and monastries, were growing up in the newly converted lands.

The Irish Missionaries

A bust of St. Patrick, from Dublin Castle, Ireland

One great center from which many missionary monks came was a land that had never been conquered by Rome. That land was Ireland, a great island west of Britain. Ireland received the Catholic Faith from a man with the Latin name of Patricius — whom we remember today as St. Patrick.

Born to a Christian family in Britain in the 300s, Patrick was kidnapped at age 16 by Irish pirates and sold into slavery in Ireland. Though for the next six years he lived the hard life of a shepherd, Patrick's Christian faith grew deeper and deeper. At last, he escaped and returned home to Britain. There, however, he received a vision calling him to return to

Ireland to preach the Gospel. For the next 14 years, he dedicated himself to his studies, especially in the Faith and the Scriptures. He then returned to Ireland as a missionary and a bishop.

The Romans had never conquered Ireland, but St. Patrick won it for the Church. His simple preaching and his love for the Irish people won them over to Christ. Patrick's use of the shamrock to describe the Holy Trinity led to the three-leafed clover becoming the national symbol of Ireland.

St. Patrick's preaching and teaching made Ireland Catholic. It was not long before monasteries dotted the island, and from these monasteries went forth missionary monks who spread the Gospel in northern and southern Britain and even into Gaul. By the 6th century, Irish monks were traveling throughout western Europe, converting pagans and preserving whatever could be saved of Roman civilization. Irish or "Gaelic" Monasteries were founded in Gaul, and the lands that became Switzerland, Belgium, and Italy. The monks in these monasteries followed a very strict way of life and prayer.

Life in Irish monasteries was similar to life in the monasteries of the East. But at the same time the Irish monasteries were spreading throughout western Europe, a new and truly western style of monastic life was coming to be in Italy. The founder of this new style of monastic life was one of the most important men in the history of the Catholic Church. His name was Benedict of Nursia.

St. Benedict and His Rule

St. Benedict (480–550) did not set out to found a religious order, but to save his soul. Born in Nursia, a town in central Italy, St. Benedict attended school in Rome but left the corrupt city as a teenager to live as a hermit in a remote cave in Subiaco, Italy. Many others followed his example, and eventually 12 small communities established themselves in the area, each with a leader chosen by Benedict.

In 525 St. Benedict moved to a mountaintop, called Monte Cassino, between Rome and Naples. There he established what would become one of the most famous and important monasteries in the history of the Church. At Monte Cassino, Benedict began writing his own rule to guide the life of his monks. The *Rule* of St. Benedict was simple — a "rule for beginners," as Benedict called it.

Like other rules for monks, Benedict's *Rule* demanded that monks live a life of prayer and manual labor; but Benedict's *Rule* is not as harsh or

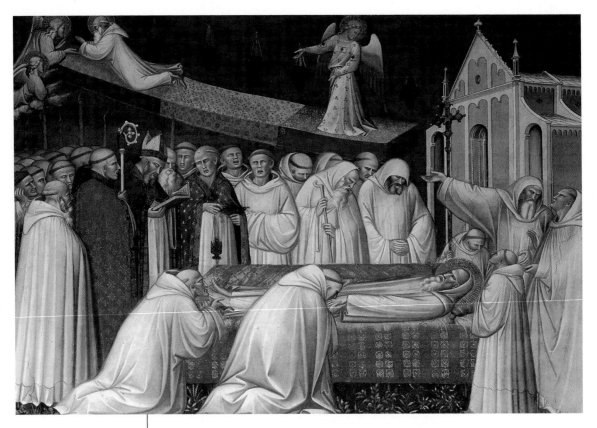

The death of St. Benedict, from St. Miniato al Monte, Florence, Italy. In the upper left, St. Benedict's soul enters heaven. Fresco by Spinello Aretino, 1387

demanding as the rules of the Irish monasteries. According to the *Rule*, the monks were to spend their days in a balanced schedule of prayer, study, exercise, manual labor, and rest in obedience to an abbot ("father"). The much harsher life of the Irish monks had attracted relatively few persons, but many more Christians could live according to the *Rule* of St. Benedict, and they did. It was not long before Benedictine monasteries were sprouting up across western Europe.

The Benedictine monasteries were important not only because of the missionary work they did but because they helped preserve Roman and Greek culture in western Europe. Monks copied ancient manuscripts of Roman literature and so kept them from being lost. Moreover, they practiced Roman methods of farming, and improved them. In this way, the monks were able to teach the people of the new barbarian kingdoms the ways of civilization.

Chapter 6 Review

Let's Remember   Please write your answers in complete sentences.
1. What do B.C. and A.D. mean?
2. List the four Gospels that tell of the life of Christ.
3. Who was the leader of the apostles to whom Jesus gave the keys of the kingdom?
4. What is the event that Christians call the birthday of the Church?
5. In what city were Jesus' followers first called Christians?
6. What is the *Didache?*
7. Who was Constantine? Why is he important to the history of the Church?
8. What Church council taught that the Son of God is equal to the Father?
9. What Mediterranean city was called the New Rome?

Let's Consider   For silent thinking and a short essay, or for thinking in a group with classroom discussion:
1. What happened during the hidden life of Jesus, before he began his public ministry?
2. How did Jesus show that he wanted to establish a church as his gift to the world?
3. How radically did St. Paul change after his conversion and how much of a surprise was it to everyone?
4. How different was the love of Christians in caring for their widows, orphans, and one another from other practices in the ancient world?
5. How rapid was the expansion of Christianity all over the known world?
6. Why did the early Church so strongly oppose heresy?

Things to Do

1. On an outline map of the Roman Empire, indicate where the following places are located: Palestine, Asia Minor, Armenia, Persia, Dalmatia, Greece, Italy, Hispania, Gaul, Britain, Ireland, and Germania. The teacher may help students with this exercise.

2. Using the same outline map or a different one, indicate where the following cities are located: Jerusalem, Antioch, Alexandria, Carthage, Rome, Milan, Nicaea, Nicomedia, and Constantinople (Byzantium).

Let's Eat!

St. Monica might have fixed this recipe; it was a favorite food throughout the Roman Empire in the early days of Christianity. It is called *Ova sfongia ex lacte* (eggs and milk) and is like an omelet or scrambled eggs. Beat 8 eggs together and add a cup of milk and 2 tablespoons of olive oil (or melted butter); mix thoroughly. Fry in a pan like an omelet and serve topped with honey and a little pepper.

Chapter 7 Byzantium and the Rise of Islam

The Byzantine Empire and the Church

From the very beginning of its history, the Church began to develop two cultures or "personalities": an eastern personality and a western one. Though both Church cultures shared the same Faith and the same sacraments, and the same kind of government (by bishops), they had some differences as well. The language of the East (Greece, Asia Minor, Syria, Palestine, and Egypt) was Greek, while the West (Italy, Spain, Gaul, Britain, and North Africa) spoke Latin. Their patterns of prayer or liturgies differed as well. From earliest times, East and West had very different liturgies of the Mass (called the Divine Liturgy in the East.)

Another difference between East and West had to do with the government of the Church. As the centuries passed, the bishops of certain local Churches came to hold authority over other bishops. By the time Constantine became emperor, the Christian Church had four great centers—Jerusalem, Alexandria, Antioch, and Rome. Constantine's new capital, Constantinople, soon joined these centers, which had come to be known as patriarchates, and their bishops as patriarchs. Four of these patriarchates were in the East and so were Greek-speaking; only one, Rome, was Latin-speaking and in the West. The four eastern patriarchates thus had more in common with each other than with Rome. Since the pope in Rome was considered to be the head bishop of the Church, the other patriarchs at times asked for his help in solving problems they

Mosaic of Emperor Constantine in the church of Hagia Sophia, Constantinople

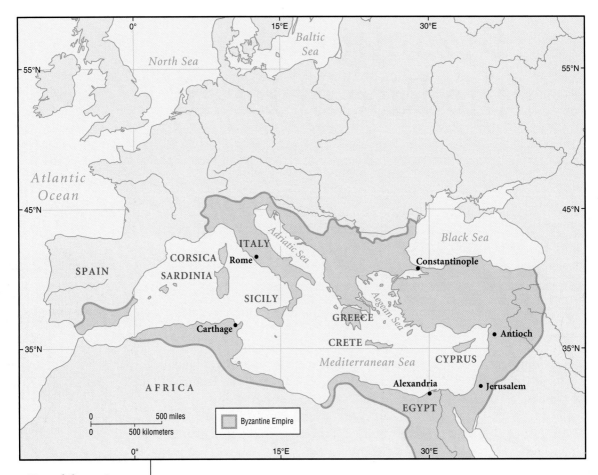

Map of the eastern Roman Empire in the 500s showing Constantinople and the three ancient patriarchal cities of the east: Jerusalem, Antioch, and Alexandria

had in the East. But, for the most part, the eastern patriarchs ruled their Churches without consulting Rome at all.

The fall of the Roman Empire in the West led to other differences between the Eastern and Western Churches. Because there no longer was any imperial government in the West, the popes had to take on political authority in Rome and its surrounding areas. The pope thus became quite independent of other political leaders. In the East, on the other hand, the emperor in Constantinople was able to exercise power over the four eastern patriarchs. It was the emperor, for instance, who chose the patriarch of Constantinople; and if a patriarch did not please him, the emperor could remove him and choose another man to take his place.

After the collapse of the western Roman Empire, the western Church evangelized and civilized the barbarians and so formed a new society in the West. At the same time, the Church in the East continued as part of the Roman Empire of the East. The four eastern patriarchs governed their Churches in a close alliance with the emperor in Constantinople — an alliance that brought them rewards but many misfortunes as well.

The Golden Mouth Defies the Emperor

As we have already seen (in Chapter 6), the Eastern Church produced some of the greatest Christian minds in history. These include St. Athanasius and St. Basil the Great — both of whom were bishops who stood up to the emperor when he commanded them to teach heresy. We have already seen what happened to Athanasius when he refused to deny his faith; but Basil, too, stood firm against the Arian Emperor Valens. Though Valens tried to bribe Basil to abandon the orthodox Faith and threatened him when he refused to do so, Basil defied him to the end.

> **eloquence:** graceful and forceful speech

A statue of St. John Chrysostom, Lichfield Cathedral, England

Another great Eastern father found out how dangerous it was to stand up to the emperor. This was St. John, called "Chrysostom" or "golden mouth" for his great powers as a preacher. John Chrysostom was born in 347 in Antioch and raised by his widowed mother, who was a Christian. After spending some time as a hermit, he was ordained a deacon and then a priest. It was shortly after he became a priest that John showed his great gift for **eloquence.**

In 387 riots broke out in Antioch when Emperor Theodosius passed a new tax. Angry people stormed through the city, damaging the statues of the emperor and his family. When the riots ended, the people waited in terror for the emperor to punish them. To comfort his terrified flock, John preached about 20 sermons that were so moving that they produced a "silence ... as deep as though not a single person was present." Eventually, through the intercession of the bishop, the people won pardon from the emperor.

It was when John Chrysostom was named bishop of Constantinople in 398 that his troubles with the emperor began. Bishop John preached eloquent sermons against the immorality of Constantinople, and he attempted to make his comfortable clergy lead strict and moral

synod: a gathering of bishops
depose: to remove a ruler from power

Justinian the Great, emperor of the Byzantine Empire, shown in an ancient mosaic from the walls of San Vitale, a church in Ravenna, Italy

The interior of Hagia Sophia as it looks today

lives. But all this made Chrysostom an enemy of the Empress Eudoxia and some Church leaders. At last, a gathering or **synod** of Eastern bishops **deposed** John, and Eudoxia's husband, Emperor Arcadius, ordered him to go into exile. But the people of Constantinople loved their bishop and threatened to riot if he were not returned. Days later, fearing a popular uprising, the emperor allowed John to reenter Constantinople.

It was not long, however, before Bishop John again angered Empress Eudoxia. She called on the bishops to condemn him once again, and they did as they were told. The Emperor Arcadius was furious with John. On the evening before Easter day in 404, the emperor's soldiers stormed the bishop's church while baptismal services were going on, forced everyone to flee, and took John prisoner. He was sent far from Constantinople, into the Armenian mountains in the far eastern part of the empire. There he lived for three years, writing more than 230 letters and welcoming those who traveled to see him. In 407, John's enemies ordered him to go to a place called Pithys, on the extreme eastern boundary of the empire. The journey was too hard for the sickly bishop, who was treated with cruelty by his captors. He died September 14, 407, on the way to Pithys. He was 60 years old.

The Byzantine Empire

The last Roman emperor who ruled both the eastern and western empires was Theodosius I, who had made the Christian Faith the official religion of the empire. When Theodosius died in 395, the empire was divided between his two sons, the Emperors Arcadius and Honorius. From

Theodora, co-ruler with Justinian of the Byzantine Empire, shown with her court. From a mosaic created in the 6th century

Constantinople, Arcadius ruled the eastern empire, while Honorius ruled the western empire from Rome. Though the eastern Roman Empire suffered from invasions by both Germans and Huns, it was not conquered by them. After 476, when Odoacer removed Romulus Augustus from power in the West, the Roman Empire was able to carry on in the East.

The eastern emperors did not give up the hope that one day the West would be restored to them. This was the dream of the greatest emperor of the East, Justinian, who began his reign in 527. It was a dream he almost made come true.

Justinian had come to Constantinople as a poor Christian peasant boy, sometime around 500. His climb to power began when his uncle, Justin, became emperor. Justinian became the emperor's close advisor and was made a consul and commander of the army in the East. It was while he was serving Justin that Justinian met Theodora, an actress in the city circus, where her father was the bear-keeper. Justinian fell in love with Theodora and at last married her in 523. Four years later, Justin I died, and Justinian and Theodora were crowned emperor and empress.

Theodora was a clever woman and Justinian gave her great authority. Theodora was known to be cruel to her enemies, but she could be courageous when Justinian was not. When a revolt broke out in Constantinople and threatened to overthrow the royal couple, Theodora refused the leave

The Art of Byzantium

Art and architecture are among the many gifts the Eastern Roman or "Byzantine" Empire gave our civilization. The greatest example of Byzantine architecture is Hagia Sophia and its great dome. The Romans were the first to place domes on buildings, but it was the Byzantine architects who discovered a way to cover very large spaces with domes of stone. Learning architecture from the Byzantines, the Muslims of the Middle East and the Christians of Russia developed the curious onion-shaped domes we see on mosques and churches.

Constantinople gave to future ages the beautiful iconic style of painting. Byzantine icons depict Christ, the Mother of God, the saints, the mysteries of the Faith and stories from Scripture and tradition. Shining in vibrant colors. Byzantine icons are not meant to be realistic images of the persons or events they portray. Instead, they show the spiritual truths behind these persons and events. Icons have been painted on wood or plaster. They also are found as **mosaics** on the walls and ceilings of churches.

> **mosaic:** a picture made of tiny tiles of colored glass and stone, set into concrete

the palace. She said she would rather die an empress than live as a commoner. In this way she encouraged Justinian not to flee, and when his soldiers went out again to stop the revolt, they succeeded.

Justinian was determined to restore the Roman Empire in the West. With his mighty army, he reconquered North Africa, the Balkans, Italy, and southern Spain. Justinian sought to unite his empire by reforming Roman law. He ordered a new code of laws to be drawn up. This new code became the model for European countries in the centuries to come.

One of Justinian's most lasting achievements was the rebuilding of Constantine's magnificent cathedral, Hagia Sophia, which had been destroyed during a revolt in Constantinople in 530. The new church took 10,000 workers and five years to complete; but when it was finished, Hagia Sophia was a wonder of glory. The new church became the model for church buildings throughout Europe.

Two of Justinian's accomplishments exist today. Hagia Sophia sill stands (it is now a museum in Istanbul) and his code of laws lives on in our modern law books and constitutions. Justinian's conquests in the West, however, did not last. After his death, the German Lombards rose up against Roman rule in Italy, as did the Visigoths in Spain. The Persians invaded the empire and conquered imperial lands in Syria, Palestine, and Egypt. In 627, Emperor Heraclius was able to drive the Persians from these lands and strengthen Roman power. But only for a short time.

The empire changed in other ways after Justinian's death. Justinian himself had come from an old western Roman family and had grown up speaking Latin. Though he ruled from Constantinople, a Greek-speaking city, he continued to write the laws in Latin—the language of ancient Rome. After Justinian, however, the Eastern Roman Empire became less Latin and more Greek. Soon, the laws of the government were written in Greek instead of Latin. Because of this change, historians have given the empire after Justinian a different name than the Roman Empire. They call it the Byzantine Empire, after Byzantium, the site where Constantine founded Constantinople. The people living in the empire, however, never called themselves "Byzantine." For the long centuries this empire existed, its people called themselves what they had always called themselves. They were *Romanoi*—Romans.

Mecca: the central holy city of the Muslim religion and the destination of Islamic pilgrims

Muhammad and the Muslims

The Story of Muhammad

In the year 570, a boy named Kuthon ibn Abdallah was born to a poor but respectable family in **Mecca**, a city in the land of Arabia. According to the story of his birth, when the baby boy was presented to his family, his grandfather called him "Muhammad," which means "one who is praised." From that time on, the boy was known by that name, although its meaning would not be understood until many years later. This Muhammad was to become the most honored and praised man in the history of his desert homeland.

Muhammad lost both of his parents when he was still very young. His father died before the boy was born, and his mother died when he was six. The orphan was taken in by his grandfather for two years and then went to live with his uncle, Abu Talib. Muhammad grew to be a hard and honest worker. As a boy he tended sheep, and as a young man he drove the camels that traveled in caravans carrying Arabian goods to be sold throughout the Byzantine Empire.

The Archangel Gabriel brings a message to the Prophet, in a 16th-century manuscript in the Topkapi Palace, Istanbul

Muhammad's skill and reputation as a cattle driver grew so great that a wealthy widow, Kadijah, hired him to lead her caravans. She then began to admire his looks and gift for leadership. Kadijah was 40 years old and had three children, yet she sent a servant to ask the 25-year-old Muhammad if he would marry her, and he agreed. They lived happily together for the next 15 years, raising children and becoming wealthy merchants in Mecca.

But Muhammed became dissatisfied. While traveling in caravans and mingling with others in the marketplaces, he had learned the teachings of

The Legend of the Kaaba

The story of Abraham from the Old Testament more or less makes up the first part of the story of the Arabian people. According to the Old Testament book of Genesis, Sarah could not believe she would conceive a child in her old age. So she allowed her Egyptian slave Hagar to become Abram's wife, and Hagar became pregnant and bore him a son, whom she named Ishmael.

After God made a covenant with Abram and changed his name to Abraham, Sarah became pregnant and gave birth to Isaac. Afraid that Isaac would have to share his inheritance with Ishmael, Sarah told Abraham to send the older son away. Abraham loved both of his sons and did not want to send Ishmael away, but God told him: "Heed the demands of Sarah, no matter what she is asking of you; for it is through Isaac that descendants shall bear your name. As for the son of the slave woman, I will make a great nation of him also, since he too is your offspring" (Gen. 21:12–13).

Abraham sent Hagar and Ishmael away into the wilderness with bread and a skin of water. After wandering far into the desert, the mother and child ran out of water, and the boy began to weep from thirst. God took pity on them and opened in the desert a well of fresh water, from which they drank.

This is the end of the story in Genesis. The Arabian legend adds the following:

Abraham heard of the miracle and came at once to build a temple to God near the well. In the temple, called the Kaaba, Abraham placed a black stone he had received from his father—a stone that was said to have come originally from the Garden of Eden, where God had given it to Adam. Hagar and Ishmael made their home near the Kaaba, and many years and descendants later, a city grew up around the temple and the miraculous well. This city was Mecca, the holiest of cities for the descendants of Ishmael, the Arabs.

> **Kaaba:** the temple Muslims believe Abraham built and in which he placed a black rock given to Adam by God

Abraham sends away Hagar and Ishmael

Each year millions of Muslims from all over the world visit Mecca, where they perform a prayer ritual centered on the Kaaba, a draped, cube-shaped stone building in the courtyard of the great mosque. The Kaaba still contains the black stone, believed by scientists to be a meteorite.

Muslim pilgrims gather around the Kaaba (the black cube in the middle) to perform Friday dawn prayers at the Grand Mosque in Mecca, Saudi Arabia

the Jews and the Christians. The moral teachings of these religions, he saw, were superior to the wicked behavior of his Arab brothers. The Arabs were pagan, worshiping idols at Mecca and other holy sites. Some Arabs had abandoned religion altogether, taking up gambling, drinking, mistreating their wives, and other abuses. Muhammad believed his people needed a leader, a prophet, to steer them toward the truth.

Muhammad began to spend hours alone in a cave on the mountain of Hira, praying. Once, he said, when he was in prayer, he heard bells and then a loud voice commanding, "Read!" When the startled Muhammad replied that he could not read, the voice recited some words, which then appeared on a flaming scroll that Muhammad was able to read. The voice told Muhammad about the one, true God, whose name in Arabic is **Allah**. All people, said the voice, were to turn from the worship of idols to the worship of Allah.

As in Jewish prayer, Muslim men worship separately from women

Allah: Arabic word for God

Saved by the Spider's Web

One legend tells how Allah intervened to protect Muhammad. When the prophet and his friend Abu Bakr first left Mecca, they hid in a cave, where they remained for three days. Immediately after they entered the cave, a spider appeared and began weaving a web across the entrance. When the Meccan soldiers came upon the cave, they decided no one could have entered it and went to look elsewhere for the fugitives.

convulsion: a violent shaking of the body
Islam: Arabic word meaning "submission," "complete obedience," "total surrender"; the name for Muhammad's religion
Muslim: Arabic word meaning "one who submits"; the name of one who follows Islam

Muhammad was so terrified by these visions that he thought he was losing his mind. But, encouraged by his wife and a Christian woman of Mecca to whom Kadijah told the story, Muhammad continued to go to the cave to pray. For two years Muhammad heard nothing more from Allah, but just as he was about to lose hope, he received what he thought were more revelations. These were so terrifying that he sometimes fainted and went into **convulsions**.

In 613, Muhammad began to go among his countrymen to preach the messages he said he had received in the cave. His message was simple: "There is no God but Allah, and Muhammad is his prophet." Muhammad encouraged his listeners to give up idol worship, lying, stealing, and drunkenness A few people — mostly family members — became his followers. Many others, however, criticized Muhammad's message and opposed him.

Over time Muhammad created a new religion that was made up of Christian and Jewish beliefs and practices, plus some beliefs and practices Muhammad added on his own. Muhammad said he was the last and greatest of the prophets — greater even than Jesus. Everyone, he said, has to worship Allah and do everything Allah commands. Because of this teaching, Muhammad's religion came to be called **Islam**, which means "submission" or "complete obedience" or "total surrender." Followers of Islam are called **Muslim**, which means, "one who submits."

Muhammad wanted to improve the moral lives of his people. He said that they were always to act justly toward others and show compassion to the poor and weak. They were not to drink alcohol or eat the meat of pigs. Arab men had many wives, and Muhammad did not forbid this. But, he said, a man could have only four wives at one time and he must treat them equally. (Muhammad, however, allowed himself to have more than four wives.)

Fearing the growing power of Muhammad and his followers, the leaders in Mecca plotted to kill him. Learning of the plot, Muhammad fled from the city by night. This event, which occurred in 622, is called the *Hejra* (**Hegira** in Latin) and is the most important date in the Islamic calendar. Just as Christians tell time from the birth of Christ (A.D. and B.C.), Muslims number their years from the Hegira. The year A.D. 2000 is the year A.H. (*Anno Hegirae*) 1378 for Muslims.

Muhammad arrived safely in the city of Yathrib, which from that time on became known as Medina, the "City of the Prophet." No longer the humble and ridiculed preacher of Mecca, Muhammad soon made himself supreme ruler of Medina. His laws followed Muslim moral teachings. For instance, they demanded care for the poor and orphaned, outlawed drinking alcohol, and forbade the Arab practice of killing unwanted babies.

With power in his hands, Muhammad decided that the best way to spread Islam was by what he called *jihad*—a holy war. Gathering an army about him, Muhammad attacked traveling caravans and looted them. Enriched by this wealth, Muhammad could afford to carry on war against Mecca.

In 624, Muhammad's forces defeated Mecca's tribesmen in the Battle of Bedr. In 630, Muhammad's army attacked Mecca, but the outnumbered Meccans simply surrendered. Crying "Allahu Akbar!" ("God is most great!"), Muhammad rode into the courtyard of the Kaaba shrine, placed his hands on the black stone, and ordered that the stone idols of the shrine be destroyed. Since then, the Kaaba (still housing the black stone) has been the spiritual center of Islam.

Though Mecca became the center of his religion, Muhammad made Medina his capital. From that city he went to conquer all the tribes of Arabia. When he died in 632, he was the religious and political leader of a small kingdom in the deserts of the Arabian peninsula.

> **Hegira:** the night flight of Muhammad and the most important date on the Muslim calendar
>
> **jihad:** a Muslim holy war

The Koran

Muslims believe that Muhammad received revelations from God for 22 years after his first vision on Mount Hira in 610. Since he could not read or write, Muhammad proclaimed what he

The practice of praying five times a day, facing the shrine of the Kaaba, dates to the year 624. When Muhammad first arrived in Medina, he yearned to unite Jews and Christians into the religion of Islam, so he had his followers pray while facing the holy city of Jerusalem. Some say that when the Jews resisted his efforts to convert them, he angrily ordered Muslims to face the Kaaba instead. Others say Muhammad had a revelation from God that his followers should face the Kaaba, and it was the Jews who grew angry. In the end, the Muslims drove out two of the three Jewish tribes from Medina and, as a punishment for suspected treason, Muhammad executed all 609 men of the third tribe.

sura: a sermon within the Koran

A copy of the Koran

learned in these revelations in sermons (called **suras**), while others wrote down what he said.

After his death, Muhammad's followers collected all the scraps, notes, and remembrances of Muhammad's sayings. The *suras* were written down, from the longest to the shortest, and put in a book. This book is called the *Qu'ran* or Koran. It is the sacred book of Islam.

Many of the *suras* resemble moral teachings and commandments found in the Christian Bible. The Koran, for instance, teaches this about generosity: "A kind word with forgiveness is better than almsgiving followed by injury. Allah is Absolute, Merciful!" Some *suras*, however, are simply primitive Arabic sayings calling for the brutal killing of enemies. Other *suras* promise very worldly rewards to faithful Muslims. One *sura*, for instance, describes heaven as a delightful garden in which beautiful maidens who never grow old will forever serve faithful Muslim men with rich foods and wine.

The Five Pillars of Islam

Although there are different groups in Islam, Muslims share common beliefs. They believe in God, good and bad angels, the Koran, prophets, and God's judgment. Muhammad laid down five commands that every Muslim has to obey. These commands are called the Five Pillars, because on them rests all of Muslim life.

1. **Belief in one God (Allah) and Muhammad as his prophet.**
   For Muslims, there is only a single, divine person, whom they call Allah. Muslims misunderstand the Christian doctrine of the Trinity — that there are three Persons in one God — and think Christians worship many gods. Muslims believe that Jesus was just a prophet and not the Son of God. They claim Muhammad is the greatest of the prophets, greater even than the "prophet Jesus."
2. **Prayer five times a day.** Wherever they are, Muslims are supposed to recite prayers at five different times of the day. In Muslim countries or wherever there are **mosques** (Muslim places of worship), a prayer leader called a *muezzin* sings out the call to prayer from

mosque: a Muslim place of worship

a tower. (Muhammad did not like bells.) Muslims may pray by themselves, but they think it is better to pray with other Muslims in a group. When Muslims pray, they kneel and bow to the ground, facing in the direction of the Kaaba shrine in Mecca.

3. **Fast of Ramadan.** During entire month of Ramadan (the ninth month of the Muslim year), Muslims fast from pleasures, including food and drink. The fast begins each day at sunrise and ends at sunset. The Ramadan fast is a time Muslims are supposed to practice virtue and "fast" from sin.

4. **Almsgiving.** Muslims believe giving **alms** to the poor is necessary for salvation.

> **alms:** money or gifts given to help the poor

5. **Pilgrimage to Mecca.** Every Muslim is required to go to the Kaaba in Mecca at least once in his or her life. Only Muslims may enter the city of Mecca.

Islam Spreads Outside of Arabia

After Muhammad's death, his followers fought over who should take his place as their leader. They ended in choosing Muhammad's friend, Abu Bakr, who became the first **caliph** or "successor" of the prophet. Although

> **caliph:** a successor of Muhammad

What Do Christians Today Think about Islam?

Along with Judaism and Christianity, Islam is one of the world's three great monotheistic religions. Christians thus can admire some of Islam's beliefs, which it shares with Judaism and the Christian Faith. Muslims also have a serious moral code; they, for instance, insist on mercy for the poor and weak and oppose abortion, just as Christians do. Christians can admire their reverent devotion to prayer and their humility before God.

Christians and Muslims, however, have important differences. Islam has no sacraments and no priests. Though it has religious leaders, Islam has no teaching authority like the pope and the bishops.

The Christian Faith shows greater respect for women than does Islam. Christians venerate Mary, who is the model for all Christian women. Though the Koran praises Mary highly as a righteous woman, Islam does not show much respect for women. Islam historically has encouraged a warlike spirit and recommended using violence to force people to submit themselves to God. For centuries, Christendom has had to fight off Muslim invasion time and time again.

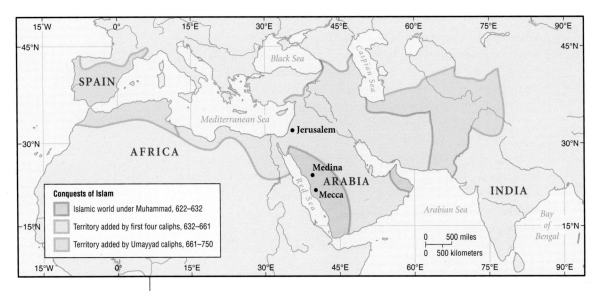

Map showing the swiftness and extent of Muslim conquest

most of Mecca and Medina accepted Abu Bakr's leadership, some tribes rebelled against him. For two years, the new caliph fought the rebellious tribes until they, at last, agreed to accept his authority. After taking full control of Arabia, Abu Bakr led a *jihad* against neighboring Persia.

A popular military leader named Omar became caliph when Abu Bakr died in 634. From 634 to 644, the Muslim army continued its conquest of

The Dome of the Rock

One of the distinctive landmarks of the Jerusalem skyline is the Dome of the Rock, an Islamic mosque built on the site of the former temples of Solomon and Herod the Great. When the Muslims conquered the city in 638, Caliph Omar himself helped clean up the site, which had been for years used as the city dump. In 691 the famous mosque was completed.

The mosque shelters a limestone rock on which, Muslims say, Abraham nearly sacrificed Isaac. The Muslims claim that the rock was also a place of prayer for all the great prophets and was the place from where Muhammad ascended into heaven. After Mecca and Medina, the Dome of the Rock is the third holiest place for Muslims.

Muslim shrine, the Dome of the Rock in Jerusalem, built on the site of the ancient Jewish Temple

Charles Martel in the Battle of Tours

The King Who Saved Christian Europe

Charles Martel (688–741) was ruler of all the Franks. His quick and effective military style earned him the nickname "the Hammer." After a series of battles against neighboring tribes from Germany, he took on the Spanish Muslims (sometimes called the Saracens) who had moved into southern Frankish territories and were approaching Tours, a city on the Loire River. Charles's army met the invaders near the town of Poitiers. In the great battle that ensued, the Muslim leader of Spain, Abd-er-Rahman, was killed, and the invaders fled in the night. In 739, the Muslims advanced again into the Burgundy region up to Lyons, but, once again, Charles drove them out of the kingdom, this time for good.

Persia and then moved west to conquer Egypt and Syria, which were parts of the Byzantine Empire. In 638, the Muslim Arabs conquered Jerusalem, which has remained a Muslim center ever since.

Omar died a violent death in 644 when he was stabbed by a Persian slave. Under the next caliph, Othman, the Arab Muslims began to grow rich from the wealth that came to them from the lands they had conquered. Othman was slain by soldiers who resented the fact that he gave too many favors to his relatives, and he was succeeded by Caliph Ali.

The new caliph not only had been the first male to accept Muhammad's teaching, but also he had married the Prophet's daughter, Fatima. But all this did not save Ali, who himself was murdered in 661. After Ali's death, Islam split into two major groups — the Sunnis, or the "traditional" believers, and the Shiites, who supported Ali's family against the Ummayad family, which had taken over the leadership of Islam. Shiites came to hold different beliefs from the Sunnis on some matters.

All this fighting among themselves did not stop the Muslim conquests. From Persia, the Muslim armies moved east into Sind (today's Pakistan). To the west they conquered the rest of North Africa, and to the north they battered the weakened Byzantine Empire and almost seized

Constantinople. In 711, the Arabs crossed the Straits of Gibraltar from North Africa and advanced into Europe. After conquering almost all of Spain, the Muslim army crossed the Pyrenees Mountains into France. This was a most dangerous moment, for if the Muslims conquered France, they could have kept the Christian Faith from becoming the religion of Europe. But in 732, in one of the most important battles ever fought, the leader of the Germanic Franks, Charles Martel, defeated the Muslims near Poitiers, a town 150 miles from Paris. The Muslims returned to Spain, and Europe was saved from Islamic conquest.

Though the Arabs were stopped from making new conquests in the West, they continued to be successful in the East. By the 9th century, the Muslim Arabs had conquered parts of India, western China, and the Malaysian and Indonesian islands in the Orient. In a little more than 100 years after the death of Muhammad, Islam covered half the known world.

The Success of Islam

Why was Islam so successful? Why did it grow so quickly and spread so far? One reason is what Islam did for the Arabs. Until Muhammad came, the Arabs were divided into tribes that struggled against and fought with one another. Islam united the Arabs so that they could turn their warlike spirit against other nations and not each other. Islam suited the desert tribesmen, for it is not a difficult or complex religion. It has clear rules for how to behave towards God and one's neighbor.

It is important to remember, too, that Islam did not spread through missionaries going out and winning unbelievers to their religion. Islam spread through warfare and conquest. Every victory they won convinced the Muslim soldiers that God was with them, and they became even bolder. "Allah is with us!" they cried, as they rode into foreign lands. Muslim soldiers did not fear death, for their religion promised them that if they died in battle, they would go straight to paradise.

When the Muslims conquered a land, they did not at first force their Islamic religion upon their subjects. They did, however, place a heavy tax on everyone who refused to become Muslim. It was much harder for non-Muslims to fit into the new Muslim society and so many Christians and Jews abandoned their faith for the new religion. So it was that Syria, Palestine, Egypt, and North Africa — lands that had been Christian — have become almost entirely Muslim.

Islam's Golden Age

When the Muslim Arabs conquered the ancient lands of Syria, Palestine, and Egypt, they did not destroy the Byzantine Roman and Greek culture they found there. They replaced Christian laws and customs with Islamic ones, but they respected the art and learning that had come down from the Greeks and Romans. In the Mediterranean lands, the Arabs went from being rough tribesmen to become civilized men. The Islamic conquerors kept the Byzantine civilization of the once-Christian lands and allowed it to continue and grow, but not in a Christian direction.

The civilization of the Muslims reached its highest point, its "Golden Age," after 750. In that year, the Abbasid family revolted against the Umayyads and took over the office of caliph. The Abbasids used their great wealth to encourage learning and culture. In 762, the Caliph Al-Mansur began building a new city he called Baghdad atop the ruins of an ancient Babylonian city on the Tigris River in Mesopotamia. Modeled on the great Byzantine cities, such as Constantinople, Baghdad became one of the grandest cities of the medieval world. It was the center of Arab Muslim literature, mathematics, astronomy, medicine, art, and architecture.

One of the most famous writings from the Golden Age is *The Thousand and One Nights*. Better known as *The Arabian Nights*, it is a collection of some 200 stories, including "Aladdin and the Lamp," "The Flying Carpet," "Sinbad the Sailor," and "Ali Baba and the Forty Thieves." The stories were based on folk tales gathered from throughout the East.

The Arabs had long loved poetry, so it is not surprising that it flourished during the Islamic Golden Age. Poets were thought to have special gifts or even to be possessed by powerful spirits, called genies. Some of the greatest poetry of Islamic civilization was written around the year 1120 by Omar Khayyam, who wrote a book of poems, called the *Rubaiyat*, in Farsi (the language of Persia). The word *rubaiyat* means "quatrain" or four-line poetry. English speakers came to know Khayyam's poetry in the 19th century, when the English writer Edward FitzGerald published a rhymed translation of 100 of the *Rubaiyat's* 1,000 quatrains.

Omar Khayyam's poetry

(translated by Edward FitzGerald)

On our powerlessness over time:
The moving finger writes, and having writ
Moves on; Nor all your piety nor wit
Shall lure it back to cancel half a line
Nor all your tears wash out a word of it.

On the joys of romantic love:
A book of verses underneath the bough,
A jug of wine, a loaf of bread—and thou
Beside me singing in the wilderness—
Oh, wilderness were paradise enow!

Scheherazade and the *Arabian Nights*

Once upon a time there was a wealthy king, called King Schariar, who ruled over Arabia. All was well in the kingdom until he made a terrible discovery. The wife whom he loved and trusted had betrayed him. Shocked and broken-hearted, he immediately ordered her execution. Yet this was not enough to erase his bitterness. He decided no woman could be trusted and so all would be punished. Each day he would marry one of the young women of the kingdom, and the following morning he would have his new bride killed. The terrible executions took place day after day, as family after family sorrowfully gave up their daughters to the bloodthirsty king.

A depiction of Scheherazade

The grand vizier, second in command over the kingdom, did his best to shield his own daughters from their sure fate. But, one day, his wise and beautiful eldest daughter, Scheherazade (pronounced Sha-Hare-a-ZAHD), volunteered to be the next bride. The vizier tried to talk her out of it, but she persisted. "Do not fear, father, for I have a plan," she told him. "If I succeed, I shall save not only my life but that of the other maidens in the kingdom." To carry out her plan she asked that her younger sister, Dunyazade, be allowed to spend the night in the palace. The vizier reluctantly agreed.

The wedding took place, and late that night Dunyazade entered the royal chamber. "What is it?" King Schariar demanded. "Oh my king," began the girl, "all my life my sister has entertained our family with the most wonderful stories. Knowing that in the morn-

ing she will be killed, I would like to ask her to tell one more tale, so that I might remember her by it." The king agreed, and Scheherazade began her tale.

The young woman's deep brown eyes shone with wonder and her hands danced as she transported the king to a magical world of a poor boy, a lamp, and a powerful genie. Through the night her melodious voice filled the room with fantastic adventures. She told of grand palaces, jewels beyond counting, carpets lifting into the air, evil magicians, and beautiful princesses. The king, his imagination utterly seized, drank in every word. When the first light edged through the curtain of the royal chamber, Scheherazade suddenly stopped, midsentence. "What?" said the king. "Don't stop now! What happens next?"

"I must end the story," the clever Scheherazade said with a sad voice. "The dawn is here, and with that, my execution."

"No, no!" he replied. "You must go on and finish the tale tonight. I can put off your execution until tomorrow."

And so that night she picked up the story where she had left off, but again the next morning she stopped in the middle of another even more exciting adventure. The king had to hear the end of it too. So once again, he postponed her execution.

The stories continued this way night after night, and lasted for 1,001 nights. By then, Scheherazade had won the heart of the king, who regretted his evil deeds and grew to love his wise and good bride. Scheherazade was allowed to live, and so, too, did her tales, known as *The Thousand and One Nights*.

Omar Khayyam was not only a poet, but an astronomer and mathematician. He was an expert in that form of mathematics known as algebra. The word, algebra, comes from the Arabic word *al-jabr*, which means "re-joining." Algebra had first been invented in A.D. 280 by a Greek mathematician, Diophantus of Alexandria, but it was further developed in the 9th century by an Arab mathematician named Muhammad ibn Musa al-Khwarizmi. Christian Europe learned algebra from the Arabs in the 12th century. It is from them that we got "zero," also called the "cipher" — which comes from the Arabic word *sifr*, meaning "empty." We also received the mathematical idea of the algorithm from the Arabs. The word algorithm comes from the name of Al-Khwarizmi.

The Arabs learned medicine as well from the Greeks, and improved on it. From the study of Greek medicine and their own experimentation, Muslim surgeons learned how to remove diseased tissue, amputate limbs, and even remove **cataracts** from the eye. They **cauterized** wounds, which means applying heat or chemicals to stop bleeding. The Arabs were advanced in dental health as well. They encouraged cleaning teeth with powders or rinses, using a softened stick, perhaps the world's first toothbrush.

> **cataract:** a disease of the eye that makes a person partly or entirely blind
> **cauterize:** to stop bleeding using heat or chemicals

Though they thought making pictures or statues of persons offended God, Muslim Arabs developed beautiful art forms. Sometimes Muslim artists made images of Muhammad and other people, but these were never shown in mosques. Pictures of Muhammad never show his eyes, nose, mouth, or ears. Instead of icons of saints, Muslim artists developed **calligraphy**, a beautiful form of writing. They made as well very complicated and colorful geometric designs. These were carved or painted or arranged in the form of mosaics. Such designs are found in elaborate rugs

> **calligraphy:** beautiful, elegant handwriting; skilled penmanship

One of the most famous Islamic physicians was Ibn Sina, born in 980 and known in Europe as Avicenna. His masterwork was a five-volume medical encyclopedia titled the *Canon of Medicine*, which contained all medical knowledge up to Avicenna's time. The *Canon* was the main textbook for medical students in the Near East and Europe for centuries. Ibn Sina was also an important philosopher. Called the "prince of philosophers," Avicenna revived interest in the Greek classical thinkers, especially Aristotle, in the Arab world.

Muslim ornamentation using Arabic script and intricately carved patterns, Cordoba, Spain

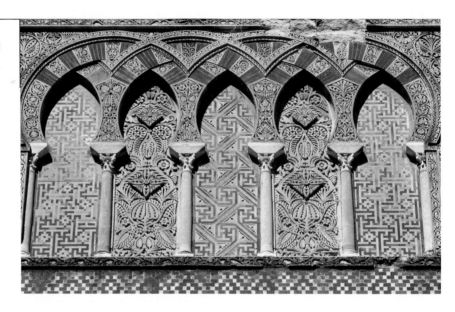

Court of the Lions, Alhambra Palace, Spain

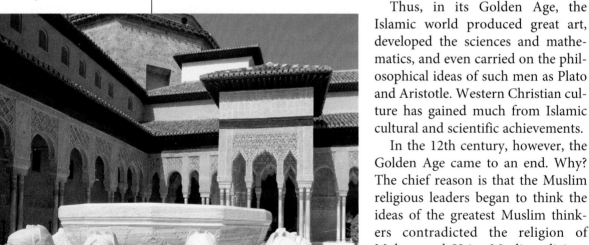

and other decorative crafts. The Muslim Arabs built grand buildings, with graceful arches, great domes, and colorful designs.

Thus, in its Golden Age, the Islamic world produced great art, developed the sciences and mathematics, and even carried on the philosophical ideas of such men as Plato and Aristotle. Western Christian culture has gained much from Islamic cultural and scientific achievements.

In the 12th century, however, the Golden Age came to an end. Why? The chief reason is that the Muslim religious leaders began to think the ideas of the greatest Muslim thinkers contradicted the religion of Muhammad. Using Muslim religious law, called *Sharia*, they stopped further developments in science and philosophy. Thus, since the 12th century, the culture of the Islamic countries has remained mostly unchanged, while, Christian Europeans, learning from the Arabs, went on to develop a rich and beautiful civilization. By the 19th century, the Muslim nations seemed very primitive to the peoples of Europe.

Chapter 7 Review

Let's Remember   Please write your answers in complete sentences.
1. What was the name of the great Byzantine preacher whose name means "golden mouth"?
2. What is another name for the Byzantine Empire?
3. What is contained in the Kaaba in Mecca, where Muslims from all over the world come to pray?
4. How do Muslims calculate time?
5. What is the name of the book that records the sayings of Muhammad?
6. What are the five pillars of Islam?

Let's Consider   For silent thinking and a short essay, or for thinking in a group with classroom discussion:
1. How much of the early Christian world was lost to the conquering Muslims?
2. Why did the Muslim religion and culture spread so rapidly?
3. Why did Islamic culture stop growing and developing after its "golden age"?
4. How are women treated in a polygamous society?

Things to Do

1. Using a blank map of the Mediterranean world, indicate the location of the five patriarchal cities: Rome, Jerusalem, Antioch, Alexandria, and Constantinople. Using a colored pencil, mark out and color in the parts of the Mediterranean world where Christians spoke Greek. Using a different colored pencil, mark out and color in the part of the Mediterranean world where Christians spoke Latin.

2. Make a map of the Middle East, showing where Mecca, Medina, Jerusalem, Damascus, and Baghdad are.

Let's Eat!

Because Muslim law forbids the drinking of alcohol, Muslims developed coffee to drink instead. The name coffee, however, means wine, even though it is not wine. Turkish coffee is very strong and sweet, like a hot, black syrup.

Chapter 8

Europe: the Middle Ages

Castles and kings, knights in armor, monks and cloisters, crusaders and saints — these are the things that come to mind when we think of the Middle Ages. The Middle Ages was all these things, but it was more. It was a time when the Church was a world power, but also the time when a little poor man, called St. Francis of Assisi, changed the world around him. It was a time when many people were superstitious and ignorant, but it was also the period when such great minds as Abelard, St. Bonaventure, St. Albert the Great, and St. Thomas Aquinas lived and worked. The Middle Ages was a time when some of the greatest works of humanity, the cathedrals, were built. It was a time when popes and bishops, kings and commoners, tried to make the Gospel of Christ the highest law in human society. The Middle Ages gave us what is called Christendom — the unique society and culture formed by the Catholic Church.

The Geography of Europe

Before we turn to the story of medieval Europe, let us take a look at the geography of the continent of Europe, where most of the events of this story took place.

If you look at a globe, you will find it is not easy to say where the continent of Asia ends and the continent of Europe begins. Because of this, Europe and Asia have sometimes been called Eurasia, to show that they actually form one great **landmass**. We do, however, distinguish between Europe and Asia. We say that the eastern border of Europe and Asia is

landmass: a large area of land

Map of Europe, showing mountains, oceans, rivers, and important countries

the Ural Mountains in Russia. The Caucasus Mountains (between the Black Sea and the Caspian Sea) and the Black Sea separate Europe from the Middle East, which is part of Asia.

Europe is a unique continent, for it is made up largely of peninsulas. In the southeast is the Balkan Peninsula, which includes Greece. The Adriatic Sea separates the Balkans from the Italian Peninsula, while the Mediterranean separates Italy from the Iberian Peninsula (Spain and Portugal). On the Atlantic side of Europe, the Iberian Peninsula and the much smaller peninsula of Brittany in France form the Bay of Biscay. Though separated from Europe by the English Channel, Great Britain is almost a great northward-pointing peninsula. Further east, is the small peninsula of Denmark, and just north of Denmark, the great curving peninsula that forms Scandinavia and is home to the nations of Norway, Sweden, and Finland.

This unique formation of Europe allows the sea breezes to influence the climate of much of Europe. On the whole, Europe is warmer in the winter and cooler in the summer than the parts of North America that lie on the same latitude. For instance, southern France and northern Spain lie on the same latitude as New England, Michigan, and Minnesota, but have far warmer climates than do these regions of North America.

An important feature of Europe is the series of mountain ranges that run from Romania in the east, through Central Europe, and into Spain and Portugal in the west. These mountain ranges are actually part of one, ancient "Alpine" range. The eastern section of this mountain range is the Carpathian Mountains, which run westward from Romania, through Ukraine, and into Slovakia. The next section of the mountain range, called the Alps, runs southwest from eastern Austria, through northern Italy and Switzerland, and into southeastern France. There it curves around to the east and connects with the Apennines in Italy. On the other side of the Adriatic Sea from Italy, the Dinaric Alps run from the Alps southward into the Balkan Peninsula. The Mediterranean Sea separates the final section of the Alpine mountain range from the Alps. This range includes the Pyrenees, which divide France from Spain.

North and northwest of Europe's great Alpine mountain range are plateaus of gently rolling or hilly country. This is generally rich farmland, though it includes features such as the great Black Forest in Germany. North of these plateaus is the Great European Plain, flat land that runs eastward across northern France, through Belgium and the Netherlands, and across northern Germany, into Poland. From Poland, the Great

Northern Plain widens out into the enormous Russian plain, which ends at the Ural Mountains.

Several great rivers have played an important part in European history. The longest of these rivers is the Danube, which rises in the Swiss Alps and then runs 1,644 miles through southern Germany, Austria, Hungary, and Serbia. It forms the boundary between Romania and Bulgaria, until it finally empties into the Black Sea. Another important river, the Rhine, also rises in the Swiss Alps, but it flows northward for over 700 miles before it enters the North Sea in the Netherlands.

Geography has played a very important part in the history of Europe. One example of this is the fact that for centuries the great Alpine mountain range separated northern Europe from the civilization of the Mediterranean country. While those lands south of the Alpine mountains developed cities early on, human life in the regions north of the mountains for many centuries centered on farming villages and did not develop important cities until well into the Middle Ages.

The Dark Ages

The Middle Ages was a long period of time—about 1,000 years. As you might expect, much happened during that 1,000-year period, many things changed. At the beginning of the Middle Ages, around the year 500, there were no knights and ladies, no castles and great soaring cathedrals. Indeed, the first 500 years of the Middle Ages were in many ways very unlike what we now imagine the Middle Ages to have been like.

The first 500 years of the Middle Ages have been called the "Dark Ages"—a name given to them many centuries later by people who knew little about them. These ages were "dark" to them. The first part of the Dark Ages was indeed a very dark time. The Roman Empire was gone in western Europe; the empire's government, education, and high culture were being forgotten. Only monasteries kept the memory of classical Greece and Rome alive.

But the Dark Ages were not actually as dark as some people think. During the period from the year 500 to the year 1000, the people of Europe, under the leadership of the Church, built up the new civilization of Christendom. The Catholic Faith united the many peoples, speaking many languages and practicing many customs, into one civilization.

King of the Franks, Emperor of the West

People in the Middle Ages told many wonderful stories about Charlemagne. They described this king of the Franks (a German tribe that ruled Gaul) as a giant of a man with flowing blond hair and a very long beard. One medieval epic, the *Song of Roland,* even described him as being 200 years old when the events of the story occurred! The real Charlemagne (a French name meaning "Charles the Great") was, in fact, large and strong, but not especially tall. His large eyes were striking, and he spoke clearly and intelligently. Charlemagne moreover was a prayerful and devoted Christian and generous to the poor. He wanted to bring his people back to the peace and prosperity of the Roman past.

Like other Frankish kings before him, Charlemagne was a defender of the Church. In 773, when the Lombards, a German tribe, were making war on the pope in Rome, Charlemagne went to the pope's defense. Marching into Italy and defeating the Lombard king, Desiderius, in battle, Charlemagne made himself king of the Lombard lands. In this way he added northern Italy to the lands he already ruled — Gaul and part of western Germany.

Charlemagne was at war for nearly all of his reign. For over 30 years, he fought the Saxons, a pagan Germanic tribe in what is now northwestern Germany. The Saxons were a fierce people who raided and robbed Frankish lands, burned churches, and killed priests and monks. In 782, Charlemagne ordered the beheading of 4,500 Saxon prisoners, most of whom had killed priests and burned churches. This was a terrible deed — the worst of Charlemagne's otherwise noble reign — and it did not end the war, which lasted for another 22 years until the Saxons were finally defeated. By the Saxon wars and other wars against other hostile neighbors,

A reliquary, or vessel to hold the relics of Charlemagne, who in some parts of France and Germany has been honored as a Blessed; created sometime after 1349

Charlemagne built up a large kingdom. At its largest, it covered all of Gaul, a strip of northern Spain, northern and central Italy, most of Germany, and what are today Austria and western Hungary.

Charlemagne helped spread the Christian Faith in the lands he conquered. Mostly this was easy because monks and other missionaries had been busy evangelizing those lands for some time. In other ways, too, Charlemagne worked to improve the lives of the peoples of his kingdom. He tried to revive the culture of the Roman Empire and so brought about what has been called the Carolingian **Renaissance** — a "rebirth" of learning and culture. Eager to restore education to the West, the king invited scholars to his palace in Aachen, where they held lively discussions on classical subjects such as mathematics, rhetoric, logic, and astronomy. Charlemagne himself learned to speak Latin and to read Greek, and he encouraged all his subjects to learn to read.

renaissance: a word meaning "rebirth." It generally refers to a rebirth of artistic and intellectual activity.

Map showing the development and extent of Charlemagne's Empire

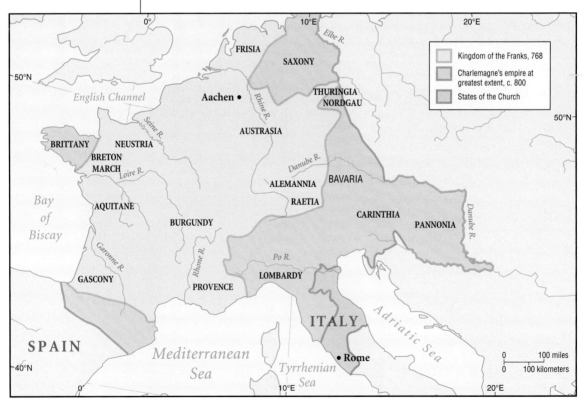

The Roman Empire Returns to the West

In the last years of his reign, Charlemagne had once again to defend the pope, Leo III, whose enemies had forced him to flee from Rome. In late 800, Charlemagne led his army into Italy to Rome, where he placed Pope Leo again on his throne.

Charlemagne had again proven that he was the Church's friend and protector. To show his thankfulness, Pope Leo III prepared a surprise for the king. It was Christmas day, 800, and Charlemagne and his men came to St. Peter's basilica for Mass. As Charlemagane knelt before the altar, Leo came forward with a crown and placed it on the king's bowed head. "God grant life and victory to Charles, Augustus, crowned by God, great and peaceful Emperor of the Romans," said pope. Then everyone cried out, "Long may he live!" and all knelt before Charlemagne.

The pope had crowned Charlemagne Roman emperor, and in this way restored the Roman Empire to western Europe. From that day on, Charlemagne was not just king of the Franks; he was Roman emperor. His task was to rule over the Christian people, bring unity and peace to western Europe, and protect the Church from her enemies.

Charlemagne reigned as king and emperor for 14 more years. When he died, his son, Louis the Pious, became Roman emperor. Louis, however, was not as strong a ruler as his father had been. During his reign, his own sons waged war against him, and after his death in 840, they fought over the empire. In 843, three of the sons signed a treaty, dividing the empire between themselves.

Though various kings held the title of Roman emperor after Charlemagne, none of them was very powerful. Western Europe had to wait another 120 or so years for an emperor to restore the power and authority of the Roman Empire of the West. That emperor was Otto I, whose empire included all of Germany, Bohemia (the modern Czech Republic), and northern and central Italy. This empire goes by different names in history; it is called the Western Roman Empire, the Roman Empire of the Germans, or the Holy Roman Empire. The empire was called "holy" because medieval people thought of the emperor as the protector of the Church. And, just as the pope was the spiritual head of Christendom, so the emperor was its the **secular** head — the supreme leader of all Christian kings.

secular: referring to activities (such as buying and selling and making laws) or things having to do with this world; not sacred

Pope Leo crowns Charlemagne Roman emperor

Statue of Roland in Bremen, Germany

The *Song of Roland*

One of the most popular medieval epic poems is based on the exploits of Charlemagne. It is the *Song of Roland*, a romantic tale of a brave nobleman, Roland, the nephew of Charlemagne.

According to the story, Roland's stepfather, Ganelon, was jealous of him. During Charlemagne's war against the Muslims in Spain, Ganelon lured Roland into a surprise ambush of Muslim warriors. Cut off from the main army, Roland and his faithful friend Oliver found themselves and their company of soldiers greatly outnumbered. They fought bravely, but their defeat was sure. At length Roland blew a horn to summon the help of his king. When Charlemagne first heard the blasts of his horn, Ganelon tried to convince him it could not be Roland. But when the blares of the horn grew quiet, Charlemagne understood what had happened, and he hurried his army to the rescue.

The king, however, arrived too late. Oliver had been killed, and Roland, after mourning his friend like a brother, likewise fell. As he died, Roland prayed to God to take his soul. While Charlemagne's troops pursued the Muslims, the king found his dead nephew on the battlefield, and Charlemagne tore his beard with grief.

Invasion and Conversion of the Norsemen

From ancient times, people had lived along the coasts of the cold northern lands of Scandinavia—Norway, Denmark, and Sweden. These peoples spoke a Germanic language and were related to the Germanic tribes that had invaded and conquered the Roman Empire. These tribes of Scandinavia shared a common name — they were Norsemen, or Northmen. They were skilled seamen, great merchant traders and explorers, and ferocious warriors who invaded foreign lands, pillaging and looting them. When they sailed from their lands, the Norsemen called themselves Vikings — a word meaning "sailors" or "travelers."

Beowulf: Hero and Epic

The Dark Ages produced a particularly memorable piece of literature, of special interest to English speakers. The epic poem, *Beowulf*, which dates to the 8th century, was written in the oldest known form of English, called Old English, or Anglo-Saxon. It is the most important sample of Anglo-Saxon writing, and it is the oldest epic of the ancient German tribes.

The story tells of a terrible monster called Grendel, half-man and half-devil, who had been terrorizing the Danes. Every night Grendel emerged from his watery lair, crossed the **fens**, and sneaked into the hall of the Danish king, Hrothgar. There Grendel seized some of Hrothgar's swordsmen, who slept in the hall, and took them home, where he devoured them. When Beowulf, a prince of the Geat (GAY-at) people of southern Sweden, heard of Grendel's deeds, he resolved to fight the monster. Gathering some companions, Beowulf set sail across the sea to the rescue of Hrothgar and his faithful men.

The story tells how Beowulf fought a great battle in Hrothgar's hall and defeated the monster, Grendel. Beowulf wrenched Grendel's arm from its socket, and the monster, fleeing the hall, returned to his watery home to die. Angry over the monster's death, Grendel's mother then came to the hall to avenge her son. She fared no better than Grendel, for Beowulf, chasing her from the hall, pursued her into her sea cave, where he slew her.

Following these victories, Beowulf returned home and became king of the Geats. He ruled his people in peace until, when he was old, a dragon entered his land and began destroying it. In a great battle, Beowulf was victorious over the dragon; but he himself suffered great wounds. In this, his last battle, Beowulf too died—a hero to the last.

> **fen:** low, wet land; a marsh or swamp

Scandinavia is a cold place, and so the Norsemen looked with envy at the rich lands of their neighbors in Britain, France (as Gaul came to be called), and Germany. For 200 years after their first invasion of England in 787, Viking pirates terrorized Europe. The barbarians who attacked the Roman Empire in the 4th and 5th centuries were cruel, but the Vikings were even more violent and destructive. They murdered, looted, and burnt down churches, monasteries, and entire villages.

In their swift and seaworthy longboats, the Vikings crossed the North Sea and conquered a large part of Britain, destroyed the culture of Ireland, attacked Frisia (now the Netherlands), and moved into France. Traveling up the Seine River, they invaded Paris three times, once with a fleet of 700 ships. They made raids into Spain, sailed into the Mediterranean and attacked Italy and Sicily.

Beginning in the 9th century, groups of Swedish Vikings went east instead of west and pushed into the forests and down the rivers of what is

To the Ends of the Earth

The Vikings developed the best ships of ancient times. The fast-moving longboats enabled the Vikings to explore farther than anyone had ever gone before. In 870, Vikings sailed across the North Atlantic to a fertile island they called Iceland. Then in 982 one of the great Viking explorers, Eric the Red, sailed farther west and found an icy country. Eric called this land Greenland, to encourage other Scandinavians to settle there. Around the year 1000, Eric's son, Leif Eriksson, who had become a Christian in Norway, returned to Greenland to spread the Gospel there. Having heard of a land even farther west, he continued to North America, where he was the first European to establish a settlement, which he called Vinland, because of the many grapevines growing there.

No one is certain where Vinland was; it may have been in New England or on Prince Edward Island, or on the Labrador coast of Canada. What we do know is that around the year 1000, Vikings landed in Newfoundland, Canada. Ruins of a Norse settlement, which date back to around 1000, were found there in 1963.

Remains of a Viking church in Greenland

now Russia. There, on the banks of the Dnieper River, they founded the city of Kiev. The Slavic people who lived in the area called these Norsemen *Rus* (meaning "red-haired"). In 907, the Viking, Oleg of Kiev, launched a fleet of 2,000 ships against Constantinople and forced the Byzantine emperor to make a trade treaty with him. In this way, Kiev developed into one of the major cities of the Middle Ages.

King Alfred and the Cakes

Legend says that after a great battle between the Viking Danes and the English, the English army scattered. The English king, Alfred, was alone as he fled through the woods. He happened upon the home of a woodcutter, and he asked the woman there to give him something to eat as well as shelter for the night. Not recognizing the ragged fellow as her king, the woman agreed to feed him if he would watch the cakes cooking on the hearth.

Alfred meant to watch the cakes, but then his thoughts about the war and his army distracted him. He forgot all about them, until the hut filled with smoke from the burning cakes. The woman came in and yelled at him: "You lazy fellow! See what you have done!" King Alfred missed his supper but not the lesson: You are never too great that you can disregard the little things.

A statue of King Alfred in Winchester, England

The Viking terrors did not last forever. Over time, the Vikings accepted the Christian Faith and became a part of Christendom. In Britain, a Saxon king in Wessex, Alfred the Great, battled the Danish Viking invasion of England. After constant battles between the Danes and Saxons, in 878 Alfred worked out an agreement with them. Each promised not to attack the other's territories, and the Danes agreed to become Christian.

In France, King Charles the Simple made a similar arrangement with the Viking, Rollo, in 911. Charles's bargain was that if Rollo and his people would stop their attacks and become Christian, they could have a large territory in northern France, over which Rollo would be duke. This land became the **duchy** of Normandy (named for the Norsemen). It later became the most powerful duchy in France. Meanwhile, in Kiev, the Grand Prince Vladimir (St. Vladimir) and his people accepted the Christian Faith in 988.

duchy: lands ruled by a duke

The Feudal Society of the Middle Ages

Invasions by Vikings from the north and by Muslims from the south shattered the power of the Roman Empire of Charlemagne. There was still an emperor, but he was powerless to protect the people of Europe. Kings, too, could not stand against the invaders — so, it is not surprising that, after a time, the common people stopped looking to their kings for help. Instead, people looked for protection from local lords. Kings, too, depended on local lords to supply them with soldiers. In this way, the power and authority of the lords became greater and greater. This led to the growth of what is called **feudalism** — the way in which society was organized in the Middle Ages. The word "feudal" comes from the Germanic word, *feod*, which means "fee." Another word for fee is **fief**.

feudalism: the form of government in the Middle Ages in which a vassal gave military service to a lord in exchange for land and protection

fief: a piece of land given by a lord to a vassal in return for military service

vassal: a person who has sworn allegiance to a lord and gives him military service

This is how feudalism developed. In order to protect his people, a lord needed soldiers. The lord would grant a fee or fief to a high-ranking soldier, or "knight," who, in return, swore a solemn oath to be loyal to the lord and serve him in war. After swearing the oath, the knight became the lord's **vassal**.

Since there was little gold or silver in western Europe during the Dark Ages, the fief was at first something like food, clothing, and shelter, or armor or weapons. In later years, the fief was a piece of land, and the vassal was not only a soldier, but a landowner and nobleman. As the vassals themselves gathered lands, they too became lords by giving out fiefs to other vassals in exchange for military service.

Feudal society can be described as a kind of pyramid. At the top of the pyramid was the king, who was the highest lord in the land. The king's vassals were the great lords (called dukes), who swore oaths of loyalty to the king and, in return, received fiefs from him. The king's vassals were themselves lords, with vassals of their own. A duke's vassals swore oaths of loyalty to *him*, not the king. The duke's vassals, in turn, might themselves be lords over other vassals. At the bottom of the feudal pyramid were the soldiers or knights, who served a lord but who themselves were not lords.

Feudal society became quite complicated, for one man could be the vassal of more than one lord; or, he might be a vassal of more than one king. A king, too, could be the highest lord in his own country, but the vassal of a king in another country. Thus, at one time, the king of England not only ruled England but had fiefs in France — which made him the vassal of the king of France.

Very few people in medieval society were lords or vassals. Most people were peasants. Not being knights, the peasants could not take feudal oaths. They lived and worked as **tenant farmers** under the protection and rule of their overlords. Some peasants were free men, but most were **serfs**, bound by law to the land and work of their fathers.

Though the word serf comes from the Latin word *servus*, meaning "slave," a serf was not actually a slave. He was not the lord's property. A serf had to do unpaid work on the lord's lands, called the **manor**, and he could not leave the manor without the lord's permission. But he had rights and was protected by law. A serf was given a portion of land for his own, which the lord could not take from him as long as the serf did what he was supposed to do. A serf had the right to pass this land down to his son, and he could acquire land for himself.

Feudalism was not the same in every part of Europe, and in some places serfs had more rights and were freer than in others. As the centuries passed, serfs became more and more free. They had to give less work to the lord and so could spend more time working their own fields.

Especially, in the early part of the Middle Ages, people had little chance to change how they lived. If you were born into a noble family, you were a noble; if you were born to a serf, then you were a serf. For a long time, the only way serfs had to rise in society was by becoming a member of the clergy of the Church. For instance, the great Pope Sylvester II (945–1003) was the son of a peasant family of southern France.

Feudalism was a necessary way of organizing society in the early Middle Ages, for it was the only way the people of Europe could defend themselves against brutal invaders. Feudalism, however, had its problems. First of all, continual small wars broke out between lords. (Today the word "feud"

> **tenant farmer:** a person who lives on and farms land owned by another and who pays rent to the owner of the land
>
> **serf:** someone who is bound to work land held by a lord and who owes work to the lord
>
> **manor:** the farmlands owned by a feudal lord

A mosaic image of a medieval peasant with a scythe, from a church floor

refs to longstanding fights between families or clans.) Second, vassals began to gather so much land and men that some of them became even more powerful than the king. This meant that the king was at times powerless to keep peace in his own kingdom.

Knights and the Code of Chivalry

In the Middle Ages, members of the **nobility** did not all have the same rank in society, but all noblemen were equal, because all were knights. The English word "knight" comes from the Anglo-Saxon word, *cnecht*, meaning a boy or a personal servant. Medieval knights, of course, were not boys or servants, but warriors who fought on horseback. Though there were foot soldiers in the Middle Ages, the most important warriors and protectors were the knights.

To become a knight, a boy from a noble family began training as a squire (from the French word for "shield bearer"). A good squire would be knighted at age 21, or sometimes at a younger age, in a religious ceremony. In the ceremony, the bishop slapped the knight on the cheek. In some places today, this custom is part of the Church's Sacrament of Confirmation, when the bishop gently slaps the cheek of the person being confirmed as if he were awakening him to live the life of faith.

You are perhaps used to seeing pictures of knights, wearing plumed helmets and full plate armor; but such armor did not come into use until the late Middle Ages. For most of the Middle Ages, knights wore coats of "mail," made from small iron rings linked together, and they carried large shields for protection. Though this chain-mail armor looked stiff, a knight could actually move easily in it because the links of rings made the armor flexible. A knight's chief weapon was the double-edged sword, but he also used the horse-lance, a pointed sword, a short ax, a mace, and a dagger.

Knighthood was not just about warfare, however. Knights swore to live by a moral code known as **chivalry** (from the French word for knight: *chevalier*). Chivalry was a Christian code of behavior, by which a knight devoted himself first of all to God and to defending the Church. The knight furthermore pledged himself to be

A bas relief of jousting knights, from Malbork castle, or Marienburg, the Teutonic Knights' fortress in the Pomerania region of Poland

brave, loyal, honest, and merciful to his defeated enemies. Knights were to be kind and gentle to all, especially the weak. They were supposed to hold women in high esteem, protect them, and treat them with great courtesy. The highest virtue of chivalry was "honor"—personal honesty and faithfulness to your promises.

The Church in Medieval Society

As we have seen, people in the Middle Ages were divided into basically two social groups—nobles and peasants. There was, however, another social group—churchmen, or the "clergy." The Church in the Middle Ages was the guide for moral life, but also an important part of the **economic** and political life of society.

> **economic:** having to do with the *economy*, which refers to the ways people produce wealth, how they distribute it among themselves, and how they use it

The clergy was divided into two major groups. First, there was the "lower clergy." These were the parish priests and monks, who prayed, administered the sacraments, and tended to people's spiritual and daily

The Legend of King Arthur

King Arthur may or may not have lived in history, but he certainly lived in the legends of England. According to some accounts, Arthur was not born but was mysteriously cast up by the sea. When he became king, he gathered noble warriors like himself into a council called the Round Table, where each knight was equal to the other knights. Arthur's enchanted sword, Excalibur, offered special protection to his people. According to legend, Arthur did not actually die, but was miraculously taken to an island to await his future rule of Britain.

A replica of King Arthur's Round Table

abbot: the head of an independent monastery, called an *abbey*

lay: from the word, *laity*—a term referring to members of the Church who are not clergy

investiture: the act of installing someone in an office

sonorous: having a full, rich sound

pilgrimage: a journey to a sacred place

needs. They provided education, refuge, and cared for the poor. The second major group was the "higher clergy," who were the bishops and **abbots**. The higher clergy were considered to be part of the nobility and were sometimes made vassals and even lords. As lords, they protected and administered their lands just like any count or baron. Many remained independent, loyal only to God and the pope, but others gave their allegiance to counts or kings and did what their lords wanted. Many **lay** nobles claimed the right to decide who would be bishops or abbots in their lands, when only the Church had that right. Kings and emperors quarreled with the pope and his representatives over who should "invest," or install a bishop into office. This conflict, called the "**investiture** controversy," lasted for many years in Europe.

From the heart of the Church beat the rhythm of daily, weekly, and yearly life for nobleman and peasant, clergy and king. There was the Sunday Mass each week, and through the year numerous saints days and feast days, sometimes with elaborate processions and, of course, feasting. Popular devotions to Mary and the saints flourished; the rosary, Stations of the Cross, and Passion plays (about the sufferings of Christ) were among the practices born during the Middle Ages.

In an age when most people could not read, the story of salvation was told in pictures. Stone statues, painted walls in the churches, and (beginning in the 12th century) stained glass windows showed scenes and figures from the Bible, from Adam and Eve to the Resurrection of Christ. The liturgy itself was splendid, with rich and colorful vestments, the smell of incense, the chant of choirs, the **sonorous** bells calling all to worship. For entertainment, "mystery plays" retelling Bible stories were acted out in the churchyards or on raised platforms in the streets.

Another feature of medieval life was the **pilgrimage**. People of all classes would leave their homes to travel, usually on foot, to holy places dedicated to Mary, the saints, and the mysteries of the Faith. Among the most popular pilgrimage sites were Rome, Jerusalem, and the shrine of Santiago (St. James, the Apostle) in Compostella, Spain. When they reached these holy places, pilgrims offered prayers of thanksgiving or petition. The journey itself, usually difficult and dangerous, was an act of faith and penance. Modern-day pilgrims still continue this pious tradition, visiting the ancient shrines as well as more recent ones commemorating Mary's miraculous appearances in Lourdes, France; Fatima, Portugal; and Mexico City.

The Heroic Hildebrand

One pope who fought against kings over the right to appoint bishops was Pope St. Gregory VII (ruled 1073–1085). Pope Gregory was born with the name Hildebrand in northern Italy in 1020. An educated and pious monk, he served Pope Gregory VI and then Pope Leo IX.

Like many other Christians in his time, Hildebrand was disturbed by the activities of immoral clergy who, among other things, bought and sold church offices and holy objects. Hildebrand thought one of the chief causes of such evil deeds was the practice by which emperors and kings, rather than the Church, appointed and invested bishops. So it was that, when Hildebrand became Pope Gregory VII, he ordered lay lords to stop investing bishops.

The pope's command angered the young king of Germany, Henry IV. In Germany, the bishops were lords and very powerful, and they supported the king against rebellious lay lords. Henry feared that if he could not choose his bishops, men who were not faithful to him might become bishops and he could lose power in Germany.

In 1075, the struggle between pope and king began. Henry disobeyed Gregory and invested a bishop against the pope's command. Though Gregory threatened to **excommunicate** him, the king refused to obey the pope and even wrote a letter calling Gregory a "false monk." Gregory then excommunicated Henry and commanded that no one in the kingdom should obey him. The German nobles told Henry that he had to get the ban lifted, or they would rebel against him. Henry had no choice but to go to Gregory to beg forgiveness.

The nobles at first tried to prevent Henry from meeting with the pope, but in 1077 the king crossed the Alps from Germany into Italy and stood, barefoot and in rags, in the snow outside a castle at Canossa, where the pope was staying. Henry waited there for three days until the pope at last forgave him and lifted the excommunication.

Henry IV, the German Emperor, doing penance before the door of the pope at Canossa

excommunicate: to forbid a member of the Church to receive the sacraments of the Church; to cut a member off from the Church

The Great Schism Between East and West (1054)

One of the greatest tragedies in Church history occurred in the Middle Ages — the splitting of what are called the Eastern Orthodox Churches from the Catholic Church. How did it happen? As we saw in Chapter 7, the early Church developed two "personalities" or cultures — an Eastern, Greek culture and a Western, Latin one. After the fall of the Western Roman Empire in 476, these two cultures of the Church had less and less to do with each other. The three Eastern patriarchs of Jerusalem, Antioch, and Alexandria fell under the direction of the patriarch of Constantinople. For the most part, they had little to do with the patriarch of Rome, the pope. The Muslim conquest of Syria, Palestine, and Egypt made communication between the pope and the patriarchs of Jerusalem, Antioch, and Alexandria even more difficult, for these cities were under Muslim rule. Now, only Rome and Constantinople were in Christian hands. They alone were free.

An ancient Byzantine mosaic showing the Empress Zoe and the Emperor Constantine Monomachus offering gifts to Christ in Hagia Sophia

Even before the Muslim conquest, the patriarch of Constantinople had been demanding more authority in the Church — even more authority than the patriarchates of Jerusalem, Antioch, and Alexandria had, though they were older patriarchates. The patriarchs of Constantinople did not claim that they held a higher place than the pope, but they began to resent it when the pope at times stepped in to settle arguments in the Eastern Churches. After all, Constantinople was a gloriously rich city, the seat of the Roman emperor, while Rome was under barbarian rulers and had suffered from warfare, plague, and famine. Many of the Eastern clergy looked down on Western churchmen, whom they thought were uneducated and rude. What could poor, unwashed sons of Germanic barbarians or the peoples they had conquered explain to the theologians of Byzantium? And what right had the pope of old, ruined Rome to tell the patriarch of Constantinople, the emperor's city, what to do?

Matters between the Eastern and Western Churches became worse after the year 1000 when popes began demanding more obedience from the entire Church, even Constantinople. Matters became especially bad when the pope and the patriarch in Constantinople took opposite sides in a dispute. Finally, the patriarch of Constantinople refused to recognize the pope's authority, and, in 1054, the pope excommunicated the patriarch, and the patriarch excommunicated the pope.

At first, only the Church of Constantinople was separated from Rome; but, as the years passed, the patriarchs of Jerusalem, Antioch, and Alexandria joined sides with Constantinople. Since Russia and other eastern European lands had received the Gospel from missionaries from Constantinople, the Churches in these lands, too, were in the end separated from the Catholic Church. For almost 1,000 years this schism has continued, tragically weakening the Church's ability to defend herself from those who have tried to destroy Christendom, both in the East and the West. In particular, the schism weakened Christendom when it had to confront the threat of Muslim conquest.

The Crusades: "God Wills It!"

From as early as the 3rd century, Christians had been making pilgrimages to the Holy Land to visit the holy places connected with the life of Christ, such as the Holy Sepulchre in Jerusalem, Mt. Calvary (where Christ was crucified), and the Church of the Nativity in Bethlehem. These pilgrimages continued even after the Muslims conquered the Holy Land in the 7th century. Though zealous followers of Islam, the Arabs generally allowed Christians in the Holy Land to practice their religion. Things changed, however, at the beginning of the 11th century, when the Seljuk Turks conquered Palestine. A Muslim people from central Asia, the Seljuks harassed and killed Christian pilgrims in the Holy Land. They took, as well, large parts of Asia Minor from the Byzantine Empire and continued to threaten it. In desperation, the Byzantine emperor finally asked for help from Pope Urban II.

In 1095, at a meeting at Clermont in France, Urban addressed a great crowd and said: Let Christians take up arms in a holy war to win back Jerusalem from the Turks! The pope not only hoped that helping the Byzantine emperor would drive the Turks out of the Holy Land but that it would reunite the Churches of Rome and Constantinople. Both knights and ordinary folk enthusiastically greeted the pope's call. "God wills it!" they cried. This war has been called the First Crusade, from the Latin word *crux*, meaning "cross." During the next two centuries there would be eight major and a few minor crusades.

A stained glass window depicting the crusader Godfrey of Bouillon, in the cathedral of Brussels

The soldiers of the First Crusade were able to drive the Turks from the Holy Land and retake Jerusalem. For about 100 years, Christian kingdoms ruled the Holy Land, parts of Syria and a region called Edessa. In 1187, however, the Muslims retook Jerusalem and the Holy Land, and then, one by one, all the other crusader kingdoms fell to the Muslims.

Later crusades failed to retake Jerusalem and the Holy Land. The crusades also failed to reunite the Eastern Churches with the Catholic Church. Instead, because the crusaders often treated Eastern Christians in the Holy Land badly and because, in 1204, one group of crusaders conquered Constantinople instead of Jerusalem, the Crusades actually increased bad feeling between Eastern and Western Christians.

Though the Crusades failed to regain the Holy Land for Christendom, they were very important for Europe. During the Crusades, Europeans came face-to-face with Islamic culture. They learned about the progress the Muslims had made in learning, art, music, and architecture and took these discoveries back to Europe. In the coming centuries, Europeans not only benefited from Muslim culture, but improved on it. The Crusades

Map of the first four crusades, showing Christian lands and Muslim-dominated lands (whose populations in some places were still mostly Christian)

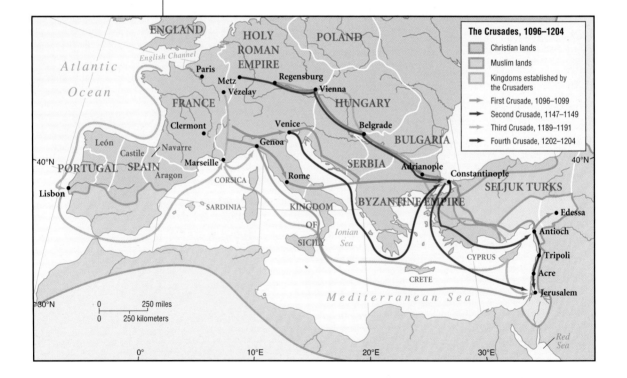

also led to trade, not only between Europe and the Muslim countries, but with the Orient — China, India, and Japan — bringing more wealth and **luxury** to European countries.

The Crusades began to change the feudal system by increasing the power of kings over feudal lords. The fact that the pope could inspire the European peoples to take up arms to fight in a Christian cause increased the authority of the **papacy** in western Europe as well.

> **luxury:** comforts and wealth beyond what people need for human life
>
> **papacy:** the office or government of the pope

The Rise of Towns and the Changing Farm

It was not only the Crusades but changes in how people farmed that brought about a period of greater wealth and cultural achievement in Europe. One of these changes was the invention of a simple farm machine: the wheeled plow. With this plow, the serfs could farm more land, produce more crops, and have more to trade with other manors. Serfs could use some of the extra crops to buy their freedom.

The farmers' markets, where goods were traded or sold, grew into busy population centers. More and more people moved to these trade centers, which grew into towns and cities. Serfs were among the people attracted to towns, for they could escape from their lords and gain their freedom in the towns. This was because kings, who gave towns special freedoms, protected peasants who lived in towns for a certain period of time from being captured by their lords. The king was only too happy to weaken the power of his vassals.

Compared to modern cities, medieval cities were not large. Modern cities have hundred of thousands, even millions of persons living in them; in 1377, the large medieval town of London had only 35,000 inhabitants. But though they were small (in comparison with our cities), the medieval towns and cities were important, for they helped increase the wealth of Europe and allowed for new achievements in culture and learning.

The New Merchant Class

In towns, people set up shops to offer services and so became tailors, butchers, bakers, and shoemakers. Other craftsmen included cloth weavers,

guild: a group of merchants or craftsmen joined together to protect their trade and for mutual aid and protection
mint: to coin money
barter: to trade by exchanging some goods for other goods without using money

glassmakers, masons (builders with stone), coopers (barrel makers), cobblers (shoe menders), and carpenters. Craftsmen began to organize themselves into groups called **guilds** to help each other out and to improve their crafts. Each kind of craftsman had its own guild. The guilds established levels of expertise, beginning with the apprentice, or student, and ending with the master craftsman. The craftsmen controlled the guild and made sure that all members of the guild charged just prices and produced quality goods. Some guilds, such as miners' guilds, tried to make sure that working conditions for members were safe. Guilds also gave aid to the families of a guild member if he fell sick or died. Guilds organized religious activities for their members.

Not only craftsmen, but also merchants (those who did not make but bought goods and sold them) had guilds. With the growth of cities, the number of merchants in Europe grew; and to make trade easier, kings and lords began to **mint** money. Before money became used widely in Europe, people relied on **barter** — the exchange of goods for other goods. For instance, someone might give a farmer a cow in exchange for a certain amount of wheat. Barter worked when one was dealing with people in his local community, but one could not easily ship cows over widespread areas. Money was far more convenient to use in such trade.

The walled city of Carcassonne, in France, has been restored to show how parts of medieval Europe appeared in those centuries.

When the use of money became common, merchants began to rely on people called bankers, who helped merchants conduct trade and loaned them money to start or improve their businesses. The most successful bankers in Europe were located in northern Italy. By the end of the Middle Ages, banking families, such as the Medici (MED•eh•chee) family in Florence, Italy, had become as rich and powerful as kings.

Most of the merchants did not have tremendous wealth and power. They formed a kind of middle class between the nobles and peasants, enriching medieval life with their goods, building fine houses, and in some cases sponsoring the highest art form of the Middle Ages, the soaring stone cathedral.

Cathedrals: Heights of Worship

The flowering of the High Middle Ages was best seen in its glorious churches, the major art form of the era. Two styles of architecture emerged between the 11th and 15th centuries: Romanesque and Gothic.

We call some of the medieval cathedrals "Romanesque" because they resemble Roman buildings. Romanesque cathedrals were built with heavy blocks of stone, strong columns, multiple arches, and sometimes domes. The ceilings in Romanesque cathedrals were made of stone and were shaped like half a barrel. Narrow aisle windows in Romanesque churches let in soft light, while the paintings, sculptures, and tapestries filled them with sumptuous color. Romanesque cathedrals were usually made in the shape of a cross, with the altar area (the apse) facing east, toward Jerusalem.

In 1140, Abbot Suger of France built the first truely Gothic-style church. Unlike the heavier, darker Romanesque churches, Gothic churches are filled with light, for they have large windows of colorful stained glass. We can recognize Gothic architecture by its pointed spires, intricate stone carvings on the outside walls, pointed arches, and immense, open interiors. Because they are supported from the outside by great half arches called "flying" buttresses, which help hold up the roof, Gothic cathedrals can be fantastically high. Their height and tall pointed spires represent the desire of medieval people to rise heavenward in worship of God.

Two of the best examples of Gothic churches are the cathedral in Chartres, France (completed in 1224), and Cologne Cathedral in Germany (begun in 1248, but not completed until 1880). The Gothic style spread all over western Europe. Italy, Spain, and England each developed their own kinds of Gothic churches.

The cathedrals of the Middle Ages were true houses of worship, large enough to fit a town's whole population at a single Mass. These churches sometimes took centuries to complete. Yet, centuries later, they still stand as testimonies to what men can do when they work for the common good with the money, time, and effort of all classes. The wealthy sponsor, who paid for the

Once a church was too high. In 1272, only 20 years after the church's completion, the record 500-foot central spire of Beauvais Cathedral in France collapsed. This disaster, however, was an exception; generally, medieval churches were successful feats of engineering.

Cologne Cathedral in Cologne, Germany

cathedral, the skilled architect, who designed it, and the laborer, who carried the stones, all played a part in the construction of these great monuments to the Catholic spirit of medieval Europe.

From Feudal Kingdoms to Nations

The weakening of feudal lords and the strengthening of the power of kings led to the formation of what are called "nation states" in Europe. A nation-state exists where people who share one language and culture are united by one government. People in a nation-state think of themselves first as belonging to that nation rather than to any part of it. For instance, in the United States, people generally think of themselves more as Americans than, say, Californians, New Yorkers, or Virginians, because all Americans share a common language, culture, and government.

Two nation-states began to form in Europe, beginning about the year 1000. They were England and France. Other parts of Europe, however, did not form into nation-states until much later. Italy, for instance, was divided into many small states, while Germany remained part of the larger Holy Roman Empire. Spain long remained divided between the Muslim-controlled areas of the south and various Christian kingdoms in the north and west.

England in the Middle Ages

England's path toward becoming a nation-state began in 1066 with William, the duke of Normandy in France. One story tells of how Harold, the earl of Wessex in England, was shipwrecked in Normandy and there promised Duke William that he could be the next king of England. Harold himself was the next in line to be king. When the king of England, Edward the Confessor, died in 1066, the English lords made Harold king. Claiming that Harold had broken his promise to him, William invaded England and, on October 14, 1066, defeated Harold's army in a battle fought at Hastings in southern England. Harold himself was killed in the battle, and William went on to make himself king of all England.

History in Pictures

The 231-foot Bayeux Tapestry, commissioned by William the Conqueror's half-brother Bishop Odo, tells the story of the Norman invasion in a series of 72 needlework scenes.

The tapestry is considered a better history than the contemporary written records. Originally hung in Bayeux cathedral, it is now at the museum of Bayeux, France.

ET FV

We remember William as King William the Conqueror because he was a harsh king who made himself the master of England. William the Conqueror divided England among lords who came with him from Normandy; he greatly weakened the power of the English lords, called barons. To strengthen his control over all England, he set up royal courts throughout the land. This weakened the lords by removing the power they had had to set up their own courts. William replaced English bishops with Norman bishops so he could have greater control over the Church in England.

Henry II, who became king of England in 1154, continued William the Conqueror's work of increasing the king's power over the lords and the Church. Henry gave more power to the royal courts and established one law for all of England. He wanted only the royal courts (not barons' courts or the Church's courts) to try all crimes, no matter where they were committed in England.

The Church in England, however, did not want to give up its authority to the king. Churchmen saw that the Church was not the servant of human governments because the Church received her authority from God. In King Henry's day, the Church had its own courts, where it tried members of the clergy. When the king demanded that at least some clergy be tried in the royal courts, the Church refused.

To help him bring the Church under kingly control, Henry chose his friend, Thomas Becket (or Thomas à Becket). An educated young man and a member of the clergy, Becket became the king's **chancellor** and served the king well. When the chief bishop of England, the archbishop of Canterbury, died, Henry had Becket made archbishop in his place. The king thought his friend would help him bring the Church under royal control, but things did not turn out as Henry expected.

Thomas seemed a changed man when he became archbishop. He was pious, a good priest, and a strong leader of the Church. Moreover, he refused to help the king take control of the Church's courts. For a time Thomas had to flee to France for his safety. After six years of exile, Thomas returned to England; but, once again, he angered the king by excommunicating everyone, including some bishops, who supported the king's attempts to control the Church.

Archbishop Thomas's excommunication of the king's friends greatly angered Henry. One night in his court, the **impetuous** King Henry cried out to his knights, saying: "Will no one here rid me of this troublesome priest?" Four of the knights took him at his word, and they hastened out to Canterbury. On December 29, 1170, while Thomas knelt in prayer in the cathedral, the knights murdered him with their swords. When the English people heard of this murder, they rose up in anger. King Henry

chancellor: the chief minister or secretary of a king

impetuous: acting hastily, rashly, or with a sudden burst of feeling

The Magna Carta (1215)

King John of England forced his subjects to pay many taxes. This, of course, angered his barons, who complained that the king was not respecting the rights they had long enjoyed. They rebelled against the king and defeated him in battle. In 1215, John was forced to meet the barons in a meadow called Runnymeade on the Thames River. There John signed the *Magna Carta*, the "great charter," in which he promised to respect the traditional rights of the barons. The *Magna Carta* did not give new rights to the barons. It said nothing about the rights of the common people. Still, it was an important document, for it underlined an idea common in the Middle Ages—that kings do not have absolute power but have to respect the laws and customs of their people.

Robin Hood

The best bowman in England shot his arrow, and it struck a hair's breadth from the center of the target. Then a stranger stepped forward, dressed in tattered scarlet clothes. He drew back his bow and shot his arrow so true that it knocked a feather off the other's shaft before landing dead center. The sheriff of Nottingham who had called the contest declared the stranger the winner, but he did not know to whom he awarded the golden arrow as prize. It was, in fact, his sworn enemy, the good Robin Hood.

Robin Hood, legend's favorite outlaw, was a green-clad forest-dweller who stole from the rich and gave to the poor, rescued damsels in distress, gathered a motley band of good-hearted men, and faithfully served King Henry II and his successor, King Richard the Lion-Heart. Robin Hood's merry adventures, told and retold in story, play, and film, recall the lively Christian spirit of the age, tweaking the noses of English nobles and clergy who were Christian in name only.

"The Passing of Robin Hood," by N.C. Wyeth

had to allow himself to be **flogged** in public, while the Church proclaimed Thomas Becket a martyr and a saint. The tomb of St. Thomas Becket became an important pilgrimage site in the Middle Ages.

flog: to beat or hit hard

Though King Henry lost this battle with the Church, he went far in making the king the supreme power in England. His sons, however, did not continue his work. Henry's eldest son, King Richard the Lion-Heart, spent more time fighting a crusade in the Holy Land than in ruling England.

When King Richard died in 1199, his brother, John, became king. John, however, was a bad king and was forced to give up some of his power to the barons. John's son, Henry III, who became king in 1216, was also a weak king. But Henry III's son, King Edward I, continued the work begun by William the Conqueror and Henry II.

Edward, who became king in 1272, conquered Wales and Scotland. He called the first parliament — a gathering of nobles, churchmen, and commoners that met to advise the king and grant him money for his wars. Edward I forced the English people to think of themselves as a united nation—as Englishmen. It was under Edward that England became a nation-state.

Feudal France Becomes a United Kingdom

France, too, was becoming a nation-state about the same time England was. When Count Hugh Capet became king of France in 987, however, France was one of the most feudal countries in Europe. The king himself ruled only a small area around the capital city, Paris, and many of his nobles were far more powerful than he.

Things began to change under the kings Louis VI (reigned 1108–1137) and Louis VII (reigned 1137–1180). These kings received help from a churchman—Abbot Suger, who was the abbot of the monastery of Saint-Denis in Paris. By his wise advice, Suger strengthened the power of the kings of France. When Louis VII was away from France on a crusade, Suger ruled France and by his wisdom made France more prosperous than it had been before.

King Louis VII's son, Philip "Augustus," who became king in 1180, devoted his life to strengthening royal power both by good means and bad. People from all of France came to love King Philip because he protected them from the power of their local lords, who were often cruel to their subjects. Philip strengthened his power by forcing King John of England to give him the lands the English kings had long held in France. In a war against the lords of southern France, Philip won for himself all of southern France—a region called Languedoc. Philip extended the power of the royal courts and was a clever ruler. By the time he died in 1223, no French lord was as powerful as the king.

Philip Augustus' grandson, Louis IX, continued the work his grandfather had begun. Louis, however, did not use dishonest means like Philip Augustus did, for Louis was a very holy man. In fact, the Church remembers him as King St. Louis of France. Louis set up a supreme court for the entire kingdom. He forced the French nobles to stop warring with one another and brought peace to the kingdom.

When King Louis IX died in 1270, France was on its way to becoming a nation-state. It was not as united as England; in fact, in the 1300s and 1400s, France had to fight a war with England that lasted 100 years, and for a time it looked as if the king of England would become king of France as well. But the war in the end strengthened the power of the

French king. When the war ended in 1453, France was well on its way in becoming a true nation-state, united under its king.

Two Saints Rebuild the Church

All was not well in the Church by the 12th century (the 1100s). Many of the clergy, bishops and priests, lived worldly lives and were more interested in power and wealth than in spreading the Gospel of Christ. Even in some monasteries, monks and nuns were not living the life of prayer and penance that was expected of them. Without good examples from the clergy and religious, lay men and women themselves did not take their faith seriously. To many living at the time, it looked as if the Church was collapsing under the weight of the sins of her members..

But in the late 12th century, two men were born who brought new light into the Christian world. They did not strive for worldly power or even to become bishops; instead, they tried to live as lowly, humble servants of Christ. Their service to God and to their neighbors showed the people of their time how Christians should live and inspired many to follow Christ more closely. These men gave a new spirit to the Church and brought new life to Christian culture. What they did changed the world of their time. Their names were Dominic, a nobleman from Old Castile, in Spain, and Francis, the son of a well-to-do cloth merchant in Assisi, Italy.

The Lord's Dog

In 1203, a 33-year-old priest in Osma, Spain, named Dominic de Guzman, joined his bishop, Diego d'Azevado, on a journey into France. The bishop was on a special mission for King Alfonso IX of Léon, but little did he know that this journey would inspire his companion with a lifelong mission for God. While passing through southern France, Dominic came in contact with the Albigensians (also called Cathars), heretics who believed that the body and the entire material world are evil. Seeing that the Albigensians were convincing many people to join their heresy, Dominic became convinced that he should dedicate his life to public preaching and teaching.

Dominic went to Rome, hoping, from there, to go as a missionary to the Muslims. Pope Innocent III, however, had other plans for the Spanish

The Holy Preacher: St. Dominic

L ong before St. Dominic was born, his mother had a very strange dream. She dreamt she would give birth to a dog that would set the whole earth afire with a blazing torch that it carried in its mouth. This "dog" was St. Dominic himself, who set the world of his time on fire with the love of Christ. Since the Middle Ages, the emblem of the Dominicans has been of a dog running with a torch in its mouth. The Dominicans have also been called *Domini canes*, the "Dogs of the Lord," both because of their name in Latin (*Dominicanes*) and because they have gone over the entire earth, "barking" the sacred knowledge of God.

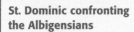

St. Dominic confronting the Albigensians

priest. Instead of to the Muslims, Innocent sent Dominic back to France, to preach against the Albigensians. For several years, Dominic preached in southern France, at least convincing some people to return to the Church.

But then, in 1208, disaster struck. The pope's representative in southern France was murdered by supporters of the Albigensians, and Pope Innocent III ordered a crusade against the heretics. This Albigensian Crusade, as it was called, became a very savage war, for the crusaders were more interested in conquering land than in saving souls. Throughout the war, Dominic risked his life by preaching to Albigensians and Catholics alike.

In 1214, a nobleman named Simon de Montfort allowed St. Dominic to take refuge in a castle near Toulouse, a city in southern France, and this became the headquarters for the new order Dominic wished to found. Unlike those in religious orders such as the Benedictines, who lived in monasteries and rarely left them, the members of Dominic's order were to travel far and wide as preachers and teachers of the Catholic Faith. Monks supported themselves by working in the fields or at crafts, but Dominic's followers were to be **mendicants**, or beggars. They would own no property but live on the alms people gave them. The Dominicans were to trust God to care for them as he does "the flowers of the field and the birds of the air" that Jesus spoke of in Matthew's Gospel. Dominic named his new order, the "Order of Preachers," and it received the approval of Pope Innocent III in 1216.

mendicant: a beggar, or someone who asks for alms

St. Dominic's Order of Preachers grew rapidly. During the next four years, Dominican houses for men and women arose throughout France, Italy, and Spain. Since its founding, The Order of Preachers, or the "Dominicans," has been one of the most important orders in the Church, and it remains active to the present day. St. Dominic himself has for centuries inspired men and women with his example. Wearing a poor **habit**, and carrying a bag of books, he traveled frequently by foot throughout Italy and France. He preached on street corners and advised bishops, popes, princes, and kings. It was as he was preparing a journey to Hungary that St. Dominic fell sick and died in the Italian city of Bologna, at the age of 51.

habit: the dress of someone who belongs to a religious order

St. Francis of Assisi: "The Little Poor Man"

As a young man, Francis Bernardone wanted nothing more than to be a soldier. When he was about 20 years old, he was wounded in a battle his city, Assisi in Italy, was fighting against a neighboring city. While he recovered, Francis spent long hours praying in the churches. In time, he began to see how empty his life was and that God was offering him a better way to live. In 1205, when he was about 24 years old, Francis gave away his belongings to the poor and began to live a life of poverty for the love of God.

St. Francis

In his eagerness to serve God, Francis not only gave away his own possessions but sold some of his father's goods to raise money to rebuild a ruined nearby church called San Damiano. This was too much for his father, the respectable Pietro Bernardone; he accused Francis of theft and dragged him before the bishop of Assisi. Francis did not defend himself; instead, he said he did

A Patroness of TV: St. Clare (1194–1253)

She was beautiful, noble, and destined for a happy marriage and motherhood. But a secret love drew the lady Clare, ever since she heard the preaching of the cloth merchant's son, Francis Bernardone. In 1212 at the age of 18, St. Clare slipped out of her father's house in Assisi at night and met St. Francis in his little chapel of the Portiuncula (por•chi•UNC•oola). St. Francis cut short her long golden hair and gave her a rough tunic to wear in place of her fine robes. By the light of the brothers' candles, St. Clare gave her life and heart to her one beloved, Jesus Christ.

At first St. Francis found a home for St. Clare in a Benedictine convent, but soon she had her own band of followers, including her sisters and her widowed mother. The women moved into a convent at San Damiano and formed the Order of the Poor Ladies, later called the Poor Clares, with St. Clare as abbess. For the remaining years of her life, St. Clare guided her fellow nuns—as a mother—and awaited approval for her strict rule of gospel poverty. In 1253 Pope Innocent IV finally approved the rule. St. Clare died two days later. Like her spiritual father St. Francis, her canonization came soon, just two years after her death.

Many wonders have been told about St. Clare. She is the patroness of television, because it happened that alone in her cell she was able to see and hear the Mass going on at the basilica. Her prayers, said the residents of Assisi, were what caused a storm to rise up and scatter the army that was prepared to attack the city. In another incident, when the convent itself was about to be stormed by the emperor's soldiers, St. Clare ran and grabbed the **ciborium** containing the Blessed Sacrament and held it up before the invaders. They were stunned by a blinding light and retreated. This is why pictures of St. Clare often show her with a ciborium.

ciborium: a closed vessel for keeping the consecrated hosts of the Eucharist after Mass

not want anything his father could give him and then stripped off all his clothes. From that time on, Francis said, he would not rely on his earthly father for anything but trust only in God.

Francis began to live a life of prayer, penance, and service to others. Dressed only in the gray, undyed tunic worn by farmers, he set about rebuilding the church of San Damiano with his own hands. It was in that church that Francis had heard the voice of Christ telling him to rebuild the Church — and Francis thought the voice meant San Damiano. He would later learn that Christ wanted him to rebuild, not San Damiano, but the Church of Christ on earth.

Francis's joy, simplicity, and unselfishness attracted many men to him. "The Little Poor Man," as he was called, was soon leading a band of men devoted to prayer and aid to the poor. Francis called his followers *fratres minores*, which in Latin means, "little brothers." It is from this name that we get the term "friars." Both the followers of St. Francis and St. Dominic are friars, a name that refers to religious brothers who live a life of service to others and, in return, receive alms.

In time, Francis asked Pope Innocent III to approve the "Little Brothers" as a new religious order, but Innocent was reluctant to do so until a dream changed his mind. In this dream, the pope saw the cathedral church in Rome, St. John Lateran, beginning to collapse, when, suddenly, a little man in a gray tunic rushed in and held up the church's walls. That little man was St. Francis. Pope Innocent approved Francis's order in the year 1209.

Like anyone else, Francis had his disappointments in life. He dreamed of converting the Muslims to the Christian Faith, and in 1219, he traveled with a group of crusaders to Damietta, Egypt. Francis did meet with the **sultan**, who was very impressed by the little, gray-clad man. But Francis's preaching was so powerful that the sultan feared he might actually convert the Muslims. The sultan thus sent Francis back with a safe conduct to the crusaders' camp.

sultan: a king or ruler of the Turks

As the years passed, the Order of Little Brothers grew rapidly and spread far and wide. In 1224, Francis resigned as head of the order and turned to a life of solitude and prayer. One day, while praying, Francis received the **stigmata**—bleeding wounds, like the wounds of Christ, that appeared mysteriously in Francis's hands and feet. Francis kept these wounds secret until his death on October 3, 1226, at the age of 44.

stigmata: miraculous bodily wounds resembling those of the crucified Christ

The Church declared Francis a saint only two years after he died. His life of holy poverty inspired many in his time and long afterwards. Just as in the pope's dream, the "Little Brother," along with St. Dominic, helped keep the Church from collapsing under the weight of the sins of Christians. Dominic and Francis were the instruments God used to preserve Catholic culture so it could be passed on from their time, through the ages, to our own.

A New Way of Learning

A medieval professor leads a class, 14th century.

trivium: a course of study in grammar, logic, and rhetoric
quadrivium: a course of study in arithmetic, geometry, astronomy, and music

In the early Middle Ages, people seeking education came to the monasteries or to schools run by the bishops in their cathedrals. Later in the Middle Ages, the growth of towns allowed the cathedral schools to grow into what are called universities. Medieval universities were divided into four colleges—the colleges of *liberal arts*, *medicine*, *law*, and *theology*. Students at these colleges could receive bachelor's, master's, and doctoral degrees in these subjects. Our modern universities come directly from these first universities.

Today young students study a collection of separate "subjects," including mathematics, reading, writing, spelling, history, geography, foreign language, science, and physical education. In the Middle Ages, education was quite different. Students did not study individual subjects, they were instead introduced to and immersed in the liberal arts. Young students (seven years of age) studied the **trivium** (*trivium* is Latin for "a place where three roads meet"): grammar, logic, and rhetoric. Grammar was the Latin language and its literature; logic was orderly thinking; rhetoric was the art of speaking and writing. Next, students studied the **quadrivium** ("a place where four roads meet"): arithmetic, geometry, astronomy, and music. The *trivium* and *quadrivium* together made up the liberal arts. After mastering the *trivium* and *quadrivium*, advanced students went on to the higher disciplines of philosophy, medicine, or law. The highest study in medieval universities—the queen of sciences—was theology, the study of what God has revealed to man.

It took time for universities to develop. At first, teachers simply traveled from town to town to give paid lectures in Latin (the language of the educated). Then students gathered to learn from certain teachers. The students and teachers organized themselves into centers of learning, or colleges, with each college specializing in a particular subject. The major universities were in Bologna, Italy; Paris, France; Salerno, Italy; and Oxford and Cambridge, in England. The University of Paris became the model for later universities throughout Europe.

St. Thomas Aquinas

Around the year 1237, a young boy of 10 or 11 years old was sent to school. The school to which he was sent was not a grammar school or even something like a high school. It was the University of Naples in Italy. The name of this extraordinary young boy was Thomas of Aquino. He was the son of the count of Aquino and, since he was five years old, he had been living in the Benedictine monastery of Monte Cassino.

While at the university, Thomas made a decision that would greatly displease his parents. He decided to enter the Order of Preachers. Now, Thomas's parents were not opposed to him becoming a religious or a priest; in fact, it was his parents who had sent him to live at Monte Cassino in order to become a monk there. But Thomas's parents hoped that he would become, not just a simple priest or monk, but the abbot of Monte Cassino. This abbot was a powerful man, for Monte Cassino controlled vast lands and wealth. Thomas's family would not want him to become one of those Dominican preachers — who, the Aquinos thought, were no better than religious beggars!

Thomas, however, believed God wanted him to be not just a priest, but a Dominican priest. When he entered the Dominican order in 1244, his mother, Countess Theodora, tried to persuade him to leave. When this did not work, she asked the pope to force Thomas to leave the order. And when this did not work, she had Thomas kidnapped and imprisoned in the family castle, Rocca Secca. At one point, his family even tempted Thomas to sin in order to get him to leave the Dominicans; but Thomas did not give in. At last, Thomas's family gave in. They freed him from the castle and let him return to his Dominican brothers.

A fresco of St. Thomas Aquinas, by Carlo Crivelli

It is hard to imagine what the history of Christendom would have been if Thomas had never rejoined the Dominicans. As a Dominican, he was able to study under the great German Dominican philosopher, St. Albertus Magnus, in Cologne, Germany, and to dedicate himself to philosophy and theology. After Cologne, Thomas studied at the University of Paris, where he became a doctor of theology. Many students eagerly attended his classes, for it was clear that Thomas was a master of Aristotle's philosophy. Among the many contributions he made to Christendom, Thomas showed that what we know by faith does not go against what we know by reason or science, and the truths of reason are not opposed to the truths of the Faith.

Eventually, Thomas returned to Italy, where he taught at a Dominican school and wrote numerous books on philosophy and theology. It was in Orvieto that Thomas began his masterwork, the *Summa Theologica* (the Summary of Theology), in which he tried to address all the questions people in his time asked about the truths God has revealed through the Church. Since the days of Thomas, the Church has seen the *Summa Theologica* as one of the most important works of theology ever written.

Thomas eventually returned to Paris, and from Paris, he went to teach in Naples. It was at the Dominican house of studies in Naples that, in 1273, he received a profound vision during prayer. Thomas had received a vision of God, after which he said, "such secrets have been revealed to me that all I have written now seems like straw." He never wrote anything in theology again. His great *Summa* was left unfinished.

It was not long after his vision that Thomas's health began to decline. In 1274, on his way to a Church council in France, he fell ill and died. The Church declared Thomas a saint in 1323 and a doctor of the Church in 1567.

A Stricken World

One day in 1347 an Italian trading ship left a port in the Black Sea and headed home to Venice. But before the boat docked, a mysterious and horrible disease had killed many of the sailors on board. Fearing that the disease would spread among its own people, Venice turned the ship away. It continued on, however, to other ports in Italy and along the Mediterranean, spreading disease everywhere it docked. As the ship unloaded its cargo in Naples, Genoa, and Marseilles, rats carrying the disease that had killed the sailors escaped into the ports. Within days the infection spread through the towns, and from the towns it passed in a few months into all of Europe. Within two years the disease had killed one-third of the population of Europe.

This disease was the bubonic plague, or "Black Death." Two weeks after being bitten by a flea infected with the disease, a person developed swellings called "buboes" in his armpits or groin and pools of blood collected under the skin in black patches. The person suffered from fever, thirst, and **delirium** and then would almost certainly die within days or even hours. The disease killed the young and the old, the poor and the rich. Some monasteries and villages were entirely wiped out. But, mysteriously, some regions, such as Poland, were never struck by the Black Plague.

delirium: a disorder of the mind where the person is confused and often sees things which are not there

Because people did not know what caused the disease, they were powerless to stop it. Some people closed themselves off in their city homes, while others fled to the countryside. Many good priests caught the disease because they stayed and ministered to the sick and dying. Many feared that the world was coming to an end. Then, by 1349, almost as quickly as the plague started, it stopped. The Black Plague, however, did not entirely disappear for a long time. Every 10 or 20 years it reappeared in certain places, and then disappeared again.

A medieval depiction of a man and woman stricken with the bubonic plague, 1411

The strange disease changed medieval society. Throughout the Middle Ages, people had generally been full of hope in the future, an attitude that could be seen in their art and philosophy. The Black Death, however filled many people with sadness and a sense of hopelessness. Painters and sculptors produced works of art that focused on death and the fear of God's judgement. Because so many people died, there were fewer farmers to work the fields. The farmers who survived were thus able to demand more freedom and even money payments from their lords. The Black Death was one of the things that brought an end to serfdom.

The Black Death had a sad effect on the Church as well. Many of the priests who ran away rather than care for the sick, survived, while many good priests died. Many more unworthy men became priests — which meant that the number of bad clergy in the Church increased. The faith of some Christians grew stronger because of the sufferings they endured, while other Christians cast aside their faith and lived lives of pleasure. So it was that Europe, which was about to enter a new and challenging age, would not have a strong Church to guide it. The Church had been deeply weakened at the very time she had to be very strong.

Chapter 8 Review

Let's Remember   Please write your answers in complete sentences.
1. Of what Germanic people was Charlemagne king before he became Roman emperor?
2. Name the seven liberal arts.

3. The Great Schism of 1054 divided the Western Church from whom?
4. Chartres Cathedral is an example of what style of architecture?
5. What was the Black Death?

Let's Consider   For silent thinking and a short essay or for thinking in a group with classroom discussion:
1. What would have caused the Norsemen to turn from trade to savage plundering?
2. Why was chivalry a Christian code of behavior?
3. Why were the Crusades fought?
4. Why was the *Magna Carta* important?
5. What were the qualities of Sts. Dominic and Francis?

Things to Do

1. Using a blank map of Europe, find the following peninsulas: the Balkan peninsula, Italy, Scandinavia, Denmark, the Iberian peninsula, and Brittany. On the same map indicate where the following mountain ranges are: the Urals, the Alps, the Apennines, and the Pyrenees. Draw in the paths of the Rhine and Danube rivers.
2. Using the map of Charlemagne's empire on page 174, take your measuring string and find the distances between the following places: Aachen and Rome, Brittany and Pannonia, Saxony and Lombardy, Gascony and Frisia.
3. Using the map on page 188, take your measuring string and measure the distances traveled by the soldiers of the First Crusade, from Vézelay in France, to Marseille, from Marseille to Sicily, and from Sicily to Jerusalem.

Let's Eat!

A Medieval Pastry: Crispels. This is a modern and easy recipe. Buy in the frozen section a package of phyllo leaves. Cut the layers into circles with a biscuit cutter. Quickly fry in vegetable oil until golden and crisp. Drain on paper towel. Drizzle honey over all and serve warm.

Chapter 9 Europe: The Renaissance, the Reformation, and the Modern World

Medieval men and women thought of themselves as citizens of the local regions where they lived, but they also thought of themselves as belonging to a greater civilization, the civilization of Christendom. The people of Europe often fought wars with each other in the Middle Ages, but they joined together in great works too. The French, English, Germans, Italians, and others cooperated to fight off invaders. They all helped create the great arts that beautified the Middle Ages. Philosophers from all over Europe sought the truth together. And all Europeans suffered together during the years of the Black Death.

But Christendom did not remain united. People in Europe began to think that the nations they belonged to were more important than Christendom. More and more, people began to think that being English, French, German, or a member of any other nation was more important than being Christian. People then began to disagree with each other about the most important ideas — they began to disagree about religion. Disagreements about religion led to disagreements in other areas of life, such as science and politics. Disagreements about ideas can split a civilization, and it split Christendom.

Yet, though it was divided, Christendom was not entirely destroyed. All Europeans no longer belonged to the Catholic Church. Some Europeans no longer believed in Christ.

A 15th century astronomical clock, on the old city hall of Prague, Bohemia (Czech Republic)

Yet, Europeans still held on to many of the Christian ideas they had first learned from the Catholic Church. These ideas still guided people and nations. Europe was in many ways becoming less Christian, but the Christian religion still played an important part in European culture.

Since the Middle Ages, the culture of Europe has spread outside of Europe. Indeed, it has spread to the entire world. Because Europe at the same time was becoming less Christian, European culture took false ideas about God, mankind, and human life with it wherever it went. At the same time, however, the Catholic Faith and Christian ideas have spread all over the world — because Europe was still basically Christian. North and South America became Christian because of the work of missionaries spreading the Faith and of European Christian colonists making their homes in these lands. The message of Christ has spread to Africa and Asia, because of European and later American missionaries. As for ideas, wherever today people speak about justice, human dignity, equality, compassion, and similar things, they are speaking of ideas that were originally Christian. Sadly, modern people do not always properly understand such ideas; but the fact that they believe in them at all is because of the Christian Faith of their ancestors.

The Search for Truth

While on earth, Jesus promised his followers that "you shall know the Truth, and the Truth shall make you free." The search for truth has always been very important in Christian European culture. Christian Europeans have sought to learn the truth about God and man; but the desire to know the truth has also led them to study the heavens above their heads, the earth beneath their feet, and the creation all around them. Like other civilizations, Christendom has long had a deep respect for **tradition** — the customs and beliefs handed down from one's ancestors. But the search for truth has led Christians to ask questions about their traditions. When they found (or thought they found) that some traditions did not respect the truth, they rejected them. For this reason, Christian European society has undergone more change than any other civilization in history.

Change, of course, is good when it is guided by truth. Such change helps people to love God and their neighbor better and makes for a better and more beautiful civilization. But oftentimes people fall into error, even

tradition: beliefs and customs handed down from parents to children over generations

when they think they are searching for the truth, and the false ideas they come up with lead to changes that harm people and the society in which they live. Christendom has suffered from both good and bad changes since the Middle Ages — changes that have helped form the world in which we live today.

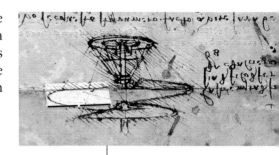

The Renaissance

One of the most important periods of change in the history of Christendom began in the 1400s and is called the *Renaissance.* The word, "renaissance," means "rebirth," for people thought the civilization of ancient Greece and Rome was being reborn in their time. The people of the Renaissance

A 1503 design for a flying machine, by Leonardo's Da Vinci

Michelangelo's famous statue of *Moses*

thought the culture of the Middle Ages was crude and barbaric and that only Greek and Roman art and literature were truly beautiful. These ideas led to many changes in Europe, some of which were good, while others ended in weakening the civilization and culture of Christendom.

When people think of the Renaissance, they think of the great paintings and sculptures made during that period. In Italy, where the Renaissance began, painters and sculptors could find many examples of ancient statues. They thought these statues from the ancient world of Greece and Rome were very beautiful, for they showed beautiful women and men as they really look. Like the Byzantine icons we spoke of in Chapter 7, medieval paintings and sculptures were not realistic. Instead, they tried to show spiritual truths. Renaissance artists, however, admired ancient classical

fresco: a painting created on fresh, moist plaster
anatomy: the structure of a plant or animal
mechanics: the study of what makes things move and how they move

art because it represented the truth of the world around us, just as it appears to us.

The great Renaissance artists we most remember are Michelangelo Buonarotti, Raphael, and Leonardo da Vinci. These and other Renaissance artists carefully studied the human body, as well as animals and plants, so that they could paint or sculpt them accurately. You can see the results of this study in Michelangelo's sculptures, such as his *Pietà,* where the Virgin Mary is seen holding the dead body of Christ. Visitors to Italy still marvel at Michelangelo's statues of Moses and the David, which he carved for the town hall of Florence. Though he was first and foremost a sculptor, Michelangelo also produced great paintings. The most famous of these are the **frescoes** found in the Sistine Chapel in Rome. On the chapel's walls and ceiling, Michelangelo painted scenes from the Old Testament as well as a gigantic picture of the Last Judgment.

Frescoes painted by Michelangelo on the ceiling and walls of the Sistine Chapel in the Vatican

Michelangelo was born and raised in Florence — an Italian city that gave the world many great artists and writers, including Leonardo da Vinci. Leonardo was not only a great painter, but he was a student of science as well. He drew pictures of the **anatomy** of birds and human beings. Based on this study and his study of **mechanics**, Leonardo came up with inventions, including machines that would allow people to travel undersea or fly through the air. His inventions, however, remained only as sketches in his notebooks. Two of Leonardo's paintings are world famous — the *Mona Lisa,* a portrait of a beautiful Florentine noblewoman, and the fresco of the *Last Supper.*

Not only the art of ancient Greece and Rome inspired Renaissance artists, but so did an idea called *humanism.* Those who accepted humanism (we call them *humanists*) did not want the Church, but human ideals of what is good or bad, to guide society. Though some humanists were devout Catholics and did not reject the Church, others did. Those who rejected the Church wanted to focus more on life in this world and less on the life of the world to come. So it was that, because of humanism, European civilization became less Christian and more secular.

Events that Changed the World

In 1453 the great city of Constantinople fell to the Turks. No one in the West could believe it. Constantinople had always withstood attack, and Europeans thought it could not fall. But fall it did, and with it the Byzantine Empire. Without the Byzantine Empire, the Turks moved into eastern Europe. They conquered Greece, the Balkan Peninsula, and much of Hungary. Over the next two centuries, the Turks invaded Christian Europe again and again. In 1529, they got as far as Vienna in Austria, but the city's brave defenders kept them from conquering the city. In 1683, the Turks again made a large-scale invasion of Europe but were again stopped at Vienna.

Johannes Gutenberg

Some people from conquered Constantinople were able to flee to Italy and other parts of western Europe. Some of these people were scholars and teachers, who brought with them the books and ideas of the ancient Greek world. New ideas and long-lost texts were suddenly the talk of the West. In Germany, a young inventor, Johannes Gutenberg, perfected a printing press using movable type. This printing press was able to make many copies of any book, and quickly it made books available to many more people than ever before. Gutenberg's Latin Bible (1455) was the first book printed in Europe.

A detail of "The Siege of Constantinople," at Moldovita Monastery in Romania

Events farther south, in Spain, led to great changes, not only in Europe, but in the entire world. Ever since Muslim Arabs conquered Spain in 711, Spanish Christians had been carrying on a war to reconquer the Iberian Peninsula and drive the Muslim invaders back into North Africa. This Christian war or "crusade" is called the **Reconquest,** and it lasted for over 700 years. By the late 1400s, Muslims controlled only the small kingdom of Granada in southern Spain. At the time, Christian Spain was divided into four kingdoms — Portugal, Navarre, Castile-León, and Aragon. The last two kingdoms were united in 1479 because of the marriage of Isabel, queen of Castile-León, and Fernando, king of Aragon.

Reconquest: the over-700-year struggle by Christian Spaniards to regain Spain from the Muslim Arabs

It was these two monarchs, Isabel and Fernando, who began the last fight of the Reconquest — the war against Granada. Together they attacked the Muslims of Granada and, in January 1492, at last took the city of Granada. The long war of Reconquest was ended. Christian monarchs ruled the entire Iberian Peninsula for the first time in many centuries.

While Isabel and Fernando were besieging Granada, a ship's captain from Italy approached them with a fantastic plan. The Portuguese were discovering a way to reach India and China from Europe by sea, by sailing around Africa's Cape of Good Hope. The Italian ship's captain, whose name was Christopher Columbus, told Fernando and Isabel that *he* could reach India (or the "Indies") by sailing west, straight across the Atlantic Ocean. The queen's geographers doubted that Columbus could do this, and Isabel at first turned him down. But, after the surrender of Granada, Isabel changed her mind. She gave Columbus three small ships and a crew to test his idea.

A metal sculpture of Columbus in Torino, Italy.

In 1492, Columbus sailed west across the Atlantic, but he did not arrive either in the Indies or China. Although Columbus did not know it, he had landed on a continent he did not previously know existed. Over the next few years, Columbus discovered

other lands, as did explorers who followed him. Yet, when Columbus died in 1506, he still thought he had reached the Indies instead of the "new" lands of North and South America.

In 1521, less than 30 years after Columbus discovered America, the Spanish explorer Hernán Cortés conquered the great Mexican Empire of the Aztecs. This was followed by Francisco Pizarro's conquest of the Inca Empire of Peru (in South America) in 1533. Other nations — England and France, as well as Portugal — soon established settlements in the Americas. European nations began to take wealth from the Americas and establish settlements and colonies there.

But more important than the wealth and the colonies was the fact that the discovery of America opened up vast new lands for the spread of European culture. That culture changed the Americas forever. Indeed, from 1492 on, European culture began changing the cultures of all the nations of the world.

Martin Luther and the Protestant Revolt

Since the 1300s, the Catholic Church in Europe had been undergoing very hard times. Many of the popes had been weak men, and some of them had been more concerned for their political power and wealth than for the holiness of the Church. Many bishops were immoral men; they did not care for their flocks and rarely visited the dioceses they ruled. A large number of priests were not faithful to their vows, and even monks and nuns were not always good examples of the Christian life. Because it seemed that popes and other churchmen were more concerned with wealth than the good of the Church, people throughout Europe lost their trust in the clergy. Heretics spoke out against Church teaching in Bohemia, Germany, southern France, and northern Italy.

By the start of the 16th century, serious Catholics were demanding great changes in the Church. Many of the changes they called for were good, but other changes would harm the Church and Christendom. About this time, a German monk and university professor, named Martin Luther, did a seemingly unimportant thing. Luther taught theology at the University of Wittenberg in Germany and, as a theology professor, he called on other

thesis: an idea presented for a debate

theologians to debate certain ideas he had about the Church. Such debates were not unusual in universities, and so when on October 31, 1517, Luther nailed his 95 **theses** (or ideas about certain issues) on the Wittenberg church door, no one thought anything of it.

Yet, Luther's ideas were heretical. In a short time, his 95 theses were printed on the new printing presses and spread throughout Germany. Luther wrote other works as well, in which he attacked the papacy and many Catholic teachings. The pope condemned Luther and excommunicated him. In 1521, the Holy Roman emperor, Charles V, called on Luther to explain his ideas at a **diet**, or parliament, in the German city of Worms [pronounced VOHRMS]. When the diet asked Luther to reject his errors, he refused. "Here I stand, I can do no other," he cried.

diet: a German parliament

Luther escaped being punished both by the Church and the empire. In the years that followed, he and his followers formed a new church and became known as "Protestants," because they had made a public "protest" *against* the Catholic Church and *for* their own ideas. Soon after, others in Germany, Switzerland, and France joined Luther's revolt, though they disagreed with Luther in different ways. One of these was a Frenchman, John Calvin, who set up a Protestant religious government in the Swiss city-state of Geneva. Calvin was a brilliant scholar and his form of Protestantism spread quickly into France, parts of Germany, and in time became the state religion of Scotland.

Martin Luther

John Calvin

Calvin agreed with Luther on many things. Both taught that faith alone is necessary for salvation, and they rejected the authority of the Church. Luther and Calvin, however, disagreed on other matters. Luther, for instance, thought Communion and Baptism are sacraments, that they bring God's grace to human souls. Calvin, on the other hand, taught that there are no sacraments at all. Baptism, he said, is only a sign of the forgiveness we receive from God; it does not cleanse us of our sins or bring us into friendship with God.

The revolt against the Church soon spread into England, where King Henry VIII abandoned his loyalty to the pope when the pope would not allow him to divorce his wife and marry another woman. Henry declared that he himself as the king, not the pope, was the true head of the Church in England. Only one English bishop, St. John Fisher, stood up to King Henry, and Fisher was imprisoned and then **decapitated**. An English lay-man, St. Thomas More, refused to swear that King Henry was the head of the Church in England and was also beheaded.

decapitate: to behead

Henry VIII led the Church of England into schism, but it was his son, Edward VI, who made the Church of England Protestant. What Edward began was completed by his half-sister, Queen Elizabeth I. It was she who made England a **bulwark** of the Protestant revolt in Europe. During Elizabeth's reign and for many years after, many Catholics were fined or tortured to death because they would not deny their Catholic Faith. Any Catholic priest found in England was executed.

bulwark: a defense or protection

The Protestant revolt split Christendom into several warring camps. Germany was divided into Protestant and Catholic regions. Even the Protestants in Germany were split between those who followed Luther and those who followed Calvin. Though most of France remained Catholic, a large number of Frenchmen became Calvinists (called Huguenots). England, Scotland, Denmark, Norway, and Sweden eventually all became Protestant. The countries that remained Catholic included Austria, Italy, Spain, and Poland. Basically, while much of northern Europe became Protestant, southern Europe remained solidly Catholic. The religious divisions led to terrible wars, the worst being the Thirty Years' War (1618–1648), which left Germany in ruins.

The Protestant revolt forced Catholic Church leaders to carry out a true reform of the Church. In 1545, Pope Paul III called on Catholic bishops to meet in a council in the Italian city of Trent to discuss how to reform the Church. The Council of Trent met at different times from 1545 to 1563 and during those years made Church teaching clearer, condemned Protestant errors, and addressed the problems in the Church. Among the fruits of the council was a catechism of the Catholic Faith. This "Catechism of the Council of Trent" was a very important work. It served the Church for four centuries and continues to be an important source of Catholic teaching to this day.

But the Council of Trent could not heal the split in the Church and in Europe. Christendom was divided into religious camps. Christendom thus

Convocation of bishops at the Council of Trent

could not be the force for good in the world it might have been, if it had stayed one, united civilization.

The Progress of Science

We have already spoken of how the search for truth has always been an important part of the civilization of Christendom. The search for truth in art helped bring about the Renaissance. The search for truth in religion brought about the Reformation — even though some people came to believe in false ideas while others came to a deeper understanding of the Catholic Faith. The search for truth led also to another important part of modern Western civilization — the study of science.

Our word, "science," comes from the Latin word, *scientia*, which means "knowledge." Europeans for centuries had been seeking a better knowledge of the world in which they lived. They tried to get this knowledge from philosophy and from theology. In the Middle Ages, some, like St. Albert the Great and the Franciscan friar Roger Bacon, tried to gain knowledge by closely observing how things worked in the world around them and by carrying out experiments. They studied plants, animals, and stones, as well as how the planets and stars move in the heavens.

What we call "modern science," however, did not begin until the 1500s. Like St. Albert and Bacon, modern scientists carefully observe the world around them and conduct very exact experiments to understand how different things in nature move and behave.

Our modern science began with a man named Nicolaus Copernicus, who asked questions about how the stars move in the heavens. For centuries, astronomers had accepted the ideas of the Greek astronomer, Ptolemy, who said Earth was at the center of the universe and around it the sun, planets, and stars all moved. Indeed, one reason Ptolemy's theory made sense was that it seems to us that Earth does not move and that the sun and stars move around it. For astronomers, Ptolemy's theory for the most part explained well what they observed happening in the heavens.

Yet, at times, Ptolemy's explanations of the motion of the planets and stars could get quite complicated. This fact led a professor at the University of Krakow in Poland, Nicolaus Copernicus (1473–1543), to come up with what he said was a simpler explanation than Ptolemy's. Copernicus wrote down his theory in a work called, *On the Revolutions of the Celestial Spheres*, which was published in 1543, the year Copernicus died. Copernicus's ideas were so new to people and so changed the way they looked at the world around them that we speak of the "Copernican Revolution."

Copernicus's revolutionary idea was that the sun, and not the earth, sits at the center of the universe. It is around the sun, not the earth, that all the planets turn. In fact, even the earth turns or revolves around the sun. Copernicus's theory was not entirely right, for modern astronomy has shown that the sun is the center of our solar system, but not of the entire universe. Copernicus said, too, that the planets and stars move around the sun in perfect circles; but another astronomer, Johannes Kepler, later showed that they move in oval-like paths, called ellipses. Yet, despite his mistakes, Copernicus did come up with a simpler way than Ptolemy's to explain how the universe works.

Another great scientist was born about 21 years after Copernicus died. This was an Italian, named Galileo Galilei (1564-1642). A brilliant young man, Galileo entered the University of Pisa at the age of 17 to study medicine. Doctoring, however, was not his chief interest; instead he turned to **physics,** the study of how bodies move. Among his discoveries was that two bodies dropped from a high place will fall at the same speed, even if one body is much heavier than the other. He also described how pendulums work. Galileo was interested as well in astronomy, and in 1609

> **Nicolaus Copernicus was a priest, medical doctor, and astronomer. In 1543 he wrote a book which proposed the theory that Earth and all the planets rotated around the sun. Thus Earth was not the center of the Universe.**

physics: the scientific study of how all the different kinds of bodies move

A page from Galileo's *Dialogue*, a debate over the two chief theories of how the universe is structured, Florence, 1632

he invented the first telescope, which he used to study the surface of the moon. He also discovered the moons of Jupiter, the spots on the sun, and the **phases** of Venus. His astronomical studies led him to accept the ideas of Copernicus and Kepler on the motion of the planets and stars in the heavens.

The 1600s and 1700s witnessed the first great flowering of modern science. Throughout Europe, scientists not only made new and important discoveries in astronomy and physics, but in **meteorology** (the study of weather), geography, **geology**, **chemistry**, and **biology**. The great scientist of this period was an Englishman, Isaac Newton, who made very important discoveries in the science of physics.

The progress of the sciences not only gave mankind a better knowledge of the physical world around them, it also led to new inventions. One of these was the steam engine. Discoveries made during this great age of science led ultimately to the world we have today — with its electricity, automobiles, medicine, computers, airplanes, and space flights. The world has received many good things from science, but science has also been responsible for some bad things as well — like pollution and weapons of mass destruction, such as the nuclear bomb. The progress of science demonstrates both how man can improve the world he lives in, and how he can make it a more unhealthy and dangerous place as well.

phase: the shape of the moon or a planet which is seen at any one time; for instance, new moon, half moon, full moon
meteorology: the scientific study of weather
geology: the study of minerals and of the earth's crust
chemistry: the study of simple substances and what happens when they are combined
biology: the scientific study of plant and animal life

The Beginnings of Modern Literature

Just as in the Renaissance, painters and sculptors tried to depict the world around them in a realistic but beautiful way, so beginning in the 16th century, poets and storytellers tried to make works that faithfully imitated how real men and women behave in the real world. This was the beginning of modern, realistic literature — a very different kind of storytelling from the epics that were popular in the Middle Ages and for centuries before. Two great masters of realistic storytelling were Miguel de Cervantes of Spain, who wrote a long novel called *The Adventures of Don Quixote*, and the **playwright**, William Shakespeare of England.

playwright: one who (makes) writes plays

Miguel Cervantes

Miguel de Cervantes Saavedra, Spain's greatest literary genius, was the author of short stories in Spanish, as well as plays, poems, and novels. Though he wrote much and is one of the most famous authors in history, Cervantes preferred to think of himself as a soldier and civil servant.

Cervantes was born in 1547. Little is known of his youth, but at age 21, he left Spain for Italy, where he worked for an Italian bishop in Rome. After a short stay in Italy, he joined Spanish troops in one of the greatest struggles against the Muslim Turks in history — the sea battle of Lepanto. Spain had joined forces with Venice, Genoa, and the papacy to stop the greatest invasion of Christian Europe since the 8th century. In 1571, the Christian fleet, commanded by the Spanish Don Juan of Austria, met a massive fleet of Turkish galleys at Lepanto at the mouth of the Gulf of Corinth in Greece. Cervantes fought bravely at Lepanto and was wounded twice in the chest by gunshots and once in the left hand — "to the greater glory of the right," he said. For the rest of his life, Cervantes remained more proud of what he did at Lepanto than of any other achievement in his full life.

When he was returning to Spain in 1575, Cervantes was taken prisoner by Muslim pirates and sold into slavery at Algiers. For five years, he was a prisoner of the Turks in Algiers. His several attempts to escape only brought him cruel punishments and torture. At last, his freedom was

Miguel de Cervantes Saavedra

purchased by the Brotherhood of the Most Holy Trinity, a Catholic society dedicated to freeing Christian slaves from the Muslims.

When he returned to Spain, Cervantes began to try to make his living as a writer. He wrote some successful plays and, in 1585, his first novel, called *Galatea*. Unable to support himself by writing, however, Cervantes went to work for the royal government and took part in outfitting a fleet and troops for King Philip II's planned invasion of England in 1588 — the Spanish Armada. Yet, for over 15 years, Cervantes lived in poverty and published only poetry. Then, in 1605, he published his greatest work — and one of the greatest works of European literature, *Don Quixote de la Mancha*. The book was an immediate success. Ten years later he published a second part to *Don Quixote*.

Cervantes never made much money from his novel, but it won readers all over Europe. An English translation that appeared in 1612 was the first of hundreds of translations of *Don Quixote* into other languages. Cervantes died at his home on April 23, 1616.

Don Quixote

Cervantes' great **romance** tells of an old and penniless country gentleman, Don Quixote, who is determined to live a life of knightly adventure like the characters in the stories he has spent years reading. Armed in old and rusty armor and accompanied by his practical and unimaginative groom, Sancho Panza, Don Quixote transforms the poor and lowly circumstances of his journey into the settings of noble romances. A simple farm girl becomes, in his imagination, the noble Lady Dulcinea del Tobosa; a flock of sheep becomes a Saracen army; and a line of windmills becomes a host of giants. Sancho rescues Don Quixote repeatedly from his confusions, and at last is himself converted to a more forgiving and loving heart by the absurd chivalry of his old master.

romance: a story of adventure

Illustration of Don Quixote and Sancho Panza, by Gustave Dore.

William Shakespeare

It is a great coincidence, but on the same day that Miguel de Cervantes died, another great writer of the century also passed away—William Shakespeare of England. Shakespeare was a **prolific** writer of plays and poems that, like those of Cervantes, have become part of world literature.

prolific: producing much or many things

Shakespeare was born in 1564 in the town of Stratford-upon-Avon in central England. His father, a successful tradesman and landowner in his county, was elected to several local offices. Later in his life, Shakespeare's father lost some of his wealth, possibly because he refused to abandon the Catholic Faith in Protestant England. Although we do not know for sure, Shakespeare was probably a Catholic—something he kept secret from the authorities because it was forbidden to practice the Faith in Elizabeth's England.

In 1582, at the age of 18, William married Anne Hathaway of Stratford, a woman eight years older than he. The couple had a daughter, Susanna; two years later they had twins, Hamnet and Judith. Stratford did not offer much chance for employment to William, and so he left his family with his father and went to London where he could practice his literary talents.

Shakespeare was a master of both **comedy** and tragedy. His first plays (*Titus Andronicus* and *A Comedy of Errors*) imitated Roman comedy and tragedy. He then wrote a series of history plays about the last years of medieval England and the birth of modern England—*Henry IV, Henry V, Richard II,* and *Richard III.* Among the questions these plays ask are, what does a people lose when a king chooses to rule selfishly and cruelly? What happens to the soul of a man who chooses to rule this way? After the historical plays, Shakespeare wrote a series of romantic comedies—*A Midsummer Night's Dream, The Merchant of Venice, As You Like It,* and *Twelfth Night.* These comedies explore how love affects human behavior and show that it cannot solve all problems.

A statue of William Shakespeare, in Leicester square, London

Shakespeare's last and greatest works include both tragedies and comedies. The tragedies, which are his greatest works, are *Hamlet, Othello, King Lear, Macbeth,* and *Antony and Cleopatra.* Among Shakespeare's last comedies, *The Tempest* is considered the greatest.

comedy: an amusing play or story that has a happy ending

The Tempest

The Tempest tells the story of Prospero, a great wizard, who was once the duke of Milan. Driven out of his duchy by his greedy brother, Prospero with his beautiful daughter, Miranda, lives in exile on a magical island, where he is served by a spirit, named Ariel, and a half-human monster, called Caliban.

Eventually, during a great storm, a ship bearing Prospero's enemies—his brother, Antonio and King Alonso of Naples—is wrecked on the island. Separated from his father because of the wreck, Alonso's son, the young Prince Ferdinand, meets and falls in love with Miranda. To test Ferdinand, Prospero puts him to work at hard tasks—all of which Ferdinand accomplishes.

In the end, after a series of adventures, Prospero's enemies have to beg his forgiveness and Prospero and Alonso agree to join Miranda

Statue of Prometheus and Ariel, characters from Shakespeare's *Tempest*, by Eric Gill

and Ferdinand in marriage. Prospero frees Ariel and prepares to return to Milan, where, he says, he will practice magic no more.

Successful and honored, Shakespeare retired from London to Stratford in 1610. He died in the home of his daughter, Judith, on April 23, 1616. The realism of Shakespeare's plays and his portrayals of human character transformed European literature.

The Dream of Democracy

A most terrifying event occurred in 1649—England killed her king. Of course, this was not the first time in history that a king had been killed, but the killing of King Charles I of England in 1649 was not like other **regicides**. Europeans of that time thought of their kings as God's anointed rulers. Standing up against the king was like standing up against God. To kill the king was thus considered a very sacrilegious act.

regicide: the killing of a king

The people of Christendom, of course, had never thought that kings had the right to do whatever they wished to do. Kings had to be just, and if they acted unjustly, the people did not have to obey them. There had been rebellions against kings in the Middle Ages — during the investiture controversy between the pope and the Holy Roman emperor, for instance, or when the English barons forced King John to sign the *Magna Carta*. Yet, medieval people generally did not overthrow their kings or kill them — they just tried to force them to do what is just.

King Charles I of England, however, thought God grants kings absolute power and that, no matter what, the people have to obey them. This notion is called the **divine right of kings**. The wealthy merchants and nobles in England's Parliament, however, disagreed with Charles. War followed. Charles was defeated. Parliament tried him and condemned him to death. In place of the king, Parliament set up a **commonwealth** or republic — a government by Parliament, a body of men elected by at least some of the people of England.

England's commonwealth only lasted until 1658, for it quickly turned into a **dictatorship** under a man named Oliver Cromwell. After Cromwell's death, Parliament asked Charles I's son, Charles II, to become king.

Both Charles II (who reigned from 1658-1685) and his brother, James II (1685–1688) had troubles with Parliament. Parliament especially did not like James, both because he believed in the divine right of kings and because he was a Catholic. Finally, Parliament forced James II to flee from England and invited his Protestant daughter, Mary, and her husband, William, Prince of Orange, to become king and queen. This "Glorious Revolution," as it is called, was a very important event, for it made it clear that Parliament from then on had power and authority over the king in England. William and Mary agreed basically that their power came from Parliament. From that time on, Parliament took on more and more power while the English monarchy grew ever weaker.

The Glorious Revolution inspired another revolution — this time, not in Europe, but across the Atlantic. In 1776, English colonists in North America began a revolution that ended in the birth of a new nation, the United States of America. Instead of a monarchy, the United States set up a republican form of government. This government was directed by a congress and a president, who were elected by the people, and a Supreme Court, which was appointed by the president. This new government was what is called a **representative democracy.** It was a democracy, because its members were chosen by the people, and it was representative

divine right of kings: the belief that because the king receives his right to rule from God, everyone must obey him without question

commonwealth: a nation where the people have the right to make the laws or elect those who make the laws

dictatorship: a government by a dictator

representative democracy: a government in which the people elect representatives who, in turn, make the laws

A mob of revolutionaries storms the Bastille prison in order to free its prisoners. This was the watershed event of the French Revolution.

because those who were elected by the people represented them in government and made laws in their name. Though not every person in the new United States was allowed to vote, far more people could vote in the United States than in England.

The American Revolution itself inspired a revolution in France, which began in 1789. The French Revolution finally overthrew the king in France and established a republic. But the French Revolution was a very bloody revolution. It attacked the Church and anyone who was opposed to the revolution. Even those who supported the revolution but who did not like the government in power were killed. From 1789 to 1794, thousands were executed in France, including many Catholic priests, religious, and laymen.

Though it was very bloody, the French Revolution inspired other revolutions in Europe and, finally, throughout the entire world. Some of these revolutions tried to set up republics where only some of the citizens had the right to elect representatives, but others were fought for democracy

—the form of government in which all citizens, rich and poor, control the government. All the revolutionaries, however, said they fought for freedom. Every person, they said, should be allowed to seek happiness in the way he or she thinks best.

The ideals of freedom and democracy have spread from Europe to all the world. Nearly all governments in our time at least say they are democracies. Nearly all the nations of Europe, Africa, Asia, and North and South America say they love freedom. Not all these nations, of course, are truly democratic, nor are all people truly free. In many countries, people think freedom means being able to do whatever one wants to do (which is called **license**), not the ability to do what one should do (which is true freedom). Yet, the fact that nearly everyone everywhere wants freedom and democracy shows how the ideas of western Europe have influenced the culture of the entire world.

license: lack of self control; the ability to follow what one desires, not what is right

Freedom and Religion

One freedom people all over the world want is the freedom to practice religion. They believe every person should be able to practice the religion he or she wants to follow. This ideal is another example of how western European civilization has influenced the entire world.

Europeans did not always believe in religious freedom. The Protestant Reformation not only divided Europe between Protestants and Catholics, but it divided the Protestants into several different groups — Lutherans, Calvinists, Anglicans, Baptists, Quakers, and others. Neither Protestant nor Catholic governments granted freedom of religion. Lutheran governments, for instance, did not allow people to practice the Catholic religion. Catholic governments did not allow people to follow Protestant beliefs.

The Catholic government of Spain, for instance, set up a court called the Inquisition to try and punish people who attempted to spread any kind of non-Catholic religion. Some of those who refused to obey the government were burnt to death. In England, Catholics could not vote, attend university, or worship freely. The government made Catholics pay heavy taxes to force them to become Protestant. Priests were tortured and put to death. The English government also persecuted Protestants who refused to belong to the Church of England.

The chief reason governments did not allow religious freedom was because people at the time believed nothing is more important than

An illustration of a scene from the Thirty Years War, by Johann Christoph Friedrich von Schiller

religion. They thought allowing people to spread false religious ideas was worse than murder — because false religions destroy the soul, which is far more valuable than the body.

Though the Netherlands granted people religious freedom in the late 1500s, it was the bloody Thirty Years' War that led more people to think that governments should permit freedom of religion. In the 1600s, the English colony of Maryland, which was founded by a Catholic, Lord Baltimore, granted religious freedom to all who lived there. In the late 18th century, Virginia, too, granted complete religious freedom, as did the Constitution of the United States of America in 1787. The French revolutionary government said everyone was free to practice whatever religion he wished, yet France persecuted Catholics from 1791 to 1803. In the 19th and 20th centuries, one European country after another granted religious freedom to its citizens. In many parts of Europe and the world, however,

Christians and others continued to suffer persecution in the 20th century. Today, even though freedom of religion has spread all over the world, people in several countries still suffer for their beliefs.

One reason religious freedom spread so quickly in the 1700s and the 1800s was because more and more people began to believe that there is no one, true religion. Many began to think that all religions are equally right and true; and if all religions are equally true, then all are equally false. Religion began to be seen as something unimportant. Instead of trusting in religion, people began instead to trust in science. Instead of seeking for eternal life in heaven, they began seeking chiefly wealth and comfort on Earth.

Chapter 9 Review

Let's Remember   Please write your answers in complete sentences.
1. What was the date of the fall of Constantinople?
2. Who printed the first moveable type printed book?
3. What two famous writers died on April 23, 1616?
4. Why was the Council of Trent called?
5. What was the Copernican Revolution?

Let's Consider   For silent thinking and a short essay or for thinking in a group with classroom discussion:
1. Compare the older icons with the later realistic human figures in painting. How do they differ?
2. What do you think it would have been like to be captured into slavery, as Cervantes was?
3. How did the printing press help Protestant ideas spread?
4. Where in the world do people still suffer for their religious beliefs?

Things to Do

1. On a blank map of Europe, find the following places: the Balkan peninsula, Greece, Constantinople, Castile, Aragon, Portugal, and Granada.

2. On a map of the world, use your measuring string to measure the distance from Spain to the islands of the Bahamas, off the coast of North America. Then measure the distance from the Bahamas to the coast of China. How wrong were Columbus's measurements of the distance from Spain to the "Indies"?

Let's Eat!

Rice pudding in the Middle Ages was just like it is today. It was eaten throughout Europe from Italy (where it was heavily flavored with almonds) all the way to England, where it was a popular dish in Shakespeare's time. In fact, Shakespeare writes about eating rice pudding in *A Winter's Tale*. Here is the recipe in the language of Shakespeare. Can you translate it? "Boyle your rice, and put in the yolkes of two or three Egges into the Rice, and when it is boyled put it into a dish and season it with sugar, synamon and ginger, and butter, and the juice of two or three Orenges, and set it on the fire againe." (Hint for today's cooking: bake it for an hour at 325°.)

Chapter 10 China: The Middle Kingdom

The ancient name for the land we call China is *Chung Kuo*—a name that means the "Middle Kingdom." The Chinese thought that their land was the center of the world. For thousands of years they met no civilized neighbors. Everything around ancient China was barbarian territory, at least as far as the Chinese were concerned.

Over the centuries, China expanded from a small kingdom along the Yellow River to its present huge size. The enormous nation of modern China, called the People's Republic of China, includes more land than the United States of America. China's neighbors on the north are the states of Mongolia and Russian Siberia. China's neighbors on the east are North and South Korea on the Korean peninsula, Japan, and the Republic of China on the island of Taiwan. South of China are the Southeast Asian nations of Vietnam, Thailand, Bhutan, and Nepal. China's western neighbors are India and Pakistan.

Examples of the geographical diversity in China

tropical: a word referring to the area around the tropics
barren: not able to produce anything
arid: having very little rainfall; dry
topsoil: the upper part of the soil; the soil on the surface

China stretches from the cold northern plains of Asia to the **tropical** jungles of Southeast Asia. China has some of the world's tallest mountains (the Himalayas), most **barren** deserts (the Gobi), and wildest rivers (the Yellow River and the Yangtze River). China has fertile lowlands and **arid** plateaus, snow-swept steppes and tropical jungles.

Two great rivers cross China from west to east—the Yellow River in the north, and the Yangtze River in the south. Civilization in China grew up along these two rivers. The valley of the Yellow River, where Chinese civilization began, has rich farmland, with deep, but dry, **topsoil**. In the beginnings of China's history, grain crops such as millet and wheat grew abundantly in the Yellow River Valley. However, annual floods have caused much hardship for the farmers and cities along the river, as they still do. The valley of the Yangtze River, which is much farther south, is

Map of modern China and its neighbors

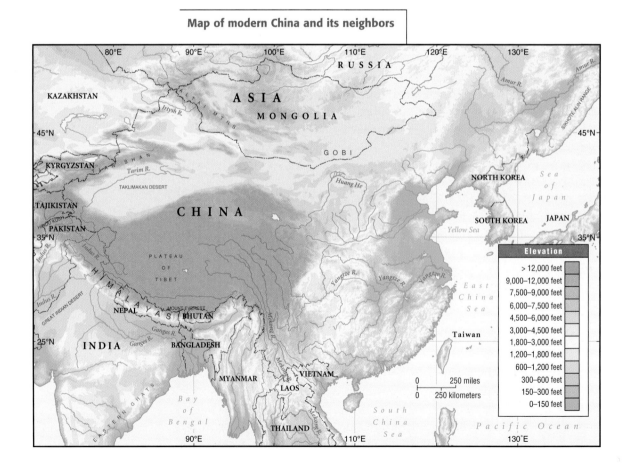

semitropical and surrounded by beautiful mountains. Rice growing made it a wealthy region. Farther south in China, tropical plants and flowers grow among the many farms and neatly ordered towns.

North of China lies Mongolia — a region of frozen plains and desert-like hills. Primitive tribes and nomads once lived in Mongolia, and the emperors of China built the marvelous "Great Wall" to keep them from invading China. In western China, the Gobi Desert and the Tibetan Mountains stretch for thousands of miles, from east to west. For centuries, these wild and desert lands made travel difficult between Europe and China and cut off almost all contact between them. The Silk Road, a great caravan route, stretched from China's capital, Changan, across the desert wastes. It ran from oasis to oasis all the way to Persia. Merchants travelling along this road brought treasured silk to the Mediterranean world in return for Western gold. Except for this trade, however, China had little contact with other civilizations. The Chinese mistrusted strangers so much that at times all foreigners were forbidden to set foot on Chinese soil.

semitropical: having hot summers and warm winters, with nearly no frost or snow

China and the Culture of Asia

For centuries, Chinese culture has influenced the culture of all of China's neighbors. They have adopted Chinese moral ideas. Their governments have been modeled on the Chinese governmental system. Chinese artistic styles and designs as well as Chinese poetry have been the standard for beauty in the Far East. The peoples of East Asia have received much from China — including one of the most important aspects of civilization, their written language.

The Chinese language is very different from the languages that have come from Europe. For instance, while English, French, and German words often have two or more syllables, Chinese words have only one syllable. Chinese, too, has no plural nouns and no verb tenses. Chinese verbs are always in the present tense.

Chinese is divided up into several dialects, but the written Chinese language is the same everywhere. Chinese does not form words from an alphabet, as European languages do. Like ancient Egyptian hieroglyphics, Chinese is written in pictures, with each picture standing for an idea. Since each picture stands for an idea and not a sound (like our letters and words do), the same picture can be used for different words in the various Chinese dialects. An example of this is if we drew a picture of a fish to express the idea of a scaly water creature with fins. Such a picture could be understood by English speakers and Latin speakers, even though an English speaker would call it a "fish" and the Latin speaker, *piscis*. In China, people could understand another person's writing even if he could not understand his speech.

ideogram: a picture or symbol that represents a thing or idea

Chinese language drawings are called **ideograms**. People who read and write Chinese learn about 2,000 ideograms. Though each ideograms stands for a simple idea, it can be joined to other ideograms to express more complex ideas. The written languages of Japan, Korea, and Vietnam are based on Chinese characters. The characters are the same though the spoken languages sound completely different.

civil servant: and official who serves a king or other form of government
literate: able to read
meritocracy: a government in which the most qualified and most talented people govern

It was difficult to learn to write Chinese, and this meant that **civil servants**, who had to be able to read and write, had to be very **literate**. After 200 B.C., one had to pass a very difficult reading test to become a civil servant, and only those who received the highest scores made it. This meant that only the most talented and capable entered the government. (We call such a system a **meritocracy**.)

Although the civil service test was open to all social classes, it cost a lot of money to prepare for it. This meant that few besides the wealthy could hope to take the test. Of course, many who did not pass the test were still very talented and intelligent, and they became teachers, musicians, and minor officials.

In traditional Chinese writing thousands of complex characters are painted with precise brush strokes.

This Chinese system of meritocracy became a model for government throughout Asia. The Japanese imitated the Chinese government, and many promising Japanese students were sent to the Middle Kingdom to study.

Early Chinese Dynasties

The Chinese divide their history into eras that are named for the principal royal families or dynasties that ruled them. Chinese history is said to have begun with mythical god-like rulers, called the Three Rulers. The Three Rulers are said to have invented civilization; and, if they existed at all, they lived

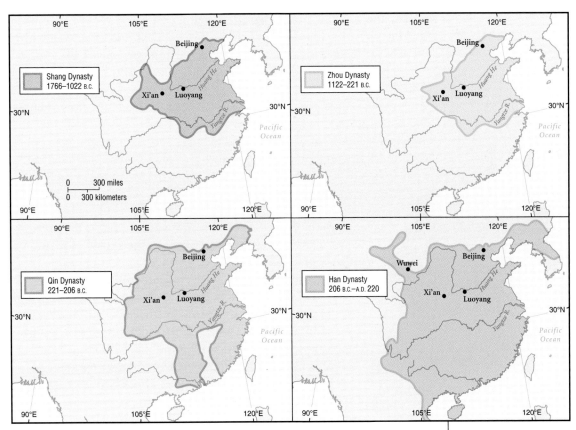

A map showing the spread of China during the rule of four principal conquering dynasties

sometime between 3000 and 2000 B.C. They were followed by human rulers, called the Five Emperors. The first dynasty for which we have certain historical evidence is the Shang Dynasty, which ruled northeastern China from about 1766 to 1022 B.C.

The Shang Dynasty (1766 to 1022 B.C.)

The Shang Dynasty ruled over a civilization that had grown up along the Yellow River in northeast China. The people of the Shang Dynasty period farmed the rich lands along the Yellow River. They began to use bronze for tools and household items at about the same time as did the people of the far-off Mediterranean. Archaeologists have discovered in China beautifully made bronze artifacts from this period. The Chinese people of the Shang Dynasty had a very strict social order; each rank or group had to obey the rank or group above it. The highest social rank had to obey the king. When a Shang king died, he had an elaborate funeral in which officials, servants, and horses were sacrificed and buried with their king.

The earliest version we have of the written Chinese language comes from the Shang period. Chinese ideograms have been found, written on bones called "oracle bones," which were used in Shang fortune-telling. The bones were thrown into the fire until they cracked, and then the cracks were "read" in order to tell someone's fortune. These oracle bones were saved as sacred objects in the royal palace libraries.

The Zhou Dynasty (1122–221 B.C.)

The kings of the Zhou Dynasty ruled for an amazingly long time — 900 years. The Zhou kings ruled China with the help of their own families and other aristocrats, as well as local leaders who were appointed and directed by the royal court. Under the Zhou kings, Chinese lords conquered lands to the south, west, and east. The Zhou Empire extended from the Pacific Ocean to the mountains of the west, and included both the Yangtze and Yellow River Valleys. Farming practices improved during this period, and industry and commerce sprang up.

The culture of China under the Zhou Dynasty was rich. In religion, besides ancestors and spirits, people worshiped a supreme God. This God, it was believed, loved good and just actions and hated evil deeds. The Zhou Chinese greatly honored the family, for they thought it the most important building block of society. China had schools, too, during this period, and artists who created works of literature, including poetry.

After a time, however, the kings grew weaker while the nobles grew stronger. The king could no longer rule the whole country and control the lords. Because a kind of feudal government developed during this period and different regions were constantly battling each other, this period of the Zhou Dynasty was called Warring States. Yet, it was during this period that the great thinkers of Chinese philosophy arose. The most important of these was a man called K'ung-tzu, whom we remember as Confucius. Confucius came up with ideas to address the turmoil into which Chinese society had fallen.

Chinese oracle bone

A Teacher of Tradition and Harmony

Confucius (551–479 B.C.) was an aristocrat from the small state of Lu in northeastern China. He wrote about morality, praising education and proper behavior toward one's parents, peers, superiors, and others. Confucius taught that a person had to respect his elders and show obedience to his superiors. According to Confucius, a person became worthy of a great position, not because he had a noble parent, but by his own talents and moral character.

Confucius took on a small band of students, who followed him from Lu to other states, and who secured for him his first government post when he was old. He devoted his old age to collecting and writing down the great poetry and ideas of China under the Zhou Dynasty. Confucius is known for a compilation of poems called *The Book of Songs*, and a history called the *Spring and Autumn Annals*. The work *Lunyu* (known in English as the *Analects*) contains sayings of Confucius that were probably brought together in a book by generations of his disciples.

Confucius gave China the social and moral ideas that have guided its civilization over the centuries since he lived. Confucius did not establish a religion, though he called on men to honor traditional religious rituals, especially reverence for ancestors. Rituals were important for Confucius, because he thought they joined people together in friendship and mutual respect.

Confucius did not come up with new ideas; rather, he saw himself as a preserver of the institutions and traditions of China. He rejected the idea that human beings are individuals who have no natural connection with one another. He wanted to give new life to the institutions that united people — the family especially, but also the local community, the school, and the kingdom. He opposed the kind of society where the rich and powerful for their own benefit rule and abuse the weak and poor.

Rulers, said Confucius, should seek first to become good men themselves and then govern more by their moral example than by force. Rulers are not to provide only for the physical needs of their people but to educate them as well. Formal education was very important to Confucius and his followers after him. Subjects, said Confucius, should show respect to their rulers, obey the laws, and participate in the rituals that tie society together. In turn, every person has the duty to show **piety** (or profound respect) to his parents, his superiors, and to the king.

Statue of Confucius at Confucian Temple in Shanghai, China

piety: the showing of reverence to God and those in authority, especially parents

Every person must strive to discipline him or herself, said Confucius, and conform to the rituals of society. By striving to be virtuous, one was being true to himself. At the same time, a person had to be considerate of others, for only in this way could everyone in society be joined together in harmony. The maxim, "Do not do to others what you would not want others to do to you," was the golden rule of Confucius's thought.

The Empire of the "Sons of Han"

currency: money that is used in a country

In 256 B.C., the last Zhou emperor died. Ten years later, a boy by the name of Zhao Zheng became king of the powerful Chinese state, Qin. Over the next 25 years, Zheng expanded the power of Qin until he had conquered all of China and established the Qin Dynasty.

Zheng's reign began with terror. He killed local rulers to force the warring states to obey him alone. He divided China into 36 provinces and placed each province under an official whom he himself appointed. Zheng unified China by requiring everyone everywhere to use the same **currency** and obey the same laws. He even commanded that axles on all carts be the same length to make it easier for them to travel along the rutted dirt roads of the Middle Kingdom.

Photo of the Great Wall of China showing the very difficult terrain the Chinese army had to defend

Zheng accomplished one of the wonders of the world: he built the first Great Wall to keep the fierce horsemen of Mongolia from invading China. The Great Wall today begins where the Yalu River runs into the Yellow Sea, and continues for 3,000 miles over the mountains and deserts to the sands of the western Gobi Desert. The first Great Wall was not as long as it was to become, but it stretched for over 1,000 miles. Zheng forced thousands of peasants and political troublemakers to work on the wall. They had to ram dirt into frames

to create bricks and haul great stones from quarries. Thousands died because of the extremely hard labor they were forced to do.

Zheng also forced peasants to dig a canal, linking rivers and lakes, so that shipping could move between the Yangtze and Yellow Rivers. The construction of the "Grand Canal," as it is called, took almost as many lives as the building of the Great Wall.

purge: to remove forcibly

The Burning of the Books

To keep people from questioning him and his deeds, Emperor Zheng forbade all his subjects to discuss philosophy. They were also not to praise what had happened in the past or criticize what was happening in their own time. Zheng, in particular, did not like Confucianism, because it encouraged people to do good just because it is right to do. Zheng wanted his people simply to obey his laws and commands. He did not want them to think about whether doing so was right or wrong.

To destroy philosophy altogether, Zheng ordered the burning of all books in China, except official documents and books of know-how. But scholars refused to give up their books and hid them from the emperor's troops. In 212 B.C., Emperor Zheng ordered 460 scholars —the greatest and most famous minds in all China—to be buried alive as a warning to those who would defy his orders. He then set a great bonfire of books ablaze on top of their burial place.

No one was safe in Zheng's Empire. From time to time, he **purged** his army officers because he did not trust them. His

Part of the clay-statue army discovered in Emperor Zheng's grave; it was created to accompany him into the afterlife.

living officers were terrified when he began to build his tomb, for they feared that he would order them all killed when he died.

Zheng's tomb was a pyramid, covered with earth, which was high enough to be seen for miles across the plain. Surrounding this tomb was Zheng's "army"—8,000 full-size, realistic **terra cotta** sculptures of soldiers, all standing in formation as if they were marching off to war. With these clay statues were hundreds of chariots with clay horses, as well as clay cavalry horses. Archaeologists did not discover the army of statues until 1974. Zheng's clay army stood 2,000 years or more beneath the farmland that surrounded the emperor's tomb.

terra cotta: a kind of clay, hardened by fire, used especially for small statues and vases

The Qin Dynasty did not last for long after Zheng's death in 210 B.C. His reign had been too cruel and terrifying and so harmful to China that it brought about a rebirth of Chinese love of tradition and sense of purpose, which led, finally, to one of the greatest periods of Chinese history—the empire of the Han Dynasty.

The Han Dynasty (206 B.C.–A.D. 220)

Zheng's son tried to rule China after his father's death, but he was murdered in 207 B.C. Civil war then broke out until a peasant, called Liu Bang, won the command of the army and united central China. He proclaimed himself emperor of China (the first time a commoner had done so), and the Chinese people generally accepted him as their ruler. They had had enough of tyranny and civil war. Liu Bang was the founder of the Han Dynasty. So great was this dynasty that, not only did it rule China for 426 years, but it gave a name to the Chinese people. Ever since, the Chinese have called themselves the "Sons of Han."

The Han emperors did not try to control every aspect of life in China, like Zheng had done. For instance, the Han allowed some local aristocrats to go back to their lands and rule them in the name of the emperor. Han laws, too, followed the philosophy of Confucius. The Han emperors wanted people to obey the laws because it was the right thing to do, not just because they were afraid of punishment.

The Han dynasty united all of central China by learning rather than by regulations. The Han emperors wanted the most capable men to serve as civil servants, and so the Han encouraged education. They were the first to use examinations to find the best minds in China for the civil service. Eventually, all of urban and rural China was included in this educational system. Passing the national exam was a way for the poorest peasant to become a leader in China. Also, over a period of several hundred years, the Chinese language spoken by the Han monarchs replaced local languages and customs.

The Han emperors carried on wars against the "barbarian" peoples in the lands northwest of central China and Central Asia. They conquered new lands in Central China and far into the south. They established trade routes that crossed thousands of miles of desert mountains and connected China with the countries of the Mediterranean. The Han Chinese traded with the Roman Empire, where Chinese porcelain and tea were greatly admired. The greatest Chinese trade item was silk, a fine cloth made from the cocoon web of a silkworm.

The Han Dynasty removed Zheng's ban on ancient books, and scholars began to copy them and write new works of their own. Poetry flourished under the Han Dynasty, as did the writing of history. Under the Han monarchs, the Chinese invented paper, water clocks, sundials, and instruments for use in studying the heavens. Painters, weavers, sculptors, and architects created beautiful works of art.

The Han Dynasty was one of the greatest periods in Chinese history. It created one of the finest civilizations the world has ever seen.

The Story of Kwang Hung

A poor boy named Kwang Hung was very fond of books and loved to study. He worked for a magistrate who paid him in books instead of money, which delighted the young boy. But the books were of little use to Kwang Hung, who was free to study only at night and had no money to buy oil to light his lamp.

At last Kwang Hung thought of a solution. He lived in a closet room beside a tavern, and the tavern was well lit with lamps all night long. Kwang made a little hole in the wall, and by moving his book back and forth in front of the hole, he caught the light that came through the hole and so was able to go on with his studies. When the examinations were held, he so distinguished himself that he was recommended to the emperor for a high appointment. He served in many important posts, and at last Kwang Hung became first minister of the empire.

A New Religion and the Golden Age of China

A new religion that entered China during the Han Dynasty grew in popularity in the years China was divided. This religion was Buddhism. It came originally from India and so Buddhist writings were originally written in Sanskrit, the language of India. The translation of the Sanskrit writings into Chinese was very difficult. Buddhism at first grew slowly in China,

Stone carving (A.D. 551) of Buddha near Taiyuan, Shanxi, China.

and it gained its greatest hold on China during the Tang dynasty. Buddhism eventually became one of the most important religions of China. (We will discuss what Buddhists believe in Chapter 12.)

Buddhist missionaries followed the trade routes from northwestern India into Central Asia, where Buddhism flourished for centuries until Islam destroyed it there. Buddhism may have come to China as early as the third century B.C.

Buddhist tradition, however, says that Mingdi, an emperor of the Han dynasty who reigned in the first century A.D., brought Buddhism to China after he dreamt of a flying god of gold that he thought was a vision of Buddha. Whether or not this story is true, Buddhism spread among many even of the common people of China, who added ideas from their own religion, Taoism, to it.

After the end of the Han Dynasty, when China was divided into more than one kingdom, non-Chinese rulers in northern China used Buddhist monks as counselors and magicians. Elsewhere in China, members of the upper classes and the learned studied and adopted Buddhist ideas and practices. In the fifth and sixth centuries, Buddhist schools and monasteries grew up in China, and even peasants adopted Buddhism. Under the Sui Dynasty (581–618), Buddhism became for the first time one of the official religions of the realm.

When the Han Dynasty came to an end around A.D. 220, it was followed by three and a half centuries in which China was divided into more than one kingdom. During this period, China suffered from civil wars and from invasions by Mongols, Turks, and people called the Hsiung Nu. China at last was reunited under the Sui Dynasty, which ruled from 589–618, and then the Tang Dynasty, which reigned from 618–907. Under the Tang, China became for a time the largest and strongest empire in the world. The Tang emperors conquered areas around China, including important trade routes that ran north of central China to Europe.

It was under the Tang Dynasty that China had its only official empress — Empress Wu, who took power in 690. By her beauty and wiles, Wu had married an emperor and then, after his death, she married his grown son. She then poisoned her young husband and killed three of her own sons. After removing her fourth and last son from the throne, Wu declared herself a man and crowned herself emperor. She put to death anyone who opposed her.

Empress Wu ruled ably and extended the territory of the empire south and north. She made Buddhism the official religion of the realm and gave much wealth to Buddhist monasteries. In 705, she was overthrown and her youngest son was made emperor in her place.

Buddhist figures from the Tang Dynasty found in the Longmen Caves of China, a place overlooking the Yi River, where more than 100,000 statues of Buddha and his disciples were carved into a cliff in A.D. 494

Seven years after Wu was overthrown, one of China's greatest emperors, Hsuan-Tsung, came to power. Emperor Hsuan-Tsung's capital city, Chang-an, in central China, became a brilliant center of culture and a fabulously rich city. The greatest Chinese poets and painters lived and worked in Chang-an — including the two poets Tu Fu and Li Po. Hsuan-Tsung supported thousands of musicians, dancers, and actors. He established China's first musical academy, called the "Pear Garden."

Many foreigners came to live in Chang-an during Hsuan-Tsung's reign — Syrians, Arabs, Japanese, Persians, Koreans, and Jews. These peoples enriched Chinese culture and practiced various religions, including Islam, Judaism, and Christianity. The first Christians had come to China in the 600s. These were heretical Christians, called Nestorians, who refused to call Mary the Mother of God. The Nestorians built the first Christian church in China in 636.

Hsuan-Tsung's reign, however, ended sadly. In 751, his armies were defeated by the Turks in western Asia, and in 755 a rebellion broke out against the emperor. The great capital, Chang-an, was **sacked**. After Hsuan-Tsung's death in 756, China suffered from invasions and civil wars. Millions of Chinese died. The empire lost a good amount of the territory it had gained under Empress Wu. The Tang Dynasty came to an end in 907.

sack: to plunder (a captured town)

The Middle Kingdom in the Middle Ages

After the end of the Tang Dynasty, China was again divided between several governments. This lasted until 960, when the Song Dynasty reunited almost all of China. During the 300 or so years the Song emperors reigned, China fought continuous wars with a nomadic people called the Tatars and, later, the savage Mongols.

Yet, under the Song Dynasty, China was prosperous and had the most advanced culture in the world. China developed the arts of shipbuilding and bridge building as well as fine poetry, beautiful paintings, and new ideas in philosophy. Under the Song emperors, the teachings of Confucius became the chief philosophy of life. The Chinese valued scholarship and moral living. Scholars made great advances in medicine and science.

Under the Song Dynasty, the wealthy lived lives of ease and beauty, and even poor farmers lived fairly good lives. But, under the Song emperors, only the wealthy were able to afford the training that was needed to take the civil service examinations. Thus, only the rich became civil servants.

The need to protect China from foreign invaders was what finally ended the Song Dynasty. Needing protection against the Tatars and other enemies, the Song emperors became allies with the Mongols. The Mongol leaders, Genghis Khan (reigned 1206–1227) and his son, Ogodei Khan (reigned 1227–1241), defeated China's enemies. But then, the Song emperors and the Mongols quarreled, and Ogodei invaded China. In 1260, Genghis Khan's grandson, Kublai Khan, set up his capital in Beijing, a city in northern China. Determined to become emperor, he invaded southern China and in a few short years conquered all of China. In 1279, The last Song emperor in despair flung himself into the sea, and Kublai Khan became emperor of China and established what he called the Yuan Dynasty.

The Yuan Dynasty—Rule of the Mongols (1206–1368)

The Mongols were masterful horsemen and the most skillful and brutal warriors of their time. A nomadic people, they traveled from place to place, killing or enslaving the peoples who lived on the land they wanted. When he became emperor of China, Kublai Khan ruled a vast territory, stretching from Eastern Europe and Mesopotamia to the Pacific Ocean.

Foot Binding

One Song emperor so much admired the way one of his wives danced on her toes, leaving prints in the snow like those of a deer, that he ordered all his wives to have their feet broken and bound so that they could all walk on their toes. For centuries afterward, upper-class Chinese women continued to follow this cruel fashion until it ended in the 1900s.

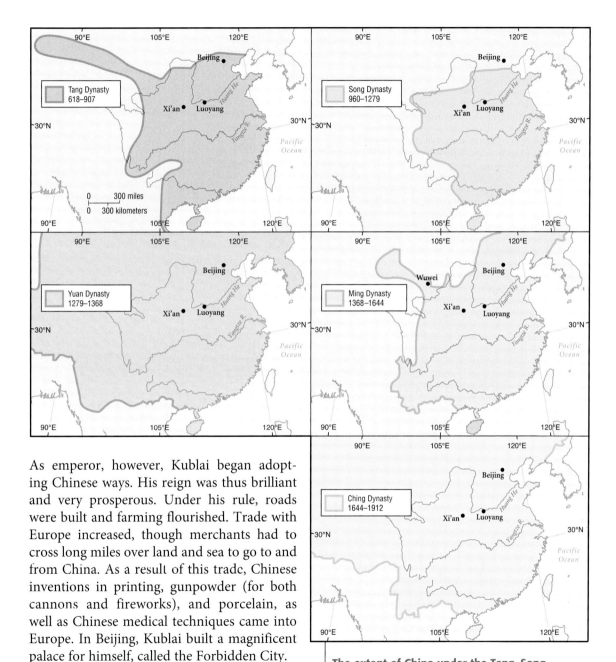

The extent of China under the Tang, Song, Yuan, Ming, and Ching dynasties

As emperor, however, Kublai began adopting Chinese ways. His reign was thus brilliant and very prosperous. Under his rule, roads were built and farming flourished. Trade with Europe increased, though merchants had to cross long miles over land and sea to go to and from China. As a result of this trade, Chinese inventions in printing, gunpowder (for both cannons and fireworks), and porcelain, as well as Chinese medical techniques came into Europe. In Beijing, Kublai built a magnificent palace for himself, called the Forbidden City.

During Kublai's reign, merchants from Europe traveled to China. The most famous of

Kublai Khan

Kublai Khan and Marco Polo

In 1275, a young Italian merchant, Marco Polo, visited the court of Kublai Khan in China. He remained there for 16 years, serving as an official in Kublai's court and travelling widely throughout China. When Marco Polo eventually returned to Europe, he told stories of inventions and wealth no one would believe. He spoke of cities without crime or sewage in the streets. He said that the Chinese dug from their hills black rocks that burned with hot flame (coal). The Chinese, he claimed, could print whole books using blocks that pressed images of letters on paper (a printing press). Chinese culture, too, said Marco Polo, was very refined. There were floating palaces and elegant dinners where the diners ate with long sticks of ivory and never touched the food with their fingers.

these merchants were Nicolo and Maffeo Polo of Venice and Nicolo's son, Marco Polo. Marco Polo remained in China for several years in the service of Kublai and later wrote a famous account of his travels there. European Catholic missionaries also traveled to China during this period. The first of these missionaries was a Franciscan priest, John of Monte Corvino, who arrived in Beijing in 1294, where he set up China's first Catholic Church. John became archbishop of Beijing, and other missionaries came to China, including the pope's representative, John Marignolli.

After Kublai's death in 1294, the Mongol empire began to fall apart. The Mongols fought among themselves and the Chinese rebelled against them. Finally, in 1368, a commoner named Hong Wu drove the Mongols out of China and made himself emperor. He set up a new, native Chinese dynasty, which he called Ming.

The Later Empire

Hong Wu's Ming Dynasty ruled China for 300 years. This was a period of peace for China. The Ming emperors encouraged agriculture and the development of new inventions. Architects built grand buildings and artists created pottery of delicate beauty. Slavery was abolished and the lives of poor farmers improved because they did not have to pay high taxes; and when their time of serfdom ended, they were allowed to move to different regions of China and seek a better life. Future generations looked back on the Ming Dynasty as a golden age.

Left: a Ming porcelain
Right: Ancient Chinese stone sculpture at the Ming Dynasty Tombs

During the Ming Dynasty, China carried on trade with many foreign nations. From seaports of the Middle Kingdom, Chinese merchants sailed out to trade with Japan and southern Asia, as well as India, Persia, and Africa. Chinese legend says that, in the early 1400s, Admiral Zheng De sailed a fleet of giant ships, some 400 feet long with nine bamboo masts, to Sumatra and Borneo. From these lands, the fleet crossed the Pacific to the coasts of an uncharted land of "fiery mountains at the feet of the dawn." Will we one day discover, perhaps, that Chinese explorers reached the Pacific coast of America or at least Hawaii several decades before Columbus landed in the New World?

At the same time, the countries of Europe were sailing eastward. Explorers from Portugal reached Asia, the Indies, and finally China. The Ming government tried to keep the Portuguese out of the Middle Kingdom, but they bribed their way in and eventually set up profitable trade with China. The Spaniards and the Dutch soon followed.

Catholic missionaries came to China with the Portuguese traders. The Catholic Church founded under the Mongols had disappeared from China, and the only Christians in China were a few Nestorian groups, who lived in the oldest Chinese cities. At first, however, no European was allowed to enter China; Portuguese traders had to stay in the port city of Macao in southwestern China. This changed in 1579, when the Chinese government allowed some Portuguese merchants to move further inland, to Canton. They were soon followed by Jesuit missionaries, one of whom was an Italian priest, Father Matteo Ricci.

Father Matteo Ricci, shown dressed in traditional Chinese robes

Matteo Ricci

Young Matteo Ricci was full of the zeal of Christ and eager to bring the Catholic Faith to the rich and vast empire of China that was so orderly and so respectful of learning and tradition. His own talents in science and mathematics won him the respect of powerful and learned men of China. Father Matteo had to learn to speak the elegant Chinese of the court and to adopt Chinese dress if he wished to be taken seriously. The Chinese knew only the roughest seamen and merchants from Europe; they thought of all Westerners as barbaric, unclean, and uneducated. Ricci and his fellow Jesuits showed the Chinese that Christian Europe, too, was a learned and civilized land. The work of the Jesuits was crowned with success when, in 1601, the emperor of China himself asked Ricci to come to Beijing, the capital of Ming China.

Father Matteo was able to show the educated men of China that their ideas of right and wrong came from a Supreme Being, the Lord of Heaven. Ricci wrote a catechism, called *The True Doctrine of God*, in which he quoted Chinese writers, especially Confucius, to show that there is only one God, that the soul is immortal, and that other teachings of the Catholic Faith are true. Finally, he gained an audience with the emperor, after 16 years of trying, and only then because the clock he had brought from Italy caught the emperor's fancy.

Matteo Ricci died in 1610, but the work of the Jesuits continued. In 40 years time, they had assembled a Church of 150,000 people, made up both of the poor and the rich and learned Chinese. To aid their work, the Jesuits translated the liturgy and the Scriptures into Chinese so that the Chinese could read and pray in their own tongue. They allowed the new Chinese Christians, too, to continue to practice ancient ceremonies that honored their ancestors and Confucius. The Chinese were very reluctant to abandon their ancient traditions. After much study, Ricci had decided that the Chinese were not practicing idol worship when they honored their ancestors and Confucius.

superstitious: having to do with *superstition*, an ignorant belief or trust in magic

But some missionaries disagreed. They thought the Chinese practice of honoring ancestors and Confucius was idolatry or, at least, **superstitious**. They complained to the pope in Rome. Arguments went back and forth, some saying Ricci was right, others that he was wrong. In 1715, Pope Clement XI ordered the missionaries in China to stop allowing the practice, and they obeyed. The result was that educated Chinese from that time on rejected the Christian Faith. In 1724, the emperor began persecuting the Church and ordered all missionaries to leave China. The work of the Chinese missionaries, it seemed, was destroyed.

Yet, the Chinese Catholic Church was not entirely destroyed. Jesuit missionaries for a while remained in the service of the emperor, who respected the priests' knowledge of mathematics and astronomy. Missionaries worked in secret among the Chinese, and native Chinese priests were ordained to minister to the people. Lay Chinese Catholics, too, catechized people in the Faith. The Church in China, however, did not grow again until the 1900s when Christian missionaries were again allowed to work in the Middle Kingdom.

The Ching, the Last Dynasty of Old China

In the 1600s the Ming dynasty fought a long war with invaders from the north, the Manchus from Manchuria, and lost. By 1662, the Manchus had completely overcome the Ming. Taking over the empire, the Manchus called themselves the Ching Dynasty. The Ching Manchus made harsh laws to keep the native Han Chinese from rebelling against them.

The Ching emperors were able rulers for about 150 years. They not only ruled Manchuria and China but added new lands to the empire. They conquered Mongolia, Tibet, and Turkestan. Korea was forced to pay tribute to the Manchu emperor. Beginning in the late 1700s, however, rebellions began breaking out throughout China. Though the Manchus had adopted Chinese culture, they never stopped treating the "Sons of Han" as a conquered people. The proud Han Chinese resented this and tried again and again to overthrow the Ching Dynasty.

Just like the Ming Dynasty, the Manchus had to deal with foreign merchants from Europe. First, it was the Portuguese and Spanish, and then the Russians. In the 1700s, Great Britain and France began trading with China. In 1784, the first ship from the United States entered a Chinese port. The Manchus feared these foreigners and would not allow them to travel from port cities into China itself. In the end, this only angered foreign countries. European countries and the United States were determined to enter China, whether the Manchu emperors liked it or not.

Chinese Emigrants

Because of famine and constant civil war throughout the 19th century, Chinese people **emigrated** in large numbers to new homes all over the world. In cities throughout the world, they set up businesses or took jobs as common laborers. Many major cities throughout the world have their Chinatowns, where Chinese families settled.

The Ching Manchus ordered all Han men to wear their hair in a long braid (a queue) at the back of the head. All Chinese who emigrated to North America and anywhere else had to keep their queue—or never return to China. Men with long queues became the image of a "Chinaman" for Westerners in the 19th and early 20th centuries.

> **emigrate:** to leave one country to go to live in another. (*Immigrate* means to enter a foreign country in order to live there.)

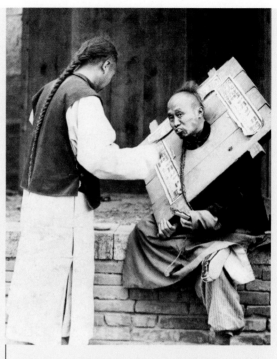

A Chinese man (wearing a queue) shows charity to a man being punished for a petty crime.

Modern China, Born in Agony

Modern China cannot be understood without some knowledge of the country's story for the last 200 years—a troubled and terrible period in Chinese history.

The last days of the Ching Dynasty were marred by civil war and foreign invasion from western Europe. To prevent Europeans from influencing the Chinese people, the Manchus for a long time only allowed European merchants to enter one seaport in China.

By the late 18th century, the mass of the Chinese people was dissatisfied with alien Manchu rule. Then, in the first half of the 1800s, China was hit by a series of natural disasters, floods, and **droughts** that caused mass famines and brought misery to the poor and middle classes. Many

> **drought:** long period of dry, rainless weather; lack of water, dryness

British forces attack
Chinese forts during the
Opium War.

Chinese slipped past the Manchu border guards and port authorities and emigrated to the islands of Malaysia and Indonesia. China was ready for civil war and uprisings.

The British added to China's problems by trading opium with the Chinese. Opium is an addictive, narcotic drug, which was grown in India. The Chinese government tried to stop the opium trade and, in one case, Chinese police seized and burned a British shipment of opium. War then broke out between Great Britain and the Chinese in which the imperial army was defeated again and again. This war led to another war, in which Chinese forces were finally overcome. Because of these wars, the Manchus had to allow the British opium trade in China and to open the country to more foreign trade. China, too, had to allow Christian missionaries to enter China. Both Protestant and Catholic missionaries, thus, began to flock to the Middle Kingdom.

The two wars with Great Britain, called the "Opium Wars," greatly weakened the power of the Manchu emperors. The wars also weakened China at the very time the empire needed to be strong enough to stand against enemies outside of China and rebellions within the empire.

The Taip'ing Rebellion

In 1845, a Chinese peasant named Hung Hsiu-ch'uan founded a new religion, called Taip'ing — "Great Peace." Hung based his religion on ideas he had learned from Protestant missionaries. For instance, he declared himself a second son of God and the successor to Jesus. Hung promised his followers that he would free them from the traditional Chinese ways that kept them poor. He promised that, in the future, there would be no private property but that all people would own property in common.

communism: a political idea that says there should be no private property but that all property should be owned together by the people

The starving poor of China were attracted to the **communism** preached by Hung. Thousands flocked to his cause. He organized his followers into an army and defeated Manchu troops. In 1851, Hung set up a revolutionary government, which he called the Heavenly Kingdom of Peace. The new political movement and religion spread through all of southern China. The Manchus were unable to fight back. Local militias had to defend their traditions and homes from Hung's armies.

The largest civil war in world history, the Taip'ing Rebellion, involved millions of combatants all over China. It destroyed the Chinese economy and weakened the imperial government. The Chinese emperor was still at the head of the government, but the country was divided into several territories under the command of local warlords and militia.

Taip'ing and its founder seemed victorious; but they did not know how to set up governments, and Hung's promises to the peasants did not come true. Finally, in 1864 a Chinese force, with the help of foreign soldiers under a British and an American commander, defeated the rebels. Plundering gangs of robbers and local warlords, called Nien, then terrorized the countryside, but the imperial government put down these bandits in bloody and destructive battles.

Manchu ladies of Peking

China, the West, and a Great Empress

Western governments had helped both the Taip'ing rebels and the Manchus during the civil war, because Westerners wanted China to be weak and disunited. Disagreements between the Chinese government and Western governments, as well as Japan, usually ended with the foreign governments seizing Chinese lands.

After 1860, more and more Protestant and Catholic missionaries entered China. By 1890, there were about 50,000 Protestant Chinese and 500,000 Catholic Chinese. The Christian successes and the fact that the Taip'ing movement used Christian ideas turned the Manchu government and many common people throughout China against the Christian Faith. They feared the Christian missionaries would destroy ancient Chinese culture. The Christians, too, supported the poor and oppressed against the rich and powerful of China. Christian ideas of social justice sowed **dissension** and friction in the already disintegrating Chinese society.

Some Chinese thought the best way to strengthen China would be to make it more like the Western countries. Such ideas were called "Self-Strengthening." These pro-Western Chinese wanted to develop factories and coal mines and to model the Chinese military after the armies and navies of countries like France and Great Britain. Yet, they also thought it was necessary to strengthen Chinese culture and the empire and return to the teachings of Confucius. China should be both modern and truly Chinese, they said. Only by moral leadership, they believed, could China again become strong. The Western governments, however, wanted China to remain weak so they could take advantage of cheap Chinese labor and take control of China's wealth.

Throughout the 19th century, however, the empire was under the control of a powerful woman, named Tz'u-hsi. She came to power in 1856 as the **regent** for her young son, the boy emperor, T'ung Chih. When he died in 1875, she stayed in power by placing another young son on the throne and ruling for him. Calling herself Wu, after the great Tang empress, Tz'u-hsi was a ruthless ruler. Favoring the "Self-Strengthening" Chinese, Tz'u-hsi's governors worked tirelessly to rebuild China. They built up modern personal armies and founded factories and mines throughout China. By the 1890s, it appeared that imperial China was about to begin another era of greatness and take its place as one of the major nations of the world.

dissension: dispute, quarreling

regent: a person who rules when the regular ruler is too young to rule or is unable to rule

The "Boxer" Rebellion

Any hope that imperial China would become again a great nation ended in 1894 and 1895, when Japan defeated China in a war over Korea. The

concession: something granted by one person or group of persons to another

war showed the European powers just how weak China really was. They demanded more **concessions** from China, and for a time it looked as if Great Britain, France, Germany, and Russia might divide up China between them.

Fearful that Western powers would destroy Chinese civilization, many Chinese decided it was time to drive the foreigners out of the Middle Kingdom once and for all. In 1900, Chinese who belonged to a political movement called the Righteous and Harmonious Fists (known to Europeans as the Boxers) rose in rebellion. The Fists attacked missionaries and Chinese Christians and threatened all Westerners in the country. The Fists lay siege to representatives of European and American governments inside the walls of the Forbidden City and for eight long and hard weeks kept Westerners from sending help to Beijing. Empress Tz'u-hsi sided with the Fists and ordered her armies to attack the European port cities. A European armed force, however, drove the Fists from Beijing and almost captured the empress. She admitted defeat on August 15, 1900. The power of the Chinese emperors was broken forever.

After the Boxer Rebellion ended, the Manchu government had to abolish many of its laws against foreign influence. Missionaries were again permitted to work in China. Chinese students were encouraged to leave China and study in schools in Europe or the United States. In time, these students formed several revolutionary societies that demanded a republic and an end to the old monarchy that had ruled the Middle Kingdom for thousands of years.

The End of the Empire

One man who helped to make China what it is today was born the son of a poor farmer in southern China. As a boy, however, Sun Yat-sen was able to go to school in Hawaii and, later, study medicine in Hong Kong, a Chinese city under British control. Sun was a Protestant Christian, the religion he followed until his death.

While studying in Hong Kong, Sun came to think that China needed to rid itself of the Manchu emperor and become a republic. He wanted China to become a true nation-state with a democratic government, like the nation-states of Europe. Sun was also a socialist — one who wanted the government to control the wealth of China. After the Boxer Rebellion, he worked to bring about a revolution in China, but failed. His ideas, however, inspired many Chinese with the desire to rid their country of the Manchu rulers.

Empress Tz'u-hsi died in 1908, and her grandson became emperor. He was, however, but a boy and his father, who was the regent, was a weak ruler. It was not long before a rebellion broke out, on October 10, 1911. Sun was in England when he heard of the rebellion, and he immediately returned to China. On February 12, 1912, the emperor abdicated. The Chinese empire passed away forever, and in its place was a new republican government with Sun Yat-sen as temporary president.

The new government, however, did not bring peace to China. Years of civil war followed as first one faction then another tried to establish a permanent government. Sun Yat-sen's political party, called the *Kuomintang* (the Nationalist Party), in the end allowed the powerful Chinese Communists to join. Supported by the Communist government in Russia, the Chinese Communists wanted the government to own all property and abolish religion. With the support of the Communists, the Kuomintang began to subdue the provincial warlords and other political opponents.

Sun Yat-sen and his wife, Sung Ch'ing-ling

Sun fell ill with cancer and died in 1925. General Chiang Kai-shek took control of the Kuomintang and expelled the Communists in 1927. Led by Mao Zedong, Chou Enlai, and Lin Piao, the Communists marched across China to safety in the far northwest, near Mongolia, where the Nationalist troops could not get at them. This journey is known as the Long March and is remembered by the Communists as a heroic flight.

Chiang Kai-shek was never able to unite all the warlords under one, Nationalist government, and the Chinese government was helpless when the Japanese army invaded China in 1937. The war against Japan was devastating to China, but it united the vast country in an effort to expel the hated foreign invader. The Nationalists fought the Japanese occupation with American aid. The China–Japan war became part of World War II in 1941, when Japan attacked the United States at Pearl Harbor. Finally after eight long years of dreadful war and huge loss of life, China saw the last of the Japanese troops leave her territory.

The joy of victory was short-lived. The Chinese Communist armies under Mao Zedong in the far northwest had grown and perfected their fighting abilities during the war with Japan. Civil war between Chiang Kai-shek's Nationalists and Mao's Communists broke out, and by 1949, the Communists, supported by the Soviet Union, were masters of all China. The Nationalists fled to the large island of Taiwan, off the eastern coast of China. There, protected by the United States, the Nationalists set up a government called the Republic of China.

regime: a system of government

Over the rest of China the Communists set up their new state, called the People's Republic of China. It was a cruel **regime** that controlled every aspect of life. Millions of Chinese died under Mao's Communist rule. The Communists persecuted not only Christians but anyone who followed a religion. There have been many Christian martyrs in Communist China, but members of other religions, such as Buddhists, have suffered as well.

Modern China was born in a long agony of disasters and civil conflict. The government of the People's Republic is still, today, officially Communist, but it allows private businesses from other countries to build factories in China, and in these factories Chinese men, women, and children work for long hours and very little pay. These factories produce many of the goods used throughout the world, and because of this, China is once again becoming one of the richest and most powerful of all the countries in the world.

But if China is growing richer, its government remains a harsh dictatorship. The government still persecutes Christians and groups like the Buddhists of Tibet. It shows no respect for human life, as can be seen in government-forced abortions, as well as concentration camps, and public executions. Little today remains of the Chinese empire, that, with its beautiful arts and architecture, its ingenious inventions and serene philosophy, was once the wonder of the world.

Chapter 10 Review

Let's Remember Please write your answers in complete sentences.
1. What was the Great Wall intended to do?
2. Who was Confucius? Where did he teach?
3. What is an ideogram?
4. Who was Kublai Khan?
5. When did the first Christian missionaries come into China? Who were they?

Let's Consider For silent thinking and a short essay, or for thinking in a group with classroom discussion:
1. How does our written language differ from the Chinese written language?
2. Why do we call China one of the great civilizations of the world?
3. What went into making the Great Wall?
4. What difficulties did Christian missionaries face in spreading the Gospel in China?

Things to Do

1. Using the map of China on page 200 and your measuring string, measure the distance (length) of China, from China's border with Kyrgyzstan and Tajikstan to the coast of the Great China Sea. How does this length compare with the length of Europe, measured from the western tip of Brittany to the Ural Mountains? (Use the map of Europe on page 170, Chapter 8.) Using the map of North America on page 350, Chapter 15, compare the length of China with that of the United States, measured from California to Maine.
2. Using a world map, find the scale, and with your measuring string measure the distance (going east) from Venice, Italy, to Constantinople (Istanbul), from Constantinople to Hormuz (the southern end of the Persian Gulf), and from Hormuz to Beijing, China. About how far did Marco Polo have to travel to the court of Kublai Khan?

Let's Eat!

Confucian philosophy says that, since, in cooking, one is combining the elements of the universe, cooking should be done with beauty and harmony. The followers of Confucius encouraged both women and men to undertake the art of cooking.

A very simple Chinese recipe is Egg Drop Soup. Bring 2 cups of chicken broth to a boil. Beat 2 eggs with 2 tablespoons of soy sauce. Drizzle the egg mixture slowly into the hot liquid. Add chopped spring onions. Serve hot.

Chapter 11 Japan: Land of the Rising Sun

Japan is a necklace of islands that run from north to south and lie to the east of the coasts of Siberia, China, and Korea. West of Japan is the Sea of Japan, which separates the Japanese islands from the Asian mainland. East of Japan is the vast Pacific Ocean.

Our name, "Japan," comes from the Chinese name for the country. The people of Japan, however, call their country Nippon, a word that means "Land of the Rising Sun." When they spelled "Nippon," the Japanese used the Chinese characters for "sun" and "source." In Chinese, those characters would be pronounced as JIH-PEN. Europeans, learning the name from Chinese speakers, called it Ja-pan.

Only a very small part of Japan is easily **habitable** by human beings. Today, Japan's over 100 million people inhabit the 15 percent of the country that is flat and fertile. The other 85 percent of Japan is mountainous, forested, and scenic. The mountains were formed from volcanoes, some of which are still active. The most famous is Mount Fuji, a beautiful, impressive volcanic mountain near Tokyo.

The soil from the volcanoes of Japan is rich, and the Japanese have learned how to get the most food they can from it. The largest crops are rice (a **staple** food of the Japanese diet), tea, soybeans, and fruit. In addition to its own farming, Japan is a major market for food and agricultural products from other nations. The Japanese harvest fish from

habitable: fit to live in
staple: most important

Mount Fuji (also called Mt. Fujiyama)

the abundant waters around the islands, both for their own needs and to sell to other nations.

Japan is made up of four islands. The northernmost island is called Hokkaido. Sapporo is its capital. The island is known for its beauty, including active volcanoes, hot mineral springs, and unspoiled lakes and forests. Its weather is cold and snowy in the winter and cool in the summer. Hokkaido is a favorite vacation spot for Japanese today.

To the south of Hokkaido lies the Island of Honshu. Honshu is by far the largest of Japan's islands and is home to the nation's capital, Tokyo. Honshu is heavily populated and currently produces much of Japan's industrial goods (cars, boats, industrial machinery, etc.) and high-tech products (such as electronics).

typhoon: a violent storm; hurricane
subtropical: a region near the tropics, having hot summers and warm winters, with nearly no frost or snow; *semitropical*

The inhabitants of Honshu benefit from an unusual feature called the Inland Sea. It is a waterway between the southeastern part of Honshu and the northern part of the next island in the chain, Shikoku. The Inland Sea, with its numerous small coves, gives Japan a waterway that is screened from the Pacific Ocean.

Shikoku is the smallest of the four major islands. It is a beautiful land, covered with lush vegetation, though its mountains and valleys make farming very difficult. The Pacific side of the island is pounded with torrential rains and storms in the summer. Snows cover the island during the winter, and rain falls often in torrents during the spring and especially the summer. These harsh rains sometimes grow into destructive **typhoons** in the Pacific Ocean.

The island of Kyushu, Japan. This view is typical of Japanese cities. Note the volcano in the background.

The southernmost of the four main islands in the chain, Kyushu, is the third largest. It has a mountainous central region with coastal plains around it. Kyushu's climate is **subtropical**, with heavy rain. The northern part of the island houses industry while the southern part produces abundant crops of rice, potatoes, and citrus, as well as livestock, and fish.

Because its islands are volcanic, Japan experiences many earthquakes. Some release just a small amount of energy and cause inconvenience,

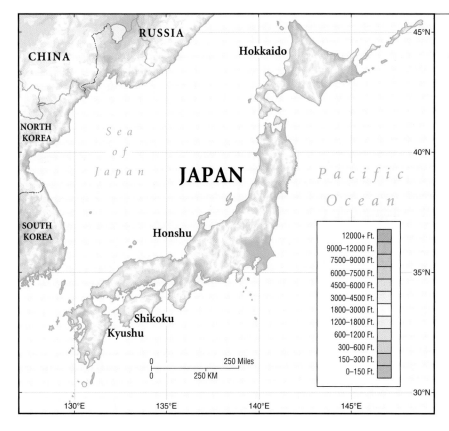

Topographical map of all the Japanese Islands with color scale keyed to elevation

while others are terribly destructive. Because their homes have been repeatedly destroyed by storms and earthquakes, the Japanese have learned to work together as an inventive and courageous team, ready to rebuild their homes as often as necessary.

Early History of Japan

The earliest inhabitants of Japan came to the islands in three waves of settlement. First, Stone Age **Caucasians** from Siberia came to the islands; then came Asian farmers. The third group of settlers was also Asian. They migrated into the south and began the process of nation building that produced Japan.

Caucasian: of or relating to the white race

Around the 3rd century A.D., a tribe living in the Yamato Plain in central Honshu made itself the chief power over most of Japan. This tribe founded a dynasty of emperors that has continued without a break into our own time. This dynasty is called Sun, because the Yamato family claimed that they were descended from the sun goddess, Amaterasu, who gave them three items that later became symbols of the emperor's power — a bronze mirror, a bronze sword, and a jeweled necklace.

mikado: emperor of Japan

The first emperor of the Sun Dynasty to rule Japan was Jimmu Tenno ("Divine Warrior"), who was called the **mikado** of Japan. Mikado means "The Honorable Gate." Since Jimmu Tenno said he came from Amaterasu, all of the emperors of Japan have been considered descendants of the gods. The mikado's cousins became chieftains of the clans, which in Japan were groups of families. Later, Japanese clans formed industrial companies, such as Toyota, Mikasa, and Mitsubishi.

piety: being pious — that is, being reverent and respectful toward God, one's parents, other elders, and those in authority

The oldest religion in Japan is Shinto, the worship of nature gods and ancestors. Shinto teaches that the gods founded Japan and will remain with the Japanese people as long as they are ruled by a mikado from the Sun Dynasty of Jimmu Tenno. Shinto continues the ancient practice of worshiping gods and spirits that are believed to inhabit such things as rivers and mountains. Shinto honors ancestors and encourages people to pray to them for aid. Even today, Shinto remains an important part of Japanese life in fostering **piety** and reverence for ancestors.

Shinto wedding, conducted by Shinto priests

China's Influence on Japanese Culture

Japan's nearest neighbors on the mainland of Asia were China and the little kingdoms of Korea. Korea had been civilized by the Chinese and was a very wealthy land in the eyes of the poor Japanese. Japanese clans began to raid Korea and try to conquer it. When they saw Chinese culture in Korea, the Japanese raiders thought it was superior to their own culture, and they began to imitate it. In that way, Chinese civilization first began to come into Japan.

One Korean king sent a number of gifts to the mikado. Among these gifts was an invaluable book, the *Thousand Character Classic*. Written in Chinese script, the book was a guide to learning and reading Chinese characters. Because only a few men in Japan were able to read, the mikado saw that the book would be very valuable to him. He sent to Korea for a scholar who might be able to teach the Japanese to read and write. The arrival of the Korean scribe Wa-ni in A.D. 405 was a new dawn for Japan. Chinese script became the first official written language of Japan.

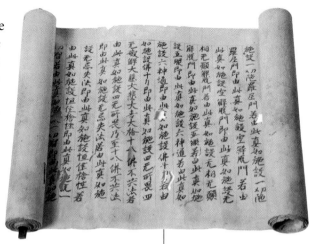

Old Japanese manuscript with Japanese calligraphy

Writing Japanese in Chinese characters is very difficult. Unlike Chinese, Japanese is an inflected language; that is, it adds syllables to words to show they are plural or to indicate what tense they are. (For instance, in English, we add –s or –es to nouns to show they are plural and -ed to verbs to show past tense.) Chinese does not do this; its words do not change form at all, and so it is easy to use ideograms with it. Japanese words, on the other hand, change form, and so ideograms do not work as well with Japanese.

In the 9th century, a Japanese monk named Kobo Daishi found a solution to the problem of how to use Chinese symbols for Japanese. Using the Indian language, Sanskrit, which has an alphabet, he came up with a **syllabary** for Japanese. Unlike a language, like our own English, which uses symbols (letters) for each sound, a syllabary uses symbols that represent syllables. English, for instance, uses *a* for the "aye" sound, *b* for the "bee" sound, *t* for the "tee" sound, etc. A language like Japanese uses one symbol for each syllable. A word such as *alphabet*, which has three syllables, would have three symbols, indicating each of the syllables, *al, pha, bet*.

syllabary: a set of written characters, each one representing a syllable

Another import from Korea was Buddhism. Around 500, a Korean king sent an image of Buddha and sacred Buddhist books to the emperor of Japan. The emperor's family decided to adopt Buddhism, partly because it was considered to be the religion of the civilized world. The Japanese ruling clans, however, feared that Buddhism might offend their native gods, spirits, and divine ancestors. This conflict between Buddhism and Shinto was a violent one.

Buddhism was finally allowed into the country when the crown prince, Shotoku, decided to make China's great civilization the model

Statue of the Buddha in Japan

for remaking Japanese society. In 593 his father, the mikado, allowed Shotoku to rule the kingdom. To change his country, Shotoku insisted that his nobles learn and observe the moral laws of Confucianism. He wrote up laws for Japan, based on Confucius's teachings. He declared Buddhism to be the religion everyone should admire, though he did not forbid people to practice Shintoism. Eventually, Buddhism became the chief religious philosophy of Japan, while Confucianism guided the laws. Shinto directed the rituals of the court and was the religion of the people.

Under Shotoku's direction, Japanese who were skilled in the arts or Buddhist studies were sent to China to complete their studies. When they returned after 10 or 20 years of training at the Chinese court, they received important government posts in Japan. Shotoku, who changed the life and culture of Japan and gave to the imperial court its ceremony and philosophy, died at the age of 48. He had been the most powerful man in the realm, though he never himself became emperor. He was always just the crown prince.

Japan in the Middle Ages

The full flowering of Chinese culture in Japan occurred during what is called the Heian period, which lasted from 794 to 1185. The mikado's court imitated the Chinese emperor's court and created poetry and music, artwork, and elegant calligraphy. In 793, a new capital city was built in the center of the Yamato plain. It was named Heian-kyo, or "Capital of Peace." Heian-kyo was the first true city in Japan. Its layout copied the Chinese capital city of Changan. It was rectangular, three miles long, and two and two-thirds miles wide. At the center of Heian-kyo sat the imperial palace. Parks and broad avenues, set at right angles, made it a lovely city. In time it came to be called simply, Kyoto, "the capital."

Though they imitated Chinese art styles, Japanese artists painted portraits that were more realistic and showed the individual character of people better than Chinese portraits did. Japan's oldest surviving portrait of an individual is the sculpture of the great Chinese Buddhist monk-missionary, Ganjin. It shows him as a **wizened** old man, wrinkled and worn, but meditating and tranquil of mind.

wizened: dry, shrunken, or wrinkled, usually on account of old age

One of the great works of Japanese classical literature appeared only a short time before the Heian period, in 760. It was a collection of 4,500 poems called *Man'yoshu*, "Ten Thousand Leaves." Most of the poems in the collection are short, five-line poems called *waka*. A few are long poems, or *choka*—though long poems do not work well in the Japanese language, and Japanese poets did not favor them. Poetry became very important during the Heian period. A **courtier,** for instance, was expected to be able to compose and recite a *waka* on command for any occasion, and to compose long poems for formal recitation when needed.

In the 900s, **prose** romances became fashionable reading, and women writers made names for themselves by writing these works. Around 1002, one woman writer, Sei Shonagun, wrote the romance, *Pillow Book,* which is now recognized as a masterpiece. The greatest prose work of the period was by another court lady, Murasaki Shikibu. It is called *The Tale of Genji* (written around 1015).

courtier: a person present in the court of a king, emperor, etc.; a court attendant
prose: writing in the ordinary form of speech; not poetry

But while the arts at the court flourished, the imperial government was weakening. The imperial family came to rely on the Fujiwara family to help them govern, and the Fujiwara gradually replaced the emperors as the real rulers of Japan. They did not remove the emperors but forced them to stay in their palace in Kyoto while the Fujiwara took care of the government of Japan. But the Fujiwara could not stand up to the growing power of the warrior

Scene from *The Tale of Genji*

The Revenge of Yoritomo

The Minamoto family found favor at court and were given honors and wealth by the mikado. But, one night, their enemy, the Taira family, surprised them and slaughtered all the family except one small boy, Minamoto Yoritomo. He was the last of the Minamoto line, and the guards were about to kill him, when he spoke up and said, "My mother and father are dead, and who but I can pray for their happiness in the next world?" The Taira grandmother, moved by the boy's **filial piety**, and remembering her own son who had died as a boy, begged for Yoritomo's life. The Taira spared him, but banished him to an island in the faraway Izu province.

In his place of exile, Yoritomo was kept under close guard. Moreover, his guards had been given orders to kill him when he reached thirteen years. But a faithful servant raised Yoritomo and taught him **martial arts** in secret. When he was thirteen, he was so **submissive** and seemingly helpless that the lord of the Taira allowed him to live. Yoritomo bided his time, waiting for the time he could take his revenge on his enemies, the Taira.

In order to get soldiers to help him carry out his revenge, Yoritomo decided to arrange a marriage with a powerful clan—which would make them his allies. There was one such clan, with two sisters, one ugly, the other, beautiful. To avoid notice and to gain the favor of the mother, Yoritomo decided he would ask to marry the ugly daughter. He thus wrote her a letter proposing

Portrait of Minamoto Yoritomo

clans from the provinces, who gradually began to make themselves the masters of Japan.

Two warrior clans came to vie with each other for the control of the imperial family through marriages and military force. They were the Taira and Minamoto clans. The story of their long feud and struggle for control of the emperor is the subject of a long story, called the *Heike Monogatori* (written about 1250). Stories from that conflict became subjects of Japanese drama.

The Era of the Shoguns

The feud between the Taira and Minamoto families ended in the victory of the great Minamoto leader, Yoritomo. Yoritomo became the most pow-

marriage and sent it by his servant. But, as events turned out, the servant had other plans than his master.

One night, the ugly sister had a dream of a pigeon flying to her with a box of gold. When she awoke, she told her dream to the beautiful sister, Masago, who said, "Let me buy your dream, little sister, and I will give you my golden mirror in exchange." The homely sister agreed, but she had barely time to say, "yes," before Yoritomo's servant appeared and handed his master's letter, not to the ugly sister, as he had been told to do, but to the beautiful one.

Masago eventually eloped with Yoritomo and began aiding him in his quest for revenge and the restoration of his house. The two of them set about collecting an army of followers and friendly lords, who were worried about the growing power of the Taira. The head of the Taira clan heard of Yoritomo's army and laughed. "For an exile to plot against the Taira is like a mouse going against a cat," he said.

But the laugh was soon Yoritomo's. Both sides gathered for battle on opposite sides of the Fuji River. On the night before the battle, two of the Taira warriors thought they would slip into Yoritomo's camp and assassinate him. They tried to cross the river through the wide shallows on their side, but their splashing stirred up the great flocks of ducks that were resting there. The sound of the birds flapping and quacking woke the Taira troops, who thought they were being surprise-attacked by their enemy. In the confusion, many ran for safety and some fought their own men in the dark. In the morning, the Taira force was dead or fled from the field. Yoritomo had won a victory without striking a blow.

In time, Yoritomo and his beautiful wife Masago built a city for themselves and their followers at Kamakura, in a valley facing the open sea. There, Yoritomo and Masago made their own court more beautiful and attractive than the emperor's court in Kyoto. Indeed, Yoritomo became more powerful than the emperor. When Yoritomo died in his bed in 1199, his Minamoto family held control not only of the capital, Kyoto, but of the entire country.

> **filial piety:** the piety shown by a son or daughter to his or her parents
> **martial arts:** the art or skill of fighting; the arts suitable to a warrior
> **submissive:** obedient, humble

erful man in Japan and the emperor in Kyoto was forced to turn to him to subdue the other warrior-chiefs and bring peace to the country. In 1192, the emperor gave Yoritomo a special title, *shogun*, or "supreme general," and with it the right to rule Japan for the emperor. The office of shogun became the chief power in the land. The emperors, though born of the ancient Sun Line, were mere figureheads without power or even enough wealth to keep up their palaces.

The period of the shoguns brought some peace and prosperity to Japan. However, noble families constantly struggled for control of the country. Each powerful clan wanted to rule Japan in the name of the emperor. In the warfare, many lords died. Their orphaned **samurai** became **ronin**, or lordless samurai. They hired themselves out as warriors or wandered the country, taking whatever they needed by force.

> **shogun:** supreme general; a military ruler of Japan
> **samurai:** the art or skill of fighting; the arts suitable to a warrior; a warrior who practices samurai
> **ronin:** a mercenary samurai without a ruling lord

The Samurai

Samurai armor

Yoritomo set up a system of government that was similar to feudalism in Europe. Nobles were to be loyal to their ruler, and the ruler to his nobles. Part of this system of loyalty was the warrior, called a samurai. The samurai followed the "code of the warrior," by which he was totally dutiful to his lord or master. A samurai's loyalty was absolute; he would unflinchingly die rather than face dishonor. The courage of the samurai may be compared to that of the Spartans.

Although the military skill of the samurai was legendary, they were much more than warriors only. They were trained in writing and in politics as well. The samurai were drawn to a sect of the Buddhist religion known as Zen. Zen Buddhism teaches that one can become enlightened through meditation and physical and mental discipline. Zen was blended with elements of the traditional Shinto religion to provide moral and artistic guidelines for the tough, yet loyal and artistic warriors —the samurai—of Japan.

Traditional Japanese Arts

Influenced by the natural beauty of Japan, the Shinto religion's appreciation of nature, and Buddhist contemplation, the Japanese developed very striking and unique arts: flower arranging (*ikebana*), growing and pruning of miniature trees (*bonsai*), poetry, and the traditional tea ceremony.

Traditional Japanese flower arranging (*ikebana*) developed from the practice of offering flowers in Buddhist temples. These flower arrangements using natural flowers and other plant materials were afterwards found in the homes of the upper classes and came to be recognized as an art form. The arrangements expressed the traditional Japanese idea of the balance of heaven and earth.

Traditional Japanese poetry expresses a strong, clear thought or emotion in verse that follows strict rules. Poetic ideas are inspired by natural objects, such as mountains, grass, or rain. The poet must express his thought in a very few words. The Japanese poetic form best known in the West today is *haiku*. A haiku poem has three unrhymed lines. The first line has five syllables; the second line, seven syllables; and the third line,

Sesshu and the Mouse

esshu (1420–1506) was one of Japan's great artists. Originally, Sesshu studied to be a monk. However, he was so busy drawing that he neglected his studies. As a punishment, his teacher tied him to a pillar at the temple. Sesshu's tears created a puddle at his own feet and, using only his toes, Sesshu drew a mouse. Legend has it that the mouse was so lifelike that his teacher, upon seeing it, gave permission to Sesshu to study painting.

Landscape by Sesshu Toyo

five syllables again. In *haiku* the poet compares and contrasts what he sees here and now with the enduring patterns of nature. The reader is challenged to find the meaning of the poem by comparing permanent things with those that pass quickly away.

Pruning a bonsai

Portrait of Matsuo Basho, by Sugiyama Sanpu

The Zen Buddhist monk, Basho, wrote one famous example of haiku:

This ancient pond here:
A frog suddenly plunges:
Plop of the water.

To understand such a poem, you need to visualize the scene. Imagine yourself standing beside the oldest pond you can think of, seeing the lichen on the trees and rocks, and the color of the dark stones. Think of how long the pond has been there and of the men of prayer and thoughtfulness who have stood, like you, beside these waters. As you are drawn deeper and deeper into the contemplation of the deep water, a frog suddenly jumps in. You do not see him; he is too quick. But the sound of his hitting the water breaks your **reverie**, and in that moment the music of the rippling water reminds you that the ancient touches the now.

Sometimes the haiku can be used to express ideas of morality as well. Here is another poem by Basho:

When a thing is said,
The lips become very cold
Like the autumn wind.

"When a thing is said"— this is not just anything that is said, but a cold thing, cold enough to chill the lips that spoke it. How often do we regret having said an unkind word almost as soon as we have said it? Here, Basho compares that moment of regret to a cold autumn wind, turning the lips, and the heart, cold with sadness, and perhaps a little fear.

reverie: dreamy thoughts, dreamy thinking of pleasant things

Woman performing the Japanese tea ceremony

The tea ceremony or *chanoyu* takes place in a small, out-of-the-way room set aside for tea. Honored guests arrive to take part in what is more than simply a social gathering. The gathering is a chance to purify the soul by appreciating nature. The ceremony is also an opportunity to appreciate the gardens surrounding the tearoom, the ceramic bowls used in the ceremony, and its decorative flowers. The tea ceremony, introduced from China, developed into its present form in the mid-1800s. It became an important form of social communication among the upper classes. The slow motions of the tea server, and the attention of the guests to every gesture, reflect the Japanese attitude to existence.

Europe Comes to Japan

Around the year 1540, a Portuguese ship, driven by a storm, landed on an island lying south of Kyushu. This was the first contact Europeans had with "The Land of the Rising Sun." Soon Portuguese merchants were trading with the Japanese.

In 1549, the Portuguese brought the Spanish Jesuit, St. Francis Xavier, to Japan. By his preaching and his holiness, as well as by many miracles, Francis Xavier won hundreds of Japanese to the Catholic Faith. He enthusiastically praised the spiritual understanding of the Japanese people and their openness to the Christian Faith. When Francis Xavier set out for China in 1551, other Jesuits came to Japan to carry on his missionary work. By 1587, there were about 200,000 Catholics in Japan.

By 1590, a Japanese feudal lord named Toyotomi Hideyoshi unified all of Japan under his power. Though at first Hideyoshi did not object to the Christians, he began to fear that Catholic priests were working to prepare Japan for conquest by Portugal or Spain. Hideyoshi feared, too, that his rivals, the samurai lords, would use the Christians against him. Hideyoshi thus began to persecute the Christians. He banished Christian missionaries from Japan and then made being a Christian a crime punishable by death.

Hideyoshi's wrath broke out against 20 Japanese Christians along with six Franciscan missionaries, who were arrested. Among these were the Japanese Jesuits, Paul Miki, James Kisai, and John de Goto. All 26 were crucified on a hill near Nagasaki on February 6, 1597. As he hung from the cross, Paul Miki preached to the crowds, inviting them to love Christ. All

Statue of Tokugawa Ieyasu at Toshogu Shrine, Nikko, Japan

26 men are today saints of the Catholic Church, known as the "Japanese Martyrs."

The desire of the Japanese government to keep Japan pure from outside influences led to further persecutions of Christians from the 1600s until the middle of the 1800s. Thousands of Christians died rather than deny their Faith. Yet, despite all the persecution against Christians, the Church in Japan was not destroyed. When Catholic missionaries entered Japan in 1865, they found about 20,000 Japanese Christians who still practiced the Faith in secret.

The Tokugawa Shogunate

After Hideyoshi's death in 1603, Tokugawa Ieyasu (a descendant of Yoritomo) emerged as the shogun of all Japan. Ieyasu moved the capital to Edo, on the eastern shore of the island of Honshu — the place where Tokyo stands today. The emperor's court remained at Kyoto, but the mikado was totally powerless. Japan kept the emperor only because the Shinto religion taught that he was sacred.

The Tokugawa shoguns continued to try to keep Japan pure of all foreign influence. They persecuted Christians and forbade contact with all foreigners. The only nation they traded with was the Dutch. Ships from all other nations were forbidden to enter Japanese ports.

Under the Tokugawa shoguns, Japanese society was divided into three classes: the nobles of the court, the samurai, and the common people. The nobles with the shogun controlled the government, while the samurai served the nobles. The commoners were divided into farmers, artisans, and merchants, of whom farmers received the most respect and merchants the least. There was also a class of "outcasts," whom everyone despised and who did the worst jobs. It was practically impossible for anyone in Japan to move from the lower classes into the higher ones.

Because Japan was closed to the outside world, the changes that occurred in Europe, the Americas, and other parts of Asia in the 17th and 18th centuries did not affect it. By the mid-19th century, Japan had none of the industry or technology that made the European countries world powers.

Commodore Perry Opens Japan

In the 18th and 19th centuries, all the great nations of Europe and the United States wanted to trade with Japan, but the shogun would not permit it. The great change came in 1853, when the United States sent Commodore Matthew C. Perry and a fleet of warships and soldiers to Japan to put pressure on the shogun to agree to a trade treaty. Faced with overwhelming military power, the shogun opened Japanese ports to the United States. Shortly thereafter, he did the same for Russia, France, and Great Britain. Japan's **isolation** from the rest of the world was ended.

In 1867, the mikado died and was succeeded by his son, Mutsuhito, who called himself Meiji, a name that means "Enlightened Rule." A group of young nobles rallied around the young emperor and demanded that real power be given to him. Faced with opposition from throughout the country, the last shogun resigned, and Meiji became the real ruler of Japan. This event is called the Meiji Restoration.

The young nobles who led the Meiji Restoration thought the young emperor would once again drive the foreigners from Japan and bring the country back to its ancient customs. They were disappointed; for Meiji, instead, banned the samurai class and abolished the **privileges** of the nobility. Instead of the samurais, Meiji built up a modern army, made up of men drafted from the common people.

Meiji allowed Christians to practice their religion for the first time in almost two centuries. Over the long years of persecution, Japanese Christians had managed to keep their little church alive—without the benefit of priests or any help from the outside. Under Meiji, the small but brave community of Catholic Christians that had endured in quiet faith was able to worship freely in the open again.

Meiji invited representatives from the European countries to Japan so that Japanese could learn a different way of government from them. He established a European-style government with a prime minister, parliament, and elections. Meiji imitated European countries, too, by building industrial factories like the Europeans and Americans had. As a result, the economy of Japan, along with its industrial and military power, grew overnight. Japan had a fully equipped modern army by the end of the 19th century, less than 50 years after Commodore Perry had sailed into Tokyo harbor.

Matthew Calbraith Perry (1794–1858). Portrait by a Japanese artist.

isolation: the condition where a nation has no contact with other nations or does not cooperate with them
privilege: a special right, advantage, or favor

Many Japanese emigrated in the last half of the 19th century and the first half of the 20th. They found new homes in the United States and in the Spanish-speaking countries of Central and South America. Japanese students traveled to Europe and America to study in universities in those places, and Japanese artists were warmly received.

Japan in the 20th Century

The new Japan under Meiji wanted to imitate the Europeans in other ways besides industry and politics. Japanese politicians wanted Japan to be an empire. In 1905, Japan fought a naval war with its new steel warships against Russia and forced the Russians to surrender. In the 1930s, Japan declared war on China, and within two years overran much of eastern China. The Japanese army committed atrocities in China that turned much of the world against Japan. A secret pact with Nazi Germany, however, allowed Japan to dominate parts of Asia.

Indochina: southeast Asia (includes Vietnam, Cambodia, and Indonesia)

By the early 1940s, Japan's military power had grown so strong that Japan invaded and occupied **Indochina** and had plans to conquer the Philippines and other lands in the western Pacific and East Asia. When the United States did not cooperate with Japan's plans, the Japanese

Modern Tokyo

fleet on December 7, 1941, attacked the United States naval base at Pearl Harbor on the island of Hawaii. This was the beginning of World War II in the Pacific, which ended when the United States dropped two atomic bombs on the Japanese cities of Hiroshima and Nagasaki on August 6 and 9, 1945. About 200,000 men, women, and children were killed or injured in the bombings, including many Catholics, for Nagasaki was the Catholic center of Japan.

Japan surrendered on September 2, 1945, its dream of conquest ended forever. Yet, since that time, Japan has grown into one of the most prosperous nations on Earth. Today, the mikado remains the ceremonial head of Japan, though he holds no real power. The government instead is a democratic one, with an elected parliament and prime minister.

Japan continues to be an industrial nation, producing automobiles, electronics, and other goods. Though they honor their ancient traditions, the Japanese have adopted much of the culture of western Europe and the United States. In return, the Japanese have shown themselves to be a very inventive and ingenious people. Their industry, inventions, and technological science have in many ways added to the well-being of all the world.

Chapter 11 Review

Let's Remember   Please write your answers in complete sentences.
1. What do the people of Japan call their country?
2. From which line do the emperors of Japan come in unbroken succession?
3. What does mikado mean?
4. Who was St. Francis Xavier?
5. Who was Commodore Matthew Perry?
6. What do people who follow the Shinto religion believe?

Let's Consider   For silent thinking and a short essay, or for thinking in a group with classroom discussion:
1. How might living on a series of islands affect people's sense of belonging to one country?
2. What might have happened in Japan had Christianity not been suppressed under Hideyoshi in the 16th century?

3. Ponder the bravery of the Japanese Christians in keeping the faith for 200 years. What does their endurance tell us about the character of the Japanese people?
4. How did the rapid development of Japan, both for good and bad, in the 20th century come about?
5. Why do you think Japanese art is focused so much on the natural world?

Things to Do

1. Between what two parallels (longitude) do the Japanese islands lie? How far distant are these parallels? Between what two latitude lines do the islands lie? About how far distant from each other are these longitude lines?
2. On a blank map of Japan, label each of the Japanese islands with its proper name. Indicate where Tokyo is. Indicate where the Inland Sea runs. Label the Sea of Japan and the Pacific Ocean.

Let's Eat!

One of the main foods of Japan is fish. Sushi and sashimi, two very popular Japanese fish foods, can now be purchased in American supermarkets and in the many Japanese restaurants in America. Some folks get mixed up with the terms sushi and sashimi. Sushi means "seasoned rice" and sashimi means "sliced raw fish."

Chapter 12 India: The World of the Rajas

India is so large that we call it a **subcontinent**—a vast and unique portion of a larger continent. India, a subcontinent of Asia, has always included several kingdoms. Today it is divided into three, separate, independent countries: Pakistan, India, and Bangladesh. Sri Lanka, a large island off the southeastern tip of India, is a fourth independent nation.

subcontinent: a vast, distinct part of a larger continent

The Geography of India

The subcontinent of India is surrounded by seas on three sides: the Bay of Bengal lies to the east, the Arabian Sea to the west, and the larger Indian Ocean to the south. India has four fairly distinct geographic regions. In the north and the northeast extend the Himalayas and their foothills. South of these mountains stretch fertile plains watered by several rivers including the Indus River and the Ganges River. A rocky triangular plateau called the Deccan Plateau lies between these plains and Tamil Nadu, a coastal plain on the southern tip of India. The northern half of India contains two great river valleys: that of the Indus River, which flows west into the Arabian Sea, and the valley of the Ganges, which is the sacred river of the Hindus. Both the Indus and Ganges rivers rise in the Himalaya Mountains.

Most of India has a **tropical climate** with frequent **monsoons** — heavy rains that occur during the summer in the north and in the winter in the south. These heavy downpours cause floods that often destroy the

tropical climate: the climate (hot and humid) of the lands near the equator
monsoon: heavy seasonal wind and rain

275

Indian woman carrying grass

farmlands on the banks of the great rivers. Up on the central Deccan Plateau, the enemy of the farmer is long drought. Because of the subcontinent's extreme climates, famines have struck India from the earliest times. The country, however, is blessed with forests of trees

Map of India

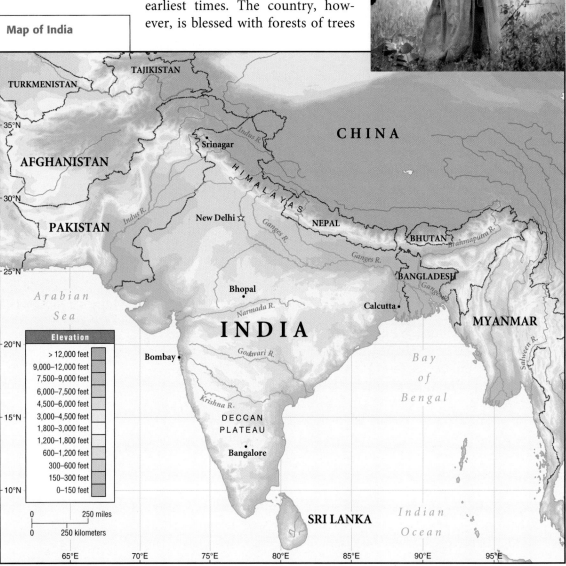

TAJIKISTAN

TURKMENISTAN

35°N

CHINA

Srinagar

Indus R.

AFGHANISTAN

HIMALAYAS

30°N

New Delhi ☆   Ganges R.   NEPAL

PAKISTAN   Indus R.

BHUTAN   Brahmaputra R.

Ganges R.

25°N

BANGLADESH

Bhopal   Ganges

Arabian Sea   Calcutta

Narmada R.   MYANMAR

INDIA

20°N

Elevation	
> 12,000 feet	
9,000–12,000 feet	
7,500–9,000 feet	
6,000–7,500 feet	
4,500–6,000 feet	
3,000–4,500 feet	
1,800–3,000 feet	
1,200–1,800 feet	
600–1,200 feet	
300–600 feet	
150–300 feet	
0–150 feet	

Bombay   Godavari R.   *Bay of Bengal*

Salween R.

Krishna R.

15°N

DECCAN PLATEAU

Bangalore

10°N   0   250 miles

0   250 kilometers   *Indian Ocean*

SRI LANKA

65°E   70°E   75°E   80°E   85°E   90°E   95°E

and bamboo, as well as a variety of mineral deposits, including iron ore, coal, silver, copper, and zinc.

Mountain ridges run across the subcontinent, dividing the country roughly in two parts: northern India and southern India. The mountain ridges also divide the people of India into two language groups. North of the mountains, the people speak a language that comes from an **Indo-European** language called Sanskrit. (Other Indo-European languages are Latin, English, and German.) The languages spoken in the lands south of the mountains come from Dravidian, a more ancient language once spoken throughout the Indian subcontinent.

> **Indo-European:** a word relating to the family of languages spoken in Europe, and some parts of Asia, including Persia and the subcontinent of India

The Beginnings of India

The Ancient Indus River Civilization

One of the four first civilizations of mankind grew up along the banks of the Indus—a river longer and mightier than the Tigris and Euphrates Rivers, and far more treacherous. The Indus River rises in the Himalaya Mountains of Nepal and rushes south and then southwest over a thousand

The Many Languages of India

Modern India recognizes many different languages as legal. Because India has so many languages, it conducts most of its business in English.

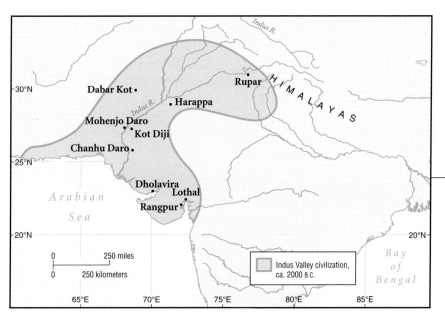

Map of Indus civilization

**View of ancient
Mohenjo Daro**

tributary: a stream or
river that flows into a
larger stream, river, or
body of water
thoroughfare: a pas-
sage, road, or street
open at both ends
citadel: a fortress

miles to the Arabian Sea. Like the Nile, the
Indus floods in the spring, leaving tons of silt
from the highlands along the banks as its violent
floods subside.

From around 2600 to about 1900 B.C., the
Indus River Valley was home to a civilization that built large cities along the river's
banks. In the past hundred years, archaeologists
have unearthed three of these cities: Harappa
and Mohenjo Daro in modern Pakistan, and
Dholavira in modern India. Historians have
named the Indus River civilization after the city
of Harappa, which stood beside the Ravi River,
a **tributary** of the Indus River.

The cities of the Harappan culture have
surprisingly similar designs. Though they are
hundreds of miles apart, Mohenjo Daro and Harappa could be twin cities,
laid out by the same architect. These ancient Indus cities were built with
set plans and had straight, north-south **thoroughfares** and almost identi-
cal dwellings for all classes of society. Each house, built around a central
courtyard, opened onto narrow, straight, crisscrossing alleys. Houses
had toilet drains that emptied into sewers, and the city had public toilets.
Each house also had a bathing platform, and the bath water ran off into
the common sewer, which emptied into the river. A bath was taken by
pouring water over the body. Daily bathing — atop a raised bathing platform — is an important custom in Indian society to this day.

Both Mohenjo Daro and Harappa are built on five mounds of brick,
which lifted the city above the floods of the Ravi and Indus Rivers.
Between the mounds, canals or dry avenues allowed floodwaters to pass
harmlessly by the city. The walls of the island-mounds were in some
areas 45 feet thick. One of the mounds held a **citadel,** with a palace and
government buildings on its platform top. Towers and gateways into the
citadel wall were reached by a ramp. Another mound held storehouses,
workshops, and barracks for laborers. Private homes rose on two other
mounds; public buildings, including a large bathing pool, were situated on
the last. One surprising feature of the Harappan cities is that they seem to
have had no fortified city wall. Were these cities never afraid of invasion?
Or had they other ways of protecting themselves?

The remains of elephants have been found in the Harappan ghost cities. This indicates that the traditional Indian practice of using elephants for work, warfare, and transport dates back to these ancient Indus valley cities. Archaeologists have discovered in the Harappan cities pictures of an elephant deity inscribed on ancient seals and tablets of clay.

Harappan civilization also developed a written language. Unfortunately, its ideograms are not intelligible to modern scholars. They are not like the writing of Mesopotamia or the later writing of Indian peoples. Only fragments of this writing survive, inscribed on clay shards that may once have been part of larger clay tablets, like those of Sumer.

Ancient pictograph from the Indus Valley civilization

All the cities of the Indus seem to have been abandoned at about the same time. Why? No one is quite sure. It does not seem that any foreign invaders overran them. Perhaps a massive flood or series of floods ruined the farmland with salts or mud so that the people had to move to new locations. Archaeologists have unearthed the bodies of many people in the ruins of Mohenjo Daro, and recent discoveries indicate that they may have died in a plague or perhaps from a massive flood. Perhaps such a flood so devastated Mohenjo Daro that its citizens simply left the city forever.

After leaving the Indus River Valley, the Harappan peoples, it seems, crossed over the mountains to the east and made new settlements in the valley of the Ganges River. Thus, they became the ancestors of the modern Indians. To their descendants they bequeathed the ancient Indus culture, with its cooperation, its gods, its farming technology, and its love of cleanliness.

The Aryan Conquerors

About the year 1500 B.C., aggressive tribes from the Asian steppes in the north pushed into India. Calling themselves *Aryas* (meaning "Noble People"), they were part of a people who overran and conquered Persia. To northern India they brought their Indo-European language, fast chariots, and bronze weapons. Eventually, through **unrelenting** warfare, they conquered this region and made it their own.

In the Indus Valley, the Aryan tribes found an existing agricultural civilization that had been around for a thousand years. The people of this ancient culture were called Dravidians. Though the Aryan language and culture became the **predominant** one in northern India, the Dravidian

unrelenting: not letting up or weakening

predominant: having more power or influence; most widespread culture survived and remained strong in areas of southern India. There, mountains and rivers defended the Dravidians from the Aryan invaders.

The Vedas: Indian poetic scriptures
couplet: a two-line stanza of a poem
proverb: a short wise saying passed down over many generations of people

The society of India today has many elements that can be traced directly to the Aryan northerners. They left a body of sacred scriptures, called the **Vedas**, which their priests learned by heart and treated as law. The word *veda* means "knowledge" in Sanskrit, the language of the Aryan people. The *Vedas* are long poems made up of many individual **couplets**, each expressing some **proverb** or religious idea. These scriptures describe the duties of men and the social order the Aryans believe was given them by their gods. Most of what we know about Aryan society comes from the longest of the *Vedas*, the *Rig Veda*. This poem deals with many aspects of Aryan life.

The Aryan priests had the task of preserving the *Vedas* in their exact wording. Written in strict meter, the poems are easy to memorize. In the priestly schools, masters taught their students to sing the verses, the master singing each line and the students repeating it until it was memorized. Hindu priests today sing the *Vedas* by repeating each line at least once.

hereditary: coming from one's parents or ancestors
raja: a hereditary prince, or king, of India
dharma: the law of the universe

Aryan society was tribal. The tribesmen enjoyed making warfare and rode horse-drawn chariots into battle. Cattle stealing and fighting were the chief occupations of Aryan warriors. Each tribe was ruled by a **hereditary** king or prince, called a **raja**. The prince had absolute power over his tribe, and the tribe had absolute power over the people they conquered. The rajas fought among themselves. Then, as their families grew and there were more sons to divide the inheritance between, they grabbed more lands from Dravidians to the south.

Between 1000 and 600 B.C. the Aryans outgrew the Indus valley and spread eastward into the Ganges plains. By the 600s B.C., there were 16 large Aryan states in northern India. A major war, probably fought around 900 B.C., became the subject of India's national epic, the *Mahabharata*. This poem, with 100,000 couplets, is the longest known poem in the world. It is moral story about ambition and duty. It speaks about the spiritual idea of **dharma**—the Sanskrit word for "the law of the universe." The war gives the characters of the poem the opportunity to find out what their

Hindu priests chanting a prayer

The *Mahabharata*

Mahabharata means "Great Epic of the Bharata Dynasty." It tells the story of two groups of cousins, the Pandavas and the Kauravas, who struggle with each other for the control of one of the kingdoms of India. The rivalry between the cousins causes the eldest Pandava, Yudhisthira, and his brothers to leave the kingdom when their father, King Pandu, dies. While in exile in a forest, the Pandavas meet the god Krishna, who appears to them as a man and becomes the charioteer of one of the brothers, Arjuna.

When at last the Pandavas return to their father's kingdom, Yudhisthira plays a game of dice with the Kauravas, to see who will control the kingdom. The Kauravas, however, cheat, and Yudhisthira loses everything in the game. Once again the Pandavas go into exile in the forest, where they must hide for 12 years, and then be unrecognized for the next year.

A long and destructive war follows between the cousins. After a terrible battle that lasts 18 days, the Pandavas are victorious, and all the Kauranas are slain on the battlefield. Yudhisthira and his brothers then rule the kingdom wisely and well for many years.

The *Bhagavad Gita*

The *Mahabharata* contains a long central section called the *Bhagavad Gita*, or "Lord's Song." It is a sermon Krishna gives to Arjuna on the battlefield. The Bhagavad Gita is the most popular sacred writing of the Hindu religion. Many have read it to discover the answer to the question of human suffering. It offers the idea of **reincarnation** (the belief that souls are born again and again in different bodies) to comfort people's doubts and fear of death.

Just before the great battle of the *Mahabharata*, Arjuna sees on the field of battle his cousins, along with their counselors and teachers, their servants, soldiers, wives, and children, and is struck with sympathy for them. "How can I take the lives of my kindred?" he says. "Would it not be better to give up the kingdom rather than cause suffering to those I care for?" But Krishna

Bas-relief in Mammallapuram, India, depicting a scene of the famous Indian epic Mahabharata, 7th century.

exclaims, "Let them perish, prince, and fight!" Krishna then gives a long sermon that gives three reasons for this cold-blooded counsel. First, says Krishna, since the soul is immortal, and only the body dies, Arjuna is doing his cousins a favor by killing them. Second, Arjuna's duty as a prince is to fight, since to be a prince is to be a killer. Third, Krishna says that, if Arjuna does not fight, he will be called a coward, not a prince. He must separate his inner "self" from the act he must do. His duty as a prince is all that matters.

Arjuna's older brother Yudhisthira is even more unhappy at what they must do in the battle, and cries out, "There is nothing more evil than a warrior's duty!" He begs Krishna to stop the carnage. He then curses *dharma*, the law of the universe that tells men what their duties are.

At the end of the *Mahabharata*, Yudhisthira comes at last to the city of the gods. There, with horror, he sees his enemies, the Kauranas, eating and drinking and feasting with the gods, while his brothers, the Pandavas, are in torment in a burning pit. The gods tell him that his cousins earned their reward by going to war as their duty demanded, but he and his brothers have earned torment for refusing to live out their appointed destiny. Yudhisthira says he would rather suffer with his brothers than feast with his enemies. The vision, however, was a test. Because of his choice to suffer with his brothers, the gods reveal to Yudhisthira that the Pandavas are not in torment but are feasting with the Kauranas in the halls of the gods.

reincarnation: the rebirth of a soul in a body

duty is and what *dharma* demands of them. The *Mahabharata* is a tragic story of defeat in victory.

The Indian Caste System

Like other ancient societies, the Aryans were very race conscious and had a rigid class structure. For instance, if your father was a farmer, you would become a farmer; if your father was a noble, you would be a noble. Yet, India's class structure was exceptionally strict and was in part based on race. The Aryans themselves were fair-skinned, large-framed, and light haired, while their conquered subjects were dark and small.

We use the word "**caste**" to describe groups in Indian society. A caste is a social group or class of people, but the Indian word for caste is *varna*, which means "color." The *Vedas* divided Indian society into three *varnas* or castes: *brahmins, kshatriyas,* and *vaishyas.* The brahmins were the highest caste — the priests who performed the sacred rituals to the gods. Next was the *kshatriyas*, the warrior class, which included kings and nobles, who ruled and fought for their tribes. The *vaishyas* were the merchant and artisan class, who carried on trade and made items to sell. These three classes had made up Aryan society even before the Aryans came to India.

Outside the three Aryan castes were two others — the *sudras* and **pariahs** or *harijans*. The *sudras* were descendants of the original Indian people

caste: a social group that excludes everyone outside of itself; a distinct class
brahmins: the highest caste in Indian society; the priestly caste
kshatriyas: the warrior caste in India
vaishyas: the merchant caste in India
sudras: the servant caste in India
pariahs: the outcasts of Indian society

She Touched the Untouchables

The Indian caste system can help us better understand the work of one of the most famous Catholics of the last century, Saint Teresa of Calcutta (1910-1997). More commonly known as "Mother Teresa," Saint Teresa worked among the poorest of the poor in the Indian city of Calcutta. She ministered not only to all the outcasts, she touched the "untouchables" and tended them with love. Today her Missionaries of Charity continue her work among the poor in India and throughout the world.

Saint Teresa of Calcutta

conquered by the Aryans. They served the brahmins, *kshatriyas*, and *vaishyas* as servants and farm workers. The pariahs were the lowest caste. They were perhaps the original inhabitants of the subcontinent, whom the Dravidian peoples had enslaved before they, in turn, were overcome by the Aryans. The pariahs were the "untouchables," avoided and despised by the members of all other castes.

The Indian caste system was very rigid. One had to be born into a caste to be a member of it and could not marry anyone outside his own caste. Very strict rules governed contact between people who belonged to different castes. Though a pariah or *sudra* could never hope to rise into a higher caste, the Indians believed that if one obeyed the rules of his caste, he could be reincarnated as a member of a higher caste. Likewise a member of a higher caste who neglected to do his duty might be reincarnated in a lower caste in a future life.

pantheon: a group of gods
petty: small and with little importance or value

Origins of Indian Religions

The religion of the Aryan people who invaded and settled India was based on the worship of nature gods. Their Aryan **pantheon** of gods and heroic stories about the gods were similar to the stories the Greeks and Romans told about their gods and heroes. The chief Indo-European gods were the three brothers, Brahman, Indra, and Varuna, who were similar in many ways to the Greek gods Hades, Poseidon, and Zeus.

Though the chief god of the Aryan people was Indra, the war god, the Brahmin priests worshiped Brahman, the god of enlightenment. The *Vedas* speak of some 33 gods, but the Aryans added the gods of conquered peoples to their pantheon until Indian civilization was worshiping hundreds of gods.

A major religious change occurred in Aryan society around the 600s B.C. While the rajas and their warriors stole cattle and waged **petty** wars to strengthen their growing kingdoms, the brahmins became more influential among the people. The people honored the priests because they knew the complex rituals for

Statue of Vishnu in Halebid (India)

controlling the gods. Kings had to listen to the brahmins' demands and buy their favor. In this way, the brahmins became the highest caste in Indian society. The religion of the brahmins is called Hinduism.

To escape the power of the brahmins, some men wandered off into the wilderness to live as hermits in search of spiritual knowledge. They undertook heroic fasts and acts of self-denial. They sang and danced unaware of anyone near them. They went into long trances. These hermits lived on what people gave them as they wandered from village to village, teaching their wisdom. Without using the ritual spells of the Brahmins, the hermits blessed those who were kind to them.

The hermits' pursuit of religious wisdom transformed Indian life. The new teaching was set forth in a series of poems called the *Upanishads*, a word meaning the "meditations." The *Upanishads* say people should trust religious insight over what one can learn through study. They counsel people who want to escape from earthly desires and pains that they should practice self-denial instead of indulging in earthly pleasures.

The *Upanishads* introduced the gods of the Dravidians into the Aryan pantheon. According to the *Upanishads*, Brahman is the creator of the universe, and with him are two other gods—Shiva, the destroyer of creation, and Vishnu, who preserves the universe that Brahman creates. Shiva's wife (called Parvati, Kali, or Durga) was the most important god of the Hindu religion.

The *Upanishads* also speak of reincarnation. Reincarnation is the belief that the immortal soul does not go to live forever in a heaven or hell after death but is reborn in another creature. The Hindus believe the soul is "reincarnated" many times. How one will live in a future life depends on how well he or she lives in this life. This belief directly supports the caste system because it teaches that every person is born into a caste based on how he lived in a previous life. If, for instance, someone is a pariah, it is because he deserves to be a pariah.

The *Upanishads* developed the idea of "the universal spirit." According to the *Upanishads*, the gods are just different "faces" of the universal spirit. Sometimes this universal spirit is called Brahman; sometimes it is presented as something greater even than Brahman.

A Hindu god in the Brihadeeswarar Hindu Temple in Thanjavur, Tamil Nadu, India

Buddhism

In the 6th century B.C., an Indian prince named Siddhartha Gautama made his own spiritual journey and taught a new way of spiritual enlightenment. This method of spiritual growth came to be named "Buddhism" from its founder, Siddhartha, who was later called Buddha, or "enlightened one."

Siddhartha wanted to know why there is sorrow and suffering in the world. His answer was that sorrow and suffering come from desire. If people want to rid themselves of sorrow and suffering, said Siddhartha, they have to purify the spirit through right thinking and right conduct. Siddhartha did not abandon all the gods of Hinduism, but he taught that

The Legend of the Buddha

At Siddhartha's birth, a **soothsayer** prophesied that the child would one day see four signs that would convince him of the misery of the world. Seeing these signs, Siddhartha would choose to be either a teacher or a tyrant. To prevent this prophecy from coming true, Siddhartha's father tried to shelter him from all sickness and decay and surround him only with youth, beauty, and pleasure.

One day, however, Siddhartha was riding in his hunting preserve when he came upon a gnarled and feeble old man who had somehow wandered into the park. Having never seen an old person, Siddhartha asked his charioteer what this creature could be. It is "Old Age," the charioteer said. On the ride home, Siddhartha passed a beggar covered with sores and shivering with fever. "What is the matter with this man?" he asked. "Sickness," replied the charioteer. Just then a funeral procession rounded the corner, and seeing the corpse, Siddhartha asked, "What is this?" "Death," was the reply.

Troubled by these sights, Siddhartha left home at the age of 29 to learn the mystery of Old Age, Sickness, and Death. Finally, in his 36th year, he sat down under a great fig tree—which Buddhists call the *bodhi*, the tree of wisdom. He vowed to sit there until he had solved the three riddles of suffering. For seven weeks he sat, fasting and thinking. At last he entered a state of mind that seemed to be neither being nor nonbeing. It was a timeless realm of meditation. Buddhism would later call that state of mind, *nirvana*—a word meaning "detachment." In that moment he became the Buddha, the "Enlightened One."

The golden Buddha of Thikse Gompa in Ladakh, India

soothsayer: one who foretells future events

religious rituals were of no use. Men of all classes flocked to his message, and the new religion spread quickly throughout northern India. People were attracted to the simple ideas of Buddhism and to the fact that, unlike Hinduism, it did not divide people into castes. Even though it did not entirely break off from Hinduism until later years, Buddhism was for several centuries the major rival to Hinduism in India.

Indian missionaries carried Buddhism to Tibet and China and to Burma, Thailand, and Southeast Asia. Buddhism became the majority religion on the island of Sri Lanka, south of the Indian mainland. Today, in Burma, Thailand, Cambodia, and Vietnam, most people are Buddhist.

Jainism

Another group of holy men began to roam through the villages of India at about the same time as the Buddha's followers were spreading

his teachings. They called themselves Jains, "conquerors." Their leader was another tribal prince, Vardhamana, who, like Siddhartha, had renounced his life of power and wealth because the sorrows of human life had horrified him. He was called the Mahavira, or "Great Hero." The way of life he founded became another major religion of India, called Jainism.

The Mahavira taught that the soul, in tiny portions, is present in all living things. Men, women, animals, flies and insects, plants and worms in the ground—all have souls that have to be reincarnated countless times because of crimes and misdeeds they have committed in life. The only way to escape reincarnation and suffering, Mahavira said, is

Jain priests in India

to refuse to destroy any living thing. Even peaceful actions such as tilling the soil or walking on the road involve committing harm, for one may disturb a worm or crush an ant.

The Mahavira's first followers thought of themselves as living symbols of respect for life. They walked about only in daylight to avoid injuring any living thing because they had not seen it. They carried brooms to sweep insects from their path and wore veils to avoid inhaling even a gnat. They refused to eat any meat, and they walked around naked, for clothing was made either from animal skins or from plants.

After his death, the Mahavira's followers took his message to all of India. Although only a few people (mostly monks) completely followed Jainist teachings, many laymen and families supported the monks and went on periodic retreats to liberate their souls. Jain missionaries went as far west as the Middle East. The Greek historian Herodotus remarked on them; he thought all Indians were Jains. Because later Jains were unwilling to be warriors or to take up the plow, they turned to trade and commerce and so formed an important part of India's merchant class.

The Christian Faith in India

The Christian Faith did not come to India for over 500 years after the death of the Buddha, but when it did, it brought a new hope to the peoples of the subcontinent. The Christian message of forgiveness of sins and redemption through Christ's death and passion showed that people are not doomed to endless reincarnation but that they are promised an eternal life in the vision of God.

Catholic Church in Basanti, West Bengal, India

Tradition says that it was the apostle Thomas who first brought the Gospel to the west coast of India. A group of Indian Christians having bishops and sacraments and called the Mar Thoma Church says it dates back to the time of St. Thomas. In the 1600s, Portuguese explorers and traders brought missionaries to India, who established the Catholic Church in the Portuguese colonies in India. One of these missionaries was the Jesuit priest, St. Francis Xavier.

Francis Xavier began his missionary work among the Indian poor in the Portuguese colonies and had his greatest success there. Ringing bells, he would walk among the people of the streets and sing hymns and play games with the children until someone would talk to him. Then he would tell them about the Savior.

In the 1800s the English brought Protestant Christianity to India. There are now Catholics, Protestants, and Mar Thoma Christians on the subcontinent.

The Great Empires of India
330 B.C.–A.D. 1948

The Mauryan Empire

The founder of India's first great empire was not a raja, nor did he belong to the caste of warriors. He was Chandragupta Maurya, the son of a common herdsman, who belonged to the sudra caste. The empire he founded has been named the Mauryan Empire in honor of him.

Mauryan Empire

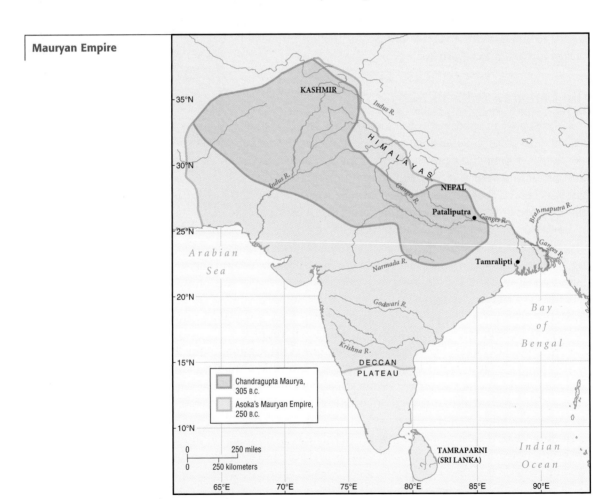

When Maurya was young, the Macedonian Greek conqueror, Alexander the Great, brought his army down out of Persia into the Indus valley, where he found small states, all at war with each other. These he easily defeated and added to his empire. When Alexander departed from the Indus valley, he left behind garrisons and commanders who made western India a Greek state.

It is said that when Chandragupta Maurya was a boy, he met and spoke with Alexander. The conqueror greatly impressed the lad. Maurya reported that some days after he met the conqueror, he fell asleep while watching over his flocks and the spirit of Alexander, in the form of a lion, came to him. When Maurya awoke, he found a real lion licking his body. The brahmins said that this was a sign that Maurya would become a king, honored by Alexander.

An ancient bust of Seleucus I Nicator

Maurya was adopted by a wise brahmin, Kautilya, who became his teacher and adviser. It was Kautilya who set Maurya on the throne of a kingdom along the Ganges River in northeast India and became his first minister. At Kautilya's urging, Maurya forged a union of several kingdoms and tribal republics in eastern India into one large kingdom. He then sent his new army into the Indus valley to bring the western Indian states under his control. Kautilya understood the best defense against invasions from the west (such as the one Alexander had led) was an Indian empire.

The Greek king of Persia, Seleucus I, tried to retake the lands Maurya had seized. But, in 305 B.C., Maurya drove Seleucus out of India forever. Maurya's chariots and elephants then moved north to the foot of the Himalayas and added Kashmir and the rest of northern India to the lands he already controlled in the Ganges and Indus River valleys.

The Mauryan capital was Pataliputra, a city on the Ganges plain. It had timber walls and large stone houses for the nobles. The gardens and parks and wide streets made Pataliputra a city of beauty. Maurya ordered all the rajas of his realm to move to his capital, where he could keep an eye on them.

A Greek ambassador, sent by Seleucus to Maurya, wrote home to his king that there was no theft or other crime to be seen in all the great city of Pataliputra. The people of the city, said the ambassador, were skilled in all the arts, lived luxuriously, and left their property unguarded and

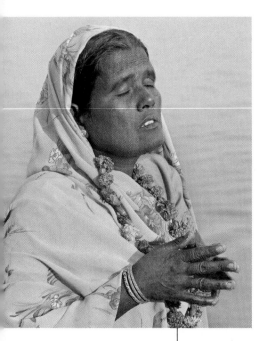

A woman prays by the Ganges River, sacred to many Indians.

doors unlocked. The crime rate was probably kept so low because Maurya visited such terrible punishments on those guilty of thieving, assault, and public drunkenness. The king believed that crime should be dealt with quickly and harshly so that those who might just think of doing harm would quake with fear.

In the Mauryan Empire women were able to read and were skilled in the arts. As in other ancient cultures, upper class women were forced to marry at a very young age. A man of 24 or older might marry a girl of eight, and most girls were married between the ages of 12 and 14.

In the Mauryan Empire, the farmlands around the capital and in the conquered lands all belonged to the king. The peasants sometimes had to give up a third or even a half of their crops to the royal collectors, but they did not have to serve in the military or serve the government in any other way. Farmers, however, along with free hermits and servants, were forced into a state of near serfdom. The empire drew its soldiers from the younger sons of the *kshariyas* caste who had lost their estates and kingdoms. Brahmins were not required to do military service or to pay taxes, but they had to be educated to serve in the government. Maurya himself was drawn to the Jain sect more than to the Hindu religion and so ignored what his brahmins told him.

As he grew older, Maurya began to fear assassins. Fearful of being poisoned, he would eat nothing that had not been first tasted by a slave. And he never slept in the same room twice in a row. Guards surrounded his sleeping rooms, where lights burned all through the night.

trivial: not important

Maurya formed a secret service of government spies to report on the activities of local governors and rajas. The spies were to keep the king informed of any plots being hatched against him. Maurya told his spies to watch and report on the most **trivial** activities of his courtiers. The slightest hint that a noble was disloyal or that he had said anything that could be understood as disloyal (even if it was not) could lead to dire consequences. The noble could be sentenced to being torn apart by lions or crushed by the feet of royal elephants. People whom the aging king thought dangerous might disappear without a trace. Ten years of such fear and watchfulness ate up Maurya's peace, while he ruled the largest empire India had ever seen.

After 20 years of rule, Maurya began to surround himself with **frivolous** entertainment. He no longer trusted his wives, not even the woman whom he had loved since his youth. He seldom left his palace except for the necessary public festivals and rituals. When India was hit by a 12-year drought and the Ganges itself dried up to a trickle, a Jain sage told Maurya that he alone could save the land by abandoning his throne and withdrawing into a hermitage. To end the drought, Maurya **abdicated** in favor of his eldest son, Bindusara, and went to live with a group of naked Jains. There, free at last of the fears that had tormented him for 10 years, the shepherd boy who became an emperor died of starvation. In 297 B.C., he fasted to death, praying for his people.

frivolous: lacking seriousness; silly

abdicate: to give up formally or renounce; resign

Ashoka the "Saint"

For 25 years, Maurya's son Bindusara ruled the empire his father had so wonderfully organized. His people called Bindusara "Slayer of Enemies," because of the many wars he fought on the borders of the empire. Bindusara ruled like his father did; and even though his laws were harsh, he brought the empire to a state of high prosperity and contentment.

View of the Great Stupa, built by Ashoka, at Sanchi, India

Bindusara named his younger son, Ashoka, to succeed him as king. This son, Bindusara thought, was the most ruthless of all his sons, and so was the most able to keep the empire together. Ashoka, who became king in about 265 B.C., followed the example of his father and set out to be a ferocious and feared master of the land. His first act was to order the death of his 95 brothers. He wanted no rivals to the throne left alive. Then he waged a brutal war on the region called Kalinga, on the southeastern coast of India. Ashoka's armies left the region burned and devastated. Whole villages and cities had been put to the sword, and thousands of people of all castes were forced to leave their homes and move to underpopulated regions of the empire the young king wanted filled up.

But when Ashoka visited the lands he had conquered, he was horrified by the suffering he saw. He recoiled from his father and grandfather's tyrannical ways and determined to change both his life and how he ruled his empire. He studied Buddhism and went on a 265-day spiritual retreat. When he returned to the throne, he issued edicts that he hoped would bring his people happiness and make his kingdom like a Buddhist paradise. He organized a council of scholars to gather Buddha's sayings and discourses, called the **sutras**, and made the philosophy of Buddhism into an organized religion.

sutras: Buddha's sayings or discourses

Buddhism did not become the official religion of the empire, though Ashoka himself became a Buddhist and supported the religion. The great king sent Buddhist missionaries to the Himalayas and to Sri Lanka, where for many years Buddhism was the official religion.

In his own kingdom, Ashoka put the **benevolent** and humane ideals of Buddhism into practice. He appointed men called "Officers of Righteousness" to oversee local officials and promote the welfare and happiness of all classes. The Officers were to be the final judges in all disputes, in order to protect people from wrongful imprisonment and undeserved punishment. Ashoka encouraged advances in medicine in all his provinces, commanding that herbs and healthful foods be planted in places they had not been known before. He gave up the ancient Aryan amusement of the hunt, which must have been a great sacrifice for a prince of his class, and forbade the killing of animals that were not to be used for food.

benevolent: kindly

In his government, Ashoka chose his officials based on their abilities, not their castes. This angered the Brahmins, but they were kept in check by the authority of Ashoka's personality and by his ruthless spy network.

The Mauryan Empire placed representatives of the central government in every village. These officials kept records of births, deaths, taxes, and

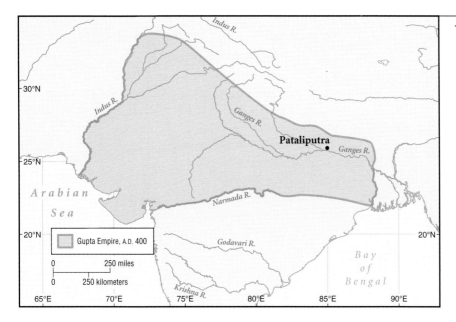

The Gupta Empire

Gupta Empire, A.D. 400

0   250 miles

0   250 kilometers

all manner of commerce. The government laid down rules and laws for every profession and line of work. For example, washers of clothes would be punished if the stones they used in their work were too sharp and ruined the clothes. And woe to the doctor whose patient died because of negligence!

Ashoka renounced war fought only for political reasons. He taught his soldiers that a man should behave toward others as he would wish them to behave towards himself. Because, however, Ashoka neglected the army, it grew weak. Ashoka died about 232 B.C., and less than 50 years later, the Mauryan Empire fell apart, as his descendants quarreled over who would be emperor. The Brahmins came back to power in the warring states. Buddhism fell out of favor, and Hinduism became once again the dominant religion of India.

The Indian Classical Period (A.D. 320–650)

After the death of Ashoka, various families struggled for control of the Mauryan Empire until, at last, a new Maurya emerged and united India by force. He was Chandragupta Gupta, whose family was to rule northern India for the next 150 years. This Gupta Empire brought prosperity and

Gupta period painting inside the Ajanta caves, India

elite: a small, socially powerful and influential group of people
despoil: to rob or plunder

relative peace to northern India and set the stage for a flowering of architecture and the arts called the "golden age" of India.

During India's golden age, leisure, learning, and courtly life became available to many people, not just a small **elite**. Educated people were expected to become good musicians, artists, and poets. The unique artistic styles of Indian sculpture and painting were first formed in this period, and fine Gupta paintings are admired even today. Stone replaced wood in the building of temples.

Mathematics and science also flourished during India's "golden age." The Indians were experts in mathematics and introduced the decimal system and the concept of zero, which was carried by Middle Eastern traders to Europe. Indian mathematicians calculated a value for *pi* more accurately than the Greeks did. And a prince named Brahmagupta taught a theory of physics that included the idea of gravity.

The Mughal Empire (1526–1707)

The "golden age" of the Guptas was followed by another period of relative peace in northern India. This period ended around 1000 when a new power, the Muslim Turks, brutally conquered and **despoiled** the cities of northern India.

In their many raids against northwest India, the Turks demolished Hindu temples, which they considered unholy, and killed tens of thousands of people. Although they totally controlled northwest India, the Turks had little impact on the rest of India at this time.

The Islamic conquerors who most influenced the culture and history of India were called the

A facade of the tomb of Akbar the Great, India

Mughals. The English word "mogul," meaning someone with great power and influence, comes from the name of these rulers. The Mughals came from central Asia and fought with fury, eventually seizing control of northern India. The Mughals were also Turkish, but their name is a form of the word "Mongol," for their king said he was descended from the famous Mongol rulers, Timur and Genghis Khan. The Mughal Empire lasted longer than other Muslim kingdoms had in India, for one of the Mughal leaders, Akbar, was wise. Akbar realized that, in order not only to conquer but to rule India, he would need the help of the Indian nobility. By respecting the Hindu religion he won the support of the Indian ruling classes.

The time of the Mughals was like a second golden age for Indian culture. This time, however, the culture was a combination of Indian Hindu culture and Turkish Moslem culture. The Indian nobles began to speak Persian, the language of their Turkish conquerors. Eventually, Persian mixed with the ancient Aryan Indo-European language to form a new language, called Urdu. Another language, Hindustani, developed from a mixture of another Indo-European language and Persian. It is now spoken throughout India.

The Mughal Empire was a period of creative achievement in art and music. The greatness of Mughal architecture can be seen in the Taj Mahal. With its dome and arches, its graceful marble tracery, and its harmonious gardens, the Taj Mahal has been called the most beautiful building in the world. It was built by the Mughal king, Shah Jehan, as a memorial to his beloved wife, Mumtaz Mahal. She was the most beautiful woman Shah Jehan had ever seen. Mumtaz and Shah Jehan loved each other deeply and had 14 children together.

distraught: agitated with sorrow or some other strong emotion

When Mumtaz died from a fever at age 39, the **distraught** king decided to build the most beautiful building the human mind could design for her tomb. He sought out and hired the greatest artists and architects of all India and set them to creating designs for his memorial. The architects presented design after design to the king, but he rejected all of them. At last, however, the perfect image was set before him, one worthy of his beloved wife. It took over 20,000 workers and 22 years to construct the Taj Mahal. Inside, the body of Shah Jehan lies in a marble sarcophagus; in another sarcophagus, exactly like his, rests his beloved Mumtaz.

The Making of Modern India

After the Mughal Empire ended, India fell into political chaos. Princes and kings made themselves independent of any central authority. The **maharajas** of larger states and the rajas of smaller ones made war on their neighbors. Into this conflict came the Europeans in the 1600s. The Portuguese had already established trading colonies in India, at Goa and Bombay. The French and the English then hastened to get a toehold in the enormously profitable trade with India—trade in precious jewels, gold, and rare spices.

maharaja: a prince that is of higher rank than a raja

The government of Great Britain placed all its activities and colonies in India in the hands of a trading company, called the East India Company. The East India Company was allowed to hire its own armies, conclude treaties with the rajas, and make its own laws for the territories it gained. By the end of the 1700s, all of India was in British hands, and the English

East India Company was running a subcontinent.

But in time, the British government took direct control over India, and for the next 150 years, India was the most important part of the British Empire. The Indian princes were put on government payroll. The British built railroads, schools, roads, and other physical improvements. They established English law courts and administrators over the Indian people. The British Indian Empire continued until 1948, when the Indians won their independence under Mohandas Gandhi and his supporters.

Old illustration of a battle between the British army and Indian rebels near Delhi, 1857

When the British gave India its independence in 1948, it divided the subcontinent into a larger Hindu state (called India) and a smaller Muslim state, called Pakistan. In 1973, eastern Pakistan declared its independence from western Pakistan and formed a new nation, called Bangladesh.

Chapter 12 Review

Let's Remember   Please write your answers in complete sentences.
1. What language today is used for doing business in modern India?
2. What are the *Vedas*?
3. What were the *varnas* in Indian society?
4. What was the first Indian Empire?
5. What is the Taj Mahal? Why was it built?

Let's Consider   For silent thinking and a short essay or for thinking in a group with classroom discussion:
1. Why are there so many languages in modern India?
2. What sort of government built cities like Harappa and Mohenjo Daro?

3. What does the fact that Hindu priests memorize *Vedas* tell us about the power of human memory?
4. What is life in a rigid caste system like?
5. How did the British Empire change India?

Let's Eat!

The distinctively Indian spice, curry, is used to season food and to help digest it. Recipe for chicken curry: Heat 3 tablespoons of oil in a skillet. Add cut-up chicken tenders (about 2 cups) and 1 sliced onion to skillet. Add a half cup of chicken broth, 1 cup of raisins, 1 sliced apple, 1 sliced green pepper, and 2 tablespoons of curry powder. Heat for a half hour; serve over rice. (Serves 4.)

Chapter 13 Africa: The Enduring Continent

The continent of Africa provides many challenges to the people who live there. Africa's hot climate is one severe challenge, but there are other challenges as well. Most of the continent is open grassland, and the vast majority of Africa's soils are poor and not suitable for farming. Africa has many tropical diseases and **voracious** insects that torment the inhabitants of most areas of the continent. The Sahara, a huge desert, lies just south of the North African coast, making transportation by land from north to south extremely difficult. Also, since water is hard to obtain in many parts of Africa (not just the vast deserts), settled life is very difficult. With these challenges, the African peoples—both present and past—require fortitude, toughness, and teamwork just to survive.

voracious: having a great, destructive appetite

The Geography of Africa

Africa is the second largest continent in the world. It is so huge that the United States, Europe, India, and Japan could easily fit into Africa with space left over. Oceans surround Africa on all sides, except for a small land bridge that connects it to Asia. The equator runs through the middle of the African continent, and all the areas of the continent are hot. In the center of the continent and along the western coast are the famous jungles of Africa.

Africa may be divided into six broad areas: North Africa, the Sahara Desert, West Africa, East Africa, central Africa, and southern Africa.

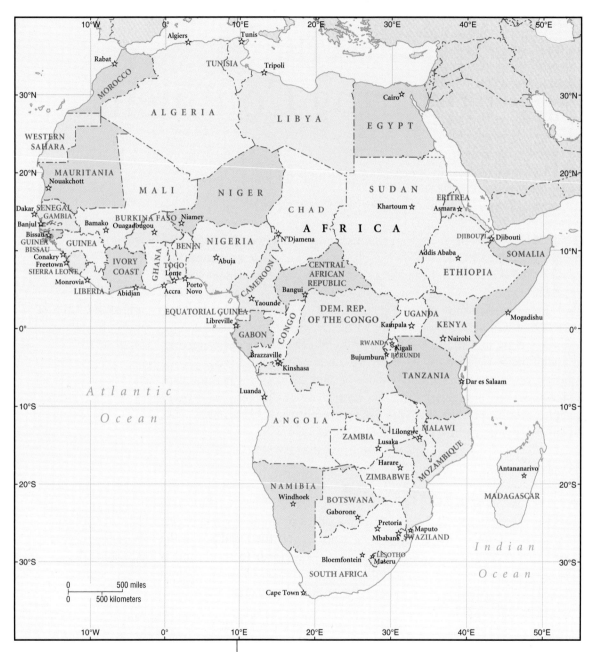

Nations and boundaries of Africa today

North Africa is the part of Africa that touches the Mediterranean Sea. Its civilization has always been part of the greater Mediterranean world. The Nile Delta that was so important to ancient Egyptian civilization is part of the North African world. Along with Egypt, ancient Phoenicia, Greece, and Rome made North Africa part of the ancient civilized world. Later, in the 7th century, Muslim Arabs conquered the entire area. Because of its rich history, North Africa has developed differently from the rest of Africa. The modern-day countries that make up this area are Morocco, Algeria, Tunisia, Libya, and Egypt.

The Sahara lies below Africa's fertile and inhabited northern coast. The Sahara is by far the largest desert in the world and stretches from the Atlantic Ocean on the west to the Red Sea on the east. It covers three and one-half million square miles. The Sahara was once a grassland, or savanna, before the end of the last ice age. There is evidence that people in the Sahara once lived in tribes as **nomadic** herdsmen. As the ice age came to an end, the earth's climate changed, and hot, dry winds turned much of the Sahara into sand wastes. Today, the southern portions of Morocco, Algeria, Libya, and Egypt, the northern half of Sudan, as well as most of Mauritania, Mali, Niger, and Chad, lie within the Sahara Desert.

nomadic: wandering; living like a nomad

West Africa is the region of the west coast of Africa, south of the Sahara, to just north of the equator. This fertile and rich area contains grasslands, rainforests, and farmlands. Many small states lie on the western coast of Africa: Senegal, Gambia, Guinea Bissau, Guinea, Sierra Leone, Liberia, Ghana, Burkina Faso, Togo, and Nigeria.

East Africa has high mountains that separate it from the Sahara to the north and west, and from the **rainforests** of western and central Africa. The Great Rift valley includes the Jordan River and the Dead Sea in the north (in Asia). It runs down East Africa from north to south and is the meeting place of the African and Indian continental plates. Volcanoes are still active there. Mount Kilimanjaro is an active and growing volcano in Kenya and the highest mountain in Africa. The farmlands of this region are very fertile because of the rich volcanic soil of the mountains and the warm but wet climate. The countries of East Africa are Sudan, Ethiopia, Eritrea, Somalia, Kenya, Uganda, and Tanzania. East Africa is the home of two of the earliest African civilizations, Kush and Ethiopia.

rainforest: a tropical woodland that receives a very large amount of rain every year. Rainforests have very tall broad-leaved evergreen trees whose branches make an unbroken roof or canopy over the forest floor.

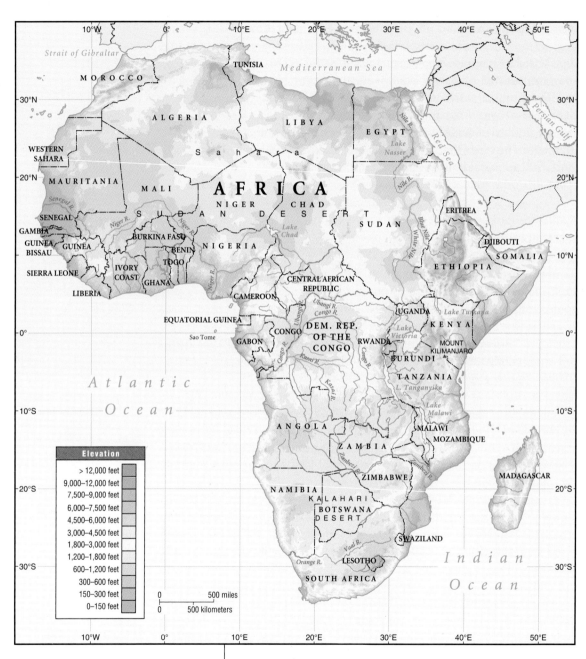

Topographical map of Africa, with color-keyed elevation table

Central Africa is the very large region drained by the Congo River basin flowing west to the Atlantic, and the Zambezi River flowing east to the Indian Ocean. The equator runs through central Africa, and it contains thick forest jungles. Beyond the forested areas are bands of grassy savannas.

Southern Africa is drier than central Africa and less mountainous than East Africa. The Kalahari Desert divides it from its neighbors to the north. Southern Africa contains the nations of Namibia, the Republic of South Africa, Botswana, Zimbabwe, Lesotho, and Swaziland. South Africa is rich in minerals and developed farmland. The Republic of South Africa has industry like Europe and North America along with modern cities and transportation. Southern Africa is home to the Bushmen, a people that roamed the whole continent and parts of Europe in prehistoric times but now live only on the fringes of the Kalahari Desert.

The Lakes and Major Rivers of Africa

In the deep chasms of the Great Rift in the eastern part of central Africa stand three large lakes: Lake Victoria, Lake Tanganyika, and Lake Malawi. The largest of the lakes is Lake Victoria, which is almost an inland sea between Kenya and Uganda. Lake Victoria is only slightly smaller than Lake Superior in North America. The waters of Lake Victoria are the source of the southern branch of the Nile River. Lake Tanganyika drains west into tributaries of the Congo, and Lake Malawi drains south and east into the Zambezi River. These three lakes are high in the mountains, and provide water for the lowlands below.

Four major rivers are an important part of the geography of Africa: the Nile, the Congo, the Niger, and the Zambezi. Although it is not a major river, the Okovango River in Botswana is very interesting, for it never reaches the sea. Instead, it ends in swamps in the Kalahari Desert in South Africa.

The Nile is the longest river in Africa, flowing approximately 4,160 miles from its farthest source until it reaches the Mediterranean Sea. The Nile starts in two places and for many miles has two branches: the southern branch, called the White Nile, and the eastern branch, called the Blue Nile. The **headwaters** of the White Nile are at Lake Victoria in the mountains of Uganda. The Blue Nile begins at Lake Tana, in Ethiopia. The

headwaters: the sources or the upper parts of a river

two branches flow northward until they meet at Khartoum, the capital of Sudan. From Khartoum, the Nile continues its long journey to the Mediterranean Sea.

The Nile provides water for living and farming for those on its banks. For centuries, it deposited the silt that made the Nile River Valley and the Nile Delta in Egypt some of the richest farmland in the world. But in 1970, the government of Egypt built the large Aswan High Dam that keeps the Nile River from flooding and provides a source of electrical power to Egypt. The dam, however, also prevents the river from depositing silt on its banks. As a result, Egypt's farmland is not as fertile as it used to be and parts of the Nile Delta are disappearing into the sea because not enough new soil comes down river to replace the soil the sea washes away.

The Congo is the second longest river in Africa. It begins in the Katanga plateau in southern Africa and flows north to the central part of the Democratic Republic of the Congo. The river then turns south and west and flows to the Atlantic Ocean. The Congo River does not form a delta like the Nile does but runs through a deep canyon to the ocean. The Congo River is the highway of the Democratic Republic of the Congo. From dugouts piloted by village people to modern riverboats and huge commercial transports, the Congo makes movement possible in the dense rain forests of central Africa.

The Niger is Africa's third longest river. It begins in Guinea in West Africa and first flows northeast through Mali. It then turns south and flows through Benin and Nigeria, ending its journey to the sea at a large delta in Nigeria. This river is very important to the people of West Africa who live on its banks. Water from the river allows farming and commercial fishing.

The Zambezi is the fourth of the great rivers of Africa. It flows east from the same high country where the Nile and the Congo begin. It passes through thick forests in Zambia and Mozambique and at last empties into the Indian Ocean.

African Resources and Food

Africa's most valuable resources are fossil fuels (such as oil and coal), precious jewels, and metals, including abundant copper and gold.

Staple African foods—peanuts, sweet potatoes, okra—are so much a part of the **cuisine** of all lands today that their origin is unknown to most. A world without the humble peanut and peanut butter is unthinkable. The sweet potato is used in many recipes. Okra and filé (a spice made from dried and ground sassafras leaves) are the essential ingredients in gumbo. This dish and blackened meat and fish are now popular in all parts of North America.

A Himba (Bantu) boy

The African Peoples and Culture

Scientists say that Africa was the first home to all members of the human race. From Africa our ancestors spread throughout the entire world. Roughly 30,000 years ago, human beings living in Africa were making sophisticated stone tools. These Africans were the Afro-Asians, Bantus, Pygmies, and Bushmen. They are ancestors of the peoples who are found on the continent today.

cuisine: a style of cooking

The Afro-Asians were ancestors of the people who live in northern Africa. They had light brown skin and were of medium height. Some older books refer to these people as "Caucasoid" or "Hamitic," but the term we use today is *Afro-Asian*.

The Bantu peoples have long lived in the sub-Saharan plateau and along the fringe of the forest region. They are tall, large framed, dark ebony in skin color and have wiry, tightly curled black hair. They are now called the Blacks, or Bantu, and inhabit most of the continent today.

The Pygmies are similar to the Bantu except for their small stature—they are only four and one-half feet tall. They have inhabited forest regions around the Congo basin and now are few in number. They have always lived by hunting and planting small plots of vegetables and maize.

A pygmy woman from Uganda

The Bushmen have made their homes in the eastern and southern savannas. They are slight of build, of medium height, and have light, copper-colored skin. Their eyes are almond-shaped, like the eyes of

A Bushman from the Hdza tribe of Tanzania lights a fire as his people has done for centuries.

Oriental peoples, and they have tightly curled dark hair. The Bushmen are a nomadic people, living by hunting and gathering only. Farming is still not their ordinary practice. Their paintings on the rock faces of cliffs and outcroppings of stone are very like the prehistoric paintings in the caves of Europe.

A Religious Family Culture

For all African societies, family and community are of the greatest importance. African peoples have believed it is a man's duty to serve his group. Not only rich ancient cultures like Christian Ethiopia but primitive tribal societies have looked upon the good of the whole community as greater than what benefits individuals alone.

Working together has thus been an important part of African culture. A French traveler to Ethiopia in the 1830s noted that the Ethiopian Africans were proud of their spirit of cooperation: "A man with no fixed obligation to his society was, in their eyes, outside of society," he said.

Most black African peoples have always believed in a supreme being, a creator god who takes special care of human beings, who are his special creation. Because of this belief, it was not difficult for Africans to accept the monotheism of Islam and the Christian Faith. Africans, of course, worshiped other gods — spirits of nature and the elements. When Africans became Muslim or Christian, they often confused these gods with Christian saints or Islamic angels and prayed to them as if they were gods. African religions thus could be a mixture of paganism and Christian or Muslim beliefs.

African religion today still includes all the acts of daily life; every human action is thought to have a religious significance. Ceremony and ritual mark the great events of life: birth, marriage, successes and failures, and death. People offer things precious to the worshiper or sacred to a spirit to recognize the important event or the on-going life of the family. Special gifts are traditionally given to each god, including animal sacrifice and (at one time) human sacrifice. Whiskey and corn meal are the traditional gifts people offer to the ancestors of the family.

Africa's Earliest Civilizations

Around 5500 B.C., the climate of the Sahara was wet and cool. Its grasslands were lush, and rivers ran across them southward into the Niger and eastward toward the Nile. (The dry riverbeds can still be seen in the desert.) Fish and game were plentiful, and generations of hunters and herdsmen lived comfortable lives. Then around 3000 to 2500 B.C. the climate changed. The rains stopped. The rivers dried up. The forests and grasses died.

The long disaster of the drying up of the Sahara helps explain the history of Africa after 2000 B.C. The peoples who lived in the once-bountiful Sahara migrated in three directions. Some went north to the coasts of the Mediterranean; some went east to the fertile valley of the Nile; and some went south into the heart of the continent.

In the Nile River Valley, the high civilization of Egypt emerged. South of the Sahara Desert, people were cut off from the ideas of the peoples of the Mediterranean. They had to cope with heat, poor soil, dense jungles, and barren mountain slopes. The deep and broad rivers were full of **predators** and **parasites**. Everywhere, **ravenous** insects brought disease with their stings and bites.

predator: an animal (such as lions and tigers) that hunts or preys on other animals
parasite: an animal or plant that lives on or in another animal or plant, from which it gets its food. (A leech is a parasite for other animals; mistletoe is a parasite that attaches to oak trees.)
ravenous: very hungry

A camel caravan crossing the Sahara

The Kingdoms of the Nile

Egypt was the first civilization in Africa, and it may have influenced two other kingdoms that grew up along the Nile River—the kingdoms of Kush and Axum. These kingdoms lay to the south of Egypt and included the lands of the modern states of Ethiopia, Sudan, and Eritrea.

Around 750 B.C., the princes of Kush made their capital at Napata, near the upper reaches of the Nile, and built a city influenced by Egyptian building styles. Greek writers referred to Kush as *Aethiopia* (Land of the Fire-Eyes), and called the Kushites, *Ethiopes*; but Kush lay to the north of what is today the nation of Ethiopia.

For a thousand years, the Kushites waged constant war with the Egyptians. Because of this contact with Egypt, the Kushites developed a civilization that looked Egyptian but had its own unique character. The Kushites, for instance, worshiped the Egyptian god Amun just as the pharaoh's court did; but the Kushites did not worship their king as a god as the Egyptians did the pharaoh.

Later, as the Sahara grew ever more dry and the pastures around Napata dried up, the Kushites shifted their capital farther south to Meroe, and there built palaces and stone cities. In Meroe, the kings built pyramids that were not as grand as the pyramids of Egypt, but had a remarkable style and dignity. Iron was abundant around Meroe, and the kings of Kush made great use of the technology of iron working. The capital grew into a great metalworking center. Heaps of iron waste may still be seen in the ruins. The kings of Kush conquered their old foes, the pharaohs, in the 8th century and for a brief time ruled both Upper and Lower Egypt.

The Kushites managed to tame the African elephant and used elephants in war. In their art, they replaced pictures of Egyptian gods with those of lions and elephants. The kingdom of Kush loved new things and sent **emissaries** to all the lands of the Mediterranean. Kushite ships sailed from ports on the Red Sea as far as India. The Acts of the Apostles (Acts 8:26–40) in the Bible tells of how the deacon Philip met an official of the queen of Meroe on the road from Jerusalem and told him the Gospel of the Lord Jesus. The Bible calls the official an Ethiopian.

emissary: a person who is sent on an errand or mission

The largest site of Kush civilization burial pyramids lies north of Khartoum, along the Nile River in ancient Meroe, Sudan.

The Kingdom of Nubia

Around A.D. 300, after suffering from invasions by wild Nubian tribes and the kings of Axum, both the kingdom of Kush and the Kushite civilization seem to have faded. No one knows how Kush came to an end. The last king of the Kushites was buried in a tiny pyramid, a sad imitation of the tombs his ancestors had built. His name was Malequerabar. That is all that we know of him.

Two hundred years later, in the 500s, Nubian invaders in the Kushite towns produced their own culture, Christian Nubia. In the 300s or 400s, monks from a region of Egypt called the Thebaid brought the Christian Faith to Nubia, and a Church was established there that had many of the same rituals as the Church in Egypt. In the 6th century, this Church adopted a heresy called "Monophysite." The Monophysites taught that Christ is only truly God, not man. In Egypt, the Monophysite Church is called Coptic, after the ancient language used in its liturgy.

In the 7th century, the Church in Nubia was cut off from the rest of the Christian world by the Muslim conquest of Egypt. For centuries thereafter, Nubia's Christian kings and bishops knew nothing of the developments of the Christian world of

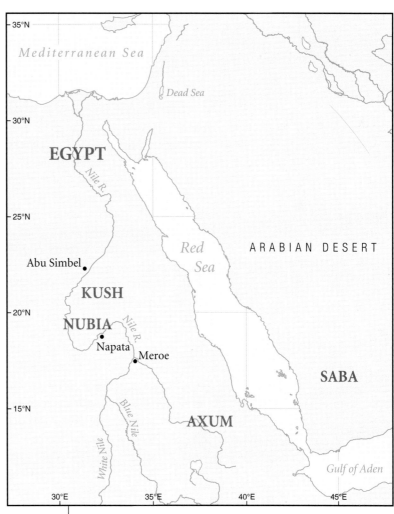

The locations of Kush, Nubia, and Axum

Europe or Constantinople. Believing the rest of the world had fallen to the Muslims, they thought they alone were left to keep the Christian Faith alive. Nubian kings made constant war on the Muslim governors of Upper Egypt and declared themselves the protectors of Egypt's Coptic Christians.

Finally, the Muslims of Egypt under the sultan, Saladin, sent troops south to stamp out the Nubian nuisance. In 1276, the Muslims overcame the first of the three Nubian kingdoms, and the middle kingdom fell a century later. The last of the Nubian Christian kingdoms fell to Muslim **scimitars** in the early 1400s. For nine hundred years, the Nubians of old Kush had held out against the Muslim armies.

scimitar: A curved sword

Axum

The kingdom of Axum arose to the south and east of Kush, in the mountains of Ethiopia. There is an Ethiopian legend that tells a strange legend about these people. The legend relates that the queen of Sheba, mentioned in the Bible, went up to Jerusalem to judge the reputation of Israel's King Solomon for wisdom (1 Kings 10:1–13). There, Solomon fell in love with her, and she bore him a son whose name was Menelik.

The queen of Sheba visits King Solomon of Israel.

The legend says that Menelik's relatives harassed him as he grew up, and he was forced to flee Sheba with the treasures that had belonged to his mother and father. He led his band of warriors into the mountains of Ethiopia, where he founded a kingdom and worshiped God like the Israelites did. Among the treasures Menelik took with him was Israel's sacred Ark of the Covenant. Solomon's Israelite son, says the legend, sent the ark to his half-brother, Menelik, to keep it safe. The legend says this Menelik became the founder of Ethiopia's line of kings. This royal line ruled Ethiopia into the 20th century. Its last emperor was Haile Selassie (who reigned from 1930 to 1974).

This legend of the queen of Sheba and her son, Menelik, is based on real history. "Sheba" is the land of the Sabaeans, a people who lived on the southern coast of Arabia. The Sabaeans set up trading posts on the African coast near their homeland. About 500 years before Christ, a number of Sabaean settlements on the African coast near the mouth of the Red Sea combined with the local peoples to develop a culture all their own. These peoples moved inland into the sparsely settled mountains of Ethiopia and built a city there, safe from Red Sea pirates and wandering nomadic tribes. By A.D. 200, the city was called Axum, and the people of the mountains that it commanded were called Amharic.

The first Christian missionary to reach Axum was St. Frumentius — St. Athanasius of Alexandria, the great defender of the Trinity, had ordained Frumentius bishop of Axum around the year 330. In the 500s, a Monophysite priest from Alexandria named Julian was sent by the Byzantine empress Theodora (Justinian's wife) to Nubia and Axum to convert them to his heresy. Since then, the Church in Ethiopia has been Monophysite. In his extraordinary report to Constantinople, Julian said that the Christian king of Axum was dressed in white linen, adorned with gold and pearls and that his throne was a gilded chariot drawn by elephants. Julian claimed that Greek was the language of the Amharic court!

A medieval Ethiopian icon of Christ

Whether the court spoke Greek or not, Ethiopia had its own literature written in Ge'ez, a **literary language** spoken by the nobles and upper classes of Axum. Ethiopia even had its own translation of the Scriptures into Ge'ez.

Axum also had unique architecture. In the 12th century, Axum's king, Lalibela, built some of the most unusual structures in the world. They were 10 churches chiseled out of the rock of the hills around his capital. Workers **excavated** down into the rock, hewing out a large, rectangular pit. In the center of this pit sits the church, sculpted out of a single rock. The roof of the church is level with the ground outside the pit. Within the churches artisans carved out huge halls with pillars and arches,

literary language: a form of a language that is more elegant than everyday speech

excavate: to make hollow by digging; to dig out

Bet Giyorgis church, one of Lalibela's rock-hewn churches

The Legend of Prester John

During the late Middle Ages in Europe, a legend grew up of a great Christian kingdom on the other side of Muslim-controlled lands from Europe. A semi-magical king named Prester John, who, it seems, could live forever, ruled this mythical kingdom. Prester John, it was said, would wage war against the Muslims until the Christian crusaders of the West joined forces with him. Then, together, they could eliminate the Muslims.

In the 1400s, Portuguese explorers ventured into the mountains of East Africa in search of Prester John. They did not find the fabled king but discovered an Ethiopia that was in many ways like the kingdoms of medieval Europe! The Portuguese found proud and independent nobles bound by oaths of loyalty to their king, along with lesser nobles and lords below them, and landless peasants laboring for all. Ethiopia had

monks, abbots, and bishops with their parish clergy worshiping as Christians, but in strange and mysterious liturgies and in an ancient sacred language.

Map of Prester John's kingdom

false windows and hidden rooms, just as if these had been erected above ground.

As with Nubia, the Muslim conquests cut Axum off from the rest of the Christian world. By the 1200s, Muslims and primitive pagan tribes surrounded the mountain kingdom, and Christian travelers from the mountains were forbidden to use ports on the Red Sea coast.

The Sudanic Civilization

Fighting to survive in the hostile climates and terrain of the continent, African societies came up with different ways of staying alive and living joyfully. Like the Ethiopians, Africans south of the Sahara Desert (the area called "Sudan" by the Arabs) developed a unique culture we call the Sudanic civilization. Four Sudanic kingdoms grew almost into empires between A.D. 700 and 1800. They were: Ghana (not the modern country with that name),

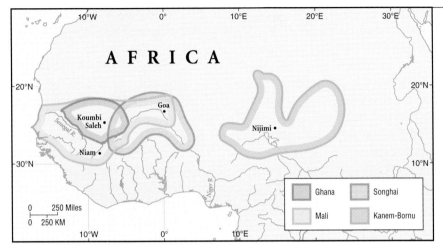

Map of West African kingdoms—Ghana, Mali, Songhai, and Kanem-Bornu

divination: the practice of trying to discover future events or hidden knowledge by means of magic

700–1200; Mali (again, not the modern country), 1200–1500; Songhai, 1350–1600; and Kanem-Bornu, 800–1800.

The Sudanic societies were headed by a king of a tribe, which might be quite small or large. Because the king was thought to be divine, he was kept from contact with the rest of the tribe. It was thought that the king needed to keep healthy to insure good weather and crops. The office of king was not passed down in families, from father to son. Instead, the king was the head priest, and the priestly class chose the king by election or magical **divination**.

Because Sudanic societies thought their king was a divine being, he ruled his people with absolute power. His subjects provided him with wives, drink, food, crafts, and items for trade. He also controlled all trade.

Burial of a Sudanic King

An African mask made by the Ndebele tribe in Zimbabwe

Kings in Sudanic cultures were not allowed to die a natural death, for the people thought that if a king died a natural death, the fertility of the land would also die. Poisoning or ritual suffocation were used to hasten death when a king's time to die was near. The king would be buried with his favorite furniture, food, and the bodies of his servants and aides, their throats slit to follow him in death.

This Sudanic order of society influenced all the peoples of West and central Africa. It became the model for all the Bantu kingdoms of central and southern Africa.

The wealth and power of the kingdoms of the Sudan were built on gold. In ancient times, the Africans had traded gold with the Phoenicians and the Carthaginians, and when the Arabs conquered North Africa in the 7th century, this trade continued. In particular, the Sudan Africans traded gold for salt, which was priceless to the Africans. On trains of camels, the Arabs carried tons of salt to the south and brought home gold beyond their dreams. Salt was not only useful to make foods **savory**, but it was essential for health among peoples who lost so much water through heavy perspiration in the intense heat.

savory: having a pleasing taste or smell

Another "product" that was not so savory was slaves. The great kingdoms of the Sudan conquered their neighbors to accumulate the gold and slaves that the traders demanded for their salt. Empires rose and fell as the price of salt and slaves went up or down.

Along with Arab merchants came Muslim teachers who converted the pagan tribes of the Sudan to Islam. The cities that grew up as trading centers and royal capitals in the Sudan became centers of Islamic learning. One such Islamic center, Timbuktu, grew world famous.

The Djinguereber Mosque dates from the early 14th century; Timbuktu, Mali

The empires of the Sudan also inspired the kingdoms on the forested western coasts of Africa to expand their borders and conquer their neighbors. The kings of Benin and Ashanti resisted Islam but waged wars to capture slaves to sell to the Muslim lands in North Africa. By the 1600s, the coastal kingdoms of West Africa were ready to trade with Europeans for gold and slaves, just as they had been doing with their Muslim neighbors.

The Slave Trade

In the 17th century, European colonists in the Americas demanded more and more slaves to work on their farms and plantations. To obtain slaves, European traders turned to western Africa. Many African chiefs collected slaves from their neighbors inland, and traded them to **slavers** on the coast in exchange for guns and other goods. Tribesmen convicted of a crime or who had debts (or whose family had debts) or whose chief did

slaver: one who makes other persons slaves

The Arab Empire in Africa

It took less than 100 years for the Arab Muslims to dominate northern Africa after they conquered Egypt in 639. The Muslim Arabs, however, did not so much conquer northern Africa as convert it. The Muslim religion rapidly replaced the Christian Faith. In fact, the Berber peoples of North Africa seemed to welcome the Arabs as liberators from the Christian Byzantine Romans who had ruled them.

As a consequence of the Arab conquests in the late 600s and early 700s, all of northern Africa became part of the larger Muslim civilization. In time, Berber tribesmen carried the Muslim faith across the Sahara to the Sudan. But the Muslim faith carried to central Africa was not a strictly Arab faith because it had been heavily influenced by the culture of the Roman and Greek Christians.

Map of Arab kingdoms and Arab influence in Africa

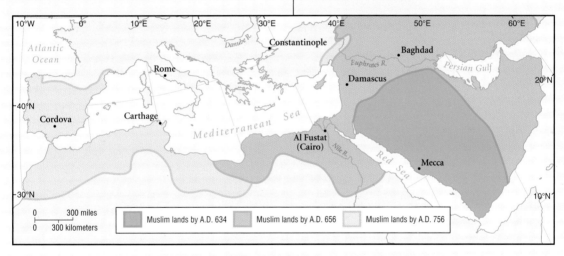

not like them, could be sold as slaves. When slaves became more valuable than gold, African kings on the coast made war on weaker neighbors to capture whole villages or peoples to sell to the slavers. The slaving wars disrupted Sudanic life and tribal allegiances for centuries.

The slave trade affected both eastern and western Africa. Arab slavers on the east coasts set up slave-trading towns from Somalia to Mozambique. But the coming of the Europeans in the 1400s had the most destructive effect on African society, since the new plantations of Brazil and the Caribbean Islands seemed to have an endless appetite for new slave labor. The Portuguese, who had first explored the African coasts, stepped in to control the new trade.

Recently purchased African slaves are transported to a European ship.

It is impossible to describe the horror of African slavery. Usually betrayed by a rival tribe, people were taken from their families and cultures, never to see them again. Then they were loaded aboard ships with too little air and space. If they survived the long trip across the ocean (and many did not), most slaves became agricultural workers with no rights, no pay, and no chance for improvement. Access to slaving areas was restricted, for it was feared that if Europeans not involved in the slave trade were to see it, it would be stopped.

The effects of the slave trade varied from place to place in Africa. Western Africa, with a large population, did not suffer terribly from the loss of people. But slaving damaged African morality, for it weakened family ties and weakened communities. In central and East Africa the loss of population to slaving was devastating. Slaving took its toll on those left behind. Villages starved because their young men and women were no longer there to work the fields.

The Kingdom of Kongo

In 1482, the Portuguese adventurer Diogo Cão, sailing down the west coast of Africa, became the first European to make contact with the kingdom of Kongo — the largest kingdom in central Africa. Portuguese interest in Kongo grew rapidly. And the kings and nobles of Kongo found everything European fascinating. They entered into trade with the Portuguese for European cloth, tools, furniture, and wine. They offered high wages to Portuguese carpenters and masons to come and build new palaces and cities for the African kingdom. They also accepted the Catholic Faith. Nzinga a Nkuwu, the supreme king (or *manikongo*), became Catholic and was baptized as João (Hongo) II, in honor of the king of Portugal, King João I.

Kongo thus became a Christian kingdom, and in the early 16th century, the grandson of the Manikongo João II, Henrique, became the first black African bishop in the Catholic Church. The nobles followed their king's lead and accepted the Faith. Many of the Bakongo people also were baptized, and a flourishing church seemed to be growing in the Congo River basin. Portuguese missionaries and Congolese converts set out into the interior of Kongo to preach the Gospel among the people there.

But the Portuguese greed for gold and slaves worked steadily against the efforts of the Portuguese government and the Catholic bishops to make Kongo into a Christian kingdom. Through the 1500s, the slave trade grew, and local African warlords and magistrates sold their people or made war on their neighbors to collect enough slaves for sale.

Seeing the bad effects slaving had on his people, the manikongo tried to limit the effects of the slave trade on his subjects. But he lost control of his provinces and local governments, and the Kongo was being drained of its manpower by slavers. In letters to the king of Portugal, the manikongo complained that the Portuguese had broken their word to his people. Committed as they were to the common good, Africans could not understand this disregard of honor.

After two centuries of Portuguese influence, Kongo was a Europeanized African kingdom, but the manikongo had little or no control of his provinces. Kongo's traditional morality was badly damaged, and its new Christian Faith had been distorted.

The manikongo, Don Alvaro, grants an audience to foreigners, ca 1650.

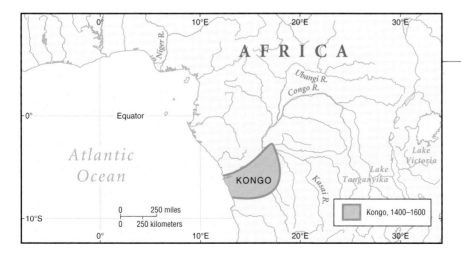

Map of the Kingdom of Kongo

African sculpture

The desperate manikongo at last decided to drive the greedy and treacherous Portuguese slave traders and mercenary soldiers from his land. The king tried to gather the Kongo army from all the provinces, but fewer than half of the army answered the call. In 1665, in the Battle of Mbwila, Kongo was defeated by the Portuguese and the head of the manikongo was cut off. It was displayed in the chapel on the bay of Luanda, where the explorer Diego Cão had first landed in Kongo.

A Warrior Queen

In the 1620s, Dona Anna de Souza Nzinga became a brilliant, warrior queen in the Kongo. She was the daughter of the king of Ndongo, a kingdom subject to Kongo. When her brother murdered her son, the heir to the throne, and made himself king, Dona Anna fled to the bush and hid. When her brother found that he could not deal with the Portuguese, he called her back and made her his deputy to negotiate with the Europeans. Because of her efforts, the Portuguese made a peace treaty with Ndongo. At this time, Dona Anna accepted baptism.

Later, when the Portuguese betrayed their treaty with Ndongo, Dona Anna found allies among the Jaga, a fierce and less civilized people, and killed her brother to avenge her son. She raised a huge army of followers made up of her Jaga allies, her own countrymen, and hundreds of escaped slaves and displaced people.

Dona Anna kept a traditional-style royal court that moved with her and her army from camp to camp. Against African custom, she dressed like a man. Though throughout all these years she kept a priest at her side and heard Mass daily, her actions were in conflict with her faith. For nine years she fought the Portuguese until she was finally defeated in 1656. She remained queen of Ndongo until her death in 1663. Her sister, Dona Barbara, became queen after Dona Anna's death and made peace with the Europeans.

The Age of Colonialism

colonialism: the control of a region by a more powerful foreign nation

As we have seen, the slave trade disrupted traditional African societies with their family-centered spirit of cooperation. This disruption left the continent open to conquest by the European powers in the 19th century. European **colonialism** was the result.

19th century European possessions in Africa

By the end of the 19th century, almost all of the African continent was divided up into colonies controlled by one or other of the European powers. European governments and companies seized the wealth of African lands and often oppressed the people, but they brought stability, peace, and a degree of civilization to Africa as well. The many different nations of Africa did not become independent until after the Second World War. Traditional African social structures and royal lines, however, no longer exist.

A Maasai woman of Kenya, wearing traditional African clothing, makes a traditional necklace.

Africa and the World

The large numbers of slave workers who came from Africa to the Americas greatly affected life in the New World. Portuguese Brazil, along with islands in the Caribbean settled by the French, Spanish, and British, have large African populations and are extensions of African culture into the New World. African immigrants have influenced life in the United States more than the Native Americans have. Elements of African culture can be seen throughout Spanish America as well. African **social mores**

social mores: the customs or practices of a society

and African religion have continued in African American communities throughout the New World.

European society both in the Americas and Europe has taken on characteristics of African musical forms and dance, as well its designs and images. For instance, early 20th century European artists imitated West African sculptures and paintings of the human form. Popular music in the United States, Europe, and in much of the world is now a blend of European melodies and African rhythms and harmonies. Bright colors in geometric patterns are so familiar in the decorative arts that it is almost forgotten that they came from Africa.

Africa's influence on art and music has been very important to the development of the culture of the world in which we live. African culture has truly become a world culture.

Chapter 13 Review

Let's Remember   Please write your answers in complete sentences.
1. Where does the Nile River originate?
2. What was the first civilization in Africa?
3. Name the four populations that make up Africa.
4. What is Timbuktu?
5. Who was Prester John?

Let's Consider   For silent thinking and a short essay, or for thinking in a group with classroom discussion:
1. Why did the Sahara become a desert?
2. Why did Kush disappear?
3. What were the effects of the slave trade upon African life.

Things to Do

1. On a blank map of Africa, indicate the regions of Africa: North Africa, the Sahara, West Africa, East Africa, central Africa, southern Africa.

2. On a blank map of Africa, draw and label the following rivers: the Nile, the Congo, the Niger, and the Zambezi. Show where Lake Victoria is.

Let's Eat!

Recipe for African peanut soup: In a large pot, place the following: 2 tablespoons oil, 1 onion and 1 green pepper (chopped), 2 cloves garlic (pressed). Sauté until brown. Add 1 can of crushed tomatoes and 4 cans chicken broth. Bring to a boil and add ½ cup uncooked rice and ¼ teaspoon pepper. Simmer for ½ hour. Add ½ cup peanut butter. Stir until smooth and serve. Sprinkle with crushed peanuts on top.

Russia: The "Third Rome"

Atheism, **Communism**, a brutal government that robbed its people of their rights—these are the ideas that often come to people's minds when they think of Russia. This is not surprising, since, for seventy-four years, from 1917 to 1991, the Russians were ruled by an atheist, Communist government called the Union of Soviet Socialist Republics. This government tried to eliminate all religion in Russia and supported violent Communist revolutions throughout the world.

It is unfortunate that many think of Russia in this way, for the Russian people have a long, heroic, and exciting history. Their ancient culture is deeply Christian, with unique and beautiful art and architecture. Russia has given the world some of its greatest writers, and the music of her composers is hauntingly beautiful. Greatest of all, however, are the Russian people, who through many hardships and sufferings have preserved their great civilization through the centuries.

atheism: the belief that God does not exist
Communism: the ideal of a political party in Russia and around the world which held that there should be no private property but that all property should be owned together by the people; Communism is also opposed to religion

The Geography of Russia

The history of Russia has been shaped by her geography. Russia is the largest country on the earth, extending from Eastern Europe, across the cold wastes of Siberia, to the Pacific coasts of Asia. Russia has vast stores of natural resources and a diverse population made up of more than 200 nationalities speaking many languages.

However, nature and geography have been harsh on Russia. More than 80 percent of the

St. Basil's Cathedral in Moscow

Russia today, along with the countries that were once under Russian control

country lies north of the latitude marking the U.S.-Canadian border. This means that most of Russia is very cold in the winter. Indeed, no protective mountain ranges stop the freezing arctic winds from coming down over a huge rolling plain stretching from the Baltic Sea in the north to the shores of the Black Sea thousands of miles to the south. This plain has only one mountain range, the Ural Mountains, which are the dividing line of Europe and Asia. Much farther to the south, in eastern Russia, rise the Caucasus Mountains.

The country falls into two regions. The first, European Russia, in Eastern Europe, is the original Russian homeland. The second is Asian Russia, which became part of the Russian Empire in the 16th and 17th centuries. The vast expanse of northern Russian Asia is called Siberia.

Asian Russia includes Siberia in the north and the Turkish steppes to the south. It is sparsely populated and has harsh weather conditions. It is a frozen waste for most of the year. The rivers that run north are frozen except for a brief summer thaw, and the plains and low mountains of Asian Russia can only be reached by air. Siberia contains the world's larg-

> 12,000 feet		6,000–7,500 feet		1,800–3,000 feet		300–600 feet	
9,000–12,000 feet		4,500–6,000 feet		1,200–1,800 feet		150–300 feet	
7,500–9,000 feet		3,000–4,500 feet		600–1,200 feet		0–150 feet	

Topographical map of Russia, with color-keyed elevation scale

est and deepest freshwater lake, Lake Baykal. The southern steppe contains two **landlocked** seas, the large Caspian Sea (which is fed by the Volga River) and the Aral Sea. The Aral Sea is much smaller than it once was because, in the 20th century, the Soviet government used the waters from the rivers that fed the sea for irrigation. The Aral Sea is no longer a part of Russia but of the independent Republic of Kazakhstan. The Caspian Sea is today surrounded by five countries: Russia, Kazakhstan, Turkmenistan, Iran, and Azerbaijan.

landlocked: completely enclosed by land; having land on all sides

Early Russian History

In the first centuries of the Russian nation, a huge forest covered all the northern half of the European Russian plain. The Slavs, a people living in southern Europe near the Carpathian Mountains, entered this forest,

The rivers of Russia with the traditional cities of Kiev, Novgorod, Smolensk, and Moscow

cleared away trees, and planted fields in the rich soil. The snowy winters were long and harsh, but the summers gave bountiful crops. The southern half of the land, the Russian steppe, was open grassland, warm and inviting. Nevertheless, the Slavs feared the steppe, because wave after wave of barbarian enemies came across it out of Asia. There was no way on the open plain for people to defend themselves against these enemies.

Over the centuries, the Russian people have had to face wave after wave of invasion. They have tried to defend themselves first against the Huns, then the Khazars, and then the Mongols, who killed and enslaved the hardy settlers. The Slavs were raided and taken into captivity so often that their name, Slav (which in the Slavic language meant "the glorious people"), became the word "slave" in western Europe.

Though it is open to invasions, Russia has one great geographical advantage: a network of easily traveled rivers. The rivers Dniester (NYEHSTER) and Dnieper (NYEPPER), the Don and the Volga, flow south into the Black Sea and the landlocked Caspian Sea. The Vistula, the Neva, and the Dvina all flow north into the North Sea and the Baltic

Sea. All these rivers begin near each other in the central **watershed** of European Russia. A traveler could go from the north up one river and then, after a simple **portage** across land, float down another river to the Black or Caspian Sea.

The Dvina and Dnieper Rivers became part of the trade route the Vikings followed to Constantinople, while the Volga River, flowing into the Caspian Sea, brought the northerners down to Baghdad. In the ninth century, a Viking, named Rurik, and his warriors sailed down the rivers of Russia and carved out a kingdom in northern Russia, called Novgorod. Rurik's warriors were called the *Rus* (meaning "red-haired) and gave their name to the people they ruled. One of Rurik's companions, a man named Oleg, moved south to the Dnieper River, on whose banks he founded the settlement of Kiev among the Slavs. Kiev was to become one of the greatest cities of medieval Russia.

> **watershed:** a region where rivers rise
>
> **portage:** a route for carrying boats overland between bodies of water

The "Constantine" of Russia

In the 800s, when two Greek brothers, St. Cyril and St. Methodius, were sent as missionaries to the Slavs who lived in Moravia, a land west of Russia. The brothers developed a written alphabet based on Greek, and using this, they translated the Scriptures and liturgical books into the Slavic language. The alphabet created by St. Cyril and St. Methodius later became the Russian alphabet.

In time, the Vikings were absorbed into the Slavic people they ruled, and the heirs of Rurik took on Slavic names. Then in the late 10th century, Prince Vladimir united all the kingdoms of the Rus under his power and made Kiev his capital. Though a pagan, Vladimir began thinking that he wanted to adopt a new religion for his people. He looked into Islam and Judaism, and rejected them. He then considered the Christian Faith, but was not impressed by practices of the Catholic Church in western Europe. Vladimir sent some emissaries to Constantinople to investigate the Church in the Byzantine Empire. So enchanted were the emissaries by the splendor of the city, the cathedral of Hagia Sophia, and the richness of the liturgy, that they ran out of words to describe it. "We knew not whether we were in heaven or on Earth," they said.

So it was that Vladimir decided that he would accept missionaries from Constantinople. In 988, he sent an army to invade Kherson, a city in the northern part of the Byzantine Empire. After taking Kherson, he sent a marriage proposal (under threat of attack) to Anna, the sister of

Icon of the Virgin Mary with hands raised in prayer in the Orthodox cathedral of St. Sophia, Kiev, Ukraine

Towers of Trinity Monastery of St. Sergius of Radonezh, founded in 1345 by St. Sergius. The Trinity Monastery has been a center of Russian Orthodoxy for hundreds of years.

the Byzantine emperor, Basil II. Basil said his sister could not marry a non-Christian, but Vladimir replied that he had decided to convert. In 988, Vladimir was baptized in Kherson, and then withdrew his troops from the city. He married Anna, and upon his return home, gave up his pagan wives. He then worked for the conversion of his kingdom to the Christian Faith. Today we remember this prince as St. Vladimir. In Russia he is called "Equal to the Apostles" for bringing the Christian Church to Russia.

Because Russia received the Christian Faith from Constantinople, Byzantine culture greatly influenced Russian politics and culture. The rituals surrounding the Byzantine emperor and imperial government were models for the Russian government for centuries. Culturally, the style of icon painting, liturgical music, church mosaics, and church architecture that developed in Russia imitated Byzantine arts.

Humility and poverty, imitating the life of Christ, and Jesus' mercy and forgiveness were Russian Christian ideals — just as they were for Christians everywhere. Russian monks sought out remote places for their hermitages and communities. Like many Russian peasants and pioneers, the monks went deeper into the forests, searching out uninhabited land farther and farther from the cities. In the 1200s St. Sergius of Radonezh founded the Holy Trinity monastery north of Moscow. Holy Trinity-St. Sergius monastery became the central community of Russian monasticism.

Russia under the Golden Horde

In the year 1223, an event occurred that changed Russia's history forever. In a battle fought on the Kalka River, Mongols from central Asia destroyed the Russian army. After the battle, the Mongols placed the

Moscow mural depicting St. Sergius blessing Grand Duke Dmitri Donskoi and his army on their way to do battle with the Mongols at Kouliobo

captured Russian princes under a heavy wooden platform on which the Mongol warriors held a victory feast, crushing the men to death.

In 1237, the Mongols returned under Batu Khan, who forced all Russia to pay tribute to him. From the "Golden Horde" (his encampment on the steppe), Batu led raids against the Russian people, whom he reduced to poverty. He then swept toward western Europe, defeated the Poles and Hungarians, and reached the Adriatic Sea. But then Batu withdrew suddenly, and the West was spared.

For two centuries after Batu, Mongol generals from the Golden Horde continued to **ravage** Russia and force Russians to pay crushing tribute. Russian slaves were regularly shipped down the rivers to the markets of Persia or marched into the interior of Asia and China. Slavers tried to hide the nationality of Russian slaves, claiming that they were "Lithuanians," or "Swedes," because the Russians had a reputation for making trouble.

ravage: to damage greatly or destroy

In 1378, the Grand Prince Dmitri of Muscovy (the name of the region around the city of Moscow), refused to pay the tribute to the Mongol **khan.** Dmitri then defeated a small Mongol army. The Mongols rode north to put down this upstart Russian; but unexpectedly, at the **juncture** of the Don and Nepryavda Rivers, Dmitri, leading a smaller Russian force, **routed** the Mongols. Because of this victory, he became known as Dmitri Donskoi — (Dmitri "of the Don.") From that time on, the princes of Moscow became the leaders of the resistance to Mongol oppression. Over the next one hundred years, the Mongols grew weaker because of wars among themselves, while the Muscovites defeated them in a series of battles and finally broke their power. Muscovy became the center of Russian life, and the chief bishop of the Russian Orthodox Church moved to Moscow.

khan: a title meaning "ruler"
juncture: the place where two things join
rout: to completely defeat

Mongol control changed Russia in many ways. Before the Mongol conquest, the Russian people had elected town governments, and the common farmer was not a serf but a free property owner. Under the Mongols, however, many Russian farmers became serfs, and Russian rulers began imitating the harsh ways of the Mongol overlords. Russia was cut off from Constantinople and from western Europe as well. Russians had to devote all their resources to defense and paying tribute money to the Mongols.

despotic: describing an absolute ruler who does what he likes; tyrannical
boyar: a landowning aristocrat of Russia
contemporary: someone who lives at the same time as another person

To escape the oppression of their own **despotic** local lords, the **boyars**, peasants fled their homes with their families and settled in lands farther north. There, in the dense forests, they could escape Mongol raids or the boyars' taxes. Peasants also moved into the broad river valleys of the Dnieper and Volga. The Russian Empire grew by accident as its people sought the liberty of the wilderness. These frontiersmen, who refused the rule or authority of the landed aristocrats, were called Cossacks. Soon large communities of Cossacks were found along the Dnieper River in the heart of Ukraine, and on the eastern and southern borders of the kingdom. Cossacks spread into the steppe with their horse herds, or turned the forests into farmland.

Ivan the Great

Ivan III, the Great

The Muscovite prince most responsible for the success of Moscow was Prince Ivan III, called Ivan the Great. Ivan became prince of Moscow in 1462 and so was a **contemporary** of Italy's Michelangelo and Leonardo da Vinci. He added the independent republic of Novgorod to Moscow's realm and conquered Tver to the northwest of Moscow. Ivan added the Kievan princedoms of Chernigov and Smolensk to his realm.

When Ivan died in 1505, he had all of the lands of Russia under his control. His nation was one people with a common language. They were united by the Orthodox Christian religion and by their resistance to Mongol oppression. With all of the Russians united under the Moscow prince, internal fighting ceased, and Russia began to see itself as a united nation.

Ivan set out to make sure that Muscovy was respected by other nations. He was unaware of developments in the West but knew how to impress the East. In 1475, he married Sophia Paleologos, niece of Constantine XI, last emperor of Constantinople. Ivan declared that this marriage made him the rightful heir of the Eastern Roman Empire. He added the imperial double-headed eagle to his family crest and took for him-

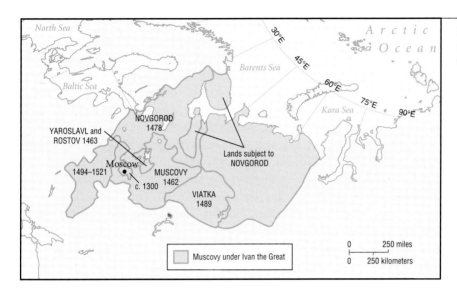

Muscovy's expansion under Tsar Ivan the Great

self the two titles of the Byzantine emperors: **tsar** (or czar, a form of Caesar) and **autocrat**.

Ivan instituted a court ceremony that imitated the pomp of Byzantine rituals. Imitating Byzantium, Ivan ordered three huge cathedrals built to adorn the **Kremlin**, his Moscow fortress-palace. Ivan's churches were impressive examples of medieval Russian architecture. The churches of the Assumption, the Archangel, and the Annunciation still stand in the modern Kremlin, a memorial to Ivan and the creation of the Russian nation.

tsar: the title of Russia's ruler, a form of Caesar
autocrat: a single ruler who has unlimited power
Kremlin: the tsar's fortress-palace in Moscow

The Kremlin in Moscow

Russian churchmen did their part to bring glory to Ivan the Great and Moscow when they began calling Moscow the "Third Rome." The Orthodox Church in Russia had followed the Orthodox Church of Constantinople into schism with the pope and the Catholic Church. The "First Rome" was thus Rome in Italy, which Russian churchmen said had fallen into heresy. The "Second Rome" was Constantinople, which had fallen to the Turks because of its sins. When Ivan became tsar, said the Russian churchmen, the world authority of Rome passed to Moscow, the "Third Rome." According to these Russian churchmen, Moscow was thus not only the center of Russia, but Russia was the leader of the world, and the Russian Orthodox Church the chief church of all Christendom.

The Russian Orthodox Church was divided, however. The Christian ideals of poverty and humility contrasted with the power of the Russian rulers and the wealth of the Russian bishops. Some churchmen argued that the Church must be wealthy in order to fulfill its obligations of charity and to attract men of quality to the priesthood. Others called for a return to the contemplative and **ascetic** life of the old monks and hermits, and a complete separation of church and state. This religious argument affected the whole of the Russian people. What Russia was becoming (powerful and worldly) seemed to betray what Russia had always been (humble and ascetic).

> **ascetic:** practicing self-denial — fasting and other penance — to achieve holiness

Ivan the Terrible

Ivan the Great's grandson, Ivan IV, was only in his late teens in 1530, when he came to the throne. Knowing that his father had been murdered by the boyars and that his mother's family had kept him prisoner in his boyhood, the young tsar set out to make the boyars completely powerless. To do this, he created a new class of **gentry** to weaken the boyars. These new gentry were made up of men who had distinguished themselves in battle. Ivan gave them great estates and peasants — but he told them that they had to furnish the tsar with soldiers and officers as needed and that their lands could be taken away whenever the tsar wished. Ivan also had a dreaded army of landless fanatics, the *oprichniks* (the "set-apart men"), who served him alone. Ivan used the *oprichniks* to terrorize the boyars and destroy those who spoke out against the tsar. After eight years of *oprichnik* terror, the boyars lost their political power. The Russian aristocracy became the servants of the throne.

> **gentry:** a member of the upper class

Tsar Ivan became fascinated with the English and sent a marriage proposal to Queen Elizabeth I. She refused, and he then tried to arrange a marriage with an English noblewoman. He brought English workmen and engineers to Russia to start factories and workshops in Moscow. He invited Germans from the Protestant states of Prussia and Brandenburg to settle along the Volga River in lands taken from the Mongols. Soon, the Russians were calling all foreigners "Germans."

Tragically, Ivan went violently insane in his later years. He carried on a 20-year war with Sweden and Poland that nearly bankrupted the treasury and cost thousands of Russian and Polish lives. His armies were sent on suicide missions or to build impossible bridges and roads.

Ivan feared everyone was trying to kill him, and he tortured his supposed enemies cruelly. He even feared that his own sons were plotting to assassinate him, and in a fit of madness he killed his eldest son with the spear-tip of his scepter-staff. He wandered howling through the halls of his palace, screaming so loudly that his cries were heard outside the Kremlin. He abandoned his Christian faith, imprisoned and killed the patriarch of Moscow (the head of the Russian Orthodox Church), and sought out witches and magicians from the pagan peoples of the far north. Told by witches that precious stones would change color if they came into contact with poison, Ivan held jewels next to his skin to see if he had been poisoned. Finally, one day he had a convulsion, fell from his throne, and died within the hour.

It is no wonder that history remembers Tsar Ivan IV as Ivan "the **Terrible**."

Ivan the Terrible (1530–84), tsar of Russia

The Dynasty of the Romanovs

After Ivan the Terrible's death, his idiot son Feodor ruled as tsar for fourteen years. When Feodor died childless, Russia was torn by civil wars until 1613, when Michael Romanov, a boyar who was distantly related to Feodor, was crowned tsar. Michael Romanov founded a line that would rule Russia until the Revolution of 1917.

terrible: causing great fear; horrible

**Russian Tsar Alexis I
(1629–1676) meets
ambassadors.**

folklore: customs, tales,
or sayings passed down
by the common people
from generation to
generation

Under the Romanovs, Russia became more autocratic and tyrannical than before, partly because it seemed that only the tsar could solve Russia's problems. There were serious quarrels among the aristocrats and the military. Ivan the Terrible's wars and how he governed Russia had brought ruin on the country. Placing all power in one man's hands seemed the only solution.

Tsar Alexis Romanov, Michael's son, had a new code of laws written up so that "law and justice shall be equal in all things." Tsar Alexis's "Code of 1649," however, brought peasants, taxpayers, army recruits, and officials tightly under the control of the Moscow government. The law code forced all peasants to be serfs. They could not leave the lands on which they lived, and sons could not leave the household of their father. Townsmen, moreover, were not allowed to move from the towns in which they lived, and they were divided into castes. Government officials regulated trade and workers in the cities. Everyone was required to carry identification and produce it on demand. Government employees handed their offices on to their sons, so that the jobs of civil servants became hereditary.

To escape from this slavery, some peasants and townsmen ran away to the south and east and joined the bands of lawless Cossacks along the Don and Volga Rivers. In the 1600s, several Cossack rebellions disturbed the peace of Russia. These rebellions became legendary in Russian **folklore**.

In 1652, Tsar Alexis began to reform Russian religious practices and so brought untold suffering to his people. Russian Orthodox Christians were deeply attached to their traditional religious rituals that had come down to them from the time of St. Vladimir. It was the brilliant and scholarly patriarch of Moscow, Nikon, who persuaded Tsar Alexis to reform Russian religious practices so that they more closely followed the practices of the Church in Constantinople. Believers were told, for instance, to make the sign of the cross with three fingers, instead of two—because that was the way it was done in Byzantium. The liturgies were rewritten so that they followed the Greek practices. Russians were told to obey these reforms on pain of death or exile. The tsar's police backed up the patriarch's demands, and punishments were swift and terrible.

To many Russians, these were not just changes in practice but changes in what they believed. A large segment of the Russian clergy and people refused to go along with Nikon's reforms. They rebelled against both

Cossacks in the 17th century—a painting titled, "Reply of the Zaporozhian Cossacks to Sultan Mehmed IV of the Ottoman Empire," by Ilya Repin

patriarch and tsar. Calling themselves "Old Believers," they asked: "Why, if Holy Russia is the third Rome, should she change her ways? Were not the reformers the true heretics? Did not Byzantium, Second Rome, fall to the Turks because it was weak in faith, while Moscow defeated the Mongols because it held fast to the true faith?"

The Old Believers did not only oppose the religious reforms; they opposed the tsar's autocracy and serfdom as well. Many clergy and aristocrats suffered for their Old Believer rebellion, and a long-lasting schism split the Russian Church. Old Believers continued to worship and communicate in secret societies over the next two centuries. They thought of themselves as being like the Christians meeting in the catacombs in the days of the Roman persecutions.

Peter the Great and the Westernization of Russia

When Tsar Alexis's son, Peter, was crowned tsar in 1696 at the young age of 24, he was determined to change the course of Russian history forever. He wanted to make Russia a truly great power, and to do this he thought he had to make Russia like the countries of western Europe. Even before

An engraving of Tsar
Peter the Great

westernization: giving
a culture or nation the
characteristics of west-
ern European culture

becoming tsar, he had set about to learn everything
he could about the West. After he became tsar, he dis-
guised himself as a simple sailor and went on a "Great
Embassy" to Germany and England. In this disguise, he
worked as a stonemason, a carpenter, a blacksmith, and
a dentist. He even kept a bag of human teeth with him
to prove his skill and talent at dentistry.

In his youth, Peter had shown great curiosity about
machines, and spent hours learning about them from the
practical German and Danish technicians of Moscow's
"German" quarter. There he learned an important idea
that he used in his later reign—that people should be
rewarded for what they could do, not because they
belonged to noble families. As tsar, he chose his army
officers from the most able of his soldiers, whether or not
they were aristocrats.

The chief goal of Peter's reign, thus, was to force Russia
to accept **westernization**. Russians had to become like
western Europeans in every area of life. For instance,
the tsar ordered Russian men to shave their beards and
to wear Western clothes. Those who refused could be
stopped on the streets and forcibly shaved by the police.
They were made to pay a "beard tax" if they refused to
shave their beards. Peter's harshness in forcing westernization on Russia
led to the outbreak of civil wars all over Russia, which he put down, one
by one, over the years of his reign.

Tsar Peter made himself absolute master of the Russian Orthodox
Church. When the patriarch of Moscow died in 1700, Peter did not
replace him. Instead, he placed the Church under a body of bishops
headed by a layman appointed by the tsar. This he called the Holy Synod.
So under Tsar Peter, the Russian Church became another branch of the
Russian government. By Peter's command, priests who heard remarks
against the government during confession were required by law to report
them to the police.

Peter wanted to make Russia a world power. He conquered the last
Mongol forces in the Crimea and built a fleet on the Black Sea, which
had been under the complete control of the Ottoman Turks. In the
north, he made war on Sweden, which at that time controlled the coast
of the Baltic Sea. In 1703 he seized the mouth of the Neva River, which

flows into the Baltic Sea, and began to build a city there, which he named St. Petersburg. St. Petersburg was built on swampy ground that had to be drained and filled. It had to be both a seaport and a fortress. To build his city, Peter forced thousands of Russian peasants to work in the cold and unhealthy swamps. He starved, beat, and drove them to their deaths for the sake of the great project.

Peter wanted St. Petersburg to be a western European city. It was to be his capital and his "Window on the West." To be able to keep a better eye on his nobles, he forced them, on pain of death or exile, to move to St. Petersburg and to build stone mansions there for themselves and their families.

St. Petersburg. *View of the Troizkoi Bridge* **by J. Schroeder**

In a series of wars, Peter defeated the Swedes, the Turks, the Poles, and his own rebellious Cossacks. His military adventures added modern Lithuania and Latvia to Russia and pushed the Russian border farther south. By building up a modern army and navy, Peter made Russia one of the great powers of Europe. For all of these achievements, this tsar has gone down in history as Peter the Great.

Peter's legacy was the westernization of Russia. Russia did become a world power, but at the heavy cost of widespread suffering and deep division among the Russian people. Russian aristocrats, who lived off the labor of their serfs, learned to speak French and to dress in French and English fashions. They traveled to foreign capitals and behaved more like western Europeans than Russians. Their peasants, on the other hand, who spoke Russian, lived in hopeless poverty. Russian townsfolk remained bound by the caste system and lived a life of little comfort and even poverty. Russian religious faith was as strong as ever, but many had lost trust in the Church. The Christian Faith remained the religion of the poor while many nobles practiced their religion without really believing in it.

So it was that, when Peter the Great died in February 1725 (at the age of 53), few of his people sincerely mourned for him.

The Empire of Russia

Peter the Great's successors as tsar were not as great as he. For 37 years after Peter's death, the Russian government was controlled by three powerful women — Peter's second wife, Catherine, his niece, Anna, and his daughter, Elizabeth. Early in her reign, Elizabeth named her nephew, called Peter, her successor on the throne. He married a German princess named Sophia. When Sophia entered the Orthodox Church, she changed her name to Catherine. A very intelligent woman, Catherine spent the next 17 years waiting for the day Peter would be tsar. Because her husband was weak-minded, Catherine thought she would be the true ruler of Russia.

When at last he became tsar in 1762, Peter did a very foolish thing — he threatened to divorce Catherine. The result was that, when he had only been tsar six months, his imperial guards took him prisoner and proclaimed Catherine as **tsarina** and empress of Russia. Tsar Peter III was taken to a country house, where he was killed in a fight.

tsarina: a female tsar or the wife of a tsar

Unlike the other women who had ruled Russia since the death of Peter the Great, Catherine did not just want to rule and enjoy court entertainment. She was determined to finish Peter the Great's work — to make Russia one of the great powers of Europe. It was because of this goal and what she achieved that we remember her as Catherine "**the Great.**"

the Great: a title given to a ruler to indicate that he or she has accomplished much. "Great," however, does not necessarily mean "good."

abolition: putting an end to or abolishing something

Catherine made many changes to Russia. In 1767, she drew up a new code of laws that called for milder punishments for crime and the **abolition** of torture. She set up schools and academies throughout Russia. She brought the Church more firmly under her control. Yet, Catherine not only did very little to help the poor, she made their lives worse. To keep the nobles on her side, she gave them even greater control over their serfs. Under Catherine, serfdom increased and became harsher than it had been before.

Catherine fought wars to increase Russia's contact with the outside world. Russia fought a six-year war with the Turks (1768-1774), in which Russia gained control of the Crimean Peninsula and other lands on the north side of the Black Sea. In this war, Russia won the right to send ships onto the Black Sea. Like Peter the Great, Catherine wanted Russia to adopt western European culture. In Catherine's time, Russia's nobles spoke French, lived in western European-style houses and adopted western European ways of thinking. By the time Catherine the Great died, Russia was what Peter the Great had wanted it to be—a powerful European state.

Russia vs. Napoleon

Catherine the Great's son, Paul III, became tsar after her death. Though historians have said that Tsar Paul was insane, he was not an entirely bad ruler. Yet, though many of his measures were wise, he committed acts of cruelty and turned many Russian nobles and military men against him. Finally, on March 23, 1801, his enemies murdered him in his palace, and his son, Alexander, became tsar.

The new tsar, Alexander I, wanted not only to make Russia a great nation but to better the lives of his people. For instance, he desired both to strengthen the Russian army and navy *and* to make the lives of the serfs easier. Alexander thus encouraged the growth of trade and manufacturing. He invited Germans and Swiss into Russia to farm the rich lands lying to the north of the Black Sea He set up schools and new universities for the Russian people. He eased the burdens placed on the serfs. Like other European rulers, Alexander began to draft Russian civilians into the army, increasing its size to 500,000 men.

During the early years of his reign, Alexander greatly admired the head of the French government, a general named Napoleon Bonaparte. The tsar's attitude changed, however, when Napoleon made himself emperor of France. In 1804, Alexander joined other European rulers in the war they were waging to destroy the power of Napoleon.

Napoleon, however, was a brilliant military commander, and in a few years he had conquered much of Europe. In 1807, Napoleon's armies defeated the Russians in battle, and Tsar Alexander made peace with the French emperor. The two even became friends. This friendship, however, ended in late 1810, and Napoleon prepared his "Grand Army" to invade Russia.

When he invaded Russia in the spring of 1812, Napoleon found the entire Russian people against him. Defending their "Holy Mother Russia" was a crusade to the Russians, and all classes eagerly joined the war effort. The armies of Tsar Alexander I fell back, luring the French deeper into

Fire of Moscow, 1812

the Russian plain as winter was approaching. Finally, at Borodino, not far from Moscow, the Russians fought Napoleon's forces, but were defeated. Napoleon entered Russia's capital, Moscow, in triumph.

But Napoleon's triumph did not last. The people of Moscow had fled the city, and the city itself caught fire. Without sufficient food and clothing to supply his army, Napoleon was forced to abandon Moscow. Forced to retreat across hundreds of miles in the bitter cold Russian winter and attacked by Russian forces, the Grand Army lost tens of thousands of men. By the time it reached the border of Russia and safety, the Grand Army had few men left.

This great war for the defense of Russia has inspired the Russians from 1812 to our own day. The Russian composer Peter Tchaikovsky celebrated this event in his famous *1812 Overture*. Russia's greatest writer, Leo Tolstoy, made the war the centerpiece of his great novel, *War and Peace*.

Following Napoleon's invasion of Russia, Tsar Alexander became one of the leaders of the European nations who at last destroyed the power of Napoleon Bonaparte. By 1814, Russia had become one of the great powers of Europe.

Alexander II, tsar of Russia (1818–1881); an active promoter of reform who was responsible for the abolition of serfdom in 1861

Russia in the 19th Century

The war against Napoleon brought more Russians into contact with the West and with Western ideas of government. The new ideas of "democracy" and "republicanism" swept through the educated classes. Secret societies of military officers wanted to overthrow the tsar's absolute government and set up a republic. Secret societies worked for reform and change in all aspects of Russian life. The universities became centers of revolutionary fervor. When Alexander I's brother, Nicholas, became tsar in December 1825, the military tried to overthrow him. This "Decembrist Revolution" was stopped only at the last moment. Ever after, Nicholas I feared the growing revolutionary movement, and he had his secret police arrest anyone suspected of revolutionary ideas or speech. Thousands were sent to the new prison camps in Siberia.

In 1861, before Abraham Lincoln's Emancipation Proclamation freed the slaves in America, Tsar Alexander II freed the serfs of Russia by imperial decree. The peasants were now free to leave the estates on which they had lived and seek employment in the cities. At the time, industry was growing in Russia and offered jobs to the newly freed serfs. But freed serfs who stayed on the land were not given free land as they had expected. Instead, they had to pay for the tiny plots they farmed, which kept them in debt to the government. Peasant resentment against the government grew.

anarchist: one who believes that any government is bad and so works for the destruction of government

In 1883, Alexander II died from a bomb thrown by a member of a revolutionary secret society of **anarchists**. His son, Tsar Alexander III, feared revolution and change as much as he feared assassination. The secret police sent even more people to Siberia. The tsar began a campaign to force all the various nationalities under Russian rule to speak Russian and to accept the Russian Orthodox faith. Many Catholics, Protestants, Jews, and Muslims were fined and arrested as disturbers of the peace. Persecution of Jews became so intense that millions of Russian Jews left their homes and emigrated to America and England.

When Alexander III died in 1895, he left his son, Nicholas II, a country raging with resentment and anger. The new tsar believed that the old Russian ways ought to be brought back again and the Russian faith revived. Nicholas II wanted to be a true Christian monarch. He was a loving family man and devoted to his German-princess wife, Alexandra, the granddaughter of Queen Victoria of Great Britain. He spent most of his time with his family away from Moscow and St. Petersburg and left the running of the country to trusted ministers. So it was that he more and more lost control of what was happening in Russia.

Nicholas II (1868–1918), tsar (1894–1917), pictured with his family: Duchess Olga, Duchess Marie, the Grand Duchess Anastasia, the tsarevitch (young tsar) Alexis, the Grand Duchess Tatiana, and his wife the Tsarina Alexandra

Industrialized Russia

By the beginning of the 20th century, Russia had become one of the industrial powers of the world. It was the fourth largest producer of iron and coal, and Russian industry employed over 2 million factory workers. Like workers the world over, Russian workers were underpaid and overworked. They wanted the right to organize into labor unions, as workers were doing in the western countries. But the secret police arrested labor organizers and broke up **strikes** with violence.

Into this boiling pot came the ideas of a 19th-century German intellectual, Karl Marx. Marx preached Communism. He said no person or family should own the kind of property that produces goods (farms, for instance, or factories) but that the working class or **proletariat** should hold all property in common. Marx said history was a story of warfare between classes, and this idea led many European intellectuals to think that only violent revolution would bring real change to society. **Marxists** were found all over Europe and, indeed, America, and secret Marxist societies, called **soviets**, sprang up in Russia. In 1905, industrial workers rose up in the cities, and Russia barely escaped revolution. The tsar and his ministers promised to loosen their control over Russia by establishing an English-style parliament; but the tsar's absolute government remained in place.

But, in 1914, suddenly and violently, the war we now call World War I broke out in Europe. Russia entered the war on the side of the French and British, facing the armies of a highly prepared and trained Germany. The war with Germany caught Russia by surprise. Russia did not have the transportation or supply systems necessary to feed and clothe her massive armies. Russian soldiers fought in the mud of the trenches through three winters without proper clothing or shoes, and with little ammunition. The death toll was staggering.

After three years of fighting, Russians were ready to make peace, but the tsar refused. In March of 1917, riots broke out in every major Russian city. The parliament declared a new government, and on March 15, 1917, Nicholas II abdicated the throne. All over Russia, the soviets took power from local governments and refused to accept the authority of the new **provisional** government. The troops at the front began to desert the army in large numbers.

strike: refusal by workers to work in order to bring employers around to giving in to their demands

proletariat: member of the working class

Marxist: one who accepts the Communist ideas of Karl Marx

soviet: a word meaning a *council*

provisional: temporary; lasting only for the time being

The Communist Revolution

To weaken Russia, the Germans urged the soviet revolution-aries to take up arms against the tsar. The Germans sent to Russia a revolutionary by the name of Vladimir Ilyich Lenin, who had been living in Switzerland to escape being arrested by Russia's secret police.

Lenin was a former law student who joined the revolu-tionaries after his brother had been arrested and executed by the tsar's secret police. Lenin then studied revolution and Marxism. A spell-binding speaker and ruthless leader, he had become well known in revolutionary circles in Russia. In November of 1917, he stirred the soviets of St. Petersburg to rise up against the provisional government. Lenin's revolution was successful. His band of revolutionaries, called Bolsheviks, seized control of the government. The November revolution marked the end of traditional Russia.

After the Bolshevik revolution, Lenin's opponents fled from St. Petersburg and gathered troops to overthrow the new gov-ernment. This led to civil war, which lasted from 1917 to 1921. During this war, the Bolsheviks had sent Tsar Nicholas and his entire family across the Ural Mountains, into the east, to keep anyone from saving them. On July 17, 1918, the tsar's Bolshevik guards executed him and his entire family — by Lenin's orders. So ended the Romanov dynasty that had ruled Russia for over 300 years. The Russian Orthodox Church considers Tsar Nicholas and his family to be martyrs for the faith.

In the end, Lenin and the Bolsheviks were victorious. Over all of Russia and the lands it ruled, they established a new government, called the Union of Soviet Socialist Republics (U.S.S.R.) or the Soviet Union. The Bolsheviks, renaming themselves the Communist Party, promised land for the peasants. Workers in industries were promised freedom from their oppressors. The Communists said that everyone in the Soviet Union was equal, for all were members of the working class. There were to be no rich or aristocrats, they said. Women were given the vote — a rare thing for that time. Yet, the only candidates that both women and men could vote for were members of the Communist Party. Lenin and his Communists wanted complete control of all aspects of life in the U.S.S.R.

Vladimir Lenin

To control the people, Lenin used a secret police force, called the Cheka, to commit acts of terror. Between 1918 and 1921, the Cheka murdered about 140,000 people throughout the U.S.S.R. Lenin persecuted Christians, especially those belonging to the Russian Orthodox Church. Churches were closed and destroyed; priests and bishops were imprisoned and murdered.

Lenin remained head of the Soviet government until his death in 1922. After Lenin's death, members of the Communist Party struggled with each other to take control of the government. Finally, one man was victorious. His name was Joseph Stalin.

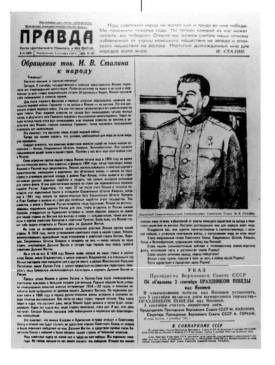

Joseph Stalin, on the front page of the Soviet newspaper, *Pravda*

The Man of Steel

The name "Stalin" was not Joseph Stalin's real name. In Russian, Stalin means "steel," and Joseph's comrades had given him this name because of his unusual strength and endurance. "Steel" was a good name for Joseph Stalin, for he was cold, hard, and cruel.

Indeed, Joseph Stalin was even more ruthless and cruel than Lenin had been. He increased the persecution of Christians; bishops, priests, and layfolk, Orthodox and Catholic, were arrested, imprisoned, and executed. By the late 1930s, the Soviets had killed about 80,000 Orthodox clergy, monks, and nuns. Stalin also attacked the people the Communists supposedly stood for—the common laborer. Stalin caused millions in Ukraine to starve to death because they refused to give up their farms to the state. Stalin went after Communists whom he feared would try to overthrow him. Stalin's "**purges**" took the lives of tens of millions of people from 1934 to 1953.

It was Stalin who led the U.S.S.R. into World II, on the side of the Allies (led by Great Britain and the United States of America) against Adolf Hitler's Nazi Germany. Russian victories in this war made the Soviet Union the second greatest power in the world, after the United States. Through Soviet power, Communism spread into Eastern Europe, China, and other regions of the world.

purge: cleansing or getting rid of something

Russia Today

The rule of the Communists over Russia formally came to an end on December 25, 1991, when the last Communist head of government, Mikhail Gorbachev, resigned. Today, Russia is a republic.

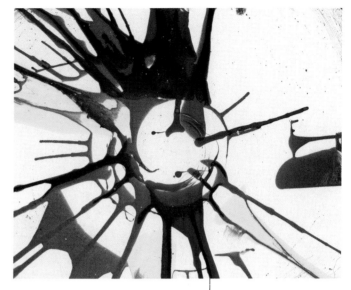

A painting by Wassily Kadinsky, an originator of modern art

As we have seen, Russia has had a rich and interesting history. The Russian people have suffered much over the centuries—and this is perhaps why they have given the world so many monuments of great beauty. Russian authors and artists have created masterpieces of human imagination. Russian painters, such as Kandinsky and Chagall in the 20th century, changed our ideas about art. Russian music continues to influence the world. The glories of Tchaikovsky, Mussorgsky, and Rachmaninoff in the 19th century, and Stravinsky, Shostakovich, and Prokofiev in the 20th will never be forgotten. Russian novelists have left a treasure house of stories for the world's edification and entertainment. Pushkin, Gogol, Tolstoy, and Dostoyevsky are the greatest names of a long list of great Russian writers and poets.

But greater than all this is the spirit of the Russian people and, especially, Russian Christians, who have endured through so much adversity, from the Mongols to the Soviets. The future destiny of so great a people remains to be seen.

Chapter 14 Review

Let's Remember   Please write your answers in complete sentences.
1. From where does Russia get its name?
2. Who created the alphabet from which the Russian alphabet comes?
3. Why did Vladimir of Kiev send emissaries to Constantinople?
4. Who were the Cossacks?
5. What is the Kremlin?

Let's Consider   For silent thinking and a short essay, or for thinking in a group with classroom discussion:

1. Why did Russia suffer so many invasions throughout its history?
2. How did the Byzantine culture of Constantinople influence Russia?
3. How did the Mongol invasions change Russia?
4. Was Peter the Great's westernizing of Russia good or bad for the country?

Things to Do

1. Using the map of Russia on page 282, indicate the direction the following rivers flow (for instance, north to south, south to north, east to west, west to east): Dnieper, Volga, Ural, Ob, and Yenisey. Indicate into what bodies of water (seas or oceans) the rivers empty.
2. By what rivers do the following Russian cities stand: Kiev, Novgorod, Smolensk, and Moscow?

Let's Eat!

Beet soup has been a staple of Russian cuisine for centuries. Here's a recipe for an easy-to-make cold beet soup, called *borscht*. Chop up fine the beets from two cans of sliced beets (save the liquid). Put chopped beets in a 2-quart covered glass dish. Add the liquid and one can of chicken broth. Stir in the juice of 1 lemon, 2 tablespoons sugar, and 1 teaspoon salt. Cover and put in the microwave for 10 minutes. Remove and chill until ready to serve. Serve with a dollop of sour cream over the top of each bowl. The recipe makes four small servings.

Chapter 15 North America: Land of Opportunity

Since the 18th century, the countries of North and South America have brought new ideas and new opportunities to the older civilizations of Europe and Asia. The United States of America, in particular, made itself a world culture, influencing the ideas and styles of living all over the world. The land and weather of the North American continent has helped the rapid growth of the United States. Few countries have had such rich farmlands, abundant **mineral deposits**, and favorable climate regions for their growth and success.

mineral deposit: a place where large amounts of a mineral (such as gold, silver, copper, etc.) are found

Pioneer homestead in the late 18th century

We will talk more fully about the countries of Central and South America in the following chapter. In this chapter we will focus on North America and, in particular, the United States. We shall show how North America has contributed to the development of the cultures of the world.

The Geography of North America

North America is a continent with many different landscapes and climates. It has towering mountains and broad, fertile plains. In the far north, the winters are long and very cold, while in the Deep South, summers are long, hot, and humid. The East Coast of North America receives abundant rainfall, while much of the west is dry. Great forests once covered much of the land east of the Mississippi River, while the west has had vast stretches of treeless grasslands and deserts.

If you look at a map of North America, you will notice that the continent extends from the Arctic Ocean in the north all the way to the Isthmus of Panama in the south. Focusing on those portions of North America covered by the United States and Canada, you will notice that they are marked out by two important mountain ranges: the Appalachian Mountains in the east and the Rocky Mountains in the west. The Appalachians run from Newfoundland in the north to northern Alabama in the south. These forest-covered mountains are not high — their highest peaks are Mt. Mitchell in North Carolina (6,684 feet) and Mt. Washington in New Hampshire (6,293 feet) Yet, the Appalachians are the dividing line between two important regions of North America — the Atlantic seaboard and the Central Plains.

The coast of the Atlantic seaboard has an irregular shape, with many bays and inlets. Several rivers rise in the Appalachians and flow eastward to the sea. In the north the land along the coasts is hilly and rocky; but as you go southward, the land widens out into plains good for farming. These lands, from Virginia to Georgia, are called the Tidewater. As you travel westward from the Tidewater toward the Appalachians, the land gets higher and more hilly and is heavily forested.

West of the Appalachians stretch the great Central Plains of North America, which extend from the Arctic Ocean to the Gulf of Mexico. In Canada, around Hudson Bay, there is a heavily forested plateau having many lakes. This is called the Laurentian Region. South of this region are the Great Lakes (Lake Superior, Lake Michigan, Lake Huron, Lake Erie and Lake Ontario) which are like freshwater seas. The waters from these lakes empty out into the St. Lawrence River, which flows northeast into the Gulf of St. Lawrence.

South of the Great Lakes lie the fertile valleys of the Ohio and Mississippi Rivers. The Ohio River rises in the Appalachian Mountains and flows westward through lands that were once covered with forests. Stretching about 2,320 miles, the Mississippi is the greatest river in North America, and one of the greatest rivers in the world. Not only the Ohio River, but other great rivers as well flow into the Mississippi. Indeed, nearly all the rivers between the Appalachian and Rocky Mountains give their water to the Mississippi.

West of the Mississippi River, the Central Plains begin to rise and become drier and drier, because they enjoy less frequent rainfall than areas east of the great river. These plains are mostly treeless. The Central Plains end at the Rocky Mountains, part of a great mountain range that extends from Alaska all the way to Central America. Unlike the Appalachians, the Rocky Mountains are very tall. Over 100 peaks in the Rockies rise higher than 12,000 feet.

West of the Rocky Mountains are the Western Highlands. In Canada, these highlands enjoy more rainfall and are greener. In the United States, however, they grow more and more arid the further south you go until they become dry deserts. Unlike the East, the Western Highlands have only two major rivers — the Columbia River, which flows into the Pacific Ocean, and the Colorado, which rises in the Rocky Mountains and then turns south and empties finally into the Gulf of California.

On the eastern border of California, the Western Highlands rise up into another great mountain range, the Sierra Nevada. Though this range of mountains is not as long as the Rocky Mountains, it is as high. Both in the north and the south, the Sierra Nevada connects with the Coast Ranges, a group of lower mountain ranges that run along the Pacific coast. The Coast Ranges and the Sierra Nevada encircle a large central plain called the Central Valley, where many of the fruits and vegetables of the United States are grown.

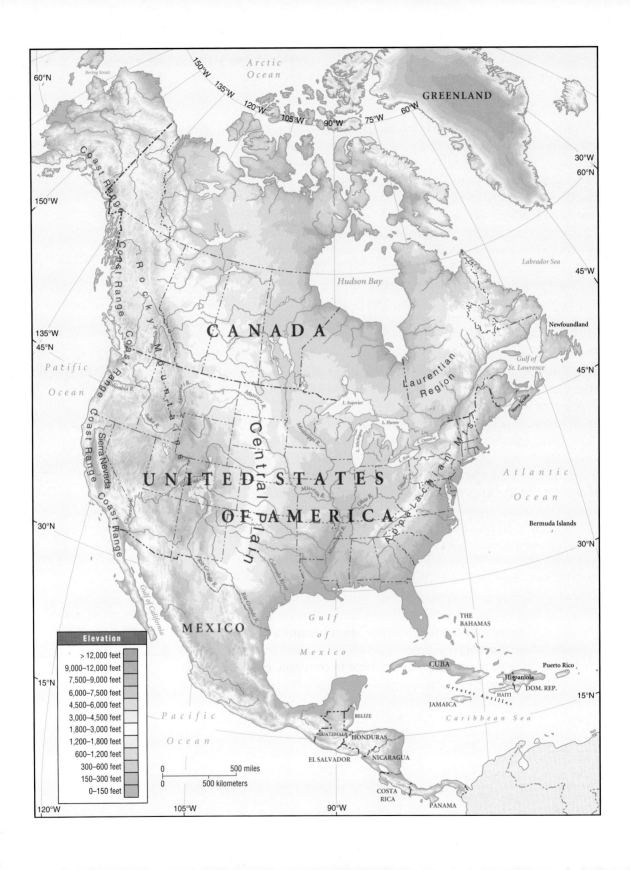

The Coast Ranges run from central Mexico, through California, Oregon, and Washington, and through Canada all the way to Alaska. North of San Francisco Bay, the region west of the Coast Ranges often receives heavy rainfall and is heavily forested. East of the Coast Ranges, the lands tend to be more arid.

How English Settlement Moved from East to West

William Penn, the founder of Pennsylvania colony, makes a treaty with the Indians.

When Europeans first came to the Atlantic coast of North America, old forests covered the land from the seacoast to the Appalachian Mountains, and far beyond those mountains. North America was not an empty continent when the Europeans arrived, for everywhere there were Native American tribes with their own cultures and ways of living that differed very much from European civilization. These tribes were unable to resist the European settlers who wanted their land, and so European civilization spread from the Atlantic coast to the Appalachians, and then from the Appalachians into the interior of North America.

The Native Americans bravely resisted the European invaders. Oftentimes Europeans did not treat these people they called "Indians" with justice or charity. Yet, the Europeans showed independence, determination, and courage in settling the wild lands, which were so different from the Europe from which they came. The settlers' independent "can do" spirit became a significant characteristic of the American people.

Too, because so much land was available to common, everyday people, aristocrats were not able to take control of the English-speaking European settlements of North America. Poorer settlers and new immigrants in the east could leave their employers and landlords and move on into the west and the free land of the wilderness. This was not the case in Europe, where aristocrats controlled most of the land and common farmers had to rent land from them.

Opposite: A map of North America, with color-keyed elevation scale

The Thirteen English Colonies

colonization: the making of a colony
eastern seaboard: the Atlantic coast of North America

English **colonization** of North America began in the 1600s. By the middle of the 1700s, there were thirteen English colonies along the **eastern seaboard**, each having its own government. The first of these colonies in the north was called Massachusetts. It was followed by the colonies of Rhode Island, Connecticut, and New Hampshire. The city of Boston was the major port and city of this region that became known as New England.

Map of the first European colonies—English, French, and Dutch—in America

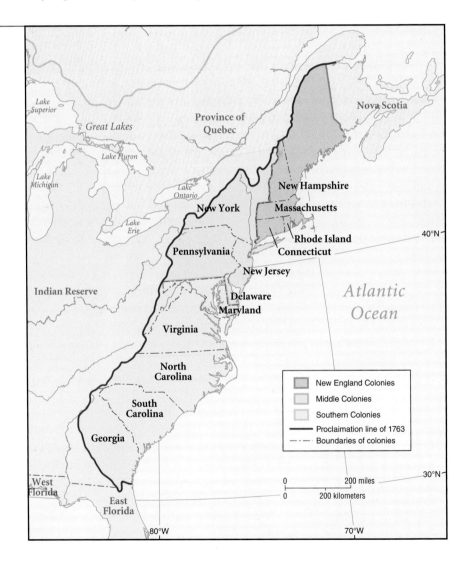

The territories that are now the states of Maine and Vermont were part of Massachusetts and New York.

It was the Dutch who originally settled the region just to the south and west of New England. They controlled the region of what is now New York City (which the Dutch called New Amsterdam), Long Island, and the Hudson River Valley. In time, the Dutch surrendered their colonies to the English, who founded the **colony** of New York. The port city of New Amsterdam changed its name to New York and became a major city and port in North America. South of New York, an Englishman named William Penn founded a colony that came to be known as Pennsylvania as a refuge for people who were persecuted for their religion in Europe. Pennsylvania was centered on a town Penn named Philadelphia, the "city of brotherly love." Philadelphia eventually grew to be the third largest city of the English colonies.

In the south, the English founded the colonies of Delaware and Maryland on the peninsula that shelters the great Chesapeake Bay. Maryland was originally a colony for English Catholics, but it soon became Protestant, like all the other colonies. Everywhere, except Pennsylvania, harsh laws were passed against Catholics. The leader of the southern colonies was Virginia, which was actually the first English settlement in North America. To the south of Virginia rose the English colonies of North and South Carolina. Last of all, to the south of Georgia lay the Spanish colony of Florida.

North of New York and New England, across the St. Lawrence River, and west across the Appalachians was the region called Canada. Canada was originally settled by the French and, even today, the province of Quebec is mostly French speaking. Though Canada later became a British possession, it was not one of the original thirteen English colonies in America.

colony: a settlement made by a people far from their native country; a territory that is distant from the country that governs it

The French in North America

Both the English and the French came to North America seeking wealth for their countries. But, while the English tended to form communities based on farming, the French were more interested in trapping animals, such as beavers, for their rich furs. Furs were very popular in Europe, where they were turned into clothing and hats.

In search of furs, French traders explored the St. Lawrence River into the West and so discovered the Great Lakes. From the Great Lakes,

Mosaic of St. Isaac Jogues, with Blessed Kateri Tekakwitha and St. René Goupil, at the Cathedral Basilica of St. Louis

they followed rivers and streams until they reached the great Mississippi River. From the Mississippi, they explored the Ohio, Missouri, and Red Rivers and eventually reached the Gulf of Mexico, where they established the city of New Orleans. They called the lands along the Mississippi Louisiana, after the French king, Louis XIV. Today, New Orleans and the state of Louisiana remain centers of French culture in North America.

French Catholic missionaries followed the explorers in their journeys — not in search of furs, but to bring the Gospel of Christ to the natives of North America. Many of the missionaries became martyrs for the Faith.

One of the great French missionaries of North America was a Jesuit priest whom we remember as Saint Isaac Jogues. Jogues came to America in 1636 and evangelized the areas around the Great Lakes, in what is now Canada and New York State. He and other brave missionaries died for Christ near what is now Auriesville, New York, during the period of 1642–1649.

The first of these North American Martyrs was St. René Goupil, a layman and doctor, whom Iroquois Indians tomahawked to death for making the sign of the cross on the brow of a child. St. Isaac Jogues was martyred in the same way in 1646. A little later, the French captured Jogues's murderer and handed him over to the Algonquin tribe, with orders not to torture him. Before his execution, one year later, the young brave was baptized, taking the name Isaac Jogues.

Another French missionary to suffer for the Faith was the Jesuit priest, St. Jean de Brébeuf. Brébeuf spent 16 years as a missionary to the Huron Indians, until 1649, when he was captured by the Huron's enemies, the Iroquois. The Iroquois put Brébeuf through many savage tortures, but never once did he cry out in pain or utter a groan. When he at last lay dead, Indians cut out his heart and ate it. They thought that by eating Brébeuf's heart they could have a portion of his courage.

Missionaries joined French explorers on their journeys deep into the continent. It was the priest Jacques Marquette, for instance, who with Louis Joliet discovered the Mississippi River. Missionaries journeyed far into the lands of Louisiana to preach the Gospel to the American Indians.

France and England were frequently at war with one another, both in Europe and in America. One of these wars, called the French and Indian War, ended in 1763 with a French defeat. France gave Canada to England, as well as all the lands between the Mississippi River and the Appalachian Mountains. France, however, gave Louisiana to Spain, to keep it from falling into the hands of the English.

Into the West

Daniel Boone

In the 1760s, frontiersmen from the English colonies began crossing the Appalachians into the lands that had been French but now belonged to England. The most famous of these wandering frontier hunters was Daniel Boone. Born in 1734, Boone had fought for the British in the French and Indian War. In 1769, Boone crossed the Appalachians and began exploring the Kentucky country.

As he passed through the Appalachians into the west, Boone looked for the best route wagons could use to get through the mountains. It was in this way that he blazed the Wilderness Road that ran from southwestern Virginia, through the Cumberland Gap, and into Kentucky. Boone's trail followed the old paths made by huge buffalo herds.

Boone was a typical example of the rugged pioneers who settled the western lands. He could barely read or write, but he knew wood-lore and survival skills that saved his life many times. Men like him had been exploring and hunting in the forests for over a century. They came to be called "Long-Rifles," after the firearms they carried and used so accurately. The Long-Riflemen made annual hunting trips into the forests in small parties of three or four men; some, like Boone, traveled alone. For months these men were cut off from civilization and their families, collecting furs to sell in the eastern cities. In the meantime, they lived off hunting animals and by the work of their own hands. Having learned a sense of independence and freedom, they came to look down on the rules

Daniel Boone (1734–1820) during his last years in the wilderness he loved and spent his entire life exploring

The Wilderness Road

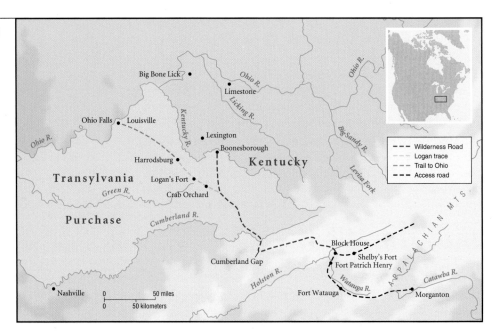

The American Bison

We think of buffalo or the American Bison as wandering in enormous herds through the Great Plains, west of the Mississippi River. But bison once roamed over much of North America, including the lands between the Mississippi and the Appalachian Mountains. These huge herds cut out paths in the Appalachians as well as the forested lands of Kentucky and Tennessee. European settlements drove the bison from the East, across the Mississippi, into the west; but the huge herds survived on the Great Plains into the late 19th century.

The bison was a major food source for the nomadic Indian tribes of North America. The Indians used bison hides for clothing and shelter and bison bones for tools or ornamentation. The Native

Americans found uses for every part of the bison. The bison also fed and clothed the new European settlers. Throughout the 19th century, however, overhunting of bison forced them almost to extinction.

Beginnings of Civilization in the Western Territories

While the English were establishing settlements on the East Coast of North America, Europeans were settling along the Pacific coast, in a place called California. Spain, Russia, and England all had hopes of colonizing California, but it was Spain's missionary efforts and the dedication of one missionary in particular, that brought California into the Spanish empire. This missionary was the Franciscan priest, Blessed Junipero Serra.

Though he was frail and suffering from poor health, Father Serra worked tirelessly to establish missions to the Indians of California. From 1769 until his death in 1784, Serra established nine missions that stretched 700 miles, from San Diego in the south to San Francisco in the north. After his death, between 1784 and 1823, Serra's successors established 12 more missions.

The missions not only were centers for spreading the Gospel. They also were centers of trade, education, and worship, all of which are needed to form a civilization. Father Serra not only greatly influenced the people of his day by baptizing and confirming thousands of new converts, he also left a great legacy that still stands today in the California Mission Trail and the Catholic Faith that is found all throughout California.

Blessed Junipero Serra

and habits of city life. Legends and popular ballads about these frontier heroes inspired the people of the colonies with a love of independence.

Boone brought his family, his wife and sons, with him to make a new life in the Kentucky wilderness. The settlers had moved into lands that several Indian nations used as sacred hunting and fighting grounds. War parties from various tribes met to fight in these lands so that war would not destroy their settlements. The Shawnee name for the territory was *Kan-tu-kee*, a word that means, "Dark and Bloody Ground."

Boone was honored as one of the first settlers of Kentucky, but his inability to read or write and lack of business skill made it easy for the dishonest men who followed the settlers into the wilderness to cheat him. He lost his lands through debt and was forced to move farther west when he was an old man. He died penniless in the western wilderness.

The Colonies Go to War

The cost of fighting the French and Indian War had been very high for the British government. Because of this, the British parliament wanted the American colonists to pay part of the cost of the war. After all, said Parliament, the war was fought to defend the English colonies from the French and their Indian allies.

So it happened that Parliament, in the name of the king, demanded that the colonists in America pay taxes they had never paid before. The colonists, who said such taxes were unjust, refused. When a mob of colonists attacked a British official in Boston, the British sent their red-coated troops into the city. The presence of British soldiers in Boston angered the colonists even more.

Bad feelings between the British and the colonists increased, especially in Boston. When Bostonians threw a shipment of tea into Boston harbor (because Parliament had put a tax on tea), the British blockaded Boston Harbor. No ships could enter or leave the harbor. To decide what to do about this blockade, which many colonists thought was unjust, Massachusetts, Virginia, and other colonies sent representatives to Philadelphia. There, they formed what was called the Continental Congress in September 1774. The Congress protested against what Parliament had done. But nothing the Congress did stopped Parliament from its attempts to force the colonies to obey its laws.

American colonists and British soldiers fight at the top of Breed's Hill (Bunker Hill). The battle was a costly victory for the British.

While the Continental Congress was meeting, the British army in Boston crossed Boston Harbor into the main part of Massachusetts. It was sent to seize illegal arms the colonists had stored in the town of Concord. Hearing of the British advance, local farmers gathered to resist it. On April 19, 1775, colonists fought the British at the towns of Lexington and Concord and drove them back to Boston.

Soon after the battles of Lexington and Concord, men from other colonies came to Massachusetts to help in the fight against the British. A British force soon landed in New York City. The conflict was spreading and the Continental Congress saw it had no other choice but to fight the war in earnest. It formed an army and at its head placed George Washington of Virginia as commander. There was now no turning back. The colonies were now at war with the powerful nation of Great Britain.

The Revolutionary War

A Virginia landowner and planter, George Washington had served as a commander of troops in the French and Indian War. He was a man of natural authority and common sense and so his men respected and were devoted to him.

It would have been hard to find a better man to command the undermanned and poorly supplied Continental Army. From the beginning, Washington faced nearly impossible odds. The Continental Army was untrained while the British Army was an experienced fighting force. Coming from different colonies, the soldiers in the Continental Army did not think of themselves as belonging to one nation. And they did not get along. Massachusetts men disagreed with Pennsylvania men; New Yorkers quarreled with Virginians. One of Washington's tasks was to keep his junior officers from shooting each other.

He also had to keep his troops from losing too many battles in the war. Congress did not understand why Washington did not fight more battles with the British and almost removed him as general. But Washington knew he had to keep his army together. As long as there was an American army, the revolution would continue. Under Washington's leadership, the army stayed together and, with the help of the French, in 1781 defeated the British at Yorktown, Virginia. After the Battle of Yorktown, the British commander surrendered to Washington and the war was ended.

At first, the colonists did not fight to form an independent country. They wanted George III as their king and to remain part of the British

Empire. But as the war progressed, the Continental Congress came to think that the colonies had to be independent from England and the king. On July 4, 1776, the Continental Congress approved a Declaration of Independence, the text of which had been written by Thomas Jefferson of Virginia.

In the Declaration of Independence, Congress stated why it was necessary for the colonies to be independent from Great Britain. Perhaps the most famous line from the Declaration is the one that speaks of the "self-evident" truth that all men are created equal and "that they are endowed by their Creator with certain **inalienable** Rights, that among these are Life, Liberty and the pursuit of Happiness." The idea that "all men are created equal" was an ideal of the frontier spirit that made up the American character. It has remained a basic part American thought from 1776 even into our own time.

inalienable: incapable of being lost, taken away, or surrendered

A New Nation

After the Continental Congress signed the Declaration of Independence, the colonies no longer thought of themselves as colonies but as independent states. During the war, these states thought it best to unite with one another for mutual protection and help. Thus, in 1781, they agreed to adopt a **constitution** to govern their union, the "United States of America." This first U.S. constitution was called the Articles of Confederation.

The Articles of Confederation, however, failed to unite the states into one nation. It did not give the government of the United States — Congress — enough power to make the states obey it. Many Americans began to think the country needed a new constitution that could better unite the states. Such a constitution had to respect the American spirit of independence and self-reliance, as well as the English tradition of respect for law.

Thus, in 1787, representatives of the various states met in Philadelphia to draw up a new constitution. The **president** of this Constitutional **Convention** was none other than the war hero, George Washington. Under his direction the convention drew up a constitution that gave more power to the government of the union while yet respecting the authority of state governments.

The Constitution of the United States of America was presented to the convention **delegates** on September 7, 1787, and sent to the separate state

constitution: the document that contains the most fundamental laws of a nation. A constitution contains the highest laws of a state.
president: the chief officer or director of a group, company, society, or nation
convention: a meeting of people who come together for a special purpose
delegate: a person who has been chosen to act for others

assemblies for **ratification**. The questions the Constitutional Convention dealt with were those raised by the American spirit of independence and equality under the law. No one wanted any one man or group of men to have too much power. No one wanted one region of the country to dominate the others, or the large states to have more power than the small states. Moreover, convention delegates wanted to guarantee each free man's right to vote for his laws and government.

ratify: to approve formally. A *ratification* is a formal approval of something.

The Constitution

After months of debate, the convention came up with a constitution that called for a three-part government, with a **legislature**, an **executive**, and a **judiciary**. The new constitution did the following things:

1. It set up a congress, made up of representatives of the people and the states. The congress makes all the laws for the new government. It is divided into two houses: the House of Representatives and the Senate.
2. The House of Representatives represents the people of the United States. The people in larger states send more representatives to the House than the people in smaller states. Each representative serves

legislature: a group of persons who make laws for a state or country
executive: a person or branch of government that has the responsibility of putting laws into effect; a president or governor is an executive
judiciary: the system of courts of law

The Constitution, an original edition from September 1787, shown as it was first issued: written entirely on one side of one large sheet of paper, in the finest manuscript handwriting

for two years. The Senate represents the states. Each state sends two senators to the Senate. Each senator serves for six years.

3. There is an executive, called the president, who does not make laws but makes sure the laws made by Congress are put into effect. The president, however, has to sign all **bills** passed by Congress before they can become laws. If the president refuses to sign (or **vetoes**) a bill, it cannot become law. The House and Senate, however, can reject the president's veto if two-thirds of both houses vote to do so, and then the bill will become a law.

4. The president is commander and chief of the army and navy of the United States.

5. The constitution said that the president is to appoint the members of the third branch of government, the Supreme Court. The Senate, however, has to approve the men the president wants to appoint. A Supreme Court **justice** can serve for as long as he or she wishes, unless the House of Representatives **impeaches** the justice and the Senate convicts him or her of having committed a serious crime.

bill: a proposed law presented to a legislature, which may vote it into law or not
veto: the act by which an executive refuses to allow an approved bill to become law

justice: a judge
impeach: the act by which the Congress accuses a president or Supreme Court justice of serious crimes

Thomas Jefferson

Slavery and a Bill of Rights

The last question the Constitutional Convention took up was the difficult question of slavery. The English colonies, like the French, Spanish, and Portuguese settlements in the New World, had accepted the ancient, but dreadful, custom of slavery. The colonists obtained their slaves from the West African coasts. All the United States had legal slavery, though the southern states had many more slaves than the northern New England states. Slavery had made large landowners in Virginia and the Carolinas (who grew tobacco, rice, and similar crops) very wealthy. Many of the founders of the United States were slave owners, including George Washington and Thomas Jefferson (though Washington freed his slaves in his will). These men disliked slavery, as did many of the other founders. Even in the southern states, many wanted to bring slavery to an end soon.

The Constitutional Convention, however, was unable to end slavery, for to do so immediately would bring poverty to the South, much of which depended on slave labor. The Constitution, however, did attack the practice of importing slaves from Africa to the United States. It said that, in 1808, no more slaves could be imported into the United States from Africa or other countries.

Many of those who opposed the new Constitution were worried that the new government would be too powerful and would violate the rights of citizens. Though the Constitution went into effect in June 1788 and shortly after George Washington was elected president, many Americans did not like the new government. To please these opponents, Congress, the president, and the state governments approved ten **amendments** to the Constitution. These amendments are called the Bill of Rights.

The Bill of Rights was meant to protect individual citizens and the states from the power of the new **federal government**. The Bill of Rights, for instance, keeps the government from persecuting people on account of their religious beliefs or forcing them to practice a particular religion. It grants people the right to speak their ideas freely, to gather in peaceful assemblies, and to own and bear arms. The Tenth Amendment says that the powers the Constitution does not give to the federal government belong to the states and the people.

Former slave quarters

The United States Expands to the West

The United States grew rapidly in the 20 or so years following the adoption of the new Constitution. In 1793 and 1794, two new states, Kentucky and Tennessee, were admitted to the Union. Then came Ohio, Indiana, and Michigan. Then, in 1803, the **ambassador** of France suggested to President Jefferson that France was willing to sell Louisiana to the United States. When asked what kind of land Louisiana had, the French foreign minister shrugged: "*Je ne sais quois.*"—"I do not know."

amendment: a change in a body of law

federal government: the central government of the United States of America established by the constitution

ambassador: a representative of a government, sent by that government to a foreign government

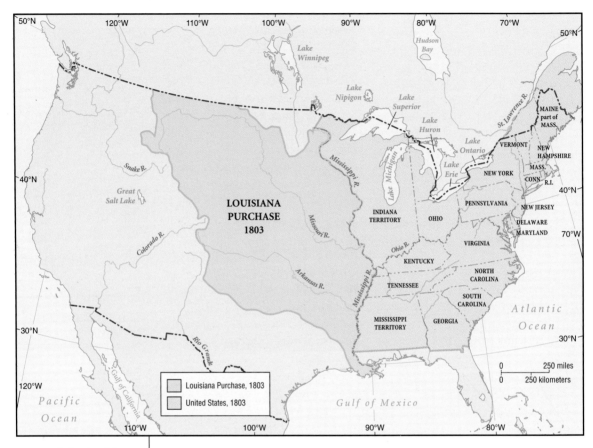

Map of the Louisiana Purchase

Louisiana was a vast territory, and the French were willing to sell it for only $15 million. President Jefferson could not pass up this deal and so he agreed to buy Louisiana. The "Louisiana Purchase" doubled the size of the country, which now spread from the Atlantic coast, across the Mississippi River, all the way to the Rocky Mountains. In 1846, the United States agreed to another treaty in which it bought from Great Britain the southern portion on the large and rich Oregon Country. With the purchase of Oregon, the United States stretched from the Atlantic Ocean to the Pacific.

The Troubling Question of Slavery

As settlers moved into the new territories, new states were formed from them. The forming of new states brought up again the troubling question of slavery.

The northern states had abolished slavery within their borders, but the southern states had kept it. Before the revolution, it had appeared that slavery would eventually die out, both in the North and the South, because it was very expensive for masters to take care of their slaves. Then in 1793, Eli Whitney of Connecticut invented a machine, the cotton gin, that made it easy to separate cotton from its seeds. With the cotton gin and slave labor, cotton growers in the South could grow and process a lot more cotton than they could before. Large slave-run plantations in the new territories of Mississippi and Louisiana brought quick wealth to their owners. The cotton gin made keeping slaves something very profitable, at least in the **Deep South**.

So it was that slavery continued in the South long after it had died out in the North. But not just because of slavery but for other reasons, the northern and southern states were growing farther apart. For one thing, the North was becoming more industrial, while the South remained mostly agricultural. The North had more people than the South, which meant the House of Representatives had more northern members than southern ones. Southerners began to think that the only way they would keep northern Americans from controlling the government was if the Senate had as many southern senators as northern ones. But for that to happen, there had to be an equal number of southern "slave" states and northern "free" ones. Some northerners, however, opposed admitting new slave states into Union, not just because these Northerners were against slavery, but because they wanted the North to control the federal government.

The fight between southern and northern states broke out in 1819 when Missouri asked to be admitted to the Union as a slave state. Some northern congressmen said, no; Missouri had to enter the Union as a free state or not enter at all, they said. Southern congressmen fought back, demanding that Missouri's request be respected.

It was the Kentucky senator Henry Clay who in 1820 came up with a **compromise** that brought peace between North and South, at least for a time. This "Missouri Compromise," which Congress approved, said that Missouri would be admitted as a slave state at the same time Maine joined the Union as a free state. More importantly, however, the compromise chose a latitude line that ran across the Louisiana Territory; slavery was forbidden north of that line, said the compromise, while south of the line, it was allowed.

The Missouri Compromise brought peace to the nation for another 25 or more years.

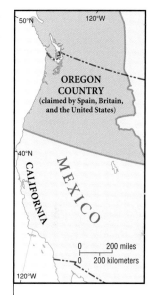

Map of the Oregon Country

Deep South: the farthest south of the American southern states; the states of Georgia, Alabama, Mississippi, and Louisiana

compromise: an agreement that settles a quarrel between two or more parties by giving each party something, but not all, of what it wants

Struggles with Mexico

In 1821, Mexico ended a ten-year revolution against Spain and became an independent state. At that time, Mexico included much of what is now the western United States, including California, Nevada, Utah, Arizona, New Mexico, Texas, and parts of Colorado and Wyoming. The area called Texas shared a border with the United States, and in the early 1820s, Americans from the United States began to settle in Texas. The Mexican government allowed them to do so.

But as more and more Americans settled in Texas, the Mexican government got nervous. Americans began to outnumber Mexicans there. The Mexican government began passing laws to discourage Americans from settling in Texas. In 1829, the Mexican government abolished slavery in all of Mexico. This law especially affected Americans in Texas, many

Map of the Republic of Texas

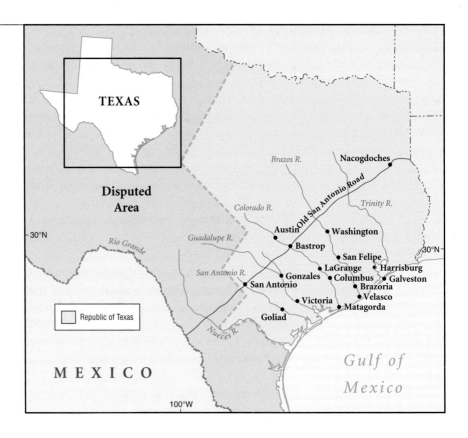

of whom were slaveholders. In 1830, the Mexican government said that Americans were no longer allowed to enter Texas as settlers.

Americans, however, continued to settle in Texas, and they became upset with the Mexican government because it would not allow them to form their own government or live by American-style laws. In 1835, Mexico's president, General Antonio López de Santa Anna, decided he would teach the rebellious Americans a lesson and, in 1835, he sent an army into Texas.

Santa Anna, however, himself had broken Mexican law by abolishing Mexico's constitution. The American Texans used this as a reason to rebel against the Mexican government. When the Texans defeated the Mexican army sent to Texas, Santa Anna gathered another army and himself led it to Texas.

While the new Mexican army was marching northward, an assembly of both English-speaking and Spanish-speaking Texans declared Texas an independent state, called the Republic of Texas. In February 1836, Santa Anna arrived in San Antonio in southern Texas and massacred the American defenders at an old Catholic mission, called the Alamo. Santa Anna then moved into eastern Texas to destroy the Texan army. But in a battle on the San Jacinto River, the Texan army led by a Tennessean named Sam Houston defeated the Mexican army and captured Santa Anna. The war ended and Texas was an independent republic.

Texas remained an independent republic for about ten years. In 1845, the Texas government asked to be made a part of the United States and was accepted into the union as a slave state. The **annexation** of Texas angered the Mexican government, which thought the United States was stealing Mexican territory.

annexation: joining or adding a small thing to a large thing, such as a smaller territory to a larger one. The verb form is *annex*.

The Conquest of Northern Mexico

Some Americans objected to making Texas part of the United States. Some of these were anti-slavery people, who did not want another slave state in the union. Others were southerners, who feared that adding more territory to the United States would stir up the quarrels over slavery. Other Americans, however, thought the United States should annex Mexican California, as well as all the Mexican territories that lay between Texas and the Pacific Ocean.

One of those Americans who wanted California was President James K. Polk. He offered to buy California from Mexico; but the Mexican

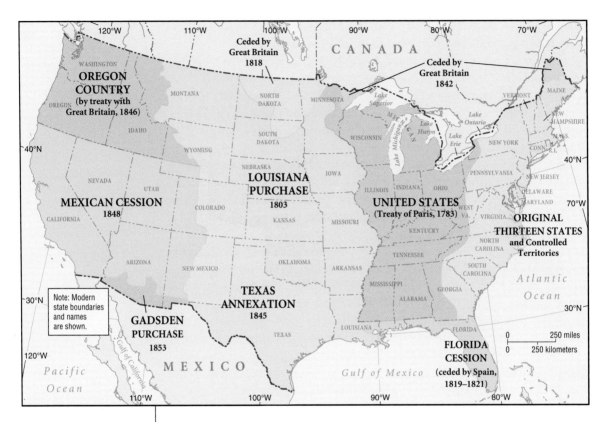

Map showing all the new territories added to the United States, including the ones ceded from Mexico

government, angry over Texas, refused. Not wanting to give up California, Polk sent the U.S. army into a part of Texas that the Mexican government said belonged to Mexico but Texas claimed was American territory. The Americans lay siege to the Mexican city of Matamoros and were in turn attacked by Mexican troops, who killed several American soldiers. Polk used this incident to get Congress to declare war on Mexico on May 11, 1846.

From 1846 to 1848, a U.S. army under General Zachary Taylor invaded Mexico from the north while another American army under General Winfield S. Scott landed on Mexico's east coast and marched toward the Mexican capital, Mexico City. In 1847, Scott's army fought its way to a bloody victory on the slopes of Chapultepec Hill, the fortress overlooking Mexico City. After fierce fighting, Scott took Mexico City. On February 2, 1848, the Mexican government signed the Treaty of

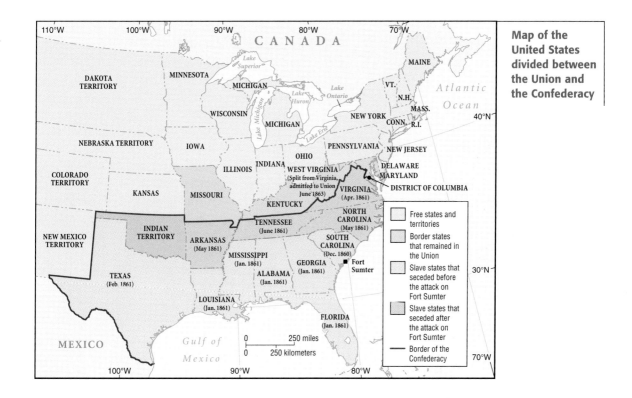

Map of the United States divided between the Union and the Confederacy

Guadalupe Hidalgo, in which it gave California, New Mexico, Arizona, and the Mexican territories to the north to the United States.

The United States of America now spread from the Atlantic to the Pacific, from "sea to shining sea."

The Civil War

As many Americans, both in the North and South, had feared, adding California and northern Mexico to the United States did stir up the controversy over slavery. Fearing that the South would lose power in the federal government if all the new territories became free states, southerners demanded that people could bring slaves into at least the southern parts of the West. Anti-slavery people, however, wanted slavery banned in all the

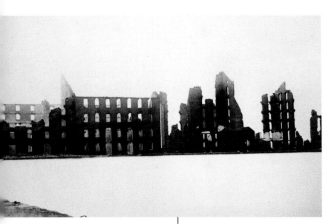

Ruins of the Gallego Flour Mills, Richmond, Virginia, April, 1865

secede: to withdraw from a group or an organization

new territories. Eventually, some northerners and southerners argued that slavery could not be banned in any of the new territories. Anti-slavery people, however, said it should be banned in all the territories. Slavery was immoral, they said, and should not be allowed to spread.

Arguments over slavery grew harsher right up until 1860, when an anti-slavery Republican named Abraham Lincoln was elected president. Fearing that Lincoln would favor measures that would destroy the South's political power and its economy, some southerners said the southern states should **secede** (that is, withdraw) from the union and form their own government. South Carolina was the first state to secede, and it was soon followed over the next six months by ten other southern states. These states formed a new federal government of their own, called the Confederate States of America.

Though southerners said that states had the right to secede from the United States, Abraham Lincoln disagreed. War between the United States and the Confederate States began when Lincoln refused to remove U.S. soldiers from Fort Sumter, a U.S. fortress in South Carolina's Charleston harbor. Considering this an act of war, the Confederate government ordered its troops in Charleston to open fire on Fort Sumter.

The first shot of the war was fired at 4:30 a.m., on April 12, 1861. Four years of fighting followed, leaving many, many thousands of dead. The war ended when the Confederate States of America, surrendered on Palm Sunday, April 9, 1865.

Equality and Human Rights

The Civil War left the southern states ruined; many thousands of southern men had died in the war and the southern economy was destroyed. The United States Congress's attempts to punish the Confederate states during the 10-year period of time called Reconstruction kept the South from prospering like the other states in the union. The war had freed the slaves, but there was little employment for them. They were "freemen" but desperately poor. Their former masters feared these men newly freed from slavery.

After Reconstruction ended, southern states passed laws that kept black people from sharing the privileges white people enjoyed. They could not attend white schools or eat in white restaurants; black people could not use the same restrooms that white people used. Such laws were passed for **segregation** — to keep the white and black races separate from one another. Even in the northern states, black people were not treated as equals to white people.

The American ideal of equality for all people did not die in the years following the Civil War, but grew stronger. Another struggle that some Americans took up was the fight to bring justice to workers. After the war, the northern states became centers of industry. Both black and white Americans as well as immigrants from other countries flocked into northern cities to work in unsafe factories, for little money. These workers and their families lived in dirty, unhealthy city slums and suffered from hunger and sickness. Workers formed unions or workers associations among themselves and fought for better wages and safer working conditions. They demanded that they be treated like human beings, with respect.

The fight for equality for blacks as well as justice for workers continued into the 20th century. Workers were able to win many victories and better their condition. In 1954, the Supreme Court said schools could no longer forbid black students from attending them. Following that ruling, segregation laws across the United States were struck down or voted out one by one.

Because of their participation in two world wars during the 20th century, Americans began to see themselves as champions of human rights, not just in their country, but around the world. After the Second World War, Americans and many people throughout the world saw the United States as the leader for the "free world" in the fight against Communism.

Even today, at the beginning of the 21st century, Americans cherish the ideals of freedom and equality — the ideals on which their country was founded.

> **segregation:** the separation of one thing from another, one person from another, or one group of people from another group of people

Chapter 15 Review

Let's Remember Please write your answers in complete sentences.

1. With what other European power did Great Britain fight a war for the control of North America?

2. Why did the English colonies in America decide to revolt against the government of Great Britain?
3. What are the three branches of government in the United States' Constitution?
4. What state was once an independent republic?
5. What does "segregation" mean?

Let's Consider   For silent thinking and a short essay, or for thinking in a group with classroom discussion:
1. How did frontier life help form the American character?
2. Why do we consider Washington a great man?
3. Could the Civil War have been avoided?
4. What are the most important ideals of American culture?

Things to Do

1. According to the map on page 352, the latitude line, 40° N runs just north of Philadelphia, Pennsylvania. Using an atlas, follow this latitude line west. What states does it pass through? Follow it east. What European countries does it pass through? Do the same with the latitude line, 50° N. Through what countries, both in North America and Europe, does it pass?
2. Using a map of North America in an atlas, identify the rivers that flow into the Mississippi River and where they begin.
3. Could one travel by boat from Lake Superior to the Atlantic Ocean? If so, how?

Let's Eat!

A recipe from colonial times is still popular today: deep dish apple pie. Pare and thinly slice 5 pounds of apples. Place ⅓ of the apples in a baking pan. Sprinkle with ⅓ cup sugar and dot with 3 tablespoons butter; sprinkle lightly with cinnamon. Continue with 2 more layers of apples, sugar and butter, and cinnamon. Sprinkle with a dusting of nutmeg before covering with a pie crust. Bake 40 minutes, or until brown and apples are thoroughly soft.

Chapter 16 Latin America: Lands of Many Cultures

I n Latin America, cultures mix in a way they do nowhere else in the world. American Indians, Europeans, Africans, Japanese, Hindus and Muslims from India, all live and work together in the huge urban areas of all the Latin American countries.

Latin American culture is found throughout Mexico, Central America, and South America, and in parts of the United States. In the 15th and 16th centuries, southern Europeans—especially Spaniards and Portuguese—began to settle in Latin America. These early settlers brought their Catholic religion and customs as well as their languages to their new homes. Since the languages of these settlers, Spanish and Portuguese, came from Latin, this cultural region of the world is called Latin America.

The Geography of Latin America

Latin America has nearly every type of landscape: mountains, jungles, plains, deserts, and coastland. It also has abundant natural resources: vast rainforests and timberlands, rich grazing and farm lands, and large deposits of valuable minerals.

South America has a wide variety of landscapes, from tropical forests to dry desert, from temperate grasslands to icy cold mountaintops. The equator runs through northern Brazil, northern Ecuador, and southern Colombia; so, in general, the weather in these regions is warm throughout

the year. Rainforests rise in the regions north and south of the equator. In contrast, the Atacama Desert in northern Chile is one of the driest places on Earth. The weather is always cold in the high Andes Mountains, which are made up of incredibly high, cold, snow-covered peaks and active volcanoes (many over 20,000 feet high.). The Andes range stretches 4,500 miles along western South America from Venezuela in the north to Tierra del Fuego on the southern tip of the continent.

South America has two other major mountain regions. One of these, the Guiana highlands, runs from southeastern Venezuela, through Guyana, Suriname, and into French Guiana. The other range is about 1,500 miles to the south in Brazil, around the cities of São Paulo and Rio de Janeiro. Plateaus, plains, smaller mountain ranges and hills cover much of Brazil between the southern mountains and the great Amazon River Basin.

The largest tropical rain forest in the world is found in the Amazon River Basin. The Amazon River is the second longest river in the world. It flows 4,000 miles, eastward from the Peruvian Andes Mountains to the Atlantic. Only the Nile River in Africa is longer than the Amazon. The hot and moist Amazon Basin covers two-fifths of the South American continent and contains more kinds of plants than anywhere else in the world.

Extending eastward from the Andes, the Central Plains cover about three-fifths of South America. These plains are drained by the huge Amazon and Plate **river systems**, which empty into the Atlantic. Argentina and Venezuela, especially, have very fertile plains and grasslands, which support many prosperous ranches and extensive farms.

The boundary between South and North America is the narrow neck of land called the Isthmus of Panama. Between this isthmus and Mexico is the region called Central America, which includes the republics of Panama, Costa Rica, Nicaragua, Honduras, El Salvador, Guatemala, and Belize. Much of Central America is covered with high mountain ranges. Among the mountains are fertile valleys. Central America has a warm tropical climate and tropical rainforests.

Mexico is geographically part of North America, but its history and traditions make it part of Latin America. Its geography is rugged but hospitable to human life. The coastal plain along the Gulf of Mexico is semitropical forest. The central plateau rises rapidly to a mile above sea level. The eruption of volcanoes has left a layer of rich soil over the plateau.

Fisherman in the Amazon rain forest

river system: a term referring to a group of rivers that all flow into a common river. The Mississippi river system, for instance, is made up of the Mississippi River and all the rivers that flow into it. The Ohio, Red, and Missouri rivers are thus part of the Mississippi river system.

Opposite: A map of Latin America, including Mexico and the Caribbean Islands

Mexico has two major mountain ranges that run from north to south. One of these ranges, on the western side of the country, is called Sierra Madre Occidental; the other range, running on the eastern side of the country, is the Sierra Madre Oriental. The region of Mexico around the capital, Mexico City, is very mountainous, with peaks rising over 17,000 and 18,000 feet. Northern Mexico is mountainous and arid, with two large deserts — the Chihuahuan and Sonoran deserts. A long peninsula on the west, Baja (BA•hah) California, forms the Gulf of California, one of the richest marine-life regions of the world.

The islands of the Caribbean Sea also form a part of Latin America. These islands include Cuba (the largest of them all), Hispaniola (divided between the nations of the Dominican Republic and Haiti), Jamaica, Puerto Rico, and the Bahamas.

Latin America Before Columbus

Sometimes we think of Native Americans as people living in tribes that travel from place to place and survive by hunting or gathering seed plants and nuts. Certainly, there were many Native American peoples who lived this way. Yet, North and South America also sheltered native peoples who farmed, lived in villages, and even built permanent houses and villages. And in Central America and northwestern South America, native peoples built great civilizations that we can admire today.

Opposite: A topographical map of South America, including Mexico and the Caribbean, with a color-keyed elevation scale

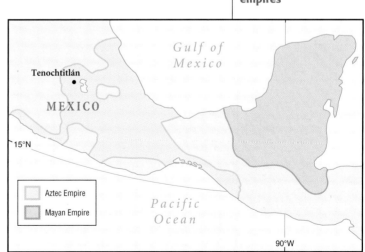

Aztec and Mayan empires

Tenochtitlán

MEXICO

Gulf of Mexico

15°N

Aztec Empire

Mayan Empire

Pacific Ocean

90°W

Inca empire

Pre-Columbian: referring to the history of the Americas before Columbus and the Spaniards arrived in the New World

maize: a plant with grain growing on large ears; corn

Latin America's story includes the tale of these three great Native American civilizations: the *Mayan* civilization of southern Mexico, the *Inca* civilization of Peru in South America, and the *Aztec* civilization in the highlands of what is now Mexico City. These civilizations are often called **Pre-Columbian**, because they existed before Christopher Columbus came to the Americas in 1492. Here, we shall discuss the Mayan and Inca civilizations. We shall address the Aztecs later in the chapter.

The Maya

Of the three Pre-Columbian civilizations (Aztec, Mayan, and Inca), the Mayan is the oldest. The Indian people called the Maya had lived on the Yucatan Peninsula for centuries, developing what became their great civilization. The Mayan civilization reached its full greatness between the years A.D. 300 and 900. The Maya were a farming people, growing **maize** (their most important crop), cotton, and other crops. Farming was not easy where they lived, for the Yucatan is covered with tropical forests. In order to farm, the Maya had to clear away the forest — and then work constantly so that their fields were not once again covered by dense jungle vegetation.

It was in the cleared spaces of the jungle that the Maya raised their cities, which were more like groupings of religious temples than anything we think of as a city. These temples, made of stone, had a pyramid shape and could be lofty. One temple ruin discovered in the Yucatan is over 200 feet high. The Mayan temples are amazing not only because they were built so skillfully but because those who built them had only wood and stone

The ruins of the Mayan Temple of the Warriors, at Chichen Itza in northern Yucatan. Notice the dense growth of tropical forest around the temple site.

tools with which to cut the temple stones. The Maya too had no vehicles with wheels or large beasts (such as oxen) to drag the huge stones from the quarry to the building site. They possessed no machines to raise the stones one on top of another.

The Maya had other arts besides architecture. They formed beautiful figurines and ornaments out of **jade.** They developed painting, both for **murals** and pottery, as well as the arts of carving and sculpture. The Maya invented a written language that used hieroglyphics.

Like nearly all ancient peoples, the Maya worshiped many gods. Along with the sun, moon, and other natural things, the Maya honored maize as a god. Human sacrifice was a part of Mayan worship. Mayan warriors raided neighboring peoples, not only to get slaves, but to gather victims to sacrifice to their gods.

Priests had tremendous power in Mayan society, both because they represented the people before the gods and because they were believed to be able to tell fortunes and predict the future. To predict the future, the priests studied the stars and, especially, the movements of the sun, moon, and the planet Venus. In this way the Maya developed a knowledge of astronomy as well as a calendar. Their knowledge of astronomy allowed the Maya to make amazingly accurate predictions of **solar eclipses**.

After the year 900, the Maya abandoned many of their settlements — no one knows exactly why. Invaders from the north took control of Mayan settlements in north Yucatan and, it seems, changed Mayan society greatly. The older Mayan settlements had no walls to protect them from invasions, but later settlements did. Human sacrifice, too, seems to have increased in the new Mayan settlements. On the whole, it seems, because of the conquest, Mayan civilization went from being a rather peaceful society to a more warlike one.

The Realm of the Inca

The high mountain valleys of the Andes in Peru were the home of another great Pre-Columbian civilization. We call this civilization "Inca" after the title of its ruler, the Inca, who was believed to be a descendant of the sun god. According to Inca tradition, the first Inca, who was the son of the Sun god and the moon goddess, established his kingdom in Peru around the year A.D. 1200.

Like the Maya, the Peruvians built cities having great stone buildings. Unlike the early Mayan settlements, however, the Inca cities had walls

A detail of an ancient carving of a Mayan prisoner, from the ruins of Palenque, Chiapas state, Mexico

jade: a hard stone used in jewelry and ornaments. Most jade is green.
mural: a picture painted on a wall
solar eclipse: a darkening of the sun in daytime that occurs when the moon passes between Earth and the sun

thatch: straw, rushes, or a similar material used as a covering or roof

aqueduct: a man-made channel or pipe used to bring water from a distance

made from uncut stones, very skillfully built without mortar. Unlike the Mayan pyramids and other buildings, the Peruvian structures had only one story; and, unlike Mayan buildings, which had stone roofs, the Peruvian buildings had **thatch** roofs. Peruvian buildings are not as impressive as the Mayan structures, but the Peruvians showed their genius in building roads and canals to make travel over their wide realm easy and swift. The Peruvians, too, raised **aqueducts** to bring water to their settlements. They built all these structures without the aid of iron, machines, and beasts of burden.

The Peruvians were ingenious farmers, cutting terraces in the sides of hills and mountains in order to grow food. In growing crops, Peruvian farmers took advantage of the different climates of their realm. The low elevations along the Pacific coast were warm, while the weather grew colder as the Andes rose to thousands of feet above the level of the sea. The Peruvians, thus, grew warm weather crops farther down the mountainsides, and crops that did better in cooler climates, farther up.

The Incan city of Machu Picchu in the Andes highlands. Notice the terraces on the mountainside at the left.

The government of Peru was very simple. The Inca was a complete **despot**, controlling the lives of all his subjects. Even the marriages of the humblest Peruvian were arranged by the Inca's government. Though, on the whole, the Inca was a rather gentle ruler, he took bitter revenge on anyone who dared to resist him. If he captured a city or region that had rebelled against him, he laid waste to it and slaughtered its inhabitants. No one was to rebel against the son of the Sun.

The chief god of the Incas was the Sun god, who had a magnificent temple in the city of Cuzco, the Inca's capital. The Inca was not only the king, but the highest priest, and he controlled religion just like he did everything else in his land. The Peruvians offered animals, grain, and flowers to their gods as sacrifices. On very solemn occasions they offered human sacrifices, generally a child or a beautiful maiden. Human sacrifice, however, was in no way as big a part of Inca religion as it was of the Mayan and Aztec religions.

Gold was very abundant in Peru and the Incas stored their houses with treasures of gold. It is said that no Inca passed his treasure down to his son. Each Inca thought he would need his treasures and even most of his houses in the next life. When the next Inca began his reign, he had to build new houses as well as gather his own treasury of gold. This shows just how much gold was to be found in Peru.

> **despot:** an absolute ruler who does whatever he likes; a ruler who is tyrannical or *despotic*

Europe Comes to Latin America

The modern history of Latin America began with Christopher Columbus's discovery of the American continents in 1492. In Chapter 9, we saw how, after much trying, Columbus was able to convince King Fernando and Queen Isabel of Spain to pay for an expedition to reach the Indies by sailing west over the Atlantic Ocean. Columbus's mission was to find gold and wealth for himself and Spain's "Catholic Monarchs" (as Fernando and Isabel were called.) Yet he had greater aim — to carry the Catholic Faith to the heathen overseas.

On August 3, 1492, in three small ships, the *Niña*, *Pinta*, and *Santa Maria*, Columbus and his crew set out on their quest across the Atlantic. It was a long and difficult voyage. As the weeks and months passed, the

Statue of Queen Isabel the Catholic, Madrid

After 35 days at sea, Columbus lands on an island, which he calls San Salvador, off the tip of Florida, taking possession of it "in the name of Our Lord Jesus Christ, for the crown of Castile"

crews feared that they would run out of water and food. They worried, too, that there would be no wind to blow them back to Spain. By October 10, the crews had had enough. They could see no land. They wanted to return to Spain. Columbus tried to calm his men. He agreed that, if they saw no land after two or three days, the fleet would return home. But, finally, at 2:00 a.m. on October 12, the crew heard the cry of "Land! Land!" They had reached land at last.

Columbus had landed on a small island, but it was just the beginning of his discoveries. In this, his first expedition and in others that he later made, Columbus discovered Hispaniola, Cuba, and the Virgin Islands. On his last expedition, he discovered the northern coast of South America. But to the day of his death, on May 10, 1506, Columbus thought he had reached the Indies instead of a "New World."

Not just Spain, but all of Europe took great interest in Columbus's discoveries. Portugal, which had been the first to reach the Indies by sea, was worried Spain would take some of its colonies in India and the Orient. To keep Spain and Portugal from quarrelling over the new lands, Pope Alexander VI in 1493 set a dividing line in the Atlantic. The pope decreed that Spain could claim all lands in the Indies that fell west of this line, while Portugal could claim all the lands that fell east of the line. Because of the pope's decision, most of Latin America came under the power of Spain. Only Brazil, which jutted out east of the line, went to Portugal. This is why, even to this day, the people of Brazil speak Portuguese, while most of the rest of Latin America speaks Spanish.

Even during Columbus's lifetime, other adventurers set out to discover new lands in the "Indies." One of these was an Italian named Amerigo Vespucci, who explored the northern coast of South America. Because of a book that told of Vespucci's adventures, people in Europe began to call the newly discovered lands *America* after him. (*Americus* is the Latin form of the name Amerigo.)

In 1513, a Spanish captain, Vasco Nuñez de Balboa, plunged into the interior of Darien (Panama) with 170 men. On September 24, 1513, standing on a mountaintop, Balboa sighted a new ocean. He called it the South Sea; later, it would be called the Pacific. It was Balboa's discovery of the Pacific that showed that what Columbus had discovered and explored was not Asia or the Indies, but an entirely new world.

The Conquest of Mexico

The Spanish explorers did not set out just to discover new lands, but to conquer them as well. Everywhere they went, these men, called **conquistadors**, claimed the lands for the crown of Spain. Like Columbus, they were eager to find riches; some, too, were interested in converting the Native Americans to the Gospel of Christ. Unfortunately, many of the explorers were cruel to the natives and forced them into slavery. They did so, even though Queen Isabel and, later, King Charles I, of Spain said the Indians should be treated with great gentleness.

conquistador: Spanish word meaning "conqueror"

One of the greatest of the Spanish conquistadors was a man named Hernán Cortés. In his youth, Cortés had been a bad student, wasting much of his time in foolish living. He dropped out of law school after only two years and then went to the Indies to seek his fortune. In 1518, Cortés became captain general of an expedition that was to seek for riches in what is now Mexico.

Cortés's fleet landed off the coast of Yucatán in February 1519. There, in what is now the state of Tabasco, Cortés's army of about 600 men fought and defeated a force of 40,000 Indians. Cortés made peace with these Indians and then sailed north along the coast of Mexico. In April 1519, he founded the first Spanish settlement on this coast, calling it Villa Rica de Vera Cruz.

Engraved portrait of Hernán Cortés

At Vera Cruz, some of Cortés's men demanded that the expedition return to Cuba. They had learned that Cortés meant to march inland, to the realm of the mighty Aztecs. In response to these men, Cortés destroyed all but one of his 11 ships. Cortés's troops cried out that he had led them to Mexico to be butchered like cattle. But Cortés refused to listen

talon: the claw of a bird of prey, such as an eagle or hawk

to them. "I will remain here," he said, "while there is one to bear me company." If any of his men, he said, were cowards, they could take the one ship left and return to Cuba. There, said Cortés, they can remain and tell "how they deserted their commander and their comrades, and patiently wait until we return loaded with the spoils of the Aztecs."

These words filled his men with courage. Nearly all of them cried out: "To Mexico! To Mexico!" They were determined to match their force against the fearsome nation of the Aztecs.

The Aztecs

The first Indians the Spaniards met when they came to the Americas were the gentle Taino people who lived on many of the islands of the Caribbean. The Indians Cortés and his men had met in Tabasco were very different from the Taino. In this land the Indians called Anahuac, the native peoples raised buildings and temple pyramids of stone instead of the dwellings of stick and thatch the Taino built. The people of Anahuac were very numerous and lived in towns surrounded by well-cultivated fields of maize.

A statue of the Aztec goddess Cihuateotl

In the center of Anahuac, in a city built in the center of a lake, dwelt a powerful, warlike people — the Aztecs. By the time Cortés arrived, the Aztec king, Montezuma II, had conquered the tribes of Anahuac, making the Aztec Empire greater than it had ever been before.

The Aztecs said that they had come to Anahuac from a land called Aztlán, far to the northwest, and had wandered into the south. In the 14th century, they came upon a lake in the high mountain valley of Mexico. There, on the shores of the lake, they beheld an eagle, perched on the stem of a prickly pear cactus, its wings spread to the rising sun and a serpent in its **talons**. For the Aztecs, this was a sign that they should settle there. They called this place and the city they would build there, Tenochtitlán.

The Aztecs were rather primitive when they arrived in Mexico. The neighboring city of Texcuco, however, had a high civilization, like that of the Maya. It was from Texcuco that the Aztecs learned the arts of civilization. By the 16th century, the Aztecs had become skilled in agriculture and architecture. They planted beautiful gardens and built the glorious city of Tenochtilán in the center of the lake. They displayed their skill in making gold ornaments and developed hieroglyphic writing with which they wrote histories and beautiful poetry. Like the Maya and Inca, however, the Aztecs had not invented the wheel.

The Aztecs worshiped many gods. One the most important of these gods was Huitzilopochtli (witsy•lo•POCT•lee), the god of war and of the sun. It was to this god that the Aztecs offered their many human sacrifices. Indeed, one of the most important reasons the Aztecs went to war was to capture victims for sacrifice. The Aztecs had many religious festivals, and each one of them had to include sacrifices of human beings, whose bodies were, afterwards, eaten. It is said that the Aztecs sacrificed about 20,000 victims each year.

Another important Aztec god was Quetzalcoatl (the "feathered serpent"), who was said to have white skin, dark hair, and a flowing beard. The legends say that Quetzalcoatl had taught people how to farm, use metals, and set up governments. The Aztecs said that under Quetzalcoatl Mexico had enjoyed a period of prosperity. But, at last, another god drove him out of Anahuac and he went east across the sea. Quetzalcoatl promised his followers that, one day, he would return to Anahuac, from the east, over the sea. It was said that when Quetzalcoatl returned, he would abolish human sacrifice.

The Spaniards Arrive

The news of Cortés's landing at Vera Cruz filled Montezuma with fear — could the Spaniard be Quetzalcoatl returned from over the sea? The strangers were white-skinned and bearded, as Quetzalcoatl supposedly had been. What's more, whatever Indian cities the strangers entered, they freed the people who were to be sacrificed. Uncertain what to do, Montezuma invited Cortés to come to Tenochtitlán.

As the Spaniards approached the Aztec capital, they were joined by the Tlaxcalan Indians who were enemies of the Aztecs. When Cortés and his men at last climbed the mountains surrounding Tenochtitlán, they saw below them the great Aztec city, with its towering temples. It was so

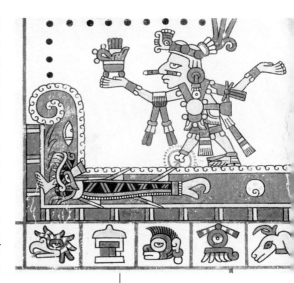

Origin of all human lands, from an Indian painted book of history showing Tezcatlipoca tempting the Earth Monster to the surface of the great waters by using his foot as bait. In swallowing his foot, the Earth Monster lost her lower jaw; hideously crippled, she was unable to sink and the Earth was created from her body. The symbols at the base of the drawing represent dates and, with the twelve dots also in the picture, signify the periods in the calendar when Tezcatlipoca was dominant over other forces.

Portrait of Montezuma II, emperor of the Aztecs

immunity: the body's ability to resist catching a disease
brigantine: a ship with two masts

beautiful that the Spaniards were in awe and felt great fear. Only a very powerful people, they thought, could build a city like that! It was Cortés's courageous spirit that encouraged his men to conquer their fear and move forward into the city.

Montezuma treated Cortés and his troops with hospitality. But though Montezuma was kind, Cortés did not trust him. Finally, fearing for his own safety, Cortés and his men seized Montezuma in his own palace. The Aztec king thus became Cortés's prisoner, though he continued to act as the king of Mexico.

The capture of their king was humiliating to the proud Aztecs. At last they rose up against the Spaniards. The streets and rooftops of Tenochtitlán were filled with armed Aztecs. Bloody fighting erupted, in the course of which, Montezuma himself was killed by his own people. The Aztec king died on June 30, 1520.

Because of the uprising, the Spaniards faced certain death if they remained in the city. On the night of July 1, 1520, Cortés led his men and their Tlaxcalan allies in a retreat from Tenochtitlán. The Spaniards later named this night *La Noche Triste* — "the sorrowful night." The Aztecs in great numbers surrounded and attacked the fleeing Spaniards, taking some of them prisoner to sacrifice to the war god. Both the Spanish and the Tlaxcalans lost many men that night; all told, 450 Spaniards and 4,000 natives were killed. A few days later, a broken and discouraged army marched into Tlaxcala.

But though he had suffered defeat, Cortés was not discouraged. He immediately began making plans to return to Tenochtitlán. Though he at first did not know it, this time he had another ally to help him in his conquest — a disease called smallpox, which struck the Aztecs. Having no **immunity** against the disease, the Aztecs died in great numbers.

At Tlaxcala, Cortés ordered 15 small ships, called **brigantines**, to be constructed so that he could assault Tenochtitlán by the waters of the lake as well as by land. His total force consisted of 818 Spaniards, together with 87 cavalry and 25,000 Indian allies. The assault on the city began on April 28, 1521. It was very hard and bloody fighting. The desperate Aztecs fought the Spaniards in every block and street of Tenochtitlán. To deprive the Aztecs of hiding places, Cortés ordered his men to destroy every house and building they came upon. When Cortés's army at last reached the center of Tenochtitlán, seven-eighths of the city had been laid waste. On August 13, 1521, the Spaniards overwhelmed what remained of the Aztec forces. Cortés had conquered Mexico.

The Beginnings of "New Spain"

In 1522, King Charles I of Spain made Cortés captain general and chief justice of "New Spain," as Mexico was now called. From 1522 to 1524, Cortés worked to rebuild Tenochtitlán, which became known as Mexico City. Using forced Indian labor, Cortés raised a city that was said to be more beautiful and rich than any city in Europe.

The Great Tenochtitlán, by Diego Rivera. Detail: a vision of life in the Aztec city of Tenochtitlán.

Encouraged by Cortés, many Spaniards came to settle in Mexico, where they mingled with the Indian population. Cortés zealously spread the Catholic Faith among the Indians. He requested the government to send over missionaries. Under Cortés, these missionaries established schools and colleges for the education of the Indians. The missionaries worked to destroy the native religion, but some of them translated the Aztec hieroglyphics and so preserved the knowledge of Aztec institutions and history. On every site of human sacrifice, the Church performed **exorcisms** and erected churches to sanctify these terrible places.

In later years, Cortés fell out of favor with the court of Spain. In 1540, he returned to Spain to plead his case before the king. Frustrated with the **rebuffs** he received from Charles I, Cortés journeyed to Seville, planning to embark for Mexico. Instead, he fell sick in a town near Seville and there died on December 2, 1547.

Spain and the Native Americans

In setting up governments in the lands they conquered in America, the Spanish monarchs faced a difficulty. Fernando and Isabel wanted the Native Americans to become Christians. They wanted to teach them European civilization so that they could fully participate in Spanish

exorcism: the act by which the Church drives demons out of persons, places, or things

rebuff: the resisting of another person's attempts to help or seek help

society. Only in this way, thought the monarchs, could Indians and Spaniards live side by side in peace.

It was Columbus who came up with a way that was supposed to civilize the Indians and make them Christians. When Columbus was governor of the island of Hispaniola, he divided up the island's lands among his men and allowed them to use Indians to work the lands. Later, the Spanish crown took over what Columbus did and gave lands to Spanish settlers. These lands were called **encomiendas**—"complimentary land grants." Someone who received an *encomienda* was called an **encomendero**. According to Spanish law, an *encomendero* was not to treat the Indians on his *encomienda* as slaves, but he could make them work for him. In return, the *encomendero* had to take care of the Indians and educate them so that they could become Christians and civilized. The idea behind this arrangement was that, in time, the Indians would take their place as full members of Spanish society.

encomienda: land that was given or granted by the Spanish king to some person
encomendero: a man who receives a land grant or *encomienda*

Unfortunately, the *encomienda* plan did not better the lives of Indians. *Encomenderos* often treated their Indian workers like slaves and were cruel to them. On Hispaniola and other islands, the native peoples were not used to such heavy labor as farming and mining. Having no immunities against European sicknesses, thousands of Indians died.

As governor of New Spain, Cortés himself established *encomiendas*. Cortés was careful not to break up native tribes but allowed the Indians to live in their villages under their native chiefs. To insure that Indian workers were treated justly, Cortés passed laws setting the number of hours an Indian was allowed to work and how much he must be paid. Cortés also required *encomenderos* to provide suitable religious instruction to their Indian workers.

Nevertheless, just like in the Caribbean islands, Indians were often abused in Mexico. The system turned the natives of the continent into serfs, bound to their lands and enslaved to their landlords. Cortés was able to keep the abuses to a minimum, but they still occurred.

Some Spaniards defended the way the Spanish treated the natives in America. They claimed that Pope Alexander VI had divided the New World between Spain and Portugal, and so these nations had the right to conquer the Native Americans. But some Spaniards disagreed. They said the pope did not give either Spain or Portugal the right to conquer but only to convert the natives to the Catholic Faith. They condemned the way the way *encomenderos* were treating the Indians. Among the Spaniards who stood up for the Native Americans was a lawyer turned priest who would become known as the "Defender of the Indians." He was Bartolomé de Las Casas.

Defender of the Indians

Bartolomé de Las Casas probably heard a sermon preached in a straw-thatched church on the island of Hispaniola in 1511. Commenting on the text, "I am a voice crying in the wilderness," the Dominican friar, Antonio de Montesinos, asked, "Are these Indians not men? Do they not have rational souls? Are you not obliged to love them as you love yourselves?"

Old engraving depicting Bartolome de las Casas

Las Casas dedicated his life to the belief that the Indians should be treated with justice and Christian charity. For 40 years or so, he argued that, as human beings, Indians had equal rights with Spaniards. The Spanish crown, said Las Casas, had no right to conquer the Indians by force. He thought Spaniards could act as **overlords** to the Indians, but they could not abolish Indian governments or enslave natives. The *encomienda* system, he said, was little better than slavery and should be abolished. No one should use force in preaching the Gospel, Las Casas said.

overlord: someone who is lord over someone else

In 1544, the Spanish king Charles I appointed Las Casas bishop of Chiapas in southern Mexico. There, Las Casas enraged colonists by setting rigid standards *encomenderos* must meet before he would **absolve** them from their sins. He basically refused to give the Eucharist to anyone who forced Indians to work on his lands.

absolve: to declare that someone is free of sin or guilt

Las Casas was a stout defender of the Indians. Sometimes, though, in defending them, he exaggerated both Indian virtues and Spanish cruelty. His most famous work, *A Short Account of the Destruction of the Indies*, is filled with many exaggerations of Spanish cruelty. This work was translated into several languages, and from it came the "Black Legend" that has been used to this day to attack Spain's reputation.

In 1550, Las Casas was in Spain where he tried to convince the Spanish king to stop all conquests of America. King Charles I did stop conquests until theologians could decide whether they were just or not. The result was that the king issued a new law for Spaniards in America. The law did not abolish conquests, but it tried to make life better for Indians in America and limit the cruelty of their Spanish rulers. It was a law inspired by the ideas of Bartolomé de Las Casas.

Juan Diego and Our Lady of Guadalupe

Because he fought for justice for the Indians, Bishop Las Casas drew many native people to the Catholic Church. Unfortunately, this did not happen all over New Spain. Because of the bad treatment they had received, many Indians were not willing to accept the Catholic Faith. They thought it was a white man's religion, that it had nothing to offer the brown-skinned natives.

Then, on December 12, 1531, something miraculous occurred. The Virgin Mary appeared to the Indian Juan Diego on Tepeyac hill near Mexico City — the site where an Aztec temple to the goddess Tonantzin had once stood. Appearing, not as a white woman but as an Aztec princess, the Virgin told Juan Diego to ask the bishop of Mexico, Juan de Zumárraga, to build a church dedicated to her on Tepeyac Hill. Bishop Zumárraga was, at first, unwilling to believe Juan Diego, but then a miracle changed his mind. On his third visit to the bishop, Juan Diego opened his **tilma**, or cloak, and a flood of roses poured forth from it. Not only was it wondrous that the Indian should find roses in December, but upon the tilma appeared the image of the lady. Bishop Zumárraga changed his mind and commanded that the church be built on Tepeyac hill.

Because of this **apparition** of the Virgin (whom we remember as Our Lady of Guadalupe), millions of Indians in Mexico were baptized into the Catholic Church. That Mary had appeared as an Aztec woman showed the Indians that the Faith was not just a white man's religion but was meant for the Indians as well.

apparition: the appearing of something that is unexpected, strange, or unusual

tilma: a cloak made of cactus fibers

Our Lady of Guadalupe

The Conquest of Peru

Cortés's conquest of the mighty Aztec kingdom inspired another Spanish conquistador to find an empire of his own to conquer. His name was Francisco Pizarro; and, in 1532, he with his brothers set off on an expedition to Peru — an empire that rivaled the glory of the Aztecs.

Climbing high into the Andes, the Pizarro brothers and their men learned that the Inca, Atahualpa, was fighting a civil war against his

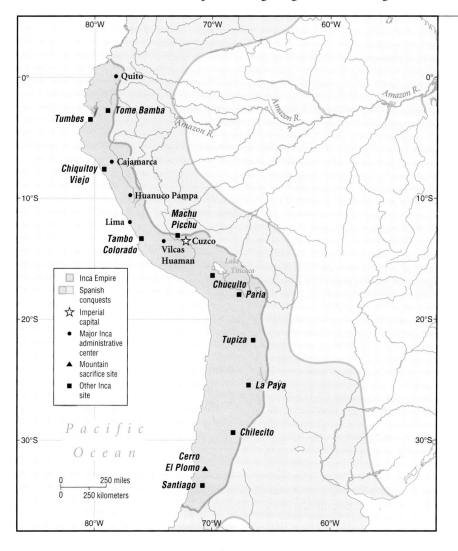

Map of the route of the conquerors of the Inca Empire

Old illustration of the funeral of Atahualpa

brother. Arriving in the Peruvian city of Cajamarca, it seemed to the explorers that the buildings were roofed with gold. The walls and roof of the Temple of the Sun, the largest building in Cajamarca, and the walls of the Inca's palace were hung with plates of gold to reflect the life-giving rays of the sun god. Hungry for treasure, Francisco Pizarro planned to seize this gold for himself.

Pizarro and his men carried out their plan in the most treacherous way. They invited the Inca into their camp. When Atahualpa entered with his bodyguard, the Spaniards slaughtered the Indians and took him captive. Pizarro said he would release Atahualpa only if he agreed to fill a room with gold. The Inca and his nobles agreed and filled the throne room of the palace with the shining metal. But when, at last, the Inca fulfilled his promise and had filled the entire room with gold, the Spaniards killed him.

After the murder of Atahualpa, Pizarro had an Inca named Manco Capac crowned king of Peru and in 1535 founded the city of Lima in Peru. Manco Capac, however, wanted to drive the Spaniards from Peru. With his Indian armies, he laid siege to the Spaniards in the cities of Cuzco and Lima. But in April 1537, the Spaniards defeated the Indians and put them to flight.

Francisco Pizarro, however, did not long enjoy his new riches and power. On June 26, 1541, he was assassinated in Lima by fellow conquistadors. The whole of rich Peru, however, remained part of the Spanish empire.

Saints of South America

Following the conquest of the Inca, the conquistadors set up *encomiendas* in Peru. The native Indians were treated as serfs, bound to the land of their villages, and forced to work in mines and on building projects. Thousands died in the first ten years of the colony. A feudal kingdom was created, rich, cruel, and far from the control of Spanish law and Spanish justice. The Church alone tried to help the Indians and improve their lot.

But despite all the evils of the time, Peru produced many holy men and women in colonial days. St. Rose of Lima (1586–1617) and St. Martin de Porres (1579–1639) are the best known.

A healer and wonder-worker, St. Martin was the son of an African slave woman and a Spanish owner. He brought comfort to the poor of Lima and inspired the rulers of the city to help their Indian serfs.

St. Rose, the **patroness** of South America and the Philippines, is remembered for the love of Christ that led her to a life of prayer and hard penance. Though she lived as a **recluse**, St. Rose knew of the sufferings of the Indian poor of Peru and spoke out against the cruelty of those who showed so little respect for their brothers and sisters.

St. Toribio de Mongrovejo (1538–1606), the bishop of Lima, risked his life fighting for Indian rights and justice. His efforts were finally rewarded when the king of Spain, Philip III, outlawed Indian servitude in 1601.

St. Francis Solano (1549–1610) carried the Gospel deep into the Chaco jungle, over the mountains, to the hostile and primitive savages who lived there. In old age he returned to Lima to preach to the wealthy of the city. His message brought about a revival of Christian faith and morality among the ruling classes of Peru.

Saint Rose of Lima

Revolution in Mexico

Like any society, 18th century Spanish America suffered from injustice and social problems. Some of these problems came from the way Spanish American society was divided culturally and socially. We will use the example of New Spain or Mexico to illustrate this.

By 1800, people of mixed Spanish and Indian race, called **mestizos,** formed the largest social group in Mexico—about 6 million people. The next largest group was the **creoles,** who were persons of Spanish blood, born in America. There were about 3 million creoles in Mexico in 1800. Besides these social groups and, of course, the pureblooded Indians, there were about 300,000 **peninsulares**—so-called because they were born on the Iberian Peninsula (Spain) and had come to live in America. Though they were the smallest group in New Spain, the *peninsulares* held by far the most political offices in New Spain. This made the creoles quite unhappy; for since they too were pure Spaniards, they thought they should at least be able to share power with the *peninsulares.* They thought they should not be deprived of power just because they were born in America.

patroness: a female who guards or protects someone or something. A man who protects and guards is a *patron.*
recluse: someone who lives alone or separated from society; a hermit

mestizo: a person of mixed Indian and Spanish heritage
creoles: American-born Spaniards
peninsulares: Spanish born people of New Spain

These internal problems in New Spain were not, however, bad enough, to cause a revolution. What finally did bring revolution to New Spain were events happening across the Atlantic. Spain, at the opening of the 19th century, was rocked with civil war.

depose: to remove from power

In 1808, the French emperor Napoleon I **deposed** the Spanish king and his son, Fernando VII. In their place, Napoleon made his own brother, Joseph Bonaparte, king of Spain. This led to an uprising of the Spanish people against the new government in which a group of leaders set up a parliament to represent both Spain and Spanish America. In New Spain, the king's representative (called the **viceroy**) tried to make himself the supreme power, but a group of *peninsulares* removed him from office. Following this, a group of creoles tried and failed to overthrow a new viceroy set up by the *peninsulares* and the Spanish parliament. This viceroy recognized both the parliament and Fernando VII as the government of both Spain and New Spain.

viceroy: an official who rules a territory in the name of the king

The two small rebellions in New Spain thus ended by keeping the old government in place. But they inspired others with more radical ideas to think of how they could change the government of New Spain. These ideas led to the first Mexican Revolution—led, oddly enough, by two priests. Their names were Padre Miguel Hidalgo and Padre José Maria Morelos.

Map of Mexico showing the major cities in 1810

Hidalgo's Rebellion

As the priest for the little village of Dolores in the Guanajuato region, Padre Miguel Hidalgo took great interest in the Indians' everyday life. While one of his assistant priests cared for the people's spiritual needs, Hidalgo helped the Indians cultivate grape vines and olive trees. According to Spanish law, however, the Indians were not permitted to engage in these activities.

Hidalgo was part of a group of creoles who had plans to overthrow the government of New Spain and form a new government. When someone told the plans of this group to the govern-

Hidalgo decided that he would not surrender or flee; he would resist. Gathering five to six hundred men around him, he marched from village to village, calling for rebellion. By September 21, 1810, 50,000 Indians, *mestizos,* and a few creoles had joined Hidalgo, marching under a picture of Our Lady of Guadalupe. As the mostly peasant army marched toward the city of Guanajuato, it slaughtered any Europeans it found. When, on September 28, Hidalgo's army took Guanjuato, a bloodbath followed. After this massacre, several Mexican bishops excommunicated Hidalgo and his followers. In this way, it appeared that the Church was the enemy of the poor.

Because of his army's atrocities, Hidalgo could convince few creoles to join his cause. Instead, they joined the forces of those called "royalists" who defended the government of Mexico.

Hidalgo achieved his greatest victory near Mexico City when, on October 30, 1810, his ragtag army of 80,000 defeated 6,000 Spaniards.

Mural of Miguel Hidalgo y Costilla by Clemente Orozco, Government Palace, Guadalajara, Mexico

Yet, despite this victory, Hidalgo did not try to take Mexico City but decided to retreat toward the city of Guadalajara. This retreat disappointed his followers. Thousands abandoned Hidalgo's army. Still, in Guadalajara, where more men joined him, Hidalgo set up a government. He promised to grant freedom to slaves and hand over to the Indians the lands they cultivated but did not own. Still, Hidalgo did not declare Mexico an independent country but promised to be faithful to King Fernando VII of Spain.

Hidalgo's government, however, did not last long. On January 11, 1810, a much smaller royalist force shattered Hidalgo's enormous army of 80,000 men. With only a small force of men, Hidalgo fled toward the north. On March 21, 1811, royalists captured Hidalgo in the hot and barren deserts of northern Mexico.

Because he was a priest, Hidalgo was handed over to the bishop of Durango. Deciding the priest was guilty of murder and treason, the bishop handed Hidalgo over to the state for execution. Standing before a firing squad on July 30, 1811, Hidalgo calmly instructed

Portrait of José María Morelos y Pavon (1765–1815), a Catholic priest and a revolutionary, who received the title of Generalissimo of the Mexican Army. He was executed by the Spanish.

pitched battle: a battle fought on a field of battle between opposing armies in formation and in close contact with each other

anonymous: having an unknown name

them to shoot him through his right hand, which he placed over his heart.

Guerrilla Warfare in the Jungles

Hidalgo was not the only revolutionary leader in Mexico. Inspired by his example, other men had taken up arms against the government. One of these was the priest, José María Morelos, who had been leading rebels in the south of Mexico since early 1810.

Unlike Hidalgo, who had come from a middle-class creole family, Morelos was a poor *mestizo*. He had worked as a mule driver until he was 25. After he was ordained a priest, Morelos took a parish in Michoacán.

Morelos formed a small rebel force around Zacatula on the Pacific coast. A skilled commander, Morelos used the hit-and-run methods of guerrilla warfare rather than **pitched battles**. Many of Morelos's soldiers were merely farmers who worked their fields until they were called to take up arms. When a battle ended, they returned to their fields. To punish and kill off these **anonymous** rebels, the Spaniards began to destroy entire villages.

Unlike Hidalgo, Morelos refused to acknowledge Fernando VII as king of Mexico. Instead, he set up a congress as the new government of Mexico. The congress declared that the law was to treat everyone in Mexico equally; it abolished slavery, and made Morelos president. The government issued a declaration of independence on December 12, 1813, the feast of Our Lady of Guadalupe, whom the declaration called "the Queen of our liberty."

Soon, however, the war turned against the rebels. In December 1813, Morelos tried to take the city of Valladolid, but was defeated. After this defeat, many lost confidence in Morelos and the rebel forces began to break into factions. In the fall of 1815, Morelos himself was captured. Loading him with chains, the royalists marched him triumphantly into Mexico City. He was executed on November 28, 1815.

Independence

It seemed that the execution of Morelos had ended revolution in Mexico. Both in Spain and Spanish America the forces of traditional government had triumphed. Fernando VII was king and ruled with absolute power. Throughout Spanish America, the royal government was firmly in control — or at least it seemed so.

But then in 1820 a rebellion in Spain forced Fernando VII to approve a constitution for the country. This constitution not only made the Spanish parliament more powerful than the king, but it allowed the government to seize lands held by the Church both in Spain and Spanish America. In Mexico, conservative creoles and members of the clergy feared that the new Spanish government would destroy the way of life and government they so loved. Union with Spain, they determined, was dangerous to the good of New Spain.

So the royalists joined the independence movement. Led by Agustín de Iturbide, the conservatives joined forces with rebel groups that had fought with Hidalgo and Morelos and carried out a "Bloodless Revolution." This revolution ended in July 1821 with a newly independent Mexico, led by Iturbide, who, soon after, was proclaimed emperor of the new country. At that time, Mexico's territory included not only the modern country of Mexico, but California, Nevada, Arizona, New Mexico, and Texas, to the north, and Guatemala, Honduras, Costa Rica, and El Salvador to the south. At that time, Mexico was a larger country than the United States.

Portrait of Agustín de Iturbide

Mexico's Agony

Agustín de Iturbide came to power offering three guarantees: independence for Mexico, protection of the rights of the Church, and equality for all citizens. Along with Iturbide, a congress made up the government of independent Mexico. The congress, however, was filled with Emperor Agustín's opponents, who refused to write up a constitution and raise taxes. Without tax money, the emperor could not pay his generals. Led by the general, Antonio López de Santa Anna, Mexican generals rose up against Iturbide, who fled into exile.

After Iturbide, Mexico became a republic. Under the first president, Guadalupe Victoria, the congress wrote up the "Constitution of 1824" that formed a government very much like the government of the United States. Mexico, however, was divided by groups that had very different ideas about the future of Mexico. One group, the conservatives, wanted to keep Mexico's Spanish traditions. In particular, they wanted to preserve the central place of the Catholic Church in Mexican society. The other group, the liberals, wanted Mexico to become like the United States and to weaken the influence of the Church in Mexico. Another problem was that Mexico had a powerful military that could overthrow governments when they did not do what the generals wanted them to do. Another problem was that powerful European governments such as Great Britain, Germany, and France took advantage of Mexico's poverty and came to control the country's economy.

One of Mexico's troublesome generals was Antonio López de Santa Anna. To gain power, he sided, sometimes with the liberals, sometimes with the conservatives. He became president at different times and, in 1834, made himself dictator. It was Santa Anna who lost Texas — and in 1846, he again became president during the Mexican-American War in which Mexico lost half its lands to the United States.

filibuster: a military adventurer
secede: to break away

Struggles Between Liberals and Conservatives

Mexico was in a very bad condition after the end of the Mexican-American War in 1848. States and regions refused to obey the government in Mexico City, and the people suffered from poverty. In the North, Indian tribes raided Mexican settlements, while **filibusters** from the United States tried to get the northern Mexican states to **secede** from the republic.

In 1853, desperate conservatives again made Santa Anna president; but he was driven out in 1855. A liberal government then took power and passed laws, forbidding the Church to own land and removing the Church's influence from the schools. These laws also hurt Indians by forcing them to sell their community lands. These lands, as well as Church lands, were bought up by wealthy men from foreign countries, who thus began to have more and more influence over the Mexican government.

In 1857, warfare between conservatives and liberals again broke out. At first, the conservatives were winning the war, but then their wealth began to run out and their troops deserted them. The war ended in 1861 when the liberal president, Benito Juárez, entered in triumph into Mexico City.

Answering the calls of Mexican conservatives, in 1862, Emperor Napoleon III of France sent French forces into Mexico, which by 1864 had driven Juárez into the far north. In place of Juárez's government, the French made an Austrian prince, Maximilian I, and his wife Carlotta the emperor and empress of Mexico. But when French troops left Mexico in 1867, Maximilian and his army could not stand up against the army

Maximilian in coronation robes

of Benito Juárez, who was backed by the United States. Juárez once again became president, had Maximilian executed, and went on to attack the Church and all of traditional Mexican society.

Juárez died of a heart attack in 1872. Four years later, one of his old allies, Porfirio Díaz, carried out a revolution against the government and made himself president of Mexico. Díaz ruled Mexico for the next 35 years. During this time, there was peace and prosperity for some—especially wealthy men from the United States, who received much of Mexico's wealth under Díaz. The poor, however, suffered great injustices. By his policy of *pan o palo* ("bread or the club") Don Porfirio rewarded his friends and destroyed his enemies. He gave more freedom to the Church than Juárez had but made sure bishops and priests did not speak out against the government.

Porfirio Díaz, President of Mexico

The Second Mexican Revolution

Though Díaz had brought peace to Mexico, his long reign ended in violence. Mexicans had grown tired of Díaz's control of the government and his injustice. In the fall of 1910, after Díaz had imprisoned a popular presidential candidate named Francisco Madero, revolution broke out in the northern state of Chihuahua. A bandit leader named Pancho Villa defeated a federal army and gradually took control of Chihuahua. Madero, released from prison, joined Villa in the north and was proclaimed president of Mexico. In the state of Morelos (south of Mexico City), the peasant leader Emiliano Zapata joined the rebellion. Rebel forces sprang up in other Mexican states and Díaz's power melted away. On May 26, 1911, he resigned as president and fled from the capital.

After this rebellion, Madero became president of Mexico. Madero, however, made powerful enemies, including the U.S. government. Zapata, thinking Madero had betrayed the revolution, rebelled against him. In February 1913, Madero was arrested by his own generals and later executed. Madero's enemy, General Victoriano Huerta, then became president. Huerta, however, was brutal, and it was not long before two generals in northern Mexico, Venustiano Carranza and Alvaro Obregón, rose up against him. Pancho Villa and Zapata also joined the rebellion,

Emiliano Zapata

which ended in August 1914. Huerta fled from Mexico, and Carranza became president.

As president, Carranza was opposed by Zapata and Villa, who for a short time seized control of Mexico City. General Obregón, however, was able to break Villa's power, and in 1919, Carranza's forces killed Zapata. In 1917, Carranza gave Mexico a new constitution that tried to destroy the influence of the Catholic Church in Mexico. By 1920, however, it was clear that Carranza did not want to give up power, and armies in Sonora rose up against him. Carranza fled from Mexico City and was later murdered.

The next president of Mexico, General Obregón, turned officially against the Church. His successor, Plutarco Elías Calles, was even more strongly anti-Catholic. From 1924 to 1936, the government of Mexico waged constant persecution against Catholics. Many martyrs died for the Faith, among them the priest, Blessed Miguel Pro. But the Mexican people, whose faith remained firm, resisted the government, and a rebellion broke out all over Mexico. The movement was called the Cristero Rebellion. Its leader, González Flores, was captured and executed. Before he was cut down by the firing squad, Flores gave out the Cristero battle cry, "*Viva Cristo Rey!*" ("Long Live Christ the King!") The rebellion lasted from 1927 to 1929.

It was not until 1979 that the Mexican government relaxed the restrictions on Catholics that had troubled the life of Mexico for 72 years.

Officers of the Cristero regiment Castañon and their banner

The End of the Revolution

One of the promises of the Mexican Revolution was that lands taken from poor farmers and Indian communities would be returned to them. Though Calles had given some land to the poor, he eventually went over to the side of the wealthy. Calles wanted to keep control of the government, even when he was not president. To do this, he and the followers of

Obregón formed a political party that became known as the Institutional Revolutionary Party (*Partido Revolucionario Institucional,* or PRI). This became the only party that could win elections in Mexico.

Calles supported a man named Lázaro Cardenas for president in the election of 1934. But, to Calles's bitter surprise, when Cardenas became president, he broke Calles's power over the PRI. In 1936, Cardenas **deported** Calles to Texas.

deport: to send out of the country

Cardenas was a very different president from Calles. He distributed millions of acres of land to peasants. He seized foreign-owned oil companies and established a government oil company. Though the laws against the Church remained, Cardenas did not enforce them. He even won the support of the archbishop of Mexico City, Luis Martinez.

In 1940, a more conservative man, Ávila Camacho, became president of Mexico. Camacho favored the growth of industry and even went so far as to say publicly that he was Catholic. Camacho's presidency basically ended the revolution. From that time until the 1990s, Mexico remained a state ruled by one party, and its government suffered much from corrupt leadership. On the other hand, because of the revolution, more peasants had land than they did in 1910. Having had to face persecution, the Church, too, was stronger. In Mexico, the old saying that "the blood of the martyrs is the seed of the Church," had again proven true.

Revolution in South America

Not just in Mexico, but in South American as well—there were those who wanted independence from Spain. In Venezuela, General Simón Bolívar organized creole leaders and formed armies to fight for independence. These struggles, beginning in 1811, lasted 13 years, until August 6, 1824, when Bolívar won a great victory over the pro-Spanish forces at Ayacucho in Peru.

The region freed by Bolívar and his allies stretched from modern-day Venezuela, west to the Pacific Ocean, and then south to the southern boundary of Peru. Bolívar's dream was to unite the several Spanish colonies in this area into a nation like the United States. He called this new nation "Colombia." But the different regions of Colombia could not agree with one another,

Simón Bolívar

and Bolívar's united colonies eventually broke up into the independent nations of Venezuela, Colombia, Ecuador, and Peru.

Argentina, led by José de San Martín, and Chile, led by Bernardo O'Higgins, had achieved independence earlier than Colombia. But Argentina, too, broke into three separate nations — Argentina, Uruguay, and Bolivia. Paraguay, a region completely cut off from the sea, also achieved independence. It immediately fell under the despotic control of General José Gaspar Rodríguez de Francia, who turned on his republican supporters and declared himself *El Supremo* ("highest one") and dictator for life.

By 1826, Bolívar and other revolutionaries had made all of Spanish South America independent. But the new, independent governments were unable to maintain order or govern wisely. Wild ideas and experiments in political organization destroyed agriculture and left the people in the Andes starving.

Just as in Mexico, South American leaders turned against the Church and angered the poor, who had received support from the Church. The Indians were worse off under the new governments than they had been under Spanish rule. The Spanish crown, at least, had protected them from the ruling classes of their countries. Revolts and **coups** occurred again and again in South America. Strongmen, supported by the army, set up despotic governments instead of states based on the rule of law and tradition. The vast wealth of South America fell into the hands of a few rich and powerful men, while much of the population was left in poverty.

coup: a military seizure of the government

The Empire of Brazil

The great South American country of Brazil had been colonized, not by Spain, but by Portugal. And, unlike the nations of Spanish America, Brazil won its freedom from Portugal without a revolution.

In 1807, when the armies of Napoleon I invaded Portugal, Portugal's king, João VI, fled to his colonies in Brazil. After Napoleon's defeat, João returned to Portugal, but he left his son, Pedro, to govern Brazil. In 1822 Pedro declared Brazil an independent empire and took his throne as Emperor Pedro I. But Pedro I was a poor ruler, and in 1831 he gave up his throne to his five-year old son, Pedro II. For the next ten years, Brazil fell into violence until Pedro II was 15. It was then he took power and showed what an able ruler he was.

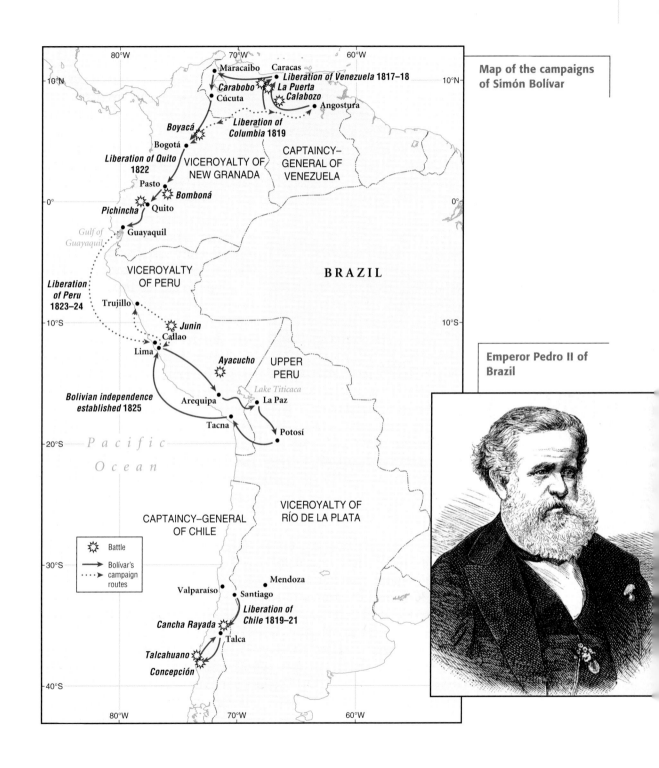

Map of the campaigns of Simón Bolívar

Emperor Pedro II of Brazil

Historical map of Brazil in the 1890s

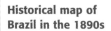

prodigy: a marvel, a wonder; exceptionally intelligent or skilled

Pedro was a **prodigy**. He had the wisdom and abilities of a much older man. Pedro II's amazing memory and brilliant mind directed Brazil for 49 years and gave Brazil a peace and prosperity unknown in the rest of South America. The emperor was also a great lover of science and the arts, both of which he promoted in Brazil. Once Pedro said, "If I were not emperor, I should like to be a schoolteacher."

Under Pedro II, Brazil encouraged immigration from Europe, and thousands of Germans, Italians, and Spanish flocked to its shores. In the 20th century, large numbers of Japanese, Syrian, and Lebanese immigrants enriched the cities of Brazil with their presence.

Because the Portuguese had brought many African slaves to work on plantations in Brazil, by the 19th century, a large part of the Brazilian population was of African descent. The Church's long opposition to slavery in Brazil gave moral strength to an abolitionist movement, and antislavery societies worked for a gradual abolition of slavery. First, the government decreed that children born to slaves were automatically free. Then, in the 1870s, the government freed all slaves over 60 years of age. Finally, in 1888, the emperor freed all slaves in Brazil.

Some wealthy and powerful families feared that neither of Pedro II's daughters would be the ruler he had been. Fearful for what might happen to Brazil after Pedro died, these families demanded an end to the monarchy. Thus, in 1889 Pedro II and his family abdicated and returned to Portugal. This was the end of the empire in Brazil. A democracy took its place, but under the new government, Brazil was not as prosperous as it had been under Pedro II. Except for the years from 1964 until 1984, Brazil has since had democratically elected presidents.

Chapter 16 Review

Let's Remember   Please write your answers in complete sentences.
1. What three major Indian civilizations were in America when the Europeans arrived?
2. What American Indian empire did Cortés overcome?
3. What American Indian empire did Pizarro conquer?
4. Why did the Cristeros rebel against the Mexican government?
5. What was Simón Bolívar's dream for South America?
6. What two countries in Latin America were for a time empires?

Let's Consider   For silent thinking and a short essay, or for thinking in a group with classroom discussion:
1. How were the ancient Indian empires of Latin America alike? How did they differ?
2. Why did the Spanish set up the *encomienda* system? Was it successful? Why or why not?
3. How were the Spanish conquistadors, Cortés and Pizarro, alike? How did they differ?

Things to Do

1. Many rivers flow into the Amazon River, as you can see using the maps on pages 374 and 376. Using these maps, make a list of the countries where the Amazon River and each of the rivers that flow into the Amazon begin.
2. Roughly, between what latitude lines does South America lie? Using a measurement string, find the distance between these lines.
3. Using a measuring string, determine the distance between the city of Recife, on the coast of Brazil, and Lima, on the coast of Peru. Measure the distance between the Mexican cities of Chihuahua and Mexico City.

Let's Eat!

The tortilla has been eaten by the people of Central America for ages and is the basis of a burrito. Spread onto a tortilla (corn or flour) 2 tablespoons of heated refried beans, seasoned with chili powder to taste. Add slices of grilled beef or chicken and pico de gallo. Top with 2 tablespoons of grated cheese. Spread sour cream over all. Roll into a burrito and enjoy.

Index